The Psychology of Radical Social Change

Since 2011 the world has experienced an explosion of popular uprisings that began in the Middle East and quickly spread to other regions. What are the different social-psychological conditions for these events to emerge, what different trajectories do they take, and how are they are represented to the public? To answer these questions, this book applies the latest social psychological theories to contextualized cases of revolutions and uprisings from the eighteenth to the twenty-first century in countries around the world. In so doing, it explores continuities and discontinuities between past and present uprisings, and foregrounds such issues as the crowds, collective action, identity changes, globalization, radicalization, the plasticity of political behavior, and public communication.

BRADY WAGONER is Professor of Psychology at Aalborg University, Denmark, and an associate editor for the journals *Culture and Psychology* and *Peace and Conflict*. He received his PhD from the University of Cambridge, where he started his line of research on the social and cultural psychology, remembering, social change, and the development of dynamic methodologies. His recent books include *The Constructive Mind: Bartlett's Psychology in Reconstruction* (Cambridge University Press, 2017), *The Psychology of Imagination* (2017), *Street Art of Resistance* (with Sarah H. Awad, 2017) and *Handbook of Culture and Memory* (2018). He was awarded the Early Career Award by the American Psychological Association (Division 26).

FATHALI M. MOGHADDAM is Professor of Psychology and Director of the Interdisciplinary Program in Cognitive Science at Georgetown University, Washington, DC, USA. From 2008 to 2014 he was Director of the Conflict Resolution Program, Department of Government, Georgetown University. In 2014 he became Editor-in-Chief of the *Peace and Conflict* journal. Prior to joining the Georgetown University faculty, he worked for the United Nations and McGill University. Among his most recent books are *The Psychology of Dictatorship* (2013), *The Psychology of Democracy* (2016), *Questioning Causality: Scientific Explorations of Cause and Consequence across Social Contexts* (with Rom Harré, 2016), and *The Encyclopedia of Political Behavior* (2017).

JAAN VALSINER is Niels Bohr Professor of Cultural Psychology at Aalborg University, Denmark. He is the founding editor (1995) of *Culture and Psychology* and the *Oxford Handbook of Culture and Psychology* (2012). He is also the Editor-in-Chief of *Integrative Psychological and Behavioral Sciences* (from 2007) and of the Springer Briefs series Theoretical Advances in Psychology. His books include *The Social Mind* (with van der Veer, Cambridge University Press, 2000), *Understanding Vygotsky* (with van der Veer, 1993), *A Guided Science* (2012), and *Invitation to Cultural Psychology* (2014). In 1995 he was awarded the Alexander von Humboldt Prize in Germany for his interdisciplinary work on human development and the Senior Fulbright Lecturing Award in Brazil 1995–1997. He is the winner of the Hans-Kilian Award of 2017 for his interdisciplinary work uniting social sciences.

The Psychology of Radical Social Change

Social Change

From Rage to Revolution

Edited by

Brady Wagoner
Aalborg University, Denmark

Fathali M. Moghaddam
Georgetown University, Washington, DC

Jaan Valsiner
Aalborg University, Denmark

CAMBRIDGE
UNIVERSITY PRESS

CAMBRIDGE
UNIVERSITY PRESS

University Printing House, Cambridge CB2 8BS, United Kingdom

One Liberty Plaza, 20th Floor, New York, NY 10006, USA

477 Williamstown Road, Port Melbourne, VIC 3207, Australia

314–321, 3rd Floor, Plot 3, Splendor Forum, Jasola District Centre,
New Delhi - 110025, India

79 Anson Road, #06–04/06, Singapore 079906

Cambridge University Press is part of the University of Cambridge.

It furthers the University's mission by disseminating knowledge in the pursuit of
education, learning, and research at the highest international levels of excellence.

www.cambridge.org
Information on this title: www.cambridge.org/9781108421621
DOI: 10.1017/9781108377461

© Cambridge University Press 2018

First published 2018

Printed in the United Kingdom by Clays, St Ives plc

A catalogue record for this publication is available from the British Library

ISBN 978-1-108-42162-1 Hardback

This book is dedicated to Michael Billig for his seminal contributions to our understanding of the role of ideology in everyday life and the intricate social-psychological processes that inhibit progressive revolutions.

Contents

Figures

Contributors

SARAH H. AWAD, Aalborg University

NIKOS BOZATZIS, University of Ioannina

SIERRA CAMPBELL, Georgetown University

MATHIEU CARON-DIOTTE, University of Montreal

ROXANE DE LA SABLONNIÈRE, University of Montreal

JOHN DRURY, University of Sussex

ROM HARRÉ, Oxford University

SÉAMUS POWER, University of Chicago

STEPHEN D. REICHER, University of St. Andrews

DONALD M. TAYLOR, McGill University

CHRISTINA TELIOU, independent researcher

DUNCAN WU, Georgetown University

TANIA ZITTOUN, University of Neuchatel

Foreword

Rom Harré

Revolution in the political or cultural sense, say, in the conventions of art, is a metaphor for a species of change. "Revolution" is not one thing. The uses of the word cover a wide field of "family resemblances," some of which are superficial and some of which are profound. In tracing its role in human life, "all history" is subsumed.

The root idea is a process by which a system, say, a wheel, returns to its original condition. In the political sense, "revolution" contrasts not only with its material sense of rotation but also with other modes of change. Evolution is a process of gradual change; that is, only some features of a system or practice change in any time, though the change may be profound if a long enough time scale is considered. The third cultural and political possibility is conservation, in which, in a fairly long period of time, no changes of consequence occur. Ancient Egyptian art and architecture seem to have maintained the same conventions for a very long time.

The very idea of political revolution depends on a belief in the possibility of social change. In turn, for this idea to make sense, there must be some conception of the roots of the social order that revolutionaries propose to change. And looking even more deeply into the presuppositions of radical movements, there must be some program of action that will change the presumptive roots of the existing social order and replace them with something different.

In a political or cultural revolution the change to the system is abrupt. At least in principle a revolution involves a total change of all the significant attributes of the system overthrown, relative to some scale of importance. This kind of revolution is the topic of the essays in this book and many other writings in political philosophy and cultural commentary.

In the political context, though it is not always the case; the revolutionaries have little idea with what to replace the system they have overthrown. Chaos and disorder appear, while the leaders search for some improvisation that will keep some sort of common life going.

An important topic for research apropos of "revolution" is to inves-
tigate the conditions for revolutionary change to break out. Following
directly on this comes the question of the conditions that are necessary
for a revolution to succeed, at least for a while. Why are some insurrections successfully repressed while others succeed? What distinguished
the Paris of 1786 from that of 1860? When a revolution has succeeded
and the old order is overthrown, what militates against the new conditions of life continuing as a new stable social order? And why do internal
conflicts among the revolutionaries occur so frequently as to negate the
change that seems to be imminent?

The intensity of revolutionary fervor is an important psychological feature of insurrections psychologists might seek to understand. Sometimes
a frenzy of destruction breaks out as the old order is broken and the constraints on public behavior seem to dissolve. This might take the form of
mass murders, such as the Terror of 1793 in Paris under the "Committee of Public Safety" or the wrecking of the plant on which the workings
of the oil industry in Bulgaria had depended prior to the collapse of the
communist regime.

Linked to all these considerations is a profound and perhaps unan-
swerable psychological question. What sort of people are the revolutionaries? Is there anything that Cromwell, Lenin, and Akhenaton had in
common other than a summoning need for change? And if they are part
of a group, why do they so often fall out among themselves?

The most important question a psychologist might attempt to answer
is why so few programs of revolutionary action succeed. In case after
case, seemingly independent of the religion, social arrangements, and
language of the culture of a society, at the historical moment of a revolutionary event, after sometimes a very short time, the very system that
was overthrown reappears. Napoleon very soon becomes emperor, and
Stalin very soon becomes the Czar by another name. And the "other
name" point is fundamental to understanding why political orders reap-
pear as if by magic.

Why do political revolutions so often seem to be succeeded, after a
period of chaos, with a regime that is very similar to the one that has
been brought down? By what means have the basic social relations that
define a certain society survived to shape postrevolutionary society? Part
of the answer lies in the necessity for everyday language to remain meaningful in order that the new situation might be intelligible both to the
revolutionaries and to their beneficiaries. The revolutionaries in France
realized something of this, renaming the days and the months and changing ordinary terms of address. The necessary language continuity is coupled with the continuity of the means for accomplishing very small-scale

necessities of everyday life. Recipes are not usually discarded while others are adopted in a revolution. A baguette is a baguette for whoever is having one for breakfast. While the leaders of a revolution are attacking the grand institutions, such as royalty or the form of the economy, the small acts that constitute everyday life continue unchanged. Their invisibility makes them potent continuants. We might call these *reductions* – the smallest social acts that are meaningful, their repetition serving to maintain the old society.

The social psychology that offers the best chance of explaining this apparently paradoxical phenomenon grounds all social arrangements in the catalog of meanings by which the populace of the time understands social events, and the rules, explicit and tacit, that express the orderliness of the customs and conventions of society at that time and place. What is the significance of burning someone alive whose opinions you dislike? What are the conventions by which an *auto da fe* is carried on? What is the meaning of the various incidents in the unfolding of a high school prom, and by what tacit rules are they managed? When can you hire a limo?

Looking closely at the social order of a particular moment at a particular time and place reveals levels of persistence through time of different kinds of customs. Those that are the longest lasting are the everyday means by which the simplest and least attended to aspects of social order are managed. How do people greet one another, and how do greeting ceremonials differ among different categories of persons – fathers and mothers, officials, friends, and so on? How is the distribution of food at mealtimes managed? And by whom? Research by such historians of culture as Peter and Iona Opie (*The Lore and Language of Schoolchildren*) reveals a stable repetition of patterns over many centuries. Again, we will call these basic and persistent elements of social life *reductons*. When we analyze an episode of real social life, what are the basic social atoms beyond which analysis will not take us? In Europe, some version of shaking hands is ubiquitous among men and some version of kissing among women. There are definite customs for greetings between men and women depending on their social relationships. But none of this applies in India even after two hundred years of the Raj and nearly a century of Westernization.

But when the revolutionaries man the barricades, it is to cries of "A bas les aristos," "Viva Fidel," and such like references to matters at the very opposite scale from the way the sans-culottes greet one another or the executioner motions the next victim to approach the guillotine. It is the persistence of reductons through moments of revolutionary fervor, because they are not attended to and their significance is not realized, that accounts in large part for the reproduction of the lineaments of the old society in the new. Once upon a time, the French rallied around the *fleur de lys*, then they flocked to the *tricouler*. But both activities were "flocking to the flag." So far as I know, the only example of a revolutionary movement that recognized this phenomenon was the French. The revolutionaries installed the goddess of reason on the altar of Notre Dame. They gave the days of the week and months of the year new names, and they tried to stamp out "monsieur" and "madame." Their rule was for so short a period that these seemingly trivial but actually deep innovations did not take. The disappearance of "thee" and "thou" from English in the eighteenth century made social space for a form of address that did not demand the overt recognition of the social status of one's interlocutor, unlike the *tu* and *vous* of the continental languages.

Though it would be impossible to devise a revolutionary program to build a society on new reductons, which did not serve as the carriers of the tacit social mores of the old regime, it is pretty clear what will not work – apparent changes in the social structure of the state. Social structures are epiphenomena of the activities of actual people, interacting according to their conceptions of the proper way to manage their lives in relation to others. The camaraderie of the munitions factories and hospitals of World War I had much more to do with the changing status of women in Britain than with any amount of demonstrations by the brave and well-meaning suffragettes.

Let us return to basics by another route. What does lead to social change? Close study of historical examples discloses something like a mutation/selection process. New customs are forever being introduced. Mostly they do not catch on outside the circle of their originators. Gender-neutral pronouns failed to change common speech. The step-by-step encroachment by women on the preserves of higher education is such an example. What began in London slowly spread to such bastions as Oxford and, later, Cambridge. Innovation and environment must match at just the right moment for a new social custom that might in the end spread to being about a fundamental social revolution. But there are no guarantees that any such coincidence will occur. The best models for social change and how to bring it about are surely the fashion and automotive industries. The couturiers invent a new style of dressing. The big clothing stores offer it, and the public affirms or rejects it. Alec Issogonis designed a car with a transverse engine. Now nearly all cars are made that way. Why? Somehow it suited the mood of the car-buying public. That is the end of the story.

1 Toward a Psychology of Revolution

Brady Wagoner, Fathali M. Moghaddam,
and Jaan Valsiner

Revolutions in a society resemble earthquakes. Suddenly – often unexpectedly – there emerges a rupture in the texture of the society that leads to turmoil in economics, the social order, and human states of mind. At all levels of a society under revolution, expectations arise that life will never be the same. But how precisely do these social transformations and changes in expectations occur? This is an open question when one looks at the history of societies, particularly because there is often a rift between the expectations that arise and the actual changes that come about through revolutions. The French Revolution of 1789 shattered the whole of Europe and led to transformations of political and social orders – as well as further revolutions in Europe (in 1830 and 1848), Latin America, and Russia (1917). Empires end – the Holy Roman Empire, the Austro-Hungarian Empire, and the British Empire are good examples – yet they turn into new forms of social organization, which sometimes begin to resemble the old ones.

Our times are not different. Since 2011 the world has seen an explosion of popular uprisings that have spread across the Middle East and North Africa. Beginning in January with the ousting of Tunisian president Ben Ali and followed by Egypt's removal of Mubarak in February, these uprisings quickly spread globally. Old regimes were toppled and new regimes could be observed in the process of their germination. In between were various efforts to create democratic forms of governance – not an easy task in societies without a tradition of openness. Acceptance of the opponent's differing political perspective and the negotiation of power through elections have not easily taken root. The chaos of public life in most of these societies has been filled with various forms of protest, some of them associated with violent radical movements.

Protests are theatrical events. They are scripted through social representations of antagonism, claims for justice and fairness, and many other reasons that could get the public to legitimize the events. In our contemporary world, they are – more often than not – directed to television cameras and, through those, to audiences in countries far away.

1

European countries saw widespread protests against governments' economic austerity programs as well for various political agendas, right or left.

In the US, the Occupy Wall Street movement emerged, followed by the readiness to "occupy Anyplace," as well as the right-wing Tea Party movement that would capture the attention of the mass media. Yet no revolution followed from these occupations. In a similar vein, Brazil experienced forceful protests leading up to the World Cup, which have intensified in the wake of widespread political scandals. Such scandals represent other forms of theatrical events in societies. Human participation in societies is organized by way of theatrical setups in the middle of ordinary living. Europe – free of wars on its territory since 1945 – participates vicariously in the conflicts in other parts of the world by observing atrocities shown on TV screens.

Social ruptures can escalate. Some recent unrests have proceeded to military conflicts and civil wars. Recent social power struggles in Ukraine, Syria, and Iraq have transformed into conflicts of devastating consequences, solutions for which are nowhere in sight. The transition from protest to military action is an orchestration skill that politicians learn by doing – and psychologists need to learn *before* politicians get involved in doing it.

Revolutions and Resolutions

Most radical social changes – "revolutions" as they quickly became labeled – tend to rapidly lead to their opposite, transforming into the reinstatement of old orders. What creates the conditions for these social upheavals, what are the dynamics of their evolution, and why do they so often fail to bring about lasting changes? Furthermore, how are these large-scale social changes related to changes in individual lives and mentalities? These are key questions asked in this volume, answers to which are sought using theories and empirical research from psychological science, situated vis-à-vis other social sciences.

The word *revolution* is itself ambiguous, as it shares family resemblances with other terms (e.g., *uprising, coup d'état, revolt, insurgency, riot, protest*), making precise definitions difficult. These terms imply different kinds and levels of societal ruptures as well as different value orientations (Valsiner, Chapter 10). Many different conditions have to be in place for a revolution to occur, whereas the other terms can be seen as parts of or precursors to revolutions. After hearing of the storming of the Bastille on July 14, 1789, Louis XVI reportedly asked, "Is this a revolt?" to which Duc de la Rochefoucauld replied, "No, sire, it is a revolution."

A much more profound transformation of society was under way than Louis XVI had imagined. The most strict definitions of revolutions say there must be mass mobilization driven by a clear ideology that changes not only the nation's leadership but also its institutions, practices, and mentalities. Few events in history satisfy these requirements – perhaps only the French, Russian, Chinese, and Haitian revolutions. More often than not, we only find a change of leadership. Taking over the existing social power positions does not necessarily transform the given society. In fact, power transfers – even violent ones – preserve the rules by which power games are being enacted. Revolutions are *conservatively bordered* so that anarchy is curtailed.

Political theorists and historians have been at the forefront of investigating revolution. Although these analyses are essential and will be commented upon here, this should not lead to a neglect of the social and psychological processes involved. Revolutions are as much about ideas, mentalities, identities, habits, and group processes as they are about economics and political calculation. One of the first distinctly psychological theories of revolution was put forward by Gustav Le Bon in his famous *The Crowd: A Study of the Popular Mind* (1896) and later *The Psychology of Revolution* (1912). Writing to understand the French Revolution and its aftermath, Le Bon formulated a theory that put collective mentalities and leader–crowd dynamics at its core (for more on Le Bon, see Chapters 2 and 5). This was followed by Ellwood (1905) and others, who saw revolution in terms of group habits and adaptability to new conditions.

This first wave of psychological theorists of revolution was largely ignored by the second wave that emerged in the 1960s. The most notable of these explained revolution through the lens of "relative deprivation" (see also Chapter 3). Davies (1962) argued that revolutions are not sparked by people living in poverty comparing themselves to those living in luxury but rather as a result of aggression following frustrated expectations. Revolutions are preceded by improvements that people expect will continue. When their situation declines, they are left with an "intolerable gap" between what they want and what they get. This is the moment in which a revolution occurs, not before. One of the major problems of this model is that it fails to explain how it works under different social-political conditions and leads to different revolutionary outcomes. A psychology that studies the emergence of revolutions needs to be contextual and developmental at its core.

More recently, social psychologists have made important contributions to a better understanding of intergroup conflict, through research on realistic conflict theory, system justification theory, social identity

theory, self-categorization theory, social dominance theory, equity theory, relative deprivation theory, terror management theory, and various
offshoots of psychodynamic theory (Moghaddam, 2008). A theme in this
research since at least the 1980s has been experimental studies on rebellion and/or collective action in the face of perceived injustice (Wright,
Taylor, and Moghaddam, 1990). One of the major challenges for social
psychologists has been to better understand how people attempt to bring
about change, and the psychology of change processes (see Chapters 2
and 13).

Central to both psychological science and revolution is change in the
ways of being and feelings about such change. The latter particularly
sets limits to the change. In assessing the psychology of change, a useful
distinction has been made between three levels of systems (Moghaddam,
2013).

A first-order system is one in which both formal law and the informal normative system justify group-based injustices. Ancient Greek
polises – based on slavery – included philosophical and rhetoric devices
of legitimizing the differential power roles of social groups. The traditions of slavery in European colonial conquests can also be seen in
the southern US until the mid-nineteenth century – until abolition of
slavery.

The second-order system has a reformed formal law, but the informal
normative system continues to justify group-based injustices. An example is the US when slavery became illegal, but discrimination against
African Americans continued and was upheld by the informal normative
system.

A third-order system is one in which both the formal law and the
informal normative system support group-based justice. Such concor-
dance can be found in some Occidental societies that have developed
solid democratic governance systems under the conditions of relative
economic prosperity. The Scandinavian countries of today are prime
examples here. This is an ideal that many participants in revolutions
strive for, but it is difficult for such a system to come out of the confrontational ethos of demolishing "the old regimes" that is usual in
revolutions.

The changes brought about by most revolutions are within-system,
not between-system. In practice, this leads, as predicted by elite theory
(Pareto, 1935), to cycles of counterelite revolution being followed by the
counterelite becoming the new elite and simply continuing to rule in the
same way. The king is dead, long live the king! The Shah is overthrown,
long reign the Supreme Leader! Mubarak is gone, hoorah for El Sisi!
Pareto (1935) warns us not to be misled by rhetoric and labels, but to

notice the continuity of elite rule over the nonelite, even though the new regime has changed the official rhetoric and now refers to the nation as "communist" or "Islamic Republic" or "democracy." From a psychological perspective, the central concern here is continuity in behavior patterns, reflecting limits to what in contemporary terminology is political plasticity (Moghaddam, 2016) but was discussed earlier by Pareto (1935) and other elite theorists using a different terminology. Thus, in a sense the chapters in this volume are building on a long line of research on limits and possibilities to dramatic social and behavioral change.

Preview of the Book

This book explores the different social-psychological conditions and processes leading up to revolutions (Part I), the different trajectories they take (Part II) and the dynamics by which they are represented to the public and would-be revolutionaries (Part III). It outlines continuities and discontinuities between present and past revolutions and uprisings, through focused analyzes of contextualized single cases. In-depth analysis of the following events are presented: French Revolution (1789), Russian Revolution (1917), North Korean Revolution (1945–1950), Iranian Revolution (1979), Velvet Revolution (1989), Hyde Park Riot (1994), Greek protests (2008), the Arab Spring (2011), Occupy Movement (2011), and Irish antiausterity protests (2014). This is by no means a complete survey of revolutions and collective movements around the world (e.g., it leaves out Latin America). But it is sufficient to draw out what new factors, such as global capitalism, the Internet and mass media, are changing the form of revolution today as well as the conditions that have remained important through the ages.

Part I, "Roots of Revolution," focuses on crowds and economic processes as conditions for revolutions, as well as global processes that neutralize them. Revolutions are rare, but precursors to them can be found in the wider phenomena of protests and collective action, which are often closely connected to economic policies and developments. Protests against fiscal strain and injustice can turn into revolutions when particular conditions are in place, such as an alienated elite that connects with the populace and provides a persuasive narrative of resisting the current system. Along these lines, major theories of crowds, collective action, relative deprivation, collective memory, globalization, and social identity are covered in this section. Contrary to Le Bon's arguments about the conservative crowd, Drury and Reicher (Chapter 2) describe how crowds can and have contributed to both social and psychological change. They develop a social identity theory of crowds, which they illustrate with the case of antiroading building protests that took place in London in the 1990s. Power (Chapter 3) then explores what factors motivate people to go out and protest in the first place, elaborating "relative deprivation" explanations with the contextual approaches of cultural psychology and collective memory. Moghaddam (Chapter 4) then asks the same question from the opposite side: why do we not find revolutions in capitalist democracies given growing wealth inequalities? He points out a number of factors created by globalization that neutralize such movements. The commentary chapter by Wagoner (Chapter 5) connects the three chapters by re-situating crowd theory within the context of cultural and economic globalization. He considers the epidemiology of revolutions – that is, how they spread to other countries, as happened in 1848, 1989, 2011, and more recently with the so-called Islamic State.

Part II, "Evolution and Involution in Social Transformations," focuses on forces driving changes in society and their relation to those that lead to reinstatement of earlier structures. It provides analyses of the dialectics of plasticity and rigidity on and between social-political and psychological levels. Case studies of the Russian Revolution, Iranian Revolution, Velvet Revolution, and French Revolution illustrate the dynamics between the two levels. The section raises the questions of the limits and possibilities of "social engineering" (Chapter 6), why so often revolutions fail to bring about lasting change, including the role of leadership (Mohaddam, Chapter 7), how revolutions shape individual life trajectories (Zittoun, Chapter 8), and what factors lead to "radicalization" in times of revolution (Wu, Chapter 9). The commentary chapter by Valsiner (Chapter 10) "Between the Guillotine and the Velvet Revolution: What Is at Stake?," combines the case studies to develop a general model that incorporates them all and explains the complex interrelationship between stability and change on individual and group levels.

Part III, "Representations of and in Revolution," then explores some ways in which revolution is communicated and represented to audiences that are both local and international, during and after its occurrence. An important influence on revolutions is the support, or none-interference, of international actors. Protests and revolutions involve active communication to bolster ones cause as well as countermessaging to delegitimize collective actions by representing them as "pathology" (Bozatzis and Teliou, Chapter 12). The media-saturated world of today includes both traditional media outlets, such as newspaper and television, as well as new media, such as Facebook and Twitter, which has been effectively used in recent revolutions especially the Arab Spring. We can also point to age-old devices of resistance such as graffiti and urban performances

(Awad and Wagoner, Chapter 11). This section considers the image politics of urban spaces and their transnational diffusion (Awad and Wagoner, Chapter 11), media coverage of protest and revolt (Bozatzis and Teliou, Chapter 12), and how individuals construct stable identities through cultural means taken over from ones group, especially historical narratives including heroes and pivotal events (de la Sablonnière, Taylor, and Caron-Diotte, Chapter 13). It thus moves from how revolutionary events are collectively represented to how individuals negotiate these representations. The commentary by Moghaddam (Chapter 14) outlines two general behavioral styles of revolutionary movements, which he calls the "shark" (expansionist) and the "octopus" (inward looking).

The world of today is filled with social tensions that at times lead to sudden ruptures – revolts, revolutions, and other forms of upsets to our mundane established ways of being. Psychology and other social sciences need to be on the forefront in making sense of the basic social processes that lead to these eruptions. Well-being and at times lives are at stake. Science here needs to be ahead of politics in such dramatic social moments. The material included in this volume is intended to provide some leads to that objective.

REFERENCES

Davies, J. (1962). Toward a theory of revolution. *American Sociological Review*, 27, 5–18.

Ellwood, C. A. (1905). A psychological theory of revolution. *American Journal of Sociology*, 11, 49–59.

Le Bon, G. (1895/2002). *The Crowd: A Study of the Popular Mind*. New York, NY: Dover.

(1912). *The Psychology of Revolution*. London: Fisher Unwin.

Moghaddam, F. M. (2008). *Multiculturalism and Intergroup Relations: Psychological Implications for Democracy in Global Context*. Washington, DC: American Psychological Association Press.

(2013). *The Psychology of Dictatorship*. Washington, DC: American Psychological Association Press.

(2016). Omniculturalism and our human path. *The Journal of Oriental Studies*, 26, 77–97.

Pareto, V. (1935). *The Mind and Society: A Treatise on General Sociology*. 4 vols. New York, NY: Dover.

Wright, S. C., Taylor, D. M., and Moghaddam, F. M. (1990). Responding to membership in a disadvantaged group: From acceptance to collective protest. *Journal of Personality and Social Psychology*, 58, 994–1003.

Part I

Roots of Revolution

2   The Conservative Crowd?

How Participation in Collective Events Transforms
Participants' Understandings of Collective Action

John Drury and Stephen D. Reicher

The events of the 1871 Paris Commune, when the working class of that
city declared a revolutionary republic separate from the French state,
were the stimulus for one of the most influential social psychology books
ever written, Gustave Le Bon's (1896/1947) *The Crowd: A Study of the
Popular Mind*. The book was an attempt not simply to explain the kinds
of (violent) crowds that Le Bon had witnessed during the Commune and
read about in accounts of the 1789 French Revolution, but to control
and combat these crowds. Yet while Le Bon and others in his class feared
that crowds threatened civilization, he also argued that their violent revolutions were incapable of bringing about real social change because of
the primitive mentality of crowd members. Thus, we are told that crowd
members "possess conservative instincts as indestructible as those of all
primitive beings. Their fetishlike respect for all traditions is absolute;
their unconscious horror of all novelty capable of changing the essential
conditions of their existence is very deeply rooted" (Le Bon, 1896/1947,
pp. 55–56). In this account, the revolutionary appearance taken on by
the rioting crowd is misleading; what motivates crowd members is ultimately their timeless "racial unconscious":

> It is difficult to understand history, and popular revolution in particular if one
> does not take sufficiently into account the profoundly conservative instincts of
> crowds. They may be desirous, it is true, of changing the names of their insti-
> tutions, and to obtain these changes they accomplish at times even violent rev-
> olutions, but the essence of these institutions is too much the expression of the
> hereditary needs of the race for them not invariably to abide by it. (p. 55)

This chapter challenges Le Bon's argument first by briefly surveying
some of the literature on social change. Here we find that the crowd
often figures as a central actor. In a number of cases, social change and
psychological change seem to be connected, so in the second section of
the chapter we describe some of the psychological transformations that
have been documented among participants involved in social change
and in collective action more generally. These transformations involve

11

embracing new ideas about the self, politics and the world, and so tell against Le Bon's claim that crowd events are associated with a conservative or regressed psychological state. We then outline an elaborated social identity model (ESIM) which specifies the intergroup processes through which many of these psychological changes occur. The remainder of the chapter illustrates the usefulness of the ESIM in explaining how participation in crowds struggling to create social change can itself change crowd participants' understandings of the meaning of their actions. The illustration consists of evidence from an ethnographic study of pacifists' experiences conflict which served to challenge their humanistic rationale for their collective actions.

Crowds and Social Change

In their study of the efficacy of nonviolent collective protest, Ackerman and Kruegler (1994) argue that "people power" helps to explain such events as the so-called velvet revolutions in Europe in 1989 (see Zittoun, Chapter 8), the fall of Marcos in the Philippines in 1986, aspects of the Palestinian Intifada and South African antiapartheid struggle, and many other key political events this century. If this is the case, why is it that the role of the crowd in history seems to be neglected? Writing in 1959, Rudé argued that most historical accounts of social change, whether favorable or hostile, "have been inclined to view these events and their participants 'from above' ... This being the case, the revolutionary crowd, whose voice was seldom reflected in the speeches of the politicians or the writings of the pamphleteers and journalists, tended to be lost sight of as a thing of flesh and blood and to assume whatever complexion accorded with the interests, opinions, or ideals of the revolutionary leaders, their critics or adherents" (pp. 4–5). Rudé therefore recommends a reversal of perspective whereby the subject of history is "seen as it were from below" (p. 5). Since the 1960s, there has been a noticeable blossoming within this "bottom-up" tradition of the literature on popular disturbance and crowd behavior. This provides many rich examples contradicting Le Bon's picture of the ineffective, conservative crowd.

For example, Rudé (1959) attributes the development and success of the French Revolution of 1789 to the participation of *sans-culottes* crowds, who intervened, through demonstrating and rioting in the streets and market places, to destroy the power of the aristocratic ruling class. In England, on a smaller scale, riots were frequently successful in forcing the authorities to alleviate particular grievances (Thompson, 1991; Sharpe, 1984). Thompson (1991, p. 292) cites the example of Devon's "classic food riots" as evidence that popular price regulation was often highly effective: crowds would seize sacks of grain from merchants by force and sell them off at what they considered a fair price. Rudé (1981) notes that the Rebecca rioters succeeded in getting rid of road turnpikes, and in some districts the actions of Swing rioters resulted in threshing machines not being restored. Reviewing the research, Thompson (1991) concludes that, since it was the absence of riot in mid-nineteenth-century Ireland and India that may have allowed dearth to pass into famine, the best aid for present-day hungry nations would be to send them experts in the promotion of riot.

Hobsbawm (1964) and Thompson (1980) suggest that, during the seventeenth and eighteenth centuries, riot was the preeminent political expression of the ruled classes.[1] Yet the twentieth century contains images of the power of the collective to shape political reality just as vivid and striking as that of Rudé's (1959) picture of the crowd in the French Revolution. Thus, the Russian Revolution of February 1917 is described by one historian as "the spontaneous outbreak of a multitude exasperated by the privations of war and the manifest inequality in the distribution of burdens" (Carr, 1950, p. 81). According to the same source, the events took place solely through the initiative of the "masses" and without the intervention or anticipation of the revolutionary parties. In another account, after weeks of strikes and conflict with police, the working-class women of Petrograd held a massive demonstration on International Women's Day; this heralded the spread of the strikes and the occupation of the factories. Eventually the police were driven out, the prisons opened and workers' councils established (Anon., 1984).

Reed (1926/1982), in his firsthand account of the revolution of October in the same year, argues that the Bolsheviks did not seize power through the organized violence of a small clique: "If the masses had not been ready for insurrection it would have failed" (p. 254). Moreover, his story speaks graphically of the participation of the "masses" in the revolutionary events. Reed describes how the previously leaderless and undisciplined Red Guards became effective once they organized themselves in the midst of conflict with the Cossacks during the revolution: "For the moment that incoherent multiple will was one will." Countless others also involved themselves in the same way: "Those who participated in the fighting described to me how the sailors fought until they ran out of cartridges, and then stormed; how the untrained workmen rushed the charging Cossacks and tore them from their horses; how the

---

[1] Hobsbawm (1964, p. 7) uses the phrase "collective bargaining by riot" to refer to the methods early trade groups used to negotiate with their employers.

anonymous hoards of the people, gathering in the darkness around the battle, rose like a tide and poured over the enemy" (p. 201).

These accounts should not be taken as indicating that the crowd's only means of contributing to social change has been through violence. Other examples alert us to the different forms that collective action can take, often within the same social movement. For instance, the suffragettes movement of 1910–1914, which led eventually to female suffrage, was characterized not only by marches and symbolic protests (such as participants chaining themselves to railings) but also by violence between crowds, police and the suffragettes (Waddington, 1992).

The apparent failure of many movements to change the social world in the way they intended does not detract from the main point being made here – that the collective is often a cause of social change and that social change often (typically?) involves collective action in the form of crowd events. Moreover, and accepting perhaps that there is a grain of truth in Le Bon's claim about the "ineffectiveness" of the French revolution, the crowds of peasants and workers involved were responsible for forcing through changes that were actually in the interests of the bourgeoisie rather than their own class.

This last example returns us to the issue, implicitly raised by Le Bon, of what counts as social change, and therefore what counts as success for a collective action. Rudé (1981) argues that we should not limit ourselves to judging crowd events merely in terms of participants' immediate intentions but in terms of their place in a broader picture; "failed" crowds can be seen as precursors or necessary moments in the development of other movements. Thus, for example, in establishing the bourgeois revolution of 1789, with its ideological expression in the notions of "Liberty, Equality, Fraternity," the crowds of *sans-culottes* prepared the way for a conscious socialist movement – a proletarian force which learned from previous "mistakes" and which was more capable of expressing the interests of the class itself. The advances of 1848 and 1871 would not have happened without 1789.

If the "successes" of a number of crowd events are sometimes only apparent in retrospect – if the immediate and subsequent social effects of collective actions are not necessarily those intended by the crowd participants themselves – then this only serves to point to the different dimensions of the "social creativity" of collective action. The examples above suggest that aims and intentions themselves might be a consequence as a much as a precondition of collective action. Now, therefore, we turn to the specific issue of participants' ideas changing in and through collective action.

Crowds and Psychological Change

One dimension of psychological change found in the literature is that of participants becoming politicized or radicalized through their involvement in strikes, occupations, and riots. For example, Malatesta (1989, p. 353) states that, during the Italian factory occupations of 1920, "the character of workers' demands soon changed" from the issue of wages to that of revolution. Schneider (1989), who participated in the naval revolt and commune at Wilhelmshaven, Germany, in 1919, comments: "There were . . . many previous prisoners of war, who were freed without any discussion of 'different races' and nationalities. Class-consciousness had solved these 'problems' on the spot" (p. 356).

Another dimension of psychological change is that of empowerment, which was noted in studies of the North American ghetto riots of the 1960s. Thus Boesel, Goldberg, and Marx (1971) document the enhanced pride in participants' identities as blacks, which seemed to be associated with what the participants now saw themselves as capable of in relation to others. Similarly, Oberschall (1968) describes how the Los Angeles riot of 1965 was seen by those involved as a "victory" for their side over the police, and how they derived a new sense of self-respect from the events.

One historical example covering both these dimensions and more, and which has been well documented, is that of the events in France in May 1968. A university protest culminated in a night of barricades and street fighting with riot police. Soon, others joined in the protest movement, and widespread occupations, wildcat strikes, and huge demonstrations almost toppled the government of de Gaulle. Among the results, Mann (1973) points not only to material rewards and worker control in matters of job regulation, but also to "an upsurge in worker interest in the construction of an *alternative* society" (p. 53, emphasis original). Despite de Gaulle's reassertion of control, Mann suggests that this radicalization did not disappear; in a "typical" day in November 1969, *Le Monde* reported that no less than seven French factories were occupied by their workers (p. 54). Accounts from within the movement point to a similar process of political transformation occurring among the students. One account states how "within a few days, young people of 20 attained a level of understanding and a political and tactical sense which many who had been in the revolutionary movement for 30 years or more were still sadly lacking"; moreover, "[t]he tumultuous development of the students' struggle . . . transformed both the relation of forces in society and the image, in people's minds, of established institutions and of established leaders" (Anon., 1968, p. 51). Occupying students displayed increased confidence in their own abilities and capacities: "The occupants of Censier suddenly cease to be unconscious, passive *objects* shaped by particular combinations of social forces; they become conscious, active *subjects* who begin to shape their own social activity" (Gregoire and Perlman, 1969, p. 37, emphasis original); "people who have never expressed ideas before, who have never spoken in front of professors and students, become confident in their ability" (p. 41).

A number of the historical examples point to the crucial role of interventions by external forces in producing these kind of changes in conceptions of self and others. Anderson (1964) describes how a nonviolent protest march to the state radio building in Hungary in 1956 became the start of a violent uprising only when state security forces fired into the crowd. Later, the decision of the government to call in Russian troops only made the Hungarian people more determined. New ideas and practices – such as the workers' councils that arose in this period – were a direct function of the struggle itself rather than a precondition for the conflict with the state: "In the society they were glimpsing through the dust and smoke of the battle of the streets, there would be no prime minister, no government of professional politicians, and no officials or bosses ordering them about" (p. 58); thus, for many people, ideas of revolution "were born out of the impact and intellectual ferment of the struggle itself" (p. 87).

Some of these examples of change are consistent with Therborn's (1980) observation about revolutionary movements: they tend not to start off with programs defining possible future societies; rather such visions arise only as a consequence of conflict with those in power over less central issues. The notion that participation in collective action may have unintended consequences – psychological or otherwise – has been central to our own research on crowds and change. This research was the basis of a model explaining both crowd dynamics and psychological change, the elaborated social identity model. We now explain the principles of this model which, we argue, makes sense of many of the phenomena described here.

An Elaborated Social Identity Model of Psychological Change in Collective Action

The elaborated social identity model (ESIM) was developed in order to explain how conflict starts and how it escalates in crowd events (Reicher, 1996b; Stott and Reicher, 1998a, 1998b). But, since such conflict often involves changes in identity in those involved, the model also sought to explain these processes of identity change, which it suggested were intimately linked to intergroup dynamics (Drury and Reicher, 2000; Reicher, 1996a, 2001).

In explicating a pattern of conflict emergence and escalation observed over a number of different crowd events, the ESIM can be broken down into three elements: *concepts, conditions,* and *dynamics.* First, concepts: *social identity* is conceptualized as the way in which people understand how they are positioned relative to others, along with the forms of action that make sense from that position; hence *context* is understood as the identity-based action of those forces external to crowd actors which enable or constrain their action.

Second, the ESIM suggests that the conditions necessary for the emergence and development of crowd conflict are twofold. The first condition is an asymmetry of categorical representations between crowd participants and an outgroup (such as the police), such that each group regards its own action as legitimate but the other's as illegitimate. The second condition is an asymmetry of power, such that the outgroup is able to impose its definition of legitimate practice on the ingroup of crowd participants – for example, through having the technology, organization, and strength in numbers to form cordons, coordinated baton charges and thereby constraining the physical movement of the crowd.

Third, there is a dynamic, meaning action and change. Outgroup actions which are perceived as treating all crowd members alike serve to extend the boundaries of the collective self (versus other) within the crowd, thus transforming a relatively heterogeneous crowd into a homogeneous one. Moreover, to the extent that such outgroup action is also seen as illegitimate (e.g., denying the right to protest and using offensive tactics to disperse the crowd) then the content of this new crowd unity is opposition to the outgroup. The dynamic therefore entails a social repositioning through which a number of dimensions of psychological change occur (Reicher and Drury, 2011). The following dimensions of change are not intended as an exhaustive list.

First, there is change in the *content* of identity ("who we are"). Those who initially saw themselves as "moderates," for example, are now positioned by the authorities as "radicals" and hence they come to understand their position and their identity accordingly (Drury and Reicher, 2000). Moreover, if "who we are" changes, there may be corresponding change in definitions of group aims and in the criteria for success (e.g., from protesting against a particular issue to overcoming the police in order to defend the right to protest; Stott and Drury, 2000).

Second, changes in the content of the collective self may mean changes in its *boundaries* – that is, in who counts as ingroup and who counts as outgroup; some now become part of "us," whereas others who were previously counted as one of "us" are now rejected (Drury, Reicher, and Stott, 2003).

Third, where these boundaries become more inclusive, and where the ingroup-outgroup distinction is highly salient, there are feelings of consensus and hence expectations of mutual support; this *empowers* crowd members to express their radical beliefs and confront the outgroup (Drury and Reicher, 1999, 2005, 2009).

Fourth, change in understandings of relations with outgroups may entail change in definitions of *legitimacy*, as beliefs about what counts as an appropriate action get redefined – for example, understandings of violence may change from "unjustified attack" to "self-defense."

These four dimensions of identity change are derived from the original statements of social identity theory (Tajfel and Turner, 1979) and self-categorization theory (Turner et al., 1987) on the nature of social identity. While the dimensions are clearly interlinked – in that those who change on one dimension often change on the others too – we will focus here on one of the four that has so far received least attention: changes in understandings of legitimate action. Thus in the final section of this chapter, we show how the intergroup dynamics of crowd conflict changed some participants' shared ideas about their social relations and hence their beliefs about legitimate actions to bring about social change.

Changing Definitions of Legitimate Action at an Anti-Roads Protest

The data presented here are part of a year-long ethnographic study of an antiroadbuilding campaign in London in the early 1990s (Drury and Reicher, 2000, 2005; Drury et al., 2003; Drury and Stott, 2001). The campaign was set up to oppose the construction of the M11 link road, which was planned to go through the districts of Wanstead, Leytonstone, and Leyton, with the loss of hundreds of houses and trees. Until the 1990s, campaigns against road schemes tended to end with the final decision of the public enquiry, but the struggle over the expansion of the M3 at Twyford Down (1991–1992) changed that. The No M11 link road campaign, which followed shortly after Twyford, took direct action including squatting houses and trees on the route of the road, occupying land and machinery, and invading construction sites.

Over the course of a year of participant observation in the campaign, we made notes, took soundtrack recordings, carried out interviews, and gathered documents, diary entries, and news materials. One of the most prevalent themes found in participants' accounts was that of "nonviolence." This section analyses the change among some campaign participants toward seeing violence as legitimate under certain conditions (conditional nonviolence), instead of seeing it as always or inherently wrong (unconditional nonviolence). This type of change by no means applied to all campaign participants, but it does show in some detail the connections between intergroup actions and psychological change.

Examples of this kind of change were scattered throughout the data set as a whole, but two particular events stand out as being important in the experience of change for a number of campaign participants: a violent eviction and the Hyde Park riot of October 1994.

A Violent Eviction

Participants attempted to prevent the demolition of houses by occupying them. In the case of this particular occupation and then eviction, which took place in August 1994, three houses that campaign participants slept in were breached by bailiffs supported by demolition workers, security guards, and police. The houses were part of a terraced row, so campaign participants then clambered onto the roofs from houses at the other end of the street to obstruct the demolition. Using a hydraulic platform, police and bailiffs attempted to pull campaign participants from the roof, using saws to cut through ropes used by participants to attach themselves to structures on the roofs.

Many of those who climbed onto the roofs said they felt their lives were threatened by the behavior of police and contractors. This fear and anger was evident from both contemporaneous soundtrack recordings and from comments made afterward. Some also said that the behavior of the demolition workers and security guards made him rethink their conceptions of the status of nonviolence. The experience of one campaign participant provides a vivid illustration.

To put the change in context, the following extract is taken from an interview carried out with the participant nine months before the violent eviction:

JD: What are the most effective ways to [take action against the road]?
CT: The non-violent direct action aspect of it
JD: Which means what?
CT: Well direct action in that you erm go and actively stop what's going on erm rather than just standing on the road and protesting where you're allowed to protest, because I think that would just be treated with contempt and ignored. Plus non-violent, cos I don't see any point at all in causing confrontation either between security guards, contractors or the police because

they're not the real enemy, they're just carrying out the wishes of the authorities involved. And to come in with a huge crowd of people and kick the shit
out of them is not valid in that it would lose support from other people and
I don't think in the long term that it would be effective.

JD: Right

CT: Erm Two-fold because if erm you lose public support and also because
they'll just bring in more people, draft in more people to come and kick
the shit out of you so [] Erm it's not their fault they're here, some of them
have got like families to feed. Things like that. I think the best way to do
to stop someone is to educate them and to talk to them, not to beat sense
into them. I don't think that ever works from the experience I've seen of erm
anti-fascist demos and things like that, I quite disagree with erm a lot of anti-
fascist tactics of just screaming abuse and going and beating up fascists. I
don't think that works. All they'll do is come round with a bigger crowd next
time.   (Interview, November 1993)

There are a number of different elements in the extract above. In the first
place, there are what might be called pragmatic arguments – that violence
by campaign participants would lose them support (and, by implication,
nonviolence enhances their support) and that it would be ineffective anyway. This is justified in terms of a simple universal – violence is never
effective (at least in his experience). But it is also underpinned by claims
about the social position and inherent nature of the possible objects of
such violence: there is the argument that security guards, contractors
and police are in some sense a neutral layer between campaign participants and the "real enemy" (the authorities whose decision it is to build
the road); and there also is the humanistic argument that the inherent
rational qualities of these people must be appealed to – through education and talking to them. Thus, the campaign participant's position was
one of unconditional nonviolence at this stage in the campaign.

Later, however, in an account of the violent eviction, the same campaign participant described how the humanistic rationale underlying
nonviolence was now unsustainable; appealing to the underlying humanity of security and contractors through talking to them over the months
was having no effect, suggesting that their group and role identities
were as real as any supposed "good" human nature in the individual
"underneath":

People were trying to guilt trip them about "How will you sleep tonight, how can
you do this?" I didn't think there was much point in doing that because there
seemed to be enjoyment in doing it. I just think if someone had been killed that
day it wouldn't have bothered them [] That in a way has very much disillusioned
me. I've been more and more getting a bit disillusioned with trying to appeal to
the security guards' [ ] better nature. (Interview, August 1994)

Worse still, the core nonviolent method of highlighting a shared humanity by making oneself vulnerable, instead of discouraging violence by
security guards and demolition workers, actually seemed to have the
opposite effect:

the thugs we have to deal with are taking advantage of our passiveness. (Personal
account, CT, autumn 1994)

However, CT argued that *pragmatic* justifications still held: nonviolence
enhanced outside support for the campaign, and campaign participants
would be even more likely to be beaten up and arrested if they used
violence:

I suppose I have become increasingly disillusioned with NVDA [nonviolent
direct action] since starting my involvement in the anti-roads movement, but
still believe that it is the best method we can use at the present time, although
my objections to violent actions are purely tactical as opposed to the moral objections I used to have. (Personal account, CT, autumn 1994)

As we have seen, the humanistic world-view did not simply delegitimize violence, but also legitimized certain other methods of collective
action, such as trying to persuade security guards, demolition contractors, police, and so on through appeals to their universal humanity and
rationality. While there was no evidence that campaign participants who
abandoned unconditional nonviolence began using violence during M11
site actions or evictions, there was a clear behavioral change evident in
their abandonment of arguments around shared individual humanity. If
argument was used, it was now based on assumptions about the reality
of groups and group interests:

I believe in appealing to things that directly effect [*sic*] them: for instance telling
police that they should be out fighting real crime and not let themselves get used
as political pawns, and pointing out to security that once the road is built they
will all get laid off, so it's in their interests to let us delay the work as much as
possible. (Diary, CT, 1994)

The Hyde Park Riot

A national demonstration against the Criminal Justice Bill (CJB) took
place in London on Sunday, October 9, 1994. Participants in the No
M11 campaign were involved in the national movement against the bill,
which was understood as an attempt to criminalize the direct action char-
acterizing the campaign: in particular the new offenses of aggravated
trespass and trespassory assembly made certain types of trespass (such

as interfering with "lawful activity") a criminal offense for the first time. There was agreement with other critics that the bill was an attack on both civil rights and unconventional lifestyles (see McKay, 1998).

Dozens of No M11 campaign participants marched with a crowd of thousands from the Embankment to Hyde Park. Toward the end of the march, a confrontation with police began over whether or not a mobile sound system could enter the park. This conflict extended to involve many more people than the small group around the sound system when mounted police entered the park and charged into the crowd as a whole. Hundreds of demonstrators then fought the police by throwing missiles and chasing them from the park. Violent conflict between riot police and demonstrators lasted for around four hours.

Both the nature of the police tactics (mounted charges into the whole crowd) and the accounts of demonstrators who were interviewed suggest that the police action was experienced as an illegitimate and indiscriminate attack on demonstrators. A number of groups and individuals on the march were advocating unconditional nonviolence; yet such people were just as vulnerable to the police charges as those who were willing to fight the police. For some of our interviewees, if the police were going to act violently whatever people did, then the humanistic rationale for nonviolence – that it prevents violence by appealing to their inherent rational nature – no longer made sense.

At the previous national demonstration against the CJB, only a month earlier, one of the groups helping co-ordinate the national campaign, and some of whose members had also been involved in the M11 campaign, distributed a leaflet offering the following advice, epitomizing the humanistic approach:

KEEP IT FLUFFY! [ ] If it turns nasty . . . remember you are an individual – don't just go along with the crowd [ ] If the violence continues, you could ALL SIT DOWN, still holding hands. [ ] As a last resort, you can form a "DOOR-MAT" by all lying on the ground, holding on to each other's arms and legs. [ ] Remember that the police are all individuals – with families, emotions and problems of their own. If you have to deal with them, try to be friendly and polite. (emphasis original)

After the October riot, while a number of the campaign participants we spoke to argued that there were good pragmatic reasons for continuing with nonviolence in the context of the M11 campaign, they also felt that, at Hyde Park, pacifist methods such as sitting down in front of the police would not have prevented the police using violence against the crowd;

violence by demonstrators against police, on the other hand, *was* effective in that situation in preventing injury to demonstrators:

JD: Should the methods of the crowd that day be used in all protest situations, and if not what was it about that situation that made violence appropriate?

DA: [ ] Obviously that wouldn't be right for every situation but given that the police did like try and charge against a whole load of just like fluffy ravers then that was probably the best thing to do. Cos I think like when you've got police on horseback if you just like offer passive resistance and you'll like be severely injured. Cos like they'd just gallop straight over the top of you.

(Interview, October 1994)

Comments from one participant can serve as an illustration of how the experience at Hyde Park buttressed views that were already changing through similar experiences of outgroup violence at the No M11 campaign. EY's nonviolence had a principled, moral-humanistic basis from the beginning of the campaign: it was unconditional. A number of statements by him and by others earlier in the campaign, scattered through the data set, attested to this. EY was present during the fighting in Hyde Park. Although he did not throw anything at the police, we noted with surprise that he did not criticize those who did. In a later interview, he described how his "rigid" approach to the question of nonviolence had changed. Although he saw nonviolence as useful and the preferred mode, his original commitment to it as an "ideology" (i.e., unconditional), he said, was grounded in social relations in which it had not been subjected to challenge. But in the light of constant attack by the police and the authorities on himself and the campaign as a whole, he said, there were times when violence counted as legitimate self-defense: nonviolence was not always enough when collectives were in conflict:

LB: Has it changed your views on nonviolence and violence at all?

EY: [ ] It has to a certain degree because I have been in contact with violence perpetrated by others against us a lot more. I mean when I wasn't involved in a full time campaign that didn't happen, so you could afford to build up certain concepts, certain ideologies [ ] when conflict isn't happening every day, when things aren't happening every day that can challenge them concepts you've built up, if you're not in contact with the police every day, if you're not in contact with the authorities every day, whereas on the campaign every day that is the case and you see the violence that's done to yourself, to your friends and your community by such people and that does challenge your ideas of non-violence or pacifism [ ] cos you have to find ways to react to that, and while I think that non-violence is definitely the best way the most constructive, I can understand people's anger and their resorting to violence, and I can certainly understand self-defence, in defence of your community, in defence of yourself, I think is a valid concept as well. But it

has sort of – I've become less dogmatic and less rigid I think in my approach
to that question.   (Interview, October 1994)

He explains that the humanistic rationale had become impossible to
maintain given what he now saw as the objecthood of the police as a
social category:

> EY: It used to be the idea you've got to treat them as individuals and not just as
> a homogeneous mass, but in fact like any group under threat they will close
> ranks and protect themselves. If if you're talking quite nicely to a policeman
> and he seems to be okay and he sympathizes with you and he's usually being
> okay, in a situation where a mate of his truncheons you over the head he'll
> protect his friend 99% of the time, and protect him in the final analysis as
> well rather than uphold the law.   (Interview, October 1994)

How Participation in Collective Action Transforms Understandings of Collective Action

In summary, in a number of cases at an antiroads direct action campaign,
the humanistic underpinnings for nonviolence gave way to a more pragmatic approach: unconditional nonviolence became conditional. In theory, pragmatism could amount to a "cynical" approach to nonviolence,
in which the participant would prefer to use violence but is unable to do
so for practical reasons, or in which there are no preferences. In practice, however, the evidence suggests that this was far from the case. The
analysis contains quotes illustrating campaign participants' criticisms of
"gratuitous" violence. For these participants, violence did not become
redefined as a neutral technique; rather, it featured as a "last resort"
only to be used in "self-defense." Nonviolence remained the preferred
approach at the No M11 campaign, given not only campaign participants' perceptions of the evidence of its tactical usefulness in appealing
to potential supporters, but also the "moral" reluctance of most campaign participants to use violence anyway.

In terms of process, features of the violent eviction and the Hyde Park
riot correspond with the principles set out in the ESIM. Thus, first,
in terms of identity, participants' pacifist norms reflected a model of
the social world comprising essentially rational individual human beings
(rather than groups). Second, while participants regarded their nonviolent direct action as both lawful and legitimate, there is evidence from
elsewhere in the No M11 data set that police regarded campaigners'
actions as both threatening and disorderly (Drury and Reicher, 2000);
and it is clear from the examples presented here that police, bailiffs, and
contractors had the organization and technology to enact their understanding that forcible removal or dispersal of protestors was lawful and

legitimate. Third, the police, bailiff, and contractor action was understood by campaign participants as illegitimate, since they felt they had the right to protest; but it was also seen as indiscriminate, on two levels: first, tactics such as mounted charges were perceived to threaten the whole crowd; and second, violent, dangerous tactics by police, bailiffs, and contractors did not discriminate between those using nonviolence and anyone else.

In terms of outcomes, for a number of participants the repositioning brought about by outgroup actions transformed what it meant to be an antiroads campaigner. They found themselves in a world not of rational, persuadable individuals but of group forces. Thus, the discarding of the humanistic rationale reflected the recognition of the objecthood of group power and group interests; these became seen as real and enduring features rather than mystified identities overlaying the supposed individual human essence. Within such repositioned relations, actions that were previously illegitimate – such as violence – now became redefined as legitimate self-defense.

Conclusions

This chapter has argued that the Le Bonian claim, that crowds are essentially conservative, is wrong in its analysis (crowds do contribute to meaningful social change) and also wrong in its premise (that the psychology of crowd members is archaic and hence essentially resistant to novelty). While most crowds are not revolutionary, social change is very often associated with crowd events and crowd behavior. And it is precisely in crowd events – in particular crowd events in which there is struggle with those in power – where the psychology of participants is recreated in the form of novel understandings of both self and appropriate action.

Though most of the examples we have provided in the chapter are of "progressive" crowds and movements, the argument being put forward here is certainly not that all crowds (or even all world-changing crowds) are left-wing, radical, or revolutionary, etc. (as in some kind of mirror-opposite of Le Bon's (1896/1947) position). By the same token, the evidence presented of "radicalization" of those involved in collective action is not intended to suggest that all such psychological changes are in one direction. Reactionary movements, such as fascism, have imposed themselves on the world through collective action and no doubt many of the participants changed their ideas about themselves and others in the process. The reason for the predominance of "radical" examples in this chapter is that such cases predominate in the literature.

The No M11 campaign did not stop the link road from being built. But, as part of the wider antiroads movement of that time, it is argued by some to have had two important social consequences (e.g., Jordan, 1998). First, it transformed our understanding roadbuilding in the UK from a merely technical matter to a profoundly political one. Roadbuilding was no longer a neutral issue. Second, and connected to this, it mortally wounded the government's massive roadbuilding program (costing £23bn and supposedly "the biggest since the Romans"), which was drastically cut (by three-quarters) in the following years.

Though these effects were only perceived some time after the events analyzed here, and the campaign was not an attempt at revolution, the analysis offered in this chapter and in our other analysis of these crowd events (see, in particular, Drury and Reicher, 2009) offers some suggestions on the links between crowds and revolutions. Specifically, where intergroup interaction – between the forces of stability and those movements struggling for change – serves to produce new relations and new understandings (of self, other, legitimacy, and power), this may form the basis of a new round of struggle in which the very reason for the struggle has changed. As we have shown, because crowd events are intergroup encounters, acting on the basis of shared social identity can have unintended consequences, including changes in identity itself. In the case of the No M11 campaign, a "local" issue (saving local houses and trees) became redefined in "global" terms (the environment, injustice, the right to protest, capitalism) following the attempt to enact that "local" issue through protest (Drury et al., 2003), paralleling the way that limited or "reformist" struggle may become revolutionary through conflict with those in power (Therborn, 1980).

REFERENCES

Ackerman, P., and Kruegler, C. (1994). *Strategic Nonviolent Conflict: The Dynamics of People Power in the Twentieth Century.* Westport, CT: Praeger.

Anderson, A. (1964). *Hungary '56.* London: Solidarity.

Anon. (1968). *Paris: May 1968.* London: Solidarity.

Anon. (1984). *The Experience of the Factory Committees in the Russian Revolution.* Cardiff: Scorcher.

Boesel, D., Goldberg, L. C., and Marx, G. T. (1971). Rebellion in Plainfield. In D. Boesel and P. H. Rossi (Eds.), *Cities under Siege: An Anatomy of the Ghetto Riots, 1964–1968* (pp. 67–83). New York: Basic Books.

Carr, E. H. (1950). *The Bolshevik Revolution 1917–1923.* Harmondsworth, UK: Penguin.

Drury, J., and Reicher, S. (1999). The intergroup dynamics of collective empowerment: Substantiating the social identity model of crowd behaviour. *Group Processes and Intergroup Relations, 2,* 381–402.

(2000). Collective action and psychological change: The emergence of new social identities. *British Journal of Social Psychology*, 39, 579–604.

(2005). Explaining enduring empowerment: A comparative study of collective action and psychological outcomes. *European Journal of Social Psychology*, 35, 35–58.

(2009). Collective psychological empowerment as a model of social change: Researching crowds and power. *Journal of Social Issues*, 65, 707–725.

Drury, J., Reicher, S., and Stott, C. (2003). Transforming the boundaries of collective identity: From the "local" anti-road campaign to "global" resistance? *Social Movement Studies*, 2, 191–212.

Drury, J., and Stott, C. (2001). Bias as a research strategy in participant observation: The case of intergroup conflict. *Field Methods*, 13, 47–67.

Gregoire, R., and Perlman, F. (1969). *Worker-Student Action Committees: France May '68*. Detroit: Black and Red.

Hobsbawm, E. J. (1964). *Labouring Men: Studies in the History of Labour*. London: Weidenfeld and Nicolson.

Jordan, J. (1998). The art of necessity: The subversive imagination of anti-road protest and Reclaim the Streets. In G. McKay (Ed.), *DIY Culture: Party and Protest in Modern Britain* (pp. 129–151). London: Verso.

Le Bon, G. (1896/1947). *The Crowd: A Study of the Popular Mind*. London: Ernest Benn.

Malatesta, E. (1989). The occupation of the factories in Italy in 1920. *The Raven*, 8(2), 353–355.

Mann, M. (1973). *Consciousness and Action among the Western Working Class*. London: Macmillan.

McKay, G. (Ed.) (1998). *DIY Culture: Party and Protest in Modern Britain*. London: Verso.

Oberschall, A. (1968). The Los Angeles Riot of August 1965. *Social Problems*, 15, 322–341.

Reed, J. (1926/1982). *Ten Days That Shook the World*. Harmondsworth, UK: Penguin.

Reicher, S. (1996a). Social identity and social change: Rethinking the context of social psychology. In W. P. Robinson (Ed.), *Social Groups and Identities: Developing the Legacy of Henri Tajfel* (pp. 317–336). London: Butterworth.

(1996b). "The Battle of Westminster": Developing the social identity model of crowd behaviour in order to explain the initiation and development of collective conflict. *European Journal of Social Psychology*, 26, 115–134.

Reicher, S. (2001). The psychology of crowd dynamics. In M. A. Hogg and R. S. Tindale (Eds.), *Blackwell Handbook of Social Psychology: Group Processes* (pp. 182–208). Oxford: Blackwell.

Reicher, S., and Drury, J. (2011). Collective identity, political participation and the making of the social self. In A. Azzi, X. Chryssochoou, B. Klandermans, and B. Simon (Eds.), *Identity and Participation in Culturally Diverse Societies: A Multidisciplinary Perspective* (pp. 158–176). Oxford: Wiley-Blackwell.

Rudé, G. (1959). *The Crowd in the French Revolution*. London: Oxford University Press.

(1981). *The Crowd in History: A Study of Popular Disturbances in France and England, 1730–1848*. Rev. ed. London: Lawrence and Wishart.

Schneider, E. (1989). The Wilhelmshaven revolt. *The Raven*, 8(2), 356–380.

Sharpe, J. A. (1984). *Crime in Early Modern England 1550–1750.* London: Longman.

Stott, C., and Drury, J. (2000). Crowds, context and identity: Dynamic categorization processes in the "poll tax riot." *Human Relations*, 53, 247–273.

Stott, C., and Reicher, S. (1998a). Crowd action as inter-group process: Introducing the police perspective. *European Journal of Social Psychology*, 28, 509–529.

(1998b). How conflict escalates: The inter-group dynamics of collective football crowd "violence." *Sociology*, 32, 353–377.

Tajfel, H., and Turner, J. C. (1979). An integrative theory of intergroup relations. In S. Worchel and W. G. Austin (Eds.), *Psychology of Intergroup Relations* (pp. 33–47). Monterey, CA: Brooks-Cole.

Therborn, G. (1980). *The Ideology of Power and the Power of Ideology.* London: Verso.

Thompson, E. P. (1980). *Making of the English Working Class.* London: Vintage Books.

(1991). *Customs in Common.* Harmondsworth, UK: Penguin.

Turner, J. C., Hogg, M. A., Oakes, P. J., Reicher, S. D., and Wetherell, M. S. (1987). *Rediscovering the Social Group: A Self-Categorization Theory.* Oxford: Blackwell.

Waddington, D. (1992). *Contemporary Issues in Public Disorder: A Comparative and Historical Approach.* London: Routledge.

3   Economic Inequality and the Rise of Civic Discontent
Deprivation and Remembering in an Irish Case Study

Séamus Power*

Sir, – Paul Krugman has compared our GDP figures to "leprechaun economics."

How ludicrous. Get with the times, Prof Krugman. Nobody believes in economics any more. – Yours, etc,

Patricia O'Riordan,
Dublin 8.

This letter, published in the *Irish Times* on Monday, July 18, 2016, encapsulated the Irish zeitgeist at the time it was published; a distrust of data reporting aggregate economic growth, frustration with official commentators on economic improvement; made manifest, in this case, with satire in the public sphere.

In this chapter, I use the Irish case study to illustrate the ways in which civic unrest occurs due to perceptions of social injustices in the form of economic inequality that generates and legitimizes protest. First I review the literature on culture and economic development. I argue that by understanding the connections between the two we can better comprehend how people perceive and respond to economic crises and what constitutes for them fair or unfair economic inequality. Next, I locate the 2008 financial crisis in historical context. I draw on economic history to illuminate the ways in which economic inequality waxes and wanes over time. This pattern is linked to the opening and closing of borders, and increased or decreased cultural and ethnic heterogeneity, which effects perceptions of perceived social injustices and the fairness of wealth and income distribution.

I situate the current Irish case within this broader cultural and economic framework. I identify a paradox from my fieldwork. When the

* This research was supported by the Society for Research on Adolescence, the Division of Social Sciences at the University of Chicago, by the Lemelson/Society for Psychological Anthropology Pre-Dissertation Award, made possible by a generous donation from the Robert Lemelson Foundation, and by a Mellon Fellowship. This manuscript benefited greatly from feedback from Michael Jindra, Richard Shweder, and Brady Wagoner.

Irish economy collapsed in 2008, there were few protests. Yet, when the Irish economy began booming once more in 2014 and 2015, there were various forms of civic unrest. This is the *deprivation–protest paradox* (see Power, 2017a). I detail two fundamental cultural psychological processes that can be used to understand this paradox. I elaborate upon classic relative deprivation theory to understand some of the dynamics of protest in the Republic of Ireland. I reveal the ways in which demonstrators expected to reap the benefits of an economic boom, having suffered harsh austerity beforehand. But this economic growth was perceived to be experienced unequally – a minority of people benefited – which created frustration that manifested in civic discontent, particularly against a new charge on water. Moreover, I apply theories of collective remembering to comprehend how protesting in Ireland is linked to historically overcoming social and political injustices in the form of uprisings and armed rebellions. Connecting relative deprivation and collective remembering informs the ways in which social groups compare and orientate themselves to one another and decide on what is and what is not fair in terms of economic distributions. Abstracting from this, I conclude by articulating a theoretical framework of unfair economic inequality and the rise of civic discontent. The perceived commodification of water in Ireland galvanized street demonstrations. Therefore, I end by discussing the increasingly special place water is likely to occupy in future social revolutions.

The global economy collapsed in 2008. Different countries and regions experienced the economic crisis in multiple ways for interrelated economic, political, financial, geographical, legal, and cultural reasons. Economic and financial analyses dominate our understanding of what happened during the 2008 financial crisis. However, understanding how culture is interconnected with economic analyses can provide a richer, more nuanced, and detailed explanation of financial and economic crises. In order to locate the localized Irish scenario within a broader framework, it is important to understand the interaction between culture and economic development.

Culture, Economics, and Development

Recent and historical work has illustrated the importance of understanding culture in relation to economic development (Banfield, 1958; Harrison and Huntington, 2000; Landes, 1999). In *The Protestant Ethic and the Spirit of Capitalism* Weber examined the impact of religious values on economic prosperity (Weber, 1905/2009). He discussed how the Calvinist belief in predestination impacted attitudes toward work. He argued economic prosperity for believers signaled they were predestined for heaven. Over time the idea of predestination faded, but the ethos of showing prosperity was maintained, and it lay at the basis of contemporary capitalism. In contrast, the basic values of Catholicism – sin followed by confession, redemption, and repeated sin – led to a less strict work ethic because forgiveness was always at hand. Protestants, unlike Catholics, valued an austere and entrepreneurial life.

Weber developed these ideas in two further studies exploring the effects of religion on culture and economic development. *The Religion of China* (1951) and *The Religion of India* (1958) further highlighted the importance of understanding culture to explain stunted economic development. He argued that Confucianism in China and Hinduism in India led citizens to explain natural phenomena with illogical and irrational supernatural belief systems. In these religious systems, the family is central and valued at the expense of the broader community, leading to a lack of entrepreneurial enterprises and, by extension, hindered economic development. Institutions capable of developing and sustaining economic growth were lacking. This theme developed in further research concerning culture and economic growth.

Banfield (1958) conducted one of the foundational studies in this area. His investigation into the poverty and lack of economic progress in a small village in southern Italy revealed the moral foundations and cultural outlook at the basis of this community. He introduced the term "amoral familism" – which originates from high death rates, harsh land conditions, and the large absence of extended family – to explain why these Italian villagers could not motivate themselves to organize politically, or economically, for the overall good of the community, and, by extension, for all individuals. By detailing the systemic problems in one rural village, he convincingly argues for the importance of understanding cultural and communal morals, in order to comprehend hindered economic development. An increasing body of literature highlights this important link, but the conclusions are contested.

In *Underdevelopment Is a State of Mind*, Harrison argued that cultural values have hindered economic development throughout Latin America (Harrison, 1985). But detractors from the importance of culture in explaining variation in regional economic development highlight geographical, political, or economic factors as being more important (Sachs, 2000). The argument is favorable geography (in terms of production of goods and work conditions), and capitalist institutions, and the feedback loop that exists between them, are of utmost importance for economic development. Not culture. And it is certainly not the most important explanatory factor in economic growth.

However, Sachs's argument is overly simplistic, because he conceptualizes culture as an explanatory variable; just one factor among many. Banfield's (1958) research illustrates the intricate ways cultural and moral beliefs – the importance of close family rather than community activism and government – meant capitalist institutions were difficult to establish in his case study in southern Italy. He does not undermine the importance of complex and preexisting reasons for the focus on the family at the expensive of the community – poverty and the low status of the manual laborer – but intertwined with, and inseparable from these forces, are culturally widespread and historically ingrained cultural and moral beliefs and values.

Similarly, Nisbett and Cohen (1996) explain higher rates of aggression and homicide in the US south, relative to the north, by examining the culture of honor that exists in the south. They use data from news reports, government institutions, legal frameworks, and experiments, to illustrate how fundamental cultural beliefs in aggressively defending honor when threatened manifests in everyday behavior. The basis of this culture of honor, according to the authors, lies in early Irish and Scot farming settlers in the American south, who, unlike their more settled neighbors in the American north, needed to physically defend any affronts to them, or against their herd, on the lawless frontier. Over time, laws and intuitions were established to keep the peace, but these were still ingrained with the moral and cultural basis of defending ones honor. Although not an explicit study of economic development, the study highlights, contrary to arguments made by Sachs (2000), that geographical topographies (i.e., farming land) are linked to the establishment of institutions (i.e., to keep law and order) and are historically interconnected with cultural and moral beliefs (i.e., the right to defend ones honor).

Cultural beliefs and economic growth are enshrined, yet the connection between the two has often been neglected in analyses of the 2008 financial crisis. Moreover, the recent focus on inequality – and cultural analyses of how it manifests, and how it is perceived – is important to comprehend in the context of the 2008 economic recession.

Cycles of Inequality and the 2008 Financial Crisis

Global inequality is increasing (Atkinson, 2015; Dorling, 2014; Picketty, 2014; Picketty and Saez, 2014). In *Capital in the Twenty-First Century* Picketty (2014) surveys data from twenty countries, dating back to the 1800s, to convincingly illustrate the ways in which global income inequality is increasing, since World War II. He argues this trend is not inevitable, and proposes a global tax on capital to help redistribution and consequently curb growing inequality. The publishing of the Panama Papers, which to some extent reveal the volume of hidden off-shore money, suggests a global tax on capital is a utopian ideal. Atkinson (2015) also identifies rising global inequality as the major problem of the twenty-first century and proposes a series of innovative and interrelated policy measures again to redistribute wealth from the few to the many. Dorling (2014), in his analysis of *Inequality and the 1%* highlights the increasing accumulation of wealth by a small minority of people since the global economic crisis of 2008. Since then, he argues, the 1 percent in the UK and the US has disproportionately increased their wealth in relation to the 99 percent. The latter have endured austerity as their economies exited formal recessions and returned to positive growth. Dorling highlights the growing frustration among the majority, who protested on the streets first in the US, then in the UK, in the form of Occupy protests. This sustained campaign in both countries was organized to highlight rising inequality – which became particularly prevalent in 2011 – when both economies reported growth, but this growth was experienced unequally. The gap between the "haves" and the "have nots" – the 1 percent and the 99 percent – became a chasm. He does not allude to the amount of wealth the 1 percent lost during the economic downturn, only what they gained during the economic recovery.

Moreover, historical economic analyses suggest the global financial crisis of 2008 was not a unique event (Aliber and Kindleberger, 2015; Reinhart and Rogoff, 2009). Reinhart and Rogoff (2009) situate the 2008 economic crash within a broad historical milieu of economic recessions and recoveries. Analyzing data ranging as far back as twelfth-century China and medieval Europe, the authors conclude that the trope "this time is different" when referring to contemporary economic booms is false: the weight of evidence suggests a cyclical – but not inevitable – pattern of economic boom and bust in the form of government defaults, inflationary spikes, and banking panics, have occurred in all nations throughout history. The role of the accumulation of debt – either by banks, governments, or the public – is one uniting theme underlying their survey of historical economic crises. Economic and social analyses of the 2008 economic crisis that claim it was a unique event grossly miss the point. The authors argue failing to remember the lessons of history results in similar mistakes being repeated. Cultural patterns of collective memory, steeped in localized history, are important to understand in order to appreciate the complexity of perceptions toward economic crises and recoveries.

These historical analyses of economic booms and busts reveal common patterns across time and countries. The literature on economic inequality suggests it is increasing since the end of World War II. Interestingly, in a theory put forth by Shweder (forthcoming), there are parallels between migration policies and income distribution. During the period 1870–1920, the US had a relatively liberal migration policy, accepting immigrants from around the world. Simultaneously, during the same period, there was an unequal distribution of income in the US. Following World War I, until the early 1970s, the US began closing its borders, and this correlated with an increase in economic redistribution. From the 1970s until the present, the US has relatively open migration policies, and again these correlate with widening gaps in income distribution (Picketty, 2014). In the US, there is a correlation between the patterns of cultural homogeneity and heterogeneity, and more or less inequality of income distribution. This is the *equality–difference paradox*: the observation that the more culturally and ethnically homogenous a country is, the greater the equal income distribution and vice versa (Jindra, 2014; Minnow, Shweder, and Markus, 2008; Shweder, forthcoming; Shweder and Power, 2013).

Following the global economic crisis of 2008, the unequal economic recovery highlighted the growing gap between "the 1 percent and the 99 percent" in many Western countries. The widening gap in income earned, with the accumulation of income in the hands of a small minority, has lead to a turn toward illiberal political and economic policies. The accumulation of wealth by a group of super-elites, who have the financial clout to influence political processes, threatens progress toward full democracies around the globe (Moghaddam, Chapter 7). In the US, both Donald Trump and Bernie Sanders gained political notoriety during the 2016 presidential election. Both potential candidates for the highest office in the US tapped in to unhappiness with large swaths of US voters who were unhappy with their economic status during the aggregate economic recovery overseen by President Obama during his two terms as president. Although the US economy improved in terms of economic growth and job creation, many voters are not experiencing this recovery in a meaningful way in their everyday lives. Bernie Sanders highlights the perceived unfair gap between a wealthy minority who are experiencing wealth gain and raising incomes during the economic recovery and those you are not. Trump wants to make America great again during his presidency by tightening US borders, controlling migration, and therefore appeasing potential voting Americans who are concerned with increasing cultural heterogeneity and increasing income inequality in the US. Similarly Britain voted to leave the European Union. The vote for Brexit was in large part a vote for greater control over British borders. Across the Western world, there has been a swing toward more extreme left- and right-wing political, economic, and social policies. Shweder's (forthcoming) model suggests the next fifty years – from 2020 to 2070 – will see a tightening of borders, control of migration, and an effect on creating greater economic equality in both the US and the UK.

Shweder (2000) suggests one plausible hypothesis to explain the pattern of open and closed borders correlating with more or less equal economic distribution. He argues that "if economic growth is contingent on accepting the deep or thick aspects of Western culture (e.g., individualism, ideals of femininity, egalitarianism, the Bill of Rights), then cultures will not converge and will not develop economically because their sense of identity will supersede their desire for material wealth" (p. 177). The implication is people will give up material economic wealth for the sake of their cultural identity. Brexit, and the election of Trump in the US, are both indicators that threatened identities and perceived eroding of social status and privilege supersede economic development. Money talks, but not always.

Encapsulated within Shweder's cyclical model of open and closed borders and correlations with greater or lesser income distribution, is the equality–difference paradox (Jindra, 2014; Minnow, Shweder, and Markus, 2008; Shweder, forthcoming; Shweder and Power, 2013). Research on this topic extends the observation that according to the Gini Index (a measure of income inequality across countries) the more culturally homogenous countries – places such as Sweden and Slovenia – have more equal income distribution. Conversely culturally heterogeneous countries, like Brazil, the UK, and the US, have greater income inequality. Indeed, there was more equal income distribution, as reported by the Gini Index, in Rwanda after the genocide by the Hutus against the Tutsis in 1994 (Shweder, forthcoming).

The finding is controversial. One implication of the equality–difference paradox might be that if you value more equal income distribution – as many left-wing politicians, and economists referred to earlier, do – you need greater cultural homogeneity. This might mean the assimilation of refugees, migrants, and other cultural groups in to the mainstream culture of the host country. It might also mean the segregation and separation of peoples. History is replete with horrific examples illustrating the homogenization of nations (Mann, 2005). Trump's discourse about building a wall on the US – Mexico border is one example. Another consequence of the equality–difference paradox is if you truly value cultural heterogeneity, one consequence might be unequal income distribution. People do not agree with, or want, to share wealth – in a variety of forms such as social welfare benefits, like Obama Care, – with people who are culturally or ethnicity dissimilar to one another (Putnam, 2007; Ziller, 2015).

One basic principle of cultural psychology is that cultures and minds make each other up (Markus and Kitayama, 1991; Shweder, 1991, 2003). Subsequently, it follows that different cultural groups have different versions of what is a true, good, beautiful, and an efficient way of life. Shweder (forthcoming) details the poorest community – as measured by mainstream economic measures – in the US. He finds that, contrary to expectations, the poorest place is a Jewish community in the State of New York. In the community of Kiryas Joel, emphasis is not placed on the accumulation of income. Religious study for the men, and child rearing for the women, are the order of the day. Communal and shared resources in this culturally homogenous community maintain a level of existence that is subsidized by the government for each member. Lack of annual earned income does not necessitate a poor life.

The Kiryas Joel example further highlights the interdependence between economics and cultural values and raises a number of questions concerning how we ought to measure income and wealth distribution; such as what are the meanings of money and what are its connection to living the good life; what are the historical dynamics of wealth and income distribution and how does this impact the conditions people think fiscal inequality is fair or unfair; and how do people think about, and react toward, these economic realities?

The Irish case study is one empirical example to explore these issues in a localized setting. In 2013, Ireland had a population of nearly 4.6 million. It is a relatively homogenous country (Alesina et al., 2003). One study ranked Ireland as number 134 from a list of 159 countries in terms of ethnic diversity (Fearon, 2003). The following section examines the curious dynamics of democratic engagement, in the form of civic unrest and protest, in this small and homogenous country, following the global financial crisis of 2008. I draw on two psychological theories to examine the dominant Irish responses to imposed austerity following the financial crisis – relative deprivation and collective remembering – and illustrate how these two psychological processes inform comparisons between social groups and lead to, and legitimize, social mobilization against perceived social injustices.

The Global Financial Crisis and the Irish Case Study

Ireland enjoyed sustained levels of high economic growth for the fifteen years preceding the 2008 financial crisis. This period was commonly known as the "Celtic Tiger." This economic growth had initially been export-led and driven by a degree of "catching up" to more developed economies. However, an unsustainable property boom marked the latter years of the Celtic Tiger. The bursting of the domestic property bubble coincided with the onset of the global financial crisis, leading to a sharp and deep recession that saw a virtual collapse of the Irish banking sector. On Monday, September 29, 2008, the Irish government made the controversial decision to safeguard all deposits, bonds, and debts in six failing Irish banks. This decision came to symbolize the difficult and unpopular policy choices successive Irish governments were forced to make over the coming years, both fiscal and banking related, which, in turn, set in motion a series of societal and cultural changes that continue to be felt today.

When the global economy collapsed in 2008, the Irish, unlike some EU neighbors, such as Greece and Spain, accepted the terms of harsh austerity without protesting (Power and Nussbaum, 2014; Power, 2015, 2016). Yet when the Irish economy became the fastest growing in Europe in 2014 and 2015 (and projected for 2016) civic discontent ran high. Hundreds of thousands protested against a new charge on water – seen as the final straw in terms of accepting austerity. There were standoffs and clashes with the police, and a refusal of a huge proportion of Irish taxpayers to register, and ultimately to pay, this new charge online. Why did the Irish rebel in this way during an economic upturn rather than the economic decline?

Previous research suggested cultural and moral reasons for the initial passive acceptance of austerity by the Irish (Power and Nussbaum, 2014; Power, 2015, 2016). Interviews with a group of public elites (i.e., TV and radio presenters, journalists, economists, outspoken academics, members of prominent financial institutions) revealed three interrelated reasons to help explain this counterintuitive process. This group drew on collective memories of an Irish past to make sense of the present and to orientate toward future action. First, when the going gets tough, the Irish hit the road. There is a collective memory of Irish people migrating in times of economic hardship. Outward migration following the latest global financial crash was seen as a culturally legitimized and reasonable response to the economic downturn. In this case history is seen to repeat itself, but not always. People do not simply remember the past. They use it (Bartlett, 1932; Halbwachs, 1992; Power, 2016; Wagoner, 2017; Wertsch, 2008).

The elites also purposefully distanced collective memories of a violent past on the island of Ireland. The Irish no longer do their bloodletting on the streets. Rather, as a maturing democracy, they take to the ballots.

Indeed, the Irish voted out the Fianna Fail and Green Party government that guaranteed the ailing banks at the expense of the taxpayer in 2011. Later, the Irish voted out the in power Fine Gael and Labour coalition government, who oversaw the economic upturn in 2016, but more on that later.

The third overarching reason given by the public elites to explain the initial Irish acceptance of austerity was a historically ingrained, culturally widespread, moral belief – with its origins in Catholicism – that in life "you reap what you sow." The application of this moral principle by the group of public elites was to suggest the Irish public were unwise with their money during the financial boom – known as the Celtic Tiger during the late 1990s and early to mid-2000s – and consequently must suffer austerity in silence as the economy collapsed. Ordinary Irish people were at least partially culpable for the economic meltdown; just like the bankers, the government, the financial regulator, the European Central Bank, the European Union, as well as a host of other possible causes. By the application of the moral principle that in life "you reap what you sow" blame was attributed to the Irish public. They do not riot or protest, unlike the Greeks and Spanish, because they have been served their just desserts.

Interviews with unemployed Irish young adults illustrate the ways in which this moral belief has become internalized (Power, 2015). Unemployed Irish youth occupy a polar opposite group to the public elites in the Republic of Ireland. Unemployed interviewees attributed blame for the financial crisis, and their poor financial position because of it, to the unscrupulous actions of bankers and the Irish government. But they also gave in-depth and intricate examples from their personal situations to suggest a proportion of blame should be attributed to the actions of individual Irish people too. For example, I asked Séan, an unemployed Irish man in his early twenties:

SP: Who, if anyone, do you blame for the recession?
SÉAN: You have to blame society in general you know what I mean, there was just no exit plan, people just kept buying and selling and giving loans, they was no expectation, or realization, that this is all going to break down . . . When the world recession kicked in and everyone is panicking and everyone is loosing jobs, no one was expecting the highlights to end so suddenly and so abruptly. So you have to put the blame on society.
SP: So who do you mean by society?
SÉAN: The Irish public.

Séan clearly blames the causes of the economic recession on the behavior and on the shortsightedness of ordinary Irish people. Although he said "it's a world recession," he blames the "Irish public" for the drastic economic decline. I asked him for an example from his own life, and he discusses his father's situation who is heavily in debt, and who suffers from clinical depression after being made unemployed. He told me:

SÉAN: "My mother and father spent what they wanted (during the economic boom, known as The Celtic Tiger), they got loans out, and the loans were so easily got, at one stage, my father told me this; he applied for an overdraft from the bank and they said "we'll get back to you." At five o clock that evening they said "James, would you like a 20,000 euro overdraft?" and my dad was like "yeah," and it's just that, that kind of naivety, that he would spend it and worry about it in the future."

So although his father is clinically depressed, and there are constant family fights and collective stress due to this financial debt, he firmly places blame for this situation is his father's actions: not the banks, the financial regulator, the European Central Bank. This is a clear example of the internalization of blame – that in life you get what you deserve. It manifests in a lack of protesting. One snippet of an interview with Mark illustrates this point. He was a young and unemployed Irish male who migrated to Canada for two years. While there he worked in a variety of manual and creative jobs. He returned to Ireland after his two-year Canadian visa expired. He had been unemployed, and living at home with his mother and two siblings, for nearly a year when I interviewed him. His response is indicative of this social group's attitudes toward protesting, democratic engagement, and social change in the localized Irish context, at the time of interviews in summer 2014. When I asked him what he thought the dominant Irish response to the economic crisis was, he said:

MARK: I don't think we have done much to be honest with you. What other response is there?
SP: Well, in some European countries, young people have protested about austerity.
MARK: It is pretty anarchist, isn't it? I don't know if it gets anything done... I don't think it's better if there are any deaths caused by it... I don't want to see anyone burnt at the stake.

These extracts, taken from a broader corpus of interview data with unemployed Irish youth, suggest that even the most vulnerable group – unemployed people on state welfare programs – accepted austerity and held easily available narratives to illustrate the actions ordinary Irish people contributed to the economic downturn. One does not protest when you feel culpable for your own situation.

Social change does not occur in the psychological laboratory. It unfolds in complex contexts, over both historical and immediate timelines, for interrelated social, cultural, economic, political, historical, and legal reasons (Power, 2011). Social change occurs in the real world. In the Irish context, a number of salient events occurred that shifted public opinion, and had an effect on the Irish public's understanding of the unfolding economic crisis, and their engagement with democratic activities, particularly in the form of demonstrating.

In summer 2013, a recorded conversation between two prominent members of Anglo Irish Bank, was leaked and was made widely available on social media. Anglo Irish Bank gave large loans to property developers during the boom years of the Celtic Tiger in the late 1990s through to the mid-2000s, in the Republic of Ireland. The conversation, recorded before the Irish government agreed to bail out the ailing Irish banks in 2008, made explicit what many Irish people had since come to expect: the bankers had lied to the government about the institutions solvency – they needed more money to shore up the bank, but lied, saying they needed a fraction of the ultimate bailout. In Ireland you're in for a penny, in for a pound.

The lie caused public outrage in the Republic of Ireland. Later, on January 27, 2016, a banking inquiry commissioned by the Irish government concluded that the Irish public was not culpable for the economic crisis. The responsibility of the financial crisis was placed on risky banking practices, and a failure of EU institutions, not on the actions of the Irish public. The banking inquiry had no power to prosecute those individuals or institutions responsible for causing and exacerbating the crisis, only to identify sources of culpability. The attribution of blame for the financial crisis, and ensuing austerity, began to change. But the most dramatic shift in context, however, was with the economy.

Following the bursting of a decade-long property bubble coinciding with the onset of the global financial crisis, Ireland suffered a sharp and deep recession that saw a virtual collapse of the domestic banking sector. Real gross domestic product (GDP) fell by almost 10 percent in 2009 and continued to contract in 2010 and 2011, while unemployment climbed from below 5 percent in 2007 to reach a peak of 14.7 percent in 2012. This compares to a contraction of 2.8 percent in the US in 2009, which was swiftly followed by a return to positive GDP growth from 2010. Given the scale of the economic headwinds, the Irish government was forced to seek shelter in the form of an EU-IMF financial assistance program as it lost access to financial markets in the face of a spiraling deficit that reached 32 percent of GDP in 2010 due to unprecedented capital injections into the banking sector.

In the context of such a sharp decline, the speed of aggregate economic recovery has been stark. The first shoots were visible in 2013, when real GDP recorded positive growth of 1.1 percent while gross national product increased by over 4 percent. However, the recovery boomed the following year, with Ireland claiming the mantle of fastest growing economy in the euro area in both 2014 and 2015, a title which it is expected to hold on to in 2016. Both GDP and, importantly, GDP per capita – a key measure of living standards – moved above its precrisis peak in 2014, a rapid turnaround given the scale of the downturn in Ireland. The improvement in economic performance was strongly led by the exporting sectors in the initial phase, but over the past year or two the recovery has broadened, with domestic demand now also making a significant contribution. While personal consumption had continued to contract in 2013, it recorded positive growth of 1.7 percent in 2014, which strengthened to an increase of 4.5 percent in 2015. Although the volatility of Irish national accounts data can make it difficult to precisely measure the strength of economic growth, the broadening of the recovery is evidenced by the performance of the labor market, where the unemployment rate has dipped below 8 percent, from a peak of 15 percent in early 2012.

This narrative of objective economic growth was omnipresent in the public sphere in Ireland since 2013. The country had formally exited the economic recession, it became the first EU country to exit the EU-IMF bailout program, and the economy was heralded as a success story for tightening belts and accepting austerity for longer-term economic growth. In the context of rapid economic growth, and a shift in the attribution of blame for the crisis toward the actions of the financial sector and government, a new charge on water was introduced.

On December 28, 2014, Michael D. Higgins, the current President of the Republic of Ireland, signed a controversial Water Services Bill into law. The Irish public would have to pay directly for the water they consume in the form of quarterly bills. The company, Irish Water, was established to oversee the introduction of water meters to quantify the amount of water used per household; to provide safe and clean drinking water and efficient wastewater treatment; and to charge people for consumed water. Ireland previously had water charges that were abolished by the Labour Party in December 1996. Irish citizens paid for their water through general taxation. Until the reintroduction of water charges in 2014, Ireland was one of the few countries in the Organization for Economic Cooperation and Development not to directly charge for consumed water.

The enactment of the Water Services Bill and the establishment of Irish Water has been met with strong opposition from sectors of the Irish public in the form of local and large-scale antiwater charges demonstrations, clashes and standoffs with police, and a refusal of many citizens to register to pay this new charge. In Ireland, water is often represented as a fundamental human right, and particularly plentiful in Ireland, an island filled with rivers and lakes, where it often rains. The charge on water acted as a concrete focal point to galvanize a broader antiausterity movement: it was the final straw.

Relative Deprivation and Civic Unrest in Ireland

I interviewed over two hundred randomly sampled Irish protestors, of a broad adult age, from all areas of Ireland, from mostly, though not exclusively, working-class backgrounds, at a series of seven national demonstrations in Dublin, Ireland. Moreover, I conducted several months of in-depth urban ethnographic work with a core group of antiwater charge demonstrators in a small Irish city. During the urban ethnography and after the nation protests, I recorded extensive notes to help contextualize my data.

The Irish suffered austerity as the economy collapsed, endured budgetary cuts, and saw their friends and family migrate, or queue for social welfare. The Irish faced austerity together. But now they hear the economy is improving. Their expectations in an economic boom are especially high, since they endured austerity, for a better tomorrow.

Yet the economic rebound was experienced unequally. Although the aggregate economic growth in Ireland in 2014 and 2015 was staggering (the letter quoted in the Irish Times at the beginning on this essay was in response to a reported 25 percent increased in Irish GDP in 2016 – a huge figure, and inaccurate of real economic growth), but this aggregate economic growth is disproportionality felt by different social groups within Irish society. The gap between expectations and lived experiences motivates and legitimizes protest in the Irish context (Power, 2017a, forthcoming; Power and Nussbaum, 2016).

Relative deprivation theory can help explain this phenomenon (Pettigrew, 2015, 2016; Power, 2017a). The skeleton of this theory predicts that when an individual or group compares themselves to salient individuals or groups, and during this comparison, they find themselves lacking, discriminated against, or disadvantaged, this leads to angry frustration. Relative deprivation is not just a contemporary phenomenon.

Aristotle discussed the connection between what people want and their penchant to revolt when they do not achieve these wants. He suggested revolutions occur when societies fail to realize equality: "the motives of gain and honor also stir men up against each other not in order that they may get for themselves, as has been said before, but because they see other men in some cases justly, and in other cases unjustly, getting a larger share of them... for when the men in office show insolence and greed, people rise in revolt against one another and against constitutions that afford the opportunity for such conduct... for men form fractions both when they are themselves dishonored and when they see others honored; and the distribution of honors is unjust when persons are either honored or dishonored against their deserts" (Aristotle, quoted in Davies, 1971, p. 87). Aristotle was not calling for blanket egalitarianism. He suggests revolutions can occur when people perceive social and economic injustices when they compare their circumstances to comparable others in society and find they are lacking.

Marx believed that people were more likely to revolt when their survival was threatened (Davies, 1971). However, he also articulated a more nuanced concept that dovetails with the concept of relative deprivation. In *Wage, Labour and Capital* Marx (1849/1973) said, "A house may be large or small; as long as the neighboring houses are likewise small, it satisfies all social requirements for a residence. But let there arise next to the little house a palace, and the little house shrinks to a hut. The little house now makes it clear that its inmate has no social position at all to maintain." People are unhappy in their contexts when their expectations are incongruent with their realities.

Alexis de Tocqueville (1857/1955) develops this concept further in the seminal *The Old Regime and the French Revolution*. He discovered that French workers revolted and overthrew their government when there was a reduction in taxes and a general loosing of Parisian rule throughout France. As a result, the French expected their lives would improve, but didn't. This incited a rage that drove this historic revolution.

Davies (1962) noted that revolutions are most likely to occur when a prolonged period of objective economic and social development is followed by a brief period of economic and social decline. This theory highlighted the temporal component of relative deprivation and the generation of frustration. Revolutions often occur when a social group's expectations of their economic or social status increases, but these increasing expectations go unfulfilled. This hypothesis chimes with contemporary social-psychological evidence that largely supports the idea that people are loss averse; they weigh losses more heavily than gains (Tversky and Kahneman, 1991).

The types of comparisons people make, to whom and why; feelings of perceived disadvantage; and the manifestation (if any) of this frustration, all depend on the wider historical, cultural, social, economic, and legal contexts and how these are oriented to, understood, interpreted, and remembered. Runciman (1966) distinguished between relative deprivations felt when individuals compare themselves to another and when groups compare themselves to other groups. In the localized context in the Republic of Ireland, protestors are making comparisons between themselves and other groups in Irish society, particularly political and wealthy elites. The division is between those who are benefiting from the economic upturn, and those who are not: between the 1 percent and the 99 percent. The protestors who I interviewed articulated a variety of social, moral, and political grievances that are culturally embedded manifestations of the growing gap – a perceived chasm – between the beneficiaries of the economic growth, and those who believed things would get better, but have not experienced it in their everyday lives.

For example, officially unemployment figures are falling in the Republic of Ireland. Despite this indicator of improvement in the Irish economy, many interviewees highlighted that although employment is increasing in Ireland, the figures disguise reality. The controversial Job-Bridge scheme requires people on social welfare to accept work that is offered to them for a small increase on their base social welfare payments. Refusal to undertake this work can mean a cancellation of social welfare payments. Many people are unhappy with being forced to work this way; many complain about the quality of jobs available, and the conditions of work. One interviewee went as far as to compare it to slavery.

The housing bubble dramatically burst in 2008 in Ireland, but during the economic recovery since 2013, property prices are once again soaring, particularly in wealthy parts of Ireland, such as south county Dublin, but not as drastically in rural parts of Ireland, or in its periphery cities. Rising housing prices, correlated with rising rent, has led to a housing crisis in Ireland, particularly, though not exclusively, in Dublin. Interviewees often moralize this dilemma: they ask how the country can be experiencing economic growth but simultaneously have increasing numbers of Irish people, including more than one thousand children, who do not have a home to sleep in.

Interviewees highlight several other salient examples that illustrate the gap between what they expected to happen during an economic recovery, and the actuality of the unequal economic boom. There are perennial problems with the health care system in Ireland; serve limitations on disability services, including respite and residential services; budgetary cuts to the arts and education; the perception the government protects corporate interests with low and nontransparent tax agreements with multinational pharmaceutical and technological companies; and in the microcosm of the installation of water meters to directly charge citizens for the water they consume, the perception that the police are on the side of this company (Irish Water), rather than supporting the public (a view contested by nonprotestor observers, who sometimes felt protestors caused more trouble than was necessary). For a full analysis of these issues, see Power (2017a, forthcoming).

Although issues of homelessness, budgetary cuts, unemployment, and other austerity measures are current problems in Ireland, they are as bound to the past, and oriented toward the future. This is because the way people remember the past has implications for how they think and behave in the present, and how they orientate their goals toward an imagined future (Bartlett, 1932; Halbwachs, 1992; Power, 2016; Wagoner, 2017; Wertsch, 2008). My earlier research suggested collective memory played a role in the initial passive Irish response to austerity. A culturally legitimized, and historical ingrained, belief in facing economic hardship with migration; of believing in reaping what you sow; and of distancing contemporary Irish society from memories of a violent past are three reasons articulated by an influential group of public elites to explain Irish acceptance of austerity without mass demonstrations (Power, 2016).

Protests are political acts (Drury and Reicher, Chapter 2). They are bound to history, yet designed to create social change in the future (Reicher and Stott, 2011; Warren and Power, 2015). The Irish antiausterity demonstrations are no different. They are framed in Irish revolutionary history, in at least three interconnected ways. I use one particular demonstration to highlight this point (Power, 2017b). The physical route of the demonstrations is purposefully charted to evoke collective memories of a revolutionary Irish past. This connection is made explicit in the speeches of left-wing politicians, community activists, and trade unionists that articulated links between the current antiausterity protests and the overcoming of perceived social and political injustices by previous generations of Irish. Third, protestors internalized these messages, and in some cases, drew explicit comparisons between overcoming previous struggles, and situating their current position within a broader political context: minorities can become majorities to effect social change (Moscovici, 1976).

Halbwachs (1992) argued that collective remembering occurs within a spatial framework. Cultural groups remember a version of their past from a spatial location, either real or imagined. Physical surroundings, steeped in cultural history, provide a framework from which groups can recall their past. This is because groups – either in their lifetime, or historically – ingrain their past upon physical structures. As such, as all recall occurs in a physical location, people remember in relation to these spatial frameworks, infused with localized meanings embedded in broader sociocultural and historical contexts. Every social group has the possibility to ascribe their own meanings on their spatial and physical locations, and even more opportunity to recall those meanings in diverse ways in the future. In this way, there are multiple ways to remember the past. Street demonstrations provide an opportunity to empirically examine these theoretical insights.

One particular protest, in summer 2015, began at The Garden of Remembrance, a park north of the river Liffey in Dublin, Ireland, – the side of the city that was traditionally more working class. The plaque outside reads "all those who gave their lives in the cause of Irish Freedom." The demonstration continued down O'Connell street; one of Dublin's main thoroughfares, named after Daniel O Connell, a well-known nationalist leader, in nineteenth-century Ireland. Most of the national antiausterity protests ended outside the General Post Office (GPO). This is one of the best-known and historical landmarks in the Republic of Ireland. On Easter weekend, 1916, Irish revolutionaries took over the building, staging a rebellion against occupying British forces. The rebellion failed from a military perspective, but achieved its ultimate goal of galvanizing an Irish War of Independence between 1919 and 1921, which led to the separation of the island of Ireland into two nations – The Republic of Ireland and Northern Ireland. The significance of ending antiausterity protests close to the centenary anniversary of the 1916 rebellion at the GPO served to create a direct link between a revolutionary Irish past, that lead to social reform and the creation Irish Free State that was governed by Irish people, to contemporary Irish protests where there is a sense of social injustice caused by the unequal economic recovery. The message is the Irish have overcome injustices before; they can do it again.

Left-wing politicians, trade unionists, community activists, and member of Right2Water (the umbrella organization set up to plan and advertise protests against water charges) gave rousing antiausterity speeches at the end of the rallies. They made explicit links between these versions of revolutionary Irish pasts – overcoming perceived social injustices – during their speeches at the end of these demonstrations.

Some interviewees also made explicit reference to this revolutionary period of Irish history to justify and legitimize contemporary Irish protests. One middle aged woman, with a working-class Dublin accent, who was carrying an Irish tricolor flag, told me that her grandfather was involved in the Easter 1916 rebellion. She explicitly justified her current involvement with antiausterity demonstrations. "This is a continuation of a longer Irish fight against tyranny. They think they can push the ordinary people around, we are here today, as we were before (in 1916), to stand up to the powers that be, to say 'we're not going to take this (austerity) anymore.'"

Comparisons are informed by how history is remembered. In the Irish case study, collective remembering reveals historical precedent over a major comparison group: "ordinary people" as self-defined by the protestors and a political elite – historically the British rulers, but in contemporary Ireland it's an Irish political elite, out of touch with the realities of the public, who continue to suffer austerity.

A history of polarization between elites and the working class in Ireland offers a template to comprehend the ways in which groups compare themselves to others. In contemporary Ireland, during the anti-austerity protests, the demonstrators did not compare themselves to other potentially salient groups within Irish society. For example, Syrian refugees – a crisis that made global headlines and was omnipresent in the public sphere during the antiausterity protests – was never mentioned. Irish people did not compare themselves to Irish celebrities or sports stars. Both of these groups are in far worse or better social and economic statuses than the demonstrators. But these are not the salient reference groups. How people remember the past has implications for how they understand, think, and rationalize in the present. Irish collective remembering during these protests, linked to physical structures in Dublin which are steeped in Irish revolutionary history, are directly evoked by antiausterity activists, and referred to explicitly, and implicitly inform, the division between "elites" in Ireland – those who are reaping the benefits of the economic recovery – and those who are not – the general Irish public. The Irish have been there before; and founded a Free State and later a republic based on a constitution conferring equality upon all citizens. Remembering history informs a contemporary perception of division between a political elite and the general Irish public. It informs who compares whom to whom.

In this way, we can comprehend the dynamics of relative deprivation if we understand the historical context in which comparisons are made, injustices are experienced, and the contexts in which angry frustration has, and can be, made manifest.

Conclusion

Economic history suggests patterns of recessions and recoveries are omnipresent throughout all societies, dating as far back as records can be reached. The 2008 economic crisis is no different. It is important to situate this economic collapse as part of a broader cyclical pattern in order to contextually understand the complex dynamics involved. Shweder (forthcoming) provides a provocative and visionary theory of open and closed societies and a correlation with lesser or greater wealth and income inequality. Painting with broad strokes, every fifty years – in the US at least – sees a shift from open to closed societies, with ensuing greater income distribution as a society becomes more closed. This fits the prediction presented by the equality–difference paradox. Simply articulated, the theory predicts the more culturally and ethnically diverse a society, the less equal income distribution there is. More culturally and ethnically homogenous societies have greater equal wealth distribution. Societies where people look and act the same are more likely to treat its citizens, and the citizens are more likely to treat each other, more fairly in terms of distributing income. One prediction of the theory is that creating a more homogenous society favors greater income distribution. This seems congruent with the British voting to leave the European Union. It is also congruent with Trump's goal to tighten US borders. Brexit and Trump's wall are two examples, both put to the popular vote in democracies. History is replete with various examples of societies turning from more open to closed societies through less democratic means. A cyclical model of societies becoming more closed seems to resonate with US and western European democracies turning toward more polarized political policies including seeking greater control of who crosses national borders and from where.

When it comes to understanding economic development, culture matters. An extensive body of literature illustrates the ways in which cultural values, beliefs, and moral reasoning are connected with policies, institutions, and versions of the good life. Economic inequality is increasing. Yet only in some cases does this seem problematic. And only in some cases it leads to protest and violence on the streets. The issues highlighted in this essay suggest it is the perception of unfair economic inequality, rather than actual inequality, that is the key to understanding democratic engagement and civic discontent.

A new theory of unfair inequality hypothesizes that civic discontent – in the form of refusing to pay taxes, protesting on the streets, as well as engaging in other democratic activities such as contacting politicians and signing petitions – occurs more frequently when the perception of unfair economic inequality is higher rather than lower. Actual or absolute inequality may be less frustrating than perceived inequality due to rising, yet unfulfilled, expectations.

The 2008 economic recession is a microcosm of these larger historical patterns and abstract theorizing. In Ireland, a small and relatively homogenous country, people suffered the yoke of harsh austerity when the economy collapsed, only to protest during a period of rapid economic recovery. This deprivation–protest paradox (Power, 2017a) has parallels in history. De Tocqueville argues the French revolution of 1789 occurred when the French government relaxed its rule on the people. The citizens' expectations of quality of life increased, but went unfulfilled. More recently, the Occupy protests across the US occurred during a time of economic recovery in 2011, rather than when the economy collapsed in 2007.

Relative deprivation theory helps to understand this paradox (Pettigrew, 2016). When a group of individual compares themselves to a salient group or individual, and concludes they are lacking or discriminated against in comparison, then this leads to angry frustration. Cultural psychological theorizing highlights the importance of understanding how this possibly universal theory manifests in localized cultural contexts. In Ireland, protestors compare themselves to political and wealthy elites in Ireland who are benefiting from the economic recovery that they expected to experience. However, despite the aggregate growth in the Irish economy, and people's rising expectations, they have not experienced this aggregate economic recovery in their everyday lives. The protestors highlight manifestations of the disjunction between the narrative of objective economic recovery, and their social realities: homelessness, the rising cost of living, tax of water, under funded health care system, and cuts to education, are easily accessible examples of the gap between expectations and social realities. The protestors, and the left-wing politicians and community organizers driving the rallies, see a gap between those who benefited from the recovery, and those who have not.

Collective remembering is a powerful tool to understand social movements, civic discontent, and how societies organize themselves in globalizing and culturally plural social worlds. The Irish initially drew on memories of a violent past to justify a peaceful acceptance to harsh austerity. But the context in Ireland changed as the attribution of blame for the crisis moved away from the actions of the public and was laid solely at the feet of a banking, governmental, and European elite. How the Irish used the past also began to change. Collective remembering helps account for what comparisons social groups make and which comparisons they do not. It also helps explain how people use to past to motivate action in the present and orientate social movements toward imagining, and creating, a future more congruent with their desires.

A theory of perceived unfair inequality has practical implications. Protests and riots can occur when people's expectations are not realized or made manifest in ways they find meaningful. As Europe and the rest of the world exists the 2008 global financial crisis at varying paces, care should be taken to create (the perception) of greater economic equality. Aggregate economic recoveries, which are not perceived to be felt fairly, can cause civic discontent. Absolute deprivation – in the case of food shortages in Venezuela in 2016 can cause people to take to the streets in the form of (violent) protest. But there is a psychological dimension too: in an oil-rich country, elites benefit, at the expense of the masses. This case contrasts with the Irish case study, yet feelings of relative deprivation are common to both. As the satirical letter at the beginning of essay illustrates, frustration can be caused by the gap between expectations and lived experiences.

It is also difficult to disentangle the timing of civic unrest in Ireland – during a period of rapid economic growth, rather than decline – from the substantive issue that finally galvanized protest: taxing water. Water was often represented as a fundamental human right by my interviewees. And it is particularly plentiful in Ireland, a small island, where it seems to rain incessantly, even in summer. Parallels were drawn with other anti–water charge demonstrations throughout the world. Protestors spoke about how Bolivian social movements developed at the turn of the millennium when they privatized their water supply, only for people to revolt and overthrow the government. The Irish protests about who controls, and pays for water, are not a unique case in the contemporary world.

Water is fundamental to the survival of humans. Droughts and floods, rising global temperatures and changing weather patterns, are altering the ways in which people conceptualize and represent water. Globalization and climate change are threatening the dynamics of water supply. Commodification of this resource, at least in the Irish case, mobilized a social movement, with ensuing claims that it was a universal human right. It is likely others think like this. Water occupies a special representational category, one that will likely become more essentialized and problematic when access to supply is more controlled, less reliable, and more salient. Access to water blurs the line between absolute and relative deprivation. How societies remember their past with water, and how they imagine their (possibly dystopian) futures when it is commoditized, privatized, controlled and limited, has implications for how future generations will comprehend this resource in a more volatile world. Shortages, or rather, perceived shortages, in the form of controlled or unfair access, could create civic discontent, and social movements. It can generate rage and drive revolution.

REFERENCES

Alesina, A., Devleeschauwer, A., Easterly, W., Kurlat, S., and Wacziarg, R. (2003). Fractionalization. *Journal of Economic growth*, 8(2), 155–194.

Aliber, R. Z., and Kindleberger, C. P. (2015). *Manias, Panics, and Crashes: A History of Financial Crises*. 7th ed. New York: Palgrave Macmillan.

Atkinson, A. B. (2015). *Inequality: What Can Be Done?* Cambridge, MA: Harvard University Press.

Banfield, E. C. (1958). *The Moral Basis of a Backward Society*. New York: Free Press.

Bartlett, F. (1932). *Remembering: A Study in Experimental and Social Psychology*. New York: Cambridge University Press.

Davies, J. C. (1962). Toward a theory of revolution. *American Sociological Review*, 27, 5–19.

(1971). *When Men Revolt and Why: A Reader in Political Violence and Revolution*. New York: Free Press.

de Tocqueville, A. (1857/1955). *The Old Regime and the French Revolution*. New York: Harper.

Dorling, D. (2014). *Inequality and the 1%*. London: Verso.

Fearon, J. D. (2003). Ethnic and cultural diversity by country. *Journal of Economic Growth*, 8(2), 195–222.

Halbwachs, M. (1925/1992). *On Collective Memory* (L. A. Coser, Trans. and Ed.). Chicago: University of Chicago Press.

Harrison, L. E. (1985). *Underdevelopment Is a State of Mind: The Latin American Case*. New York: Madison Books.

Harrison, L. E., and Huntington, S. P. (Eds.) (2000). *Culture Matters: How Values Shape Human Progress*. New York: Basic Books.

Jindra, M. (2014). The dilemma of equality and diversity. *Current Anthropology*, 55, 316–334.

Landes, D. S. (1999). *The Wealth and Poverty of Nations: Why Some Are So Rich and Some So Poor*. New York: W. W. Norton.

Mann, M. (2005). *The Dark Side of Democracy*. Cambridge: Cambridge University Press.

Markus, H., and Kitayama, S. (1991). Culture and the self: Implications for cognition, emotion, and motivation. *Psychological Review*, 98(2), 224–253.

Marx, K. (1849/1973). *Wage, Labour and Capital*. New York: International.

Minnow, M., Shweder, R. A., and Markus, H. (2008). *Just Schools: Pursuing Equality in Societies of Difference*. New York: Russell Sage Foundation Press.

Moscovici, S. (1976). *Social Influence and Social Change*. London: Academic Press.

Nisbett, R. E., and Cohen, D. (1996). *Culture of Honor: The Psychology of Violence in the South*. Boulder, CO: Westview Press.

O'Riordan, P. (2016). Statistics and "leprechaun economics" [letter to the editor]. *Irish Times*, July. www.irishtimes.com/opinion/letters/statistics-and-leprechaun-economics-1.2725047.

Pettigrew, T. (2015). Samuel Stouffer and relative deprivation. *Social Psychology Quarterly*, 78(1), 7–24.

(2016). In pursuit of three theories: Authoritarianism, relative deprivation, and intergroup contact. *Annual Review of Psychology*, 67, 1–21.

Piketty, T. (2014). *Capital in the Twenty-First Century* (A. Goldhammer, Trans.). Cambridge, MA: Belknap Press.

Piketty, T., and Saez, E. (2014). Inequality in the long run. *Science*, 344(6186), 838–842.

Power, S. A. (2011). On social psychology and conflict resolution. *Psychology and Society*, 4(1), 1–6.

(2015). To understand the Eurozone crisis, consider culture. *Capital Ideas*, June, 63– 65. www.chicagobooth.edu/capideas/magazine/summer-2015/to-understand-theeurozone-crisis-consider-culture?cat_policy&src_Magazine.

(2016). A violent past but a peaceful present: The cultural psychology of an Irish recession. *Peace and Conflict: Journal of Peace Psychology*, 22(1), 60–66.

(2017a). The deprivation–protest paradox: How the perception of unfair inequality leads to civic unrest. Unpublished manuscript.

(2017b). Using the past: Motivating anti-austerity protests by remembering revolutionary Irish history. Unpublished manuscript.

(forthcoming). Actual democracy and a United Europe of States: A case study of austerity and protest in the Republic of Ireland. In B. Wagoner and I. Bresco (Eds.), *The Road to Actualized Democracy: A Psychological Perspective*. Charlotte, NC: Information Age.

Power, S. A., and Nussbaum, D. (2014). The Fightin' Irish? Not when it comes to recession and austerity. *The Guardian*, July 24. www.theguardian.com/science/head-quarters/2014/jul/24/thefightin-irish-not-when-it-comes-to-recession-and-austerity.

(2016). "You reap what you sow": The psychology of Irish austerity protests. *The Guardian*, March 15. www.theguardian.com/science/head-quarters/2016/mar/15/economics-as-a-morality-play-austerity-protest-in-ireland.

Putnam, R. D. (2007). E pluribus unum: Diversity and community in the twenty-first century. *Scandinavian Political Studies*, 30(2), 137–174.

Reicher, S. D., and Stott, C. (2011). *Mad Mobs and English Men? Myths and Realities of the 2011 Riots*. London: Constable and Robinson.

Reinhart, C. M., and Rogoff, K. S. (2009). *This Time Is Different: Eight Centuries of Financial Folly*. Princeton, NJ: Princeton University Press.

Runciman, W. G. (1966). *Relative Deprivation and Social Justice: A Study of Attitudes to Social Inequality in Twentieth-Century England*. Berkeley: University of California Press.

Sachs, J. (2000). *Notes on a New Sociology of Economic Development*. New York: Basic Books.

Shweder, R. A. (1991). *Thinking through Cultures: Expeditions in Cultural Psychology*. Cambridge, MA: Harvard University Press.

(2000). Moral maps, "First World" conceits and the New Evangelists. In L. Harrison and S. Huntington (Eds.), *Culture Matters: Cultural Values and Human Progress* (pp. 158–177). New York: Basic Books.

(2003). *Why Do Men Barbecue? Recipes for Cultural Psychology*. Cambridge, MA: Harvard University Press.

(forthcoming). The risky cartography of drawing moral maps: With special
reference to economic inequality and sex selective abortion. In J. Cassaniti
and U. Menon (Eds.), *Universalism without the Uniformity: Explorations in
Mind and Culture*. Chicago: University of Chicago Press.

Shweder, R. A., and Power, S. A. (2013). Robust cultural pluralism: An interview with Professor Richard Shweder. *Europe's Journal of Psychology*, 9, 671–
686.

Tversky, A., and Kahneman, D. (1991). Loss aversion in riskless choice: A reference dependence model. *Quarterly Journal of Economics*, 107(4), 1039–
1061.

Wagoner, B. (2017). *The Constructive Mind: Bartlett's Psychology in Reconstruction*.
Cambridge: Cambridge University Press.

Warren, Z., and Power, S. A. (2015). It's contagious: Rethinking a metaphor
dialogically. *Culture and Psychology*, 21(3), 359–379.

Weber, M. (1905/2009). *The Protestant Ethic and the Spirit of Capitalism*
(T. Parsons, Trans.). New York: W. W. Norton.

(1951). *The Religion of China: Confucianism and Taoism* (H. H. Gerth, Trans.).
New York: Free Press.

(1958). *The Religion of India: The Sociology of Hinduism and Buddhism* (H. H.
Gerth and D. Martindale, Trans.). New Delhi: Munshiram Manoharlal.

Wertsch, J. (2008). The narrative organization of collective memory. *Ethos*, 36,
120 135.

Ziller, C. (2015). Ethnic diversity, economic and cultural contexts, and social
trust: Cross-sectional and longitudinal evidence from European regions,
2002–2010. *Social Forces*, 93(3), 1211–1240.

4 The Globalization-Revolution Paradox
No Revolutions in Capitalist Democracies

Fathali M. Moghaddam

For my friends, everything; for my enemies, the law.

– President Vargas

The above quotation from the Brazilian dictator Getúlio Vargas (1882–1954), seems puzzling from a conventional perspective; surely the law is something beneficial, so why would the dictator want the law for his enemies? The puzzle is explained when we consider that those who enjoy great power and resources can shape and apply laws, and create the larger conditions of life, to benefit themselves at the expense of other people. *Globalization*, the increasing economic, cultural, and technological integration and interdependence of different countries and regions of the world, is leading to the growth of the global super-rich, who have tremendous international power and the ability to shape international laws and life conditions in their own interests. At the heart of globalization lies a paradox: globalization is creating greater wealth inequality, but at the same time thwarting revolutionary movements in response to increasing inequality. I explore the complex factors behind this paradox, with particular focus on trends in the US, the leading capitalist democracy.

A starting claim in this discussion is that all major societies began as dictatorships, and some progress has been made by some countries to reach "actualized" or full democracy (Moghaddam, 2013, 2016). However, there are no absolute dictatorships or absolute democracies. The road from dictatorship to fully developed democracy is long and extremely difficult, including in contemporary Western societies where democratic progress remains unfinished and is in serious danger because of increasing resource inequalities. It is ironic that in this so-called age of democratization, democracy has come under increasingly serious assault.

The threat to democracy arises from a number of different sources. First, the growth of dictatorships around the world is a direct challenge to the long-term survival of democracies. The rising power on the world stage is of course China, an absolute dictatorship. A resurgent Russia is collaborating with Iran and a number of other thriving dictatorships, in the context of the collapse of the Arab Spring and the re-emergence of dictatorships in the Muslim world. At the same time, the US continues to prop up a number of dictatorships around the world, including oil-rich nations such as Saudi Arabia. The twenty-first century has heralded a relative decline in American prestige and power, in part because of catastrophic foreign policy mistakes and very costly foreign wars. At present, it is not at all certain that a democratic US will be the global superpower in the twenty-second century. As with all previous world powers, the US will sooner or later experience decline, and at present the country most likely to replace American supremacy on the global stage is a dictatorship. China and other readily recognized dictatorships represent the "conventional" threat to democracy.

A new and rising threat is increasing resource inequalities. Over the last half-century, the rich have been getting richer, the middle class has been struggling not to get poorer, and the bottom one-third or so of the population have been left further behind. This trend is well documented in Thomas Picketty's *Capital in the Twenty-First Century* (2014), Danny Dorling's (2014) *Inequality and the 1%*, and Anthony Atkinson's (2015) *Inequality: What Can Be Done?* About 80 super-rich individuals now own as much wealth as the poorer half of humankind, about 3.5 billion people (Oxfam, 2015).

The individuals whose wealth makes them part of the global super-rich do not all see themselves as belonging to one group (for an alternative view, see the discussion on the "transnational capitalist class" by Robinson and Harris, 2000), but irrespective of how they see themselves they are interconnected through mutual material interests. It is these mutual material interests that lead them to take action to further their collective political interests. In a detailed analysis of the international ownership network, researchers discovered that the control of transnational corporations can be represented by a bow-tie structure, with much of the control being held by financial institutions, and more particularly by key owners in these institutions, situated at the tightly knit core of the bow-tie (Vitali, Glattfelder, and Battiston, 2011). Research has shown not only high interconnectedness of board of directors of major corporations, but also that social connections make it less likely that chief executive officers will face negative consequences because of poor performance (Nguyen, 2012). Research also demonstrates that major corporations that have more international connections also make more donations to politicians in US elections (Murray, 2014). The broad picture emerging from research is of the global super-rich increasing their relative wealth advantage, their interconnectedness, and their political clout.

The objective of the global super-rich is to maximize their own profits. This is to some degree achieved by moving their assets from country to country to make use of the cheapest labor, a strategy that puts pressure on the wages of lower- and middle-class groups (they also do this to avoid taxes). In countries with higher-middle- and lower-class incomes, such as those of North America and the European Union, there is inevitable pressure to decrease incomes and/or increase productivity in order to compete with middle- and lower-class employees internationally. The global super-rich use their enormous resources to ensure that national and local groups, elected or unelected, represent their interests rather than the interests of the middle and lower classes. With very few exceptions, the global super-rich act to weaken democracies and to increase their own political influence (it could be argued that George Soros and a few other billionaires have acted to strengthen rather than weaken democracy, but these are exceptions). This is not because the global super-rich are consciously involved in a conspiracy against democracy, but because in pursuing the maximization of their profits they inevitably run up against democratic processes and practices that protect middle- and working-class interests.

Despite being unelected and often not holding any official government positions at all, the global super-rich have enormous influence on economic, political, and cultural developments around the world. The role of this elite has become more important through globalization. Whereas the global super-rich is enabled by globalization to more effectively maneuver and mobilize their resources to better use global opportunities for accumulating financial wealth and political influence, the majority of middle-class and lower-class people find themselves weakened by globalization, forced to compete in a larger and far more fierce international labor market. In addition, as highlighted by Pope Francis's June 18, 2015, encyclical on climate change, the poor are being disproportionally harmed by global warming. Calls for a rethinking of economic "progress" as it is taking place, with massive wealth accumulation in the hands of the few and continued damage to the natural environment, have of course been repudiated by a variety of right-wing political groups – vilifying Francis as the "Red Pope" (The Pope's encyclical on climate change was aggressively attacked by the political right. Pope Francis was lambasted as being in league with communists; see http://thinkprogress.org/climate/2015/06/19/3671144/the-pope-freaks-out-climate-deniers/).

Old Dictatorships and the New Global Super-Rich

The word "dictator" brings up images of Hitler and Stalin from the twentieth century, or Putin and other twenty-first-century heads of state who camouflage their iron rule by staging elections. Mention "dictatorship" and people think of the personality or the "mind" of the individual dictator. Such focus on the characteristics of an individual has a certain logic to it. After all, it is the individual dictator who gives the orders and inspires deadly repression. I still remember listening to Khomeini in Iran after the revolution, cold-bloodedly encouraging his forces to wipe out all opposition. There was not the slightest hint of emotion or compassion in his voice. When he returned to Iran as absolute ruler on February 1, 1979, after fourteen years of exile, his response to the question, "What do you feel?" was "Nothing." He was being sincere; he felt nothing.

Khomeini, Saddam Hussein, Putin, the clique who govern China—these are all dictators of the old style. The traditional definition I have provided in *The Psychology of Dictatorship* fits them well, "Dictatorship is rule by a single person or a clique that is not elected by the subject population and not removable through popular election, with direct control of a security apparatus that represses political opposition, without any independent legislative and judicial checks, adopting policies that reflect the wishes and whims of the dictator individual or clique rather than popular will, with a high degree of control over the education system, the mass media, the communication and information systems, as well as the movement of citizens, toward the goal of continuing monopoly rule by the regime" (Moghaddam, 2013, p. 18).

The Old Dictatorships rely predominantly on brute force to maintain a monopoly on power. The countries that still practice dictatorship in the old style, including Russia, North Korea, Saudi Arabia, Iran, and China, periodically resort to naked violence, as well as routine daily practice of arrest and intimation, in order to re-establish the ruling elite's control over the majority of the population. Demonstrations by opponents of the regime are brutally put down, journalists and political opposition leaders are imprisoned or assassinated, the police and the military are engaged to protect the regime against the will of the people by infiltrating and violently assaulting any form of organized democratic movement. Individuals can often informally criticize the regime in taxis, shops, coffee houses, and other such places, but they are brutally hammered into silence if they try to organize and publicize their criticisms through outlets that could potentially reach large numbers of fellow citizens.

The Old Dictatorships know that a public could quickly gather in support of critics who dare organize to create a more open society.

Consequently, the Old Dictatorships do not allow anyone the opportunity to become a potential leader of organized dissenters; they smash down organized opposition with open savagery. The Old Dictatorships are typically clumsy, crude, and obvious, and most people see them for what they are. But conditions in the twenty-first century are nurturing the emergence of a powerful global super-rich, which has tremendous influence internationally. Whereas the Old Dictatorships are multiple, the new global super-rich is emerging as one global phenomenon. The *global* scale of the interests and influence of the new global super-rich is putting in danger Western democracies, including the US and the countries of Western Europe. The economic, cultural, technological, and in some ways political integration of nations, means that the actions of the global super-rich impact trends around the world, not just single nations.

The Common Interests of the New Global Super-Rich

Of course it could be argued that the interests of the global super-rich around the world are not all the same, and it is wrong to assume they constitute one group. There is no doubt that there is some competition between the members of the global super-rich, just as there is competition between members of the middle class and members of the working class around the world. But the global super-rich have certain foundational common interests, and these manifest themselves through their often interlocking ownerships across different international and national corporations. The "superordinate" common interest of maximizing profits through their interlocking ownerships of corporations, banks, and other financial institutions, means that the individuals constituting the global super-rich do not need to perceive themselves as belonging to one group; they inevitably act as one group in pursuit of common economic goals. This includes, using their resources to support certain policies within and across nations and oppose others. What is new about this influence, then, is that globalization has facilitated the treatment of the world as one economic unit, by a global super-rich that has international ownership throughout this one unit.

The global super-rich indirectly enjoy tremendous influence, without being elected by, or responsive to, the people, and with their own interests as the primary guide. Of course the influence of the global super-rich is not blatant or direct, as is the case with the Old Dictators, the likes of Stalin and Hitler. It is supremely ironic that in the "age of democratization," there is an insidious attack against democracy through a process and from a source that is more difficult to detect.

The assault on democracy in the US and other Western democracies involves depriving ordinary people of power to change the way resources are distributed in their societies, but at the same time allowing people freedom of expression. The illusion of power is maintained by allowing people opportunities for free expression and free participation in elections. However, what voters can change through elections is extremely limited because the viable candidates for elected office typically represent the very narrow interests of one or another faction of the global super-rich. For example, in the US any politician who advocates higher taxes for the rich or any other type of even moderate wealth redistribution is immediately attacked as a "communist" by a media predominantly controlled by Murdoch family and other global super-rich members, such as the Koch brothers.

The key components of the globalization-revolution paradox is:

1 Increasing resource inequalities between the rich and the rest at both national and international levels.

2 The emergence of the global super-rich with the ability and motivation to influence national political trends in major ways; to act as an unelected source of influence on national and regional elections and national and regional governments.

3 Political activities of the global super-rich in support of their own interests and toward the expansion of their global, regional, national, and local influence.

4 Corporatization and neutralization of universities and other centers that could have acted to launch countermovements against the new global super-rich.

5 Global transformation of the meaning of freedom from "political freedom" to "freedom to consume."

6 Global spread of self-help and individualism as the dominant ideology.

7 Preoccupation of people and governments with various "threats" and "security issues," including Islamic radicalization, terrorism, environmental collapse, and "invasions" of refugees and immigrants, that seem to require greater surveillance, police control, stronger and more aggressive leadership, and less freedom for citizens.

8 Movement toward informal "governance" through major banks and other financial institutions, international corporations, thinks tanks and elite gatherings (such as the World Economic Forum's annual meeting, Davos, Switzerland, and TED conferences; as well as even more exclusive private elite meetings, such those of the Bildderberg Group and the Boao Forum) by a global super-rich who are unelected, not answerable to local, national, and regional governments, and primarily concerned to further increase their own international resources.

Whereas the Old Dictatorships operate primarily within national borders, such as within the borders of Russia, China, Iran, Saudi Arabia, and North Korea, the new global super-rich is not bound by national borders. Nor is the new global super-rich as clearly visible, and therefore as recognizable a target for attack, compared to the Old Dictatorships. Rather, the new global super-rich operate loosely and globally, using enormous international resources and networks above and beyond nation states. The new global super-rich is not headed by a single person, such as Putin in Russia or Khamenei in Iran, or even a clique, as in China. Rather, it is emerging out of the mutual political interests of the global super-rich.

The Influence of the New Global Super-Rich

The global super-rich use their enormous resources to further their own interests. Of course, they also use their wealth and power to hide their influence. For example, on January 2, 1981, Margaret Thatcher, the UK prime minister, held a secret lunch meeting with Robert Murdoch, the media magnate (http://theguardian.com/media/2012/mar/17/rupert-murdoch-margaret-thatcher). This meeting was persistently denied by both Thatcher and Murdoch and only became public thirty years later. The purpose of this covert meeting was to pave the way for News International, Murdoch's company, to purchase the Times Newspapers despite laws intended to prevent exactly this kind of monopoly ownership in the media. Murdoch's control of the Fox Broadcasting network, as well as major film studios, book publishers, satellite-television providers, hundreds of newspapers and news outlets operating around the world, gives him tremendous national and international power. Murdoch continued his private dealings with the next major successful Tory prime minister; he was one of the first to visit the newly elected prime minister David Cameron at 10 Downing Street after his election win in 2010, although Murdoch remained unseen by the public because he used a back entrance.

But Murdoch's extensive dealings with Prime Minister Tony Blair and President Bill Clinton and President Hillary Clinton, as well as many other "progressive" politicians, reveals that the media mogul does not discriminate when it comes to political influence; he had strong ties with politicians of both left and right, including Tony Blair (www.newyorker.com/magazine/2006/10/16/murdochs-game). He has hosted fund-raising events for the Clintons (Democrats), as well as supported their Republican rivals. Whatever the outcome of elections, Murdoch is part-owner of the winner.

Rupert Murdoch and his sons (to whom he is passing on his empire) represent the more public face of the global super-rich. The Murdochs are part of a mobile international elite which is unelected, not bound by or loyal to any nationality, able to exert global influence in political, economic, educational, and cultural trends through its influence over the international mass media and international financial markets.

Increased wealth concentration, and the greater influence of the global super-rich, is emerging as part of globalization and particularly the relatively free flow of capital around the world. As the world becomes more integrated economically, the global super-rich are able to move their investments more efficiently from country to country, and region to region, to take advantage of cheaper labor and lower production costs. Manufacturing has moved from North America to China, Vietnam, India, and other countries with lower labor costs. This is in a context where in the year after the 2008 "great recession" when so many lower- and middle-class people around the world suffered financially, the twenty-five "top" hedge fund managers were each paid an average of $1 billion (yes, billion). Local and national allegiances have become meaningless for the global super-rich and their international business interests, as they pursue higher profits. The increased mobility and agility of global business has placed pressure on labor unions, which still tend to operate within national and regional boundaries. In many parts of the world, lower income employees feel increasing pressure, as they compete with lower income workers from distant lands without the support of strong labor unions. While productivity increases have created a larger "national income pie" in most countries, the share of labor in the national pie has decreased (Anastasia, 2006).

At a time when labor struggles, the rewards of the current system are enabling the global super-rich to purchase more and more expensive toys, such as *Octopus*, the 414-foot yacht, which has a submarine, helicopters, and a swimming pool, owned by Microsoft co-founder Paul Allen. Worldwide the sale of luxury yachts is booming, helped by demand from China.

In countries such as the US and the UK, the theatrical show of national politics continues, but the votes cast in elections have very little impact on the behavior of the global super-rich, and the growing divide between the super-rich and the rest of humanity. In the US, this divide has come to have a more direct impact on democracy, since the Supreme Court in 2010 concluded that spending money in elections is a form of free speech and cannot be limited. The outcome of this decision is that both Republicans and Democrats are now far more beholden to the donors who give the largest amounts of money to their political campaigns. All American politicians face the same plight: they have to accept huge donations to have a realistic chance of success in important elections. Irrespective of whether a Republican or Democrat wins the race to the White House in 2016, the winner's political campaign will have been funded by billions of dollars donated by fantastically rich people.

The "Occupy Movement" and Responses to It

Given the growing rift between the richest and the rest, and given antidemocratic power and influence of the global super-rich, why have people in Western societies, where there is freedom to protest, not reacted more vehemently against this situation? There has been some attempt to protest against the unbalanced economic trends and the growing power of the super-rich: that is in large part what the Occupy Wall Street movement was and is about. Starting from the protest at New York City's Zuccotti Park in September 2011, the Occupy Movement quickly became international as protests against "Wall Street economics" spread to dozens of different countries.

The global super-rich did not sit idly by, but responded to the Occupy Wall Street movement by supporting opposing movements. The most prominent of such opposing movements in the US is the Tea Party movement, which takes conservative antigovernment, "free market" positions and supports ultra-conservative political candidates. The Tea Party movement is supported by global super-rich funders, such as the Koch brothers.

The most common slogan of the international Occupy Movement has been "We Are the 99 Percent," clearly pitting the majority against the rich minority. Although Occupy Movement protests have involved hundreds of thousands of people across many nations, particularly in New York and Washington, DC, in the US, the impact of the movement has been limited. One reason why more of the 99 percent have not been involved in protests against economic trends that increasingly favor the super-rich have to do with globalization trends and particularly the preoccupation with various "security threats." The new global super-rich is gaining influence opportunistically, taking advantage of concerns with security and terrorism to divert attention away from political issues such as resource inequalities and social justice. The "corporatization" of universities has enabled and accelerated this trend.

The Corporate University

The "corporate university" also has an important role in the decline of democracy in twenty-first-century societies. Universities have often served as centers of opposition to antidemocratic movements. But particularly since the 1970s universities in the US, and increasingly in the UK and elsewhere, are becoming "corporate" and business oriented, rather than strong supporters of progressive movements. Academic ideals of free thinking, independence, and critical engagement with authorities over issues of resource inequalities have faded. New assistant professors soon learn that according to the value system of twenty-first-century universities they must aspire to be entrepreneurs, not scholars; they are hired for their abilities to generate income for the university. To label an assistant professor a "scholar" is to hint that this person is out of place in the twenty-first-century university. To describe a new assistant professor as "entrepreneurial" is to signal that this person is a success in the new "academic" culture. Entrepreneurial types work with, not against, the global super-rich. In essence, universities in Western societies have been "neutralized" through corporatization, which is far more lethal and effective than the readily observable physical attacks against universities I experienced in the Iranian dictatorship.

The new global super-rich deals with freedom in a novel way compared to the Old Dictatorships. The new global super-rich does not try to end freedom but to re-direct how it is used, to ensure that freedom does not challenge the increasingly unequal distribution of power and resources around the world. In the globalized world, the primary meaning of freedom is "free to consume" in the marketplace. "Choice" has come to mean "choice of goods and services to consume," rather than choice among a wide variety of viable political candidates. In societies where people are free to express their opinions, this has not translated to action that creates fairer resource distribution. Why resort to brute force and open aggression when you can keep control and monopolize resources through far more subtle means?

Globalization and modernization have spread a "self-help" ideology, based on the idea that the status and resources of people depend on their personal efforts and merits. This trend was facilitated and supported on a world scale by the collapse of the USSR and communist societies, the emergence of a more open economy and entrepreneurship in China, and the globalization of "Hollywood" culture with its American Dream ideology. The impact of these factors has been to strengthen the idea that differences in wealth and status are based on individual characteristics, so that it is because of their own personal efforts and merits that the super-rich have huge resource and power advantages. Major social science research projects funded by and biased in favor of right-wing sources have been used to bolster the idea that intelligence is inherited and power and status differences across individuals are "inborn." A good example is the research of Herrnstein and Murray (1996) attempting to portray American society as a meritocracy in which people with higher intelligence, which they claim is largely inborn, "rise to the top." If we take this view seriously, we must conclude that the likes of George W. Bush "rose to the very top" because of their superior intelligence.

Immigrants, Terrorists, and Other "Threats"

Enormous movements of populations across national boundaries, regions, and even continents have resulted in the native people in many countries feeling threatened by an "invasion" of immigrants and refugees. Sixty million people are fleeing wars and persecution, and tens of millions more are fleeing their homelands because of economic hardship (for reports of the latest global refugee trends, see www.unhcr.org/2016trends). The impact of climate change is starting to become more serious, and this also results in massive migrations as people flee environmental disasters, ruined agriculture, and famines. The flood of newcomers is leading to backlashes against "outsiders," with the consequences of threatened collective identity and higher support for strong leadership, hierarchical decision-making, ethnocentrism and a focus on interethnic differences, with a corresponding neglect of resource disparities between the super-rich and the rest. These trends all strengthen dictatorial rule, by giving power to particular individual leaders rather than to the mass of citizens.

A related trend is "terrorist threats" as a distraction from issues of increase resource inequalities. Particularly since the September 11, 2001, attacks against targets in New York and Washington, DC, the threat of terrorism has been used to justify wars, the expansion of military culture in everyday life, and the invasion of privacy and attacks on basic civil liberties. These trends all further weaken democracy.

There is a robust relationship between external threat and internal cohesion and support for more right-wing leadership and movements. The spread of "freedom as consumption" and "self-help ideology," as well as increased perceived security threats from the invasion of immigrants and refugees, all contribute to this shift to the political right and change in culture so that more and more politicians openly attack "government," "taxes," "social welfare," and everything else not in the interests of the super-rich.

Increasingly, even in democracies most people view politics as a spectator sport; they feel helpless to change the system so it benefits the masses more and the super-rich less. Trust in politicians and government institutions have declined (Americans are less trusting of both other people and major institutions, Paxton, 2005; although there are some age and race differences, Wilkes, 2011); there has also been a decline in communities and social capital generally (this argument has been forcefully developed by Putnam, 2000, but critics point out that electronic and other communities are evolving as new forms of social capital). Voters recognize that there is a huge disconnect between their wishes, their motives, and their interests, and those of the "elected politicians." In the 2014 mid-term congressional elections in the US, for example, the approval rating for Congress went down to the low teens, but a congress representing more or less the same interests was returned after the election. The people are saying "We don't trust or approve of these politicians," but politicians representing the interests of the super-rich keep getting voted back in. The national political theater of Republican versus Democrat, Conservative versus Labour, and the like, has lost significance, and many voters have realized that real power lies elsewhere.

The solution is a two-pronged attack: grass-roots and local on the one hand and global on the other hand. This is feasible, even though pro-democracy forces have been slow to take advantages of the opportunities offered by globalization. For example, many labor unions are pro-democracy, but have tended to remain within national and even local borders, and have weak international connections. The international movement of labor, with the endless connections it creates, is an enormous asset waiting to be utilized.

Central Elements of the Globalization-Democracy Paradox

Ask people around the world about globalization and its consequences, as I have done repeatedly over the last few decades, and they invariably mention a wide variety of positive and negative changes. Some respondents talk about job outsourcing and the movement of manufacturing industries from Western to Third World societies where the cost of labor is still much cheaper. Others mention the global spread of electronic communications, mobile phones, and the interconnectedness of our twenty-first-century world. Some people highlight the spread of Western popular culture, the influence of Hollywood icons and the Americanization of youth everywhere. The ubiquitous use, and even monopoly status in some areas, of the English language is often criticized, particularly by people who feel that their own mother tongue is threatened with decline or even extinction. Older people often complain about the faster "unhealthy" pace of life they believe is associated with globalization. Many Westerners mention security threats, terrorism, and the spread of extremist Islam. However, missing from these many different discussions is the surprising role played by globalization in the assault on democracy. Even the conservative author Francis Fukuyama (2012) recognizes this connection: he has commented that "the current form of globalized capitalism is eroding the middle-class social base on which liberal democracy rests" (p. 2).

On the surface, globalization should be helping the spread of democracy. After all, globalization is generally seen as associated with the spread of information, increased interconnectedness, and a higher level of environmental awareness among people around the world. Furthermore, education and health levels are improving globally and some types of violence have declined, and presumably these changes are also conducive to spreading democratic values and practices. However, the foreseen growth of genuine democracy is not happening. Indeed, unexpectedly, democracy has been weakened as a result of globalization. In this chapter, I discuss the main reasons for this worrying trend. At the heart of my discussion is the growth of the global super-rich.

Some argue that resource inequalities have nothing to do with democracy: as long as every citizen has a vote and the system is one-person-one-vote, then it does not matter how much money the rich and the rest have. This perspective is not just naive, it is misleading. First, the rich use their wealth and power to influence not just who gets elected, but who becomes a viable candidate in the first place. Becoming a viable candidate for political office needs funding, and in the US presidential elections billions of dollars are needed. The 2015 UK general elections were the most expensive ever. Obviously the super-rich have a huge advantage to influence who becomes a viable candidate and who ultimately gets elected. Second, being super-rich means having the material resources to mount effective campaigns against elected politicians who want to implement policies that go against the interests of the super-rich. The poor are relatively powerless, so that politicians find it much easier to implement policies that go against the interests of the poor. For example, personal and corporate tax rates have been lowered in the last few decades in OECD countries (Brys, Mathews, and Owens, 2011; Piketty, 2014). Top corporate tax rates in the 1980s were seldom less than 45 percent, but in 2011 the average OECD rate was 26 percent. Obviously the major shareholders in corporations reap the benefits of this lower corporate tax rate.

Increasing inequality is not just about unequal incomes, but also about increasingly unequal political influence. The clearest sign that politicians from all the viable political parties represent the interests of the same small group of people, the rich, is that the huge rift between the richest and the rest is becoming larger and larger, as is the amount of money needed to seriously compete in political elections (Kang, 2013). Of course, the rich are happy to supply the money that politicians need to win elections – several billion dollars will be needed to win the 2016 US presidential elections. Increasingly, it is the global super-rich who provide the money that directly or indirectly influences national elections. "US-style electioneering" is spreading around the rest of the "democratic world," where political campaigns are increasingly run according to Madison Avenue style marketing plans. The result is terrible for ordinary people, because the global super-rich are primarily concerned with own profits, national and regional problems. No wonder ordinary people are feeling disenchanted and approval rating for Congress in America is in the teens (www.gallup.com/poll/162362/americans-down-congress-own-representatives.aspx).

The disenchantment with "gridlock on the hill" in the US and with the inability of democracy to improve the lives of ordinary people, who are falling further behind from the rich, is occurring in the context of global changes that put a spotlight on the successes of China, a dictatorship. There is a lot of secret admiration of China, in the business sector and even among ordinary people in Western societies. The extraordinary growth of the Chinese economy stands in contrast to the stagnant standard of living of ordinary people in democratic societies, both in the West and in the rest of the world. In the 1960s, India and China had comparably poor economies and the majority of Indians and Chinese people struggled to find enough to eat, but half a century later "democratic India" has fallen well behind "dictatorial China" economically, so that in 2014 the GDP per head in India was $1,700 compared to $7,700 in China. The "success" of the Chinese dictatorship in channeling the aspirations of the Chinese people toward consumerism and away from politics, has served as a lesson for some people in Western societies. I am struck by how often over the last few years I have been told by Westerners in all walks of life – business people, students, government officials, everyday working people – that the Chinese model is working very well and perhaps "we should give up on democracy for a while and try the Chinese way of doing things." This sentiment has most often been expressed to me by Americans fed up with "government gridlock" and Europeans frustrated by the "bureaucrats in Brussels."

The Size Factor

The decline of trust and the disenchantment of ordinary people with central governments and politicians in the US and many other democracies is to some extent a result of the world becoming increasingly integrated and influenced by events and factors originating in distant lands, societies becoming larger and larger, and people feeling they are far away from the most important decision makers who impact their lives. During the golden age of Athenian democracy about twenty-five hundred years ago, the total population of Athens and the rest of Attica was probably not more than three hundred thousand (Thorley, 1996, p. 1). The population of the US at the time the US Constitution was ratified was about one million. The US population is now about 320 million, and India, the world's largest democracy, has a population of about 1.3 billion. The twenty-eight-member European Union (EU), represented by the European government in Brussels, has a population of about 505 million. No wonder Indians, Americans, and Europeans feel that "their" governments are far away. Not surprisingly, the countries with the most inclusive and robust democracies, the Scandinavian countries and Switzerland, have much smaller populations. Throughout the ages, authors who have formulated ideas about utopias have had smaller societies in mind, starting with Plato who had in mind a Republic of about five thousand people.

The technology now exists to close the gap between citizens and governments (Linders, 2012). Ordinary citizens can be more directly involved in decision-making, at least on the most important decisions such as taxation and resource distribution. Of course, there is the risk that ordinary citizens might develop the ability to take decisions that favor their own interests, resulting in lower profits for the global super-rich. But despite the fact that research evidence showing greater inequality results in slower growth (Ostry, Berg, and Tsangarides, 2014) and greater health problems for the poor (Marmot, 2005), it is not clear that most people favor redistribution of wealth as a way to temper inequality. A 2015 *New York Times/CBS News* poll found that Americans do want more equal wealth and income distribution; www.nytimes.com/2015/06/04/business/inequality-a-major-issue-for-americans-times-cbs-poll-finds.html). However, other research finds less support for redistribution (Kuziemko et al., 2013). Below I discuss key factors influencing this situation.

Reasons for Inaction

Why in this age of "democratization" have people not prevented the growth of the global super-rich with extraordinary international influence above and beyond national governments, in the US and other major nations? Part of the answer is that people have been entangled and distracted by changes brought about through globalization. These changes have brought threatened collective identities, which has preoccupied the masses. A series of external threats, from floods of immigrants and refugees to terrorism and economic instability, has resulted in host populations even in relatively "democratic" societies to becoming more ethnocentric, defensive, and more supportive of more authoritarian leadership. I discuss this theme in more depth below.

What about the argument that "globalization is not new"? The answer is that globalization *is new* in ways that matter for threatened collective identities. First, the speed at which vast movements of people take place in the twenty-first century, facilitated by modern transportation systems, is very different from the much slower pace of transportation in earlier eras. As I argue in more detail below, this rapid movement of enormous number of people raises serious threats for host populations. Second, security threats raised by twenty-first-century globalization are very different and far more serious than in earlier eras. For example, in the nineteenth century, Great Britain, the world superpower of the time, was concerned about Afghanistan and surrounding regions (including what is now Pakistan) because they were on the trade route to India. In this sense, these areas were "security concerns." But at no time in the nineteenth century did the British government or people worry that attackers originating from Afghanistan or surrounding regions would inflict serious human and material damage in Britain. The technology for such an attack (e.g., jet planes) simply did not exist. The threat of something like a "dirty bomb" makes twenty-first-century globalization very different from all earlier forms of globalization. The changed security situation means that the political focus stays away from the increasing gap between the super-rich and the rest, and more on "security threats."

The next two major sections of this chapter deal with, first, globalization and the focus on various threats confronting people and, second, the transformation of the meaning of freedom and the spread of self-help as the dominant ideology around the globe.

Collective Threatened Identity and Mutual Radicalization

In this first part, I examine how globalization is resulting in perceptions of threats, and how these perceptions are leading to mutual radicalization.

Perceived Threats

Integral to globalization are a number of benefits, such as increased flow of information and greater exchange of goods and services. However, there is also a negative side to globalization, particularly arising out of the rapid movement of enormous numbers of people across national borders, regions, and even continents. These changes have led to complex psychological reactions, which directly and indirectly distract attention from the issue of wealth inequalities.

Endless waves of immigrants and refugees, extremist ideologies spreading through electronic networks, international sex and drug trafficking, fast mutating and dangerous diseases streaking across national borders: these are some of the negative changes associated with twenty-first-century globalization. Historical, economic, political, environmental, and cultural circumstances have combined to create serious and continuous threats to local populations. The outcome is a powerful emotion well known to psychologists: fear. People feel fear because of economic instability and apparent decline, terrorist threats, global warming, decreased opportunities for their children, an increasing gulf between the rich and themselves, the "invasion" of millions of refugees and immigrants, and serious threats to their native culture and language.

Fear is the most powerful force strengthening the Old Dictatorships. President Franklin D. Roosevelt (1882–1945) said famously in his first inaugural address in 1933, "The only thing we have to fear is fear itself." People gripped by fear become especially vulnerable to manipulation. Dictators know the power of fear and use the iron grip of fear to control their populations. Behind the surface of law and order on the streets of Moscow, Beijing, Tehran, Riyadh, Pyongyang, and the capitals of other major dictatorships is the real probability that political dissenters will experience imprisonment, torture, and execution – or assassination in broad daylight. Fear is woven into the fabric of everyday life and forms the backbone of the Old Dictatorships.

Fear can play a constructive role in some instances. For example, fear of global warming could lead to more serious efforts to control environmental degradation. But fear in the political sphere is poison to democracy because it can lead people to become ethnocentric, closed-minded, and unquestioning toward authority. Fear leads people to look the other way when they see mismanagement, it leads to tolerance for inept leaders who blunder into huge policy mistakes. This is what happened after September 11, 2001, when so many people in the US and the UK went along with the decision to invade Afghanistan and then Iraq. The fear of terrorist attacks resulted in a knee-jerk reaction to unquestioningly support Bush and Blair in their disastrous war policy, the results of which have been catastrophic for the entire Near and Middle East.

Globalization and Collective Fear

Globalization is bringing many changes with the potential to increase our collective fears, starting with vast and rapid movements of people across nations and continents. The sheer volume of immigrants and refugees rapidly moving from country to country has increased large-scale and sudden intergroup contact, often resulting in feelings of instability and threat to the home residents. For example, an estimated 30 million Muslims now live in the European Union, from just a few million in the 1960s. One outcome of this rapid change has been "mutual radicalization," with right-wing and nationalist Europeans reacting against Islamic and traditionalist immigrants, taking more and more extreme positions. This process is also most clearly apparent in the European Union, where the National Front in France, the UK Independence Party (U-KIP) in the UK, and other extremist groups throughout Europe are steadily gaining influence, particularly in Brussels, the EU capital, and changing mainstream European politics. Collective fear of outsiders has resulted in mainstream European political parties to move further to the right and adopt more conservative policies.

What many native Europeans see as an "invasion" of European countries by refugees and immigrants, particularly Muslims, has even led to extremist nationalist attempts to "fight back" to stop the Muslim tide. This is apparently what led to an attack by Anders Behring Breivik, the thirty-two-year-old Norwegian right-wing extremist who killed seventy-seven people in terrorist attacks on July 22, 2011. Those killed and injured were actually not Muslims, but mostly the children of Norwegian left-wing politicians. Breivik was attempting to "wake up" the European mainstream, so they would see the "Muslim invasion" the way he saw it. Timothy McVeigh and Terry Nichols, who blew up a federal government building, killing 168 people and seriously injuring many hundreds more, in Oklahoma City on April 19, 1995, had similar ideas about "waking up" the American mainstream to the takeover of America by non-Whites and non-Christians. These extremist attacks are examples of reactions against "sudden contact," when dissimilar groups with little or no history of contact suddenly find themselves face-to-face with one another.

Of course immigration has always been part of the historic tradition of immigrant receiving countries such as the US, Canada, Australia, and New Zealand. There have been huge influxes of immigrants to these countries in the past, at times then first-generation immigrants made up a larger percentage of existing population. What is new in the twenty-first century is the speed at which enormous numbers of immigrants and refugees suddenly arrive in the adopted land. This is made possible through the much faster transportation systems, which can move millions of people in a matter of weeks.

When I visit the National Museum of the American Indian in Washington, DC, I feel both sad and inspired. I feel sad because evidence from the lives of hundreds of different American Indian tribes tells me of vanished cultures and languages. Entire tribes were wiped out, mostly by disease, but also by massacre and forced displacement as newly arrived settlers of European stock – the invasives – swept across the American continent. But I also feel inspired, because a number of American Indians have shown communal resilience and are fighting to survive in the longer term.

The invasion of traditional Native American lands by the settlers took centuries, because transportation and technology was much slower than it is now in the twenty-first century. Despite the relatively slow pace of invasion, the American Indians did not have enough time (or want) to adapt to the new situation or were prevented from doing so. They ended up being herded together and shunted aside in reservations. Those American Indians who fought back, sometimes with tactics that we might today call "terrorism," proved too weak and too small in number to resist the march of settlement.

Communications and transportation systems in the twenty-first century allow for much faster movement of people and ideas, and so influx of migrants can in some instances be even more dramatic and frightening – for all sides. For example, traditional and fundamentalist Muslims in some parts of the world are suddenly finding their lives and lands being invaded by secular Western Hollywood style culture, and in some instances, of course, by Western troops and bombs. No matter how hard the traditionalists and fundamentalists try to stop the process, Westernization continues and even speeds up – through the Internet, television, radio, imported goods, and through the arrival of Westerners on their doorsteps.

I witnessed this type of "invasion" in Iran in the 1970s, when I used to return to visit my family from my studies in England. On each return trip I would witness dramatic changes in Iranian society. The oil price increase of 1973 had given the Shah enormous additional income, and the newly acquired wealth was being used in wildly misconceived and mismanaged "modernization" projects, which all involved enormous numbers of Western companies and their Western employees working in Iran. Huge cultural disparities and divisions appeared in Iranian society. In some parts of Tehran, young men and women were openly living "free sex and free thinking" Westernized lives, imported wholesale from

London, Paris, and New York, while in other parts of Tehran there were Iranians following the same behavioral patterns and values as their ancestors hundreds of years earlier. The Shah and his "American masters" were seen to favor Westernization, and traditionalist and fundamentalist Muslims clearly saw this movement as a threat, perhaps a fatal one, to their way of life and their religion.

Sitting in London, Washington, DC, Paris, or some other part of the Western world, it is very difficult to appreciate the high levels of threat experienced by people in non-Western societies. From a Western perspective, it seems improbable that vast non-Western societies could feel threatened. But history shows non-Western societies have good reason to feel threatened: bring to mind the fate of native people in North and South America, at least 95 percent of whom were annihilated by the end of the nineteenth century. Islamic traditionalists and fundamentalists have this history in mind when they feel threatened by the global spread of Western secular culture.

Particularly since the takeover of Iran by Islamic fundamentalists in 1979, the tide of radicalization and anti-Western sentiment has surged stronger and stronger across the Islamic world. Islamic radicalization and terrorism is a reaction to the perceived threat to traditional and fundamentalist Muslim ways of life. The traditionalists and fundamentalist Muslims clearly see the writing on the wall: globalization is bringing Westernization and modern gender roles, and if this is allowed to continue it will mean the end of traditional and fundamentalist Muslim ways of life. Liberated women will transform the Muslim family, reform socialization practices, and change Muslim societies. Traditional and fundamentalist Muslim men are fighting against such an outcome.

This is why in Iran the fundamentalists took over the government to prevent democracy taking root. The constitution they set in place in Iran gives absolute power to the "Supreme Leader," an unelected "spiritual guide" with complete authority over all aspects of government. The fundamentalists in Iran and in the rest of the Islamic world see themselves, their culture, and their religion to be in a fight for survival. Of course culture is difficult to measure, so it is difficult to pinpoint the decline of something like "Islamic culture" or other non-Western cultures. How do we know non-Western cultures are really threatened? One way to assess such a threat is to focus on language, because language change is far easier to measure than "culture change."

Symbolic of the global sweep of Western culture is the plight of minority languages, in the face of the onslaught of the English language. The Islamic fundamentalists do not want to become like the nine thousand or so languages that have disappeared from the earth over the last five hundred years. There are now approximately six thousand languages left alive in the world, and most of these "survivors" will probably be dead by the end of this century. The research area known as "language death" tracks this decline in language diversity around the world. The speakers of hundreds of minority languages can already see their languages dying. In a similar way, traditionalist and fundamentalist Muslims can see the signs: globalization means Westernization, which means death for them.

Sudden contact has not only resulted in increased sense of threat and radicalization in the Islamic world, but the same process is evident in Western societies.

Mutual Radicalization: Antidemocratic and "Automatic"

The process of mutual radicalization inevitably leads to a weakening of democracy and a strengthening of dictatorial trends. During mutual radicalization, extremist groups exaggerate and highlight threats from "outsiders." For example, extremist French nationalists exaggerate and highlight threats from "Islamic invaders taking over France" and extremist Muslims in France exaggerate and highlight threats from "Westerners attacking Islam." These trends are speeded up by "crisis incidents," such as the Muslim terrorist attacks against the French satirical magazine *Charlie Hebdo* in 2011 and 2015. When 12 people were killed in the second attack, support for the extremist right-wing National Front increased and hate crimes against Muslims spiked in France. This radicalization on the nationalist side resulted in Muslim communities in France feeling threatened, and with a continuation of young Muslims showing an interest in traveling from France to fight "for Islam" in Syria. The result has been the growth of radical, antidemocratic forces in France. So far these antidemocratic forces are operating without real power, but they represent a real longer-term threat.

Both the extremist French nationalists and the extremist Muslims living in France are at the core against democracy. Psychologically there is deep similarity between the different extremists and why they oppose democracy: they have low tolerance for differences and ambiguity; they want a world in which everyone is clearly divided into "us" and "them," "good" and "bad," "friend" and "enemy." Groups such as the National Front are extremely ethnocentric, and not just anti-Semitic but also anti-all minorities. They use the ballot box because they have to for the present, but if they ever attain power their basic ideology will inevitably lead to an attempt to shut down democratic rights – as happened in Germany in the 1930s and in Vichy France 1940–1944. Similarly, the ideology of radical Islam inevitably opposes democracy. This is clear from the experiences of countries where radical Islamic forces have taken over: the representatives of God on earth, such as the Supreme Leader in Iran, do not feel they need democracy, even though they are forced by twenty-first-century values to organize "elections" and put on a show of allowing the people to "vote."

Groups such as the extremist nationalists and the Islamic fundamentalists in Europe are fighting democracy the old way. They are crude and obvious in their intentions, and present visible targets for pro-democracy forces. The forces supporting the influence of the global super rich are far more difficult to recognize and defeat.

Freedom Transformed

Vastly improved communications and transportation systems, integral to globalization, is leading to the spread of a transformed view of freedom, particularly in how people live their everyday lives. Freedom of choice in the consumer marketplace is now getting priority, with the mass media and mass advertising celebrating the enormous "freedom of choice" afforded by the vast array of goods and services on offer. The "free market" presents consumers with choices of enormous numbers of different cereals, salad creams, automobiles, washing machines, and every other kind of consumer product, as well as vast varieties of services.

Freedom without Political Influence

In the globalized world that is emerging people enjoy freedom of speech. They can criticize whatever and whoever they want, including the individuals and groups at the head of the government. Indeed, there are almost countless outlets, from traditional newspapers to Internet blogs, chatrooms, and newsletters, through which diverse points of view and complaints about all kinds of local, national, and international issues can be expressed. In the globalized world, what people say or think does not really matter; it is more or less inconsequential and does not lead to "real" change. What is "real" change?

Real change is about how resources are distributed in society; it is about who owns what. If freedom is supposed to be part of a more just democratic world, how is it that freedom of speech, enjoyed by so many and expanded through the global Internet, has not prevented this historic concentration of global wealth and power in the hands of fewer and fewer people? How is it that the global reach of the Internet and the spread of smartphones have not prevented the Gini Index, the most widely accepted measure of economic inequality, from steadily rising?

The Gini Index for households in the US rose from 0.386 in 1968 to 0.476 in 2013, the highest of any industrialized society. This is in the same period that the computer revolution, the Internet, smartphones, Facebook, Twitter, Snapchat, Yik Yak, and scores of other new high tech developments were giving Americans additional avenues to exercise free speech. These parallel trends, with growth in "freedoms" taking place at the same time as increasing resource and power inequalities, mean that we have to rethink our assumptions about the "democratizing" consequences of the electronic revolution and globalization. Only some interpretations of freedom lead people to seek greater fairness in society.

Also, although people are free to express themselves in any way they want, the impact of what they have to say is actually declining (of course, the views of the people are supposed to be reflected in the mass media). The traditional reason given for this limited impact is that the media is monopolized by a small number of owners, with the richest owning hundreds of media outlets in many different countries. But there are other, more subtle reasons. The first factor is the increasing specialization and narrowing of interest and communications groups, and the second is the transformed meaning of freedom.

Until the late 1960s, you could count the main television channels in both the US and the UK using the fingers of one hand. Most people got their news from these few television stations. In the twenty-first century, there are hundreds of different television channels available to Americans and Europeans, and indeed to people in many other countries. The sources of news are increasing daily, as are the ways in which ordinary people can communicate and spread information globally.

Although anyone can use the Internet and other open communications tools to reach an audience, the fragmentation of the media means that critics often end up in "echo chambers." Universities used to be places where such trends were disrupted and people with competing and different points of view would be forced to challenge one another. But increasingly, "safe spaces" are being created in universities, to ensure that students do not feel "threatened" by views that oppose their own. The "need" to make universities a "safe space" has spread to how some students evaluate research. After leading a seminar discussion on psychological research by Stanley Milgram, Phil Zimbardo, and others that suggests even people with normal personalities can be pressured to obey and do very serious harm to others, I was told by a student that such "anxiety-provoking" research should not be discussed in class.

Will university classes soon also become "safe spaces," where "troubling" ideas are avoided, right-wing critics chat with other right-wing critics, left-wing critics chat with other left-wing critics, and the majority remains apathetic toward controversial issues? This tragedy to the idea of an informed public may not matter to members of the ruling elite, because they are not affected by apathy. By the 2014 mid-term elections in the US, the approval rating for Congress had fallen to the low teens, but the vast majority of incumbents were returned anyway. "They don't approve of us," these incumbents might ask, "Why should we care, we're in safe electoral districts." My point is not that politicians should change policies in line with public opinion in every situation, but that we have reached a crisis point with respect to resource inequalities, the accumulation of wealth in fewer hands, and the growing influence of a global super-rich. On these issues, the interests and views of the majority do not seem to matter.

The emerging globalized world has become immune from criticism. The inequalities characteristic of the globalized do not change in response to criticism. These growing inequalities are well documented, but little attention is being given to how little effect the people freely expressing their dissatisfaction have on these trends. Critics discuss increasing inequalities, but this has not prevented inequalities from growing.

The second reason why freedom of expression now has more limited impact on political outcomes has to do with a foundational reinterpretation of "freedom" and a re-direction of energies in search of "freedom."

Consumption as Freedom

Civilians stuck in war-torn Third World countries find themselves in a continuous search of the black market for things they need, and my life in war-torn Iran was no different. Everything could be found, but often at a high price that only a tiny minority could afford. To cope with the severe shortages that were part of our daily lives, we had to have a lot of ready cash, preferably in American dollars, or know somebody high up in the regime. Some people in Iran had both. Anything and everything, from onions and electricity to baby food and dentures, suddenly and without warning became scarce. "Choice" had a very limited meaning in the marketplace of war-torn Iran, because the vast majority of people had almost no choice or selection of goods and services compared to consumers in Western societies. Of course, for most of human history the vast majority of people have had similar levels of very limited choice when it came to goods and services. The affluence of modern Western societies, however, has led to "consumer choice" having a very different meaning and it now extends far beyond the West.

I am disappointed at how I now treat as normal the enormous variety of goods and services on offer in the US. I find it difficult to remember that the vast majority of humanity, now and throughout history, has not enjoyed the same kinds of choices. I am now used to walking into grocery stores that offer hundreds of different types of salad dressing, cereals, cookies, jams, vegetables, and fruits all year round, cheeses, and endless varieties of meat, fish, and poultry. I get annoyed when the local pharmacy does not have the exact medicine I need immediately available, or the local car dealership does not have ready for me today the color car I want, or the book I order takes an extra day to arrive at my home. Conforming to local norms, I have come to see such "shortcomings" and "delays" as violations of my rights.

How dare they not have the brand of toothpaste I need? How dare they hold up delivery of my green tennis shoes? How dare they not offer me a greater variety of pasta sauces? I will be taking action – shopping elsewhere–to show my displeasure.

The role of the consumer has taken center stage, and rights and duties have been redefined in relation to consumerism. "Choice" now means being able to choose between a greater variety of cheeses, wines, ovens, jeans, and washing machines. People now spend more time thinking about and choosing between their computers, cells phones, and wireless packages than they do thinking about and choosing between their political representatives.

"Consumer choice" has taken central place in the everyday lives of most of us, whereas "political choice" has become marginal and even insignificant in the actual realm of our everyday activities. Consumer choice derives meaning from actual decisions we make or aspire to make every minute of our lives. The countless advertisements bombarding us directly and indirectly "nudge" us to think and dream about the choices we have made or could have made. The market presents us with hundreds of car models and countless options, endless varieties of foods, computers, holidays, clothing, sports equipment, jewelry, entertainment options, smart watches, and cell phones.

It does not matter that most of us can't afford most of what is on the market, the illusion of freedom and choice still feeds our dreams. If Joe and Jane have to work three full-time jobs between them, and also use food stamps, to be able to feed themselves and their two children, and are never able to take holidays, they still feel better because they live in an "open" society and one day they, or their children, could be affluent enough to take holiday excursions. Joe and Jane feel they have choices in the marketplace, because so much is on offer to everyone. In the land of opportunity everyone benefits from having so many choices on the marketplace, or so it is said.

Compared to our choices as consumers, our political choices seem utterly meager and meaningless. When we are not satisfied with a cereal or a pair of jeans, we feel we can switch to one of the many different brands available on the market. We can and do make such choices every day, even if the array of choice is limited by what is expected to be profitable to the seller. But there are comparatively long intervals between political elections with little meaningful opportunity to participate in political processes, and there is, often at best, an extremely limited choice of political representatives on offer. In most elections, the candidates from the two major parties do not offer policies that are substantially different from one another, and certainly not policies that reflect the needs of the less affluent. The policies they offer represent the interests of the people who pay for their political campaigns, mostly covertly.

The choices offered in politics are few and far between, and seem not to really represent what most people need at all. Nor do the choices people face in the marketplace of politics line up with their dreams and aspirations. Politics continues to be shaped by elites with enormous financial resources such as the Koch brothers who in 2010 were given license by the US Supreme Court to spend as much as they want in American political elections, because apparently spending money is a form of free speech; in the "land of the free," freedom to buy elections must never be curtailed. So people show up for elections – about 20 percent every two years for local elections and 40–50 percent for national elections – and cast votes to choose between candidates who continue with policies that favor the elites.

The "choice" voters have among politicians is so narrow that the entire election process is often a mockery. The reinterpretation of "freedom to choose" from political to consumer markets is accompanied by an illusion of openness and free movement of individuals up and down the social hierarchy.

The Illusion of Mobility

A remarkable feat achieved in societies moving toward the globalized world is the continued illusion that we live in an open society, where individuals move up and down the social hierarchy based on their individual hard work and talent. This illusion is strongest in the US, where the American Dream continues to be trumpeted by politicians and businesses, assisted by right-wing researchers. Despite the enormous wealth divide and the huge jump in the cost of higher education, 52 percent of Americans still believe there is plenty of opportunity for "average Joes" to get ahead (this is down from 81 percent in 1998).

As research clearly shows, the American Dream is in trouble, because equality of opportunity has faded in America (see Bartels, 2008; Putnam, 2015). The traditional path of education has been blocked because of rapidly rising costs, with tuition prices at the "top schools" rising at least 4.5 percent annually since the 1980s (Clotfelter, 1996), reaching a total tuition of more than $200,000 for a bachelor's degree in the 2010s – well above what most American families could pay. The outcome is inevitable: from 1970 to 2012, the proportion of American twenty-four-year-olds who came from low-income families and had a bachelor's degree rose from 6 percent to just 8 percent, but the increase for twenty-four-year-olds from wealthy families was from 40 percent to 73 percent (Pell Institute, 2016).

Social mobility, the probability of a person born into an economically poor family rising to become a member of the middle class or the rich, is lower in America than in most of Europe and about the same as in the UK (McNamee, 2014). Inheritance is often more important than talent. Even though left-wing critics disagree with right-wing critics about why social mobility in America has not improved, they both agree improvement is needed. Left-wing critics point to the enormous and increasing cost of education, the huge advantages enjoyed by the children of the rich, and other environmental factors that influence the success rates of children from rich and poor families. Right-wing critics point to individuals marrying other individuals with similar levels of intelligence and drive, having children who (supposedly) inherit the intelligence and drive of their parents, with the consequence that there is stratification based on merit. Whether we are persuaded by left-wing explanations that focus on environmental factors or right-wing explanations that give priority to "built in" individual difference factors, the bottom line is that social mobility is not in line with the American Dream.

The American Dream tells us that it does not matter where you come from or what your group memberships are, in America you have a fair shot at rising to the top. I have interviewed many groups of immigrants in North America, as well as many people who are outside America but would like to be let in, and the story that really fires their imaginations is the American Dream. Like all dreamers, those who are inspired by the American Dream believe themselves to be the exceptions, one of the few who will win a big-prize lottery ticket.

How is it that the American Dream continues to motivate vast numbers of people, when the facts tell us that the probability of starting poor and moving up to the middle and upper classes is lower in the US than in most European countries? In practice, a poor child in America has about a 9 percent chance to make it to the top quintile (about half as much chance as a poor child in Denmark). Most people who start poor, stay poor – that is a fact generally ignored by the millions of poor people who cling to the American Dream. Surely it is only the economically poor and the poorly educated who fall for this? Not so; many affluent and well educated individuals can fall into the same trap, as reflected by the "Hollywood pipeline."

There are hundreds of different university undergraduate and graduate programs in the US training young people in acting. These include programs at Harvard, Yale, Brown, and many other "top" universities. Thousands of students graduate from these universities every year. Every few years, one of these graduates becomes successful and makes it big in Hollywood, but the vast majority never earns enough money from acting to even support a middle-class lifestyle. They either abandon acting completely, or do other work to supplement the meager living they make from acting. Despite the presence of this huge army of people who never succeed in acting, every year more students compete to enter acting programs and every year another huge cohort of graduates start on what they believe to be the path to Hollywood. The odds are heavily against them, just as the odds are heavily against people buying lottery tickets, but the Hollywood dream keeps them inspired and they keep buying lottery tickets.

The American Dream ideology portrays society as meritocratic, as a place where anyone who works hard and has talent will make it to the top. Anyone can become a star in Hollywood, anyone can become President of the US, anyone can become rich and successful. This illusion is maintained by a few exceptional cases, the token "rags-to-riches" examples that are constantly celebrated. The global super-rich pass on enormous wealth, power, and advantages to their own children, who if current trends continue will become richer and more powerful, and have even greater influence on national and local politics. The richest 0.1 percent increased their share of total wealth in the US from 7 percent in 1970 to 22 percent in 2012. This is largely achieved through inheritance, and the result is that those born rich benefit from huge advantages. The top rate of estate tax fell from 55 percent in 2001 to 35 percent in 2012. Even though the top rate was at 40 percent in 2015, this only applies to inheritance above $5,430,000. Of course, the global super-rich have done much better for themselves than the "mere rich" by hiding much of their wealth offshore; according to a 2012 estimate as much as $21 trillion, the size of the American and Japanese GDPs put together, is hidden offshore by the global super-rich, out of reach of national tax authorities.

China Points the Way

Today, one can wake up in a large hotel in New York, or Istanbul, or Moscow, or Tokyo, or London, or Beijing, or in any other major city in the world, and momentarily forget which country one is in – there is now so much similarity in goods and services around the world. The similarity in clothing, cars, buildings, and many other things is tangible and visible. But a more important similarity is less visible, and often remains hidden: the globalization of the new meaning of freedom, as "freedom to consume."

This new meaning of freedom is most apparent in China, the rising superpower of the twenty-first century. The people in China do not have a voice in the political sphere, but they do have increasing choices in the consumer marketplace. Even though growth in the Chinese economy has slowed from 10–11 percent per annum to about 7–8 percent per annum, the standard of living for the vast majority of the 1.2 billion Chinese has been steadily increasing, as has the range of goods and services available to them. This new "freedom to consume" has become the foundation of a sense of "progress" in China, but the Chinese people have experienced no improvements in their political freedoms.

Of course the "Chinese model" is deceptive, because the "freedoms" it offers people are shallow and will vanish as soon as there is a major economic crisis in China. It is deceptive because the veneer of communism is being used to camouflage one of the most gigantic and corrupt concentrations of wealth in modern history: wealth amassed by the ruling clique in China. This is achieved through a hidden "gray economy," worth about $1.5 trillion and mostly controlled by elite government officials. "Communist" China has about 430 billionaires, the second largest among nations after the US. But China is catching up fast, adding a billionaire a week.

The leadership in twenty-first-century China monopolizes political power and enjoys unparalleled personal wealth. For example, the businessman Wang Jianlin has a personal fortune of about $35 billion, spread in investments around the globe (www.nytimes.com/2015/04/29/world/asia/wang-jianlin-abillionaire-at-the-intersection-of-business-and-power-in-china.html). Whereas the so-called Great Helmsman Mao Zedong tried to channel the energies and aspirations of the people into "perpetual" revolution, such as the destructive "Cultural Revolution" and the "Great Leap Forward," the new Chinese leadership channels the aspirations of the people for freedom into consumerism. China is pointing the way to the future of the emerging new world.

Concluding Comment

Although there have been super-rich individuals and families in other historical eras, twenty-first-century globalization is creating something completely new: a *global* super-rich. Never before has globalization resulted in this level of integration, allowing the world to be treated by the global super-rich as one economic unit.

Globalization is bringing changes that have so far benefited the global super-rich more than the rest of humanity. This is in part because the increasing interconnectedness of the world, the improved communications and transportations systems, the economic integration and global banking and financial systems, all facilitate the movement of capital in search of lower labor costs, lower taxes, and higher profits. Labor unions representing the interests of lower and middle class have remained mainly within national boundaries rather than global, and their power relative to employers has declined. One author describes this as "Disintegrating democracy at work" (Doellgast, 2012). Even global warming is detrimentally impacting the poor more than the rich, as pointed out by Pope Francis. Rather than lift democracies, globalization is lifting the global super-rich to increased wealth and potentially sinking genuine democracy.

REFERENCES

Anastasia, G. (2006). Effects of globalization on labor's share of national income. Working Paper WP/06/294. International Monetary Fund.

Atkinson, A. (2015). *Inequality: What Can Be Done?* Cambridge, MA: Harvard University Press.

Bartels, L. M. (2008). *Unequal Democracy: The Political Economy of the New Gilded Age.* Princeton, NJ: Princeton University Press.

Brys, B., Mathews, S., and Owens, J. (2011). Tax reform trends in OECD countries. OECD Taxation Working Papers 1. Paris: OECD Publishing.

Callick, R. (2013). *The Party Forever: Inside China's Modern Communist Elite.* New York: Palgrave Macmillan.

Cingano, F. (2014). Trends in income inequality and its impact on economic growth. OECD Social, Employment, and Migration Working Papers 163. Paris: OECD Publishing.

Clotfelter, C. T. (1996). *Buying the Best: Cost Escalation in Elite Higher Education.* Princeton, NJ: Princeton University Press.

Crystal, D. (2000). *Language Death.* Cambridge: Cambridge University Press.

Diamond, L. (2015). Facing up to the democratic recession. *Journal of Democracy*, 26, 141–155.

Doellgast, V. (2012). *Disintegrating Democracy at Work: Labor Unions and the Future of Good Jobs in the Service Economy*. Ithaca, NY: Cornell University Press.

Dorling, D. (2014). *Inequality and the 1%*. London: Verso.

Forbes. (2015). 500 richest people in the world. www.forbes.com/sites/chasewithorn/2015/03/02/forbes-billionaires-full-list-of-the-500-richest-people-in-the-world-2015/

Fukuyama, F. (2012). The future of history. *Foreign Affairs*, January/February, 1–12.

Herrnstein, R. J., and Murray, C. (1996). *Bell Curve: Intelligence and Class Structure in American Life*. New York: Free Press.

Kang, M. S. (2013). The year of the super PAC. *George Washington Law Review*, 81, 1902–1929.

Kurlantzick, J. (2013). *Democracy in Retreat: The Revolt of the Middle-Class and the Worldwide Retreat of Representative Government*. New Haven, CT: Yale University Press.

Kuziemko, I., Norton, M. I., Saez, E., and Stantcheva, S. (2013). How elastic are preferences for redistribution? Evidence from randomized survey experiments. Working Paper 18865. Cambridge, MA: National Bureau of Economic Research.

Linders, D. (2012). From e-government to we-government: Defining a typology for citizen coproduction in the age of social media. *Government Information Quarterly*, 29, 446–454.

Marmot, M. (2005). *The Status Syndrome: How Social Standing Affects Our Health and Longevity*. New York: Owl Books.

McNamee, S. J. (2014). *The Meritocracy Myth*. 3rd ed. New York: Rowman and Littlefield.

Moghaddam, F. M. (2013). *The Psychology of Dictatorship*. Washington, DC: American Psychological Association Press.

(2016). *The Psychology of Democracy*. Washington, DC: American Psychological Association Press.

Mudde, C. (2013). Three decades of populist radical right parties in Western Europe: So what? *European Journal of Political Research*, 52, 1–19.

Murray, J. (2014). Evidence of a transnational capitalist class-for-itself: The determinants of PAC activity among foreign firms in the Global Fortune 500, 2000–2006. *Global Networks*, 14, 230–250.

Nguyen, B. D. (2012). Does the rolodex matter? Corporate elite's small world and the effectiveness of board of directors. *Management Science*, 58, 236–252.

Ostry, J. D., Berg, A., and Tsangarides, C. G. (2014). Redistribution, inequality, and growth. Staff Discussion Note SDN/14/02. International Monetary Fund.

Oxfam (2015). Wealth: Having it all and wanting more. www.oxfam.org/en/research/wealth-having-it-all-and-wanting-more.

Paxton, P. (2005). Trust in decline? *Contexts*, 4, 40–46.

Pell Institute (2016). Indicators of higher education equity in the United States. www.pellinstitute.org/downloads/publications-Indicators_of_Higher_ Education_Equity_in_the_US_2016_Historical_Trend_Report.pdf.

Piketty, T. (2014). *Capital in the Twenty-First Century* (A. Goldhammer, Trans.). Cambridge, MA: Harvard University Press.

Piketty, T., and Saez, E. (2014). Inequality in the long run. *Science*, 344, 838–843.

Piketty, T., and Zucman, G. (2014). Capital is back: Wealth-income ratios in rich countries 1700–2010. *Quarterly Journal of Economics*, 129, 1255–1310.

Putnam, R. D. (2000). *Bowling Alone: The Collapse and Revival of American Community* New York: Simon and Schuster.

(2015). *Our Kids: The American Dream in Crisis*. New York: Simon and Schuster.

Robinson, W., and Harris, J. (2000). Toward a global ruling class: Globalization and the transnational capitalist class. *Science and Society*, 64, 11–54.

Thorley, J. (1996). *Athenian Democracy*. New York: Routledge.

Vitali, S., Glattfelder, J. B., and Battiston, S. (2011). The network of global corporate control. *PLoS ONE*, 6(10), e25995.

Wilkes, R. (2011). Re-thinking the decline in trust: A comparison of Black and White Americans. *Social Science Research*, 40, 1596–1610.

5 From the Age of the Crowd to the Global Age

*Brady Wagoner**

> While all our ancient beliefs are tottering and disappearing, while the old pillars of society are giving way one by one, the power of the crowd is the only force that nothing menaces, and of which the prestige is continually on the increase. The age we are about to enter will in truth be the ERA OF CROWDS.
>
> – Le Bon, *The Crowd: A Study of the Popular Mind*

> Politics is a rational way of exploiting the basic irrationality of the masses
>
> – Moscovici, "Discovery of the Masses"

The actions of crowds have been a key component of radical social change throughout world history, especially in the modern era. When Le Bon wrote the famous lines quoted above, France had experienced over a century of successive revolutionary upheavals, instituting various forms of government (monarchies, republics, dictatorships, etc.) and numerous constitutions. It had seen dramatic regime changes in 1789–1794 (French Revolution overthrowing King Louis XVI), 1802–1804 (Napoleon declared "first consul for life" and then "Emperor of France"), 1830–1831 (July Revolution overthrowing King Charles X), 1848–1851 (February Revolution overthrowing Louis Napoleon and creating the Second Republic), and 1870–1871 (formation and destruction of the Paris Commune). Yet despite all this or because of it, the elite saw little progress being made when compared with France's rivals Britain and Germany, who had made clear economic and social gains over the century. It was this turbulent history that early crowd psychology[1] aimed to understand – in particular the causes and consequences of the French Revolution. Le Bon was by no means the first to tackle the subject – Taine and Sighele were clearly forerunners (see van Ginneken, 1992) – but his *The Crowd: A Study of the Popular Mind* has

* I am grateful to Sarah H. Awad and Ignacio Bresco for their comments on an earlier draft of this chapter.

[1] It has also been refered to as "mass psychology," especially within the German tradition.

been by far the most influential.[2] It has served both as a fertile source of scientific ideas and was widely taken up by politicians from the far right to far left, though most notoriously by Hitler and Mussolini (Moscovici, 1981).

In *The Crowd*, Le Bon set out principles for the statesmen to govern mass societies, much like Machiavelli's *The Prince* had advised rulers of an earlier era. The voice of the masses now dictated the behavior of rulers and kings rather than the reverse, such that political leaders needed tools to manage them. Crowd society had emerged through urbanization, rapid social changes, and improved means of communication, which freed people from traditional authority and brought them together as a mass in centers of political power. Le Bon's originality was to see the crowd not as criminal, insane or made up of social outsiders (as had been done before him) but as a group mentality that any person, regards of background, could enter into. The contrast was between what an individual will do alone versus in the thrall of a group. As Moscovici (1986, p. 19) put it: "The behavior of individuals in a crowd is shaped by their culture. When man is alone he can elude it; in a crowd he cannot escape it." The crowd mentality was not exactly irrational as it is usually understood, but rather obeyed a form of thought distinct from individual reasoning. It could lead its members to the extremes of violence but could also direct them to great heroism, sacrificing themselves for the collective cause (cf. Awad and Wagoner, Chapter 11). In this way, Le Bon argued that the crowd should not be defined in common language terms as a simple aggregate of people in a common place, but "psychologically" as a submergence into collective thoughts and emotions. Thus, nations can be crowds while people co-habiting a square may not be.

In this chapter, I use the semantics of crowd psychology to comment on the three other chapters of Part I. While Drury and Reicher (Chapter 2) focus on the dynamics of protest crowd events and their psychological impacts on participants, Power (Chapter 3) steps back to consider the broader social and economic conditions under which protests arise, nuancing "relative deprivation" theory with concepts from cultural psychology and memory studies. Moghaddam (Chapter 4) then extends the socioeconomic discussion of revolutionary conditions to an international level, pointing out how globalization is both creating greater wealth inequalities (especially, the global super-rich) and at the same time thwarting movements against this tendency. Although his

---

[2] By 1921 *The Crowd* had gone through twenty-nine editions and been translated into sixteen languages. A similar but more rigorous and academic formulation of crowd psychology was put forward by Le Bon's contemporary Gabriel Tarde.

argument is not about crowds as such, some of the tactics the global rich use to maintain their privilege (e.g., promoting consumption, individualism, and security fears) can be fruitfully seen through the lens of crowd semantics. Moreover, processes of radicalization he discusses fit squarely into crowd psychology, but the theory requires updating to account for how modern technologies and global connectedness make possible for networked crowds (as happens with diffuse terrorist groups). These are new forms of "imagined communities" (Anderson, 1983).

I aim here to outline a crowd psychology for the twenty-first century that includes processes of collective memory and globalization. The argument begins by outlining the main characteristics of crowd thinking, especially the importance of ideational images for forging affective group attachments and motivating action in a common direction. It proceeds to elaborate the important place of a group's traditions in crowd theory with the concept of collective memory, where a reservoir of past images serves to orient action in the present, thus moderating social changes. In a globalized world, images are quickly transmitted around the world, where they enter into the social-politic dynamics of different localities, becoming symbols for new causes. Under these conditions, an uprising in one part of the world can spark one elsewhere. Some of these images and symbols may even become a part of global collective memory. Finally, the chapter highlights how Moghaddam's concept of "mutual radicalization" can be read through the lens of globalized crowd psychology.

Suggestion, Images, and the Group Mind

The metaphor of suggestion is at the heart of crowd psychology (Feber, 1996). Its meaning does not differ from its lay use in French and English to denote a proposal that typically leads to some action being done. However, the concept of suggestion was taken from the more specific context of hypnotism. At that time, there was a public debate between the Paris and Nancy schools in France over whether hypnosis could be applied simply to pathological cases or to the broader population. Le Bon sided with the latter position and used the model of hypnotizer/patient (at the interpersonal level) to understand the relation of leader/crowd (at a macro level). This was an extremely generative analogy in a number of ways: the effective hypnotizer or leader could get people to believe almost anything (which also explains collective illusions, such as seeing the Virgin Mary), and to suggest actions that would be carried out with no conscious memory of the instructions (which explains the seemingly irrational actions people will do in the name of "faith") (see also Moscovici, 1981, p. 83ff.).

These striking effects are brought about, both in hypnosis and groups, through the medium of vivid images implanted in people's minds.[3] The leader does not win over the crowd by reasoning with them but by suggesting spectacular images that connect up with deeply held beliefs. It is mainly because of this that images are so effective at sparking people's passions (see also Awad and Wagoner, Chapter 11). All the statistics of growing wealth inequality (see Moghaddam, Chapter 4) mean little against the concrete case of the person who made it in the American mind steeped in rags-to-riches stories. Le Bon (1885/2002) remarked:

Whatever strikes the imagination of crowds presents itself under the shape of a startling and very clear image, freed from all accessory explanation, or merely having as accompaniment a few marvelous or mysterious facts: examples in point are a great victory, a great miracle, a great crime, or a great hope. Things must be laid before the crowd as a whole, and their genesis must never be indicated. A hundred petty crimes or petty accidents will not strike the imagination of crowds in the least, whereas a single great crime or a single great accident will profoundly impress them, even though the results be infinitely less disastrous than those of the hundred small accidents put together. (p. 37)

Providing statistics and weighing up different explanations, points of view and possible actions will not be well received by the crowd, which is intolerant of ambiguity. It wants decisive leaders who present simple causes to complex problems. This explains the widespread phenomena of scapegoating throughout history, whatever the religious, ethnic, or national group being targeted. Likewise, through such tactics Moghaddam (Chapter 4) describes how people's attention is diverted from democratic issues to "security threats" (of immigration and terrorism). Security threats are made more salient through images of "hordes" of people flooding into a country or images of devastation following terrorist attacks transmitted through the news media. Trump's statement "build a wall" is a straightforward example of a concrete image that in the mind of the crowd provides a flawless solution to a simple problem.

In fact, Trump's overall communication style of *suggestion, assertion,* and *repetition* of phrases (e.g., "crooked Hilary" and "the dishonest media") without evidence or consistency fits Le Bon's analysis. Through such rhetoric "a lie can travel half way around the world while the truth is still putting on its shoes," as Mark Twain was credited with saying. This

---

[3] Reich (1946) points out how the Nazis hypnotized the masses through dramatic effects created by speeches delivered at night surrounded by people carrying torches. Images of these events would be exposed to more people through the powerful new tool of cinema which is also watched in the dark.

is not to say that other politicians do not use tactics out of Le Bon's play-book. No US president can avoid repeating the word "freedom"[4] and other national symbols in their speeches, in order to tap into historically rooted ideas of the US imagined community (for an analysis of figurative language in Obama's speeches, see Ritchie, 2012). It is only by pack-aging ideas in pithy formulas and vivid images that strong feelings are evoked and beliefs are given a durable form. Although the Occupy Wall Street movement was quickly disbanded (Moghaddam, Chapter 4), its language of "1 percent and 99 percent," "Wall Street and Main Street," showed up in the 2012 and 2016 US presidential debates and continues to be used today.[5] It has become part of the collective currents of thought and feeling that move us, just as the notions of "liberty" and "equality" have since the French Revolution. Drury and Reicher (Chapter 2) argue that even if a protest action is not successful it can still have lasting effects on participants' psyches. How protest ideas are incorporated into collec-tive currents will be further explored below.

In short, it is through the mechanism of suggestion that individuals are submerged into the mind of the crowd. Suggestion is different from the contemporary concept of social influence in that the latter is focused on the exchange of information between normally rational individuals; in contrast, suggestion transports the person into a new psychological state and engulfs them in a group mind (Moscovici, 1986, p. 14). The whole group comes under the spell of a belief that motivates it in a sin-gle direction and makes it intolerant to all those who would refute it. Social movements just like nations need powerful symbols to bring them together for a common cause. National flags and religious symbols oper-ate in the same way as cautionary global warming communications fea-turing images of the world on fire, stranded polar bears, and cities under water. These images speak to our emotions and direct us to action rather than reasoning. For an image to be successful, however, it has to tap into ideas already deeply embedded in a group's tradition. In the case of global warming images, I would argue they are firmly anchored in the

---

[4] Le Bon (1885/2002, p. 61) comments: "The power of words is bound up with the images they evoke, and is quite independent of their real significance. Words whose sense is the most ill-defined are sometimes those that possess the most influence. Such, for example, are the terms democracy, socialism, equality, liberty, etc., whose meaning is so vague that bulky volumes do not suffice to precisely fix it. Yet it is certain that a truly magical power is attached to those short syllables, as if they contained the solution of all problems. They synthesise the most diverse unconscious aspirations and the hope of their realisation."

[5] In the 2016 democratic party primaries, Bernie Sanders was energetically supported partly by the young. Earlier he would have likely been easily dismissed as a "socialist" or "communist" within US society.

ancient religious trope of apocalypse.[6] It is for this reason that Le Bon saw crowds to be inherently conservative: "fundamental ideas resemble the volume of the water of a stream slowly pursuing its course; the transitory ideas are like the small waves, forever changing, which agitate its surface, and are more visible than the progress of the stream itself although without real importance" (Le Bon, 1885/2002, p. 30). The next section will venture into this deep water of a group's "fundamental ideas."

Collective Memory as a Group's Fundamental Ideas

Why do so many revolutions end by reinstating a social order similar to what had come before? Le Bon's answer was that deeply held traditions and social habits hold the most sway over the crowd mind (together with the crowd's ultimate desire to return to an idealized, distant past). Although he often used the awkward language of "racial" characteristics – such as the "Latin" race's excitability – we can replace this nineteenth-century pseudo-biological notion of a group with the twentieth-century concept of "collective memory." According to Halbwachs (1925/1992), who coined the term, groups do not share a mentality because of some biological unconscious, but because of "social frameworks" that transmit traditions from one generation to another through age overlap and socialization. Despite this difference between the thinkers, there are commonalities in the importance both ascribed to concrete images and formulas in creating a group mentality that fosters affective bonds between members. Halbwachs (1925/1992, p. 59) famously described how such phrases as "'In our family we are long lived,' or 'we are proud,' or 'we do not get rich'" create for the family group an inherent physical and moral property that is transmitted to its members. According to him, these operate not only as images of the family's past but also as models and examples that guide its members' actions in the present. Clearly, the same processes apply to national groups. The conservativeness of crowds has to do with them being primarily moved

---

[6] Social representations theory has powerfully analyzed how scientific ideas are transformed as they become lay knowledge or common sense (see, e.g., Moscovici, 2000). The two main processes involved are "objectification" and "anchoring." The former describes how concrete images are found to express the abstract ideas, while latter describes how the unfamiliar is made familiar by linking it to the group's existing framework of knowledge. For example, when psychoanalysis entered the French public in the 1950s it was anchored to the more familiar ideas of conversation and confession (Moscovici, 2008).

by the images that constitute their collective memory, and for this reason "the most violent rebellions merely end in a changing of words and terms" (Le Bon, 1885/2002, p. 47). He continues:

> The most redoubtable idols do not dwell in temples, nor the most despotic tyrants in palaces; both the one and the other can be broken in an instant. But the invisible masters that reign in our innermost selves are safe from every effort at revolt, and only yield to the slow wearing away of centuries. (p. 47)

Le Bon was thinking here of the French revolutionaries' attempts to eradicate religion through the destruction of churches and the expelling, converting or guillotining of priests. Yet only a few years later the abolished system of worship was reinstituted by popular demand. The revolutionaries' attempts to "socially engineer" a new society on rational principles was of marginal success in most areas (see also Campbell and Moghaddam, Chapter 6), but their efforts to do so are instructive for our purposes. The French revolution had the ambitious goal of creating a society based on reason rather than religion, something that had never been done before. However, leaders such as Robespierre intuitively understood the importance of collective symbols and created a new Enlightenment religion, the "cult of the supreme being," to stand in for Roman Catholicism. It is little wonder that Le Bon (1885/2002) himself described *crowd psychology as secularized religion*! The new cult was a form of Deism based on Enlightenment philosophies and was to become the new state religion. It had its own churches ("temples of reason"), festivals, rituals and moral code based on the civic duty to liberty, democracy, and justice. Yet these new practices failed to take hold, as they did not adequately connect to the deeper currents of French customs – the new religion died on the guillotine with Robespierre in 1794.

The French Revolution also instituted many more mundane practices in an attempt to rupture collective memory and bring about a society based on liberty, equality, and fraternity. They broke down the existing social order by erasing symbols of privilege, instating new forms of address – everyone was to be referred to as "citizen" (*citoyen*)[7] in the place of "my lord" (*Monsieur*) – and new styles of clothing which were worn by all regardless of status. Previously, people of the "third estate" (the 98 percent of the population who were neither nobles or clergy) would habitually make way for members of the other estates in the streets. The new clothing had a carnival flair that encouraged people to transgress established norms and suspend ranks and privilege. The third estate was thus empowered to stand their ground on city streets

---

[7] The Russian Revolution instituted the word "comrade" as a form of address for similiar purposes.

and even taunt members of the other estates. Connerton (1989) points out that these were direct interventions into embodied practices, which he argues are highly resilient to change because they work unconsciously and habitually – and as such they are easily transmitted intact from one generation to the next. Even the trial and public execution of the king can be seen as a ritual statement that both physically and symbolically severed the head of royalty. It drew on and subverted images of the king's coronation ceremony, where he was crowned and his body was proclaimed sacred by the church, powerfully objectifying and naturalizing the royal order. Finally, the revolutionaries targeted houses of the rich and churches (especially bell towers) that stood as insults to the republican morals of equality. The newly finished Pantheon in Paris was repurposed to be a monument to reason: Voltaire's body was reburied there in an elaborate ceremony; later the same was done for Rousseau. In all this, we see how old images and symbols are refashioned to serve contemporary aims; in times of radical social change they may even be used to subvert their original purpose (cf. Wagoner, 2017).

Any social movement today also draws on deeply rooted collective images that speak to people's emotions and in so doing motivates action in a common direction – something frequently accomplished with national flags (Awad and Wagoner, Chapter 11) but a variety of images can fill the role. In Latin America, one commonly finds the hammer-and-sickle symbol of the Soviet Union during left-leaning protests, which stands for resistance to oppression there. The same symbol has the exact opposite meaning in Eastern Europe because of the distinct historical relation to communism (Carretero and van Alphen, 2018). In the US, labeling something "communist" or "red" essentially disqualifies it without the need for further argument – such is the legacy of the Cold War on the American mind. Moghaddam (Chapter 4) notes how it was even applied to the Pope Francis after his encyclical on climate change and its disproportionate impact on the poor! In all three contexts, people react to symbolic images that carry forward a group's history in an affective response – an image's impact varies widely across cultures given the divergent historical experiences of the groups concerned. From Power's (Chapter 3) study it is also noteworthy that the ultimate trigger of the 2014 Irish protests against austerity was the tax on water, which served as a symbol of a basic human right in the rainy and lake filled nation, in spite of the fact that most other countries in the Organization for Economic Cooperation and Development charge for water consumed. As Power describes in Chapter 3, these protests were carefully choreographed to pass by important historical sites commemorating Irish resistance to British occupation, thus subtly conveying through affective images that "the Irish have overcome injustices before; they can do it again." This clearly illustrates how images from the group's collective memory were used to channel people's emotions and actions against current government polices.

Globalization, Revolution, and Memory

A focus on collective memory and its conservative force only tells part of the story – radical social change does happen and often rapidly. This section will focus on one factor that brings about significant social changes: globalization and the increasing interconnectedness of people and ideas. At the time of the French revolution, news traveled over land at the speed of a horse. By contrast, revolutions today are almost instantly broadcast to the whole world – at least to those countries that do not censor them. This creates a problem for leaders aiming to retain the status quo. For example, China forbid coverage of the 2011 Arab uprisings and invested heavily in blocking news of it on the Internet. In the nineteenth century, the Papal States (of what is today Italy) decided against introducing railroads for fear that they would bring radical ideas to its citizens. Both states were right to be wary: Contact between peoples has been one of the major forces of social change throughout human history and its influence is only growing in the globalized world of today (Wagoner, 2017).

The process involved in the global spread of ideas and practices is more complex than is allowed for by the concept of *imitation* that Le Bon and other crowd psychologists used. New ideas and practices enter into preexisting social dynamics and cultural understandings of the group concerned and must also be considered relevant to people's aspirations there to be adopted (Bartlett, 1923). For example, Arab countries did not participate equally in the 2011 uprisings nor did they lead to the same outcomes. The protests in Saudi Arabia were easily neutralized by the strong state and by being associated with the Shia minority group. Syria, Libya, and Yemen are highly sectarian societies, and have all fallen into civil war given this starting point. By contrast, Tunisia and Egypt seemed to have followed a similar and comparatively more stable revolutionary trajectory, but diverged paths when Muslim Brotherhood president Morsi was ousted in Egypt. Hearing of this event led the Islamist politicians in Tunisia to compromise with the other political factions, such that the country today remains the only success story of the uprisings, though still a fragile one.

The successive uprisings in each Arab country were preceded and fueled by slogans, images and the stories they told, as crowd psychology would have predicted (see also Awad and Wagoner, Chapter 11). In Tunisia, a fruit vendor Mohamed Bouazizi set himself on fire in protest of the police's confiscation of his cart for refusing to pay bribe. Bouazizi's image has since become a powerful reminder of the revolutionary cause and has even been included on Tunisian postage stamps. Although his self-immolation happened in a small town, his image and the story of humiliation quickly spread throughout the country, motivating nationwide protests with the chant "the people demand the down of the regime." This phrase would soon be used in protests throughout the Arab world. The conflict in Syria in fact started when a group of teenagers, under the age of fifteen, were arrested for spray-painting the phrase on a city wall. In Egypt, the protests that started the revolution were organized on the Facebook page "We Are All Khalid Said," commemorating an activist of who was brutally killed by police for his activities the previous summer. Outside the Middle East, protestors were also inspired and borrowed some of the symbolic imagery from the Arab uprisings. For example, Madrid's Plaza del Sol was renamed Tahrir by antiausterity protestors.

The phrase "Arab Spring" itself is interesting as it makes an analogy with the 1848 "Springtime of the People" revolutions. It was first applied in the immediate aftermath of the 2003 Iraq war, which US leaders promised would spread democracy throughout the Middle East. That failed. But in 2011 the phrase found a better fit, both in terms of the spread of uprisings and ultimate outcomes. In this example we see how phrases become part of *global memory*, borrowed and adapted to make sense of contemporary events and create a future orientation on the basis of a narrative from the past. This requires decontextualizing symbols from the situation of origin and re-contextualizing them into new places for different ends. The prototypical case of this is the French revolution, which has become the mold through which earlier and later radical social changes were understood in both popular culture and social scientific theory. When we are confronted with a revolution today we ask who are the new Jacobins? When is this revolution's "Thermidorian Reaction"? Who will be their Napoleon? Before the French Revolution, the very word "revolution" used to be conceptualized as part of a cyclical process – "a turning around" as the name implies. It then became wedded to Enlightenment ideas of progress and took on associations of modernization. This new schema of revolution was projected back in time to understand the English and American revolutions as well as forward to those that followed.

A recently emerged global memory is that of the 9/11 terrorist attacks. 9/11 has become the schema into which new terrorist attacks are preformed in our understanding. For example, the terrorist attack by extreme nationalist Anders Behring Breivik on Norwegians (mentioned by Moghaddam, Chapter 4) was first reported by the news media as an Islamic Terrorist attack. 9/11 is primarily solidified in our memories through the dramatic statement and circulation of images (Mitchell, 2005). Most will instantly recognize the images of a plane hitting the twin towers in New York City, which will in turn activate a network of meanings surrounding the event. New York City has since been active in constructing their own images of the site, including a temporary instillation of two airy light beams in the sky where the tours once stood. On the ten-year anniversary of 9/11, a memorial composed of infinity pools in the footprints of the towers was unveiled, which provides an image of loss and resilience to the world. Thus, both the attackers and the victims aimed to create images to memorialize the event and transmit it to the world. These images can then be used to foster affective bonds of identification across global networks and can function as analogies to understand a host of current events and concerns.

Mutual Radicalization and Terrorism

Moghaddam (Chapter 4) argues that the "sudden contact has not only resulted in increased sense of threat and radicalization in the Islamic world, but the same process is evident in Western societies." At the time of writing this chapter, three jihadists plowed a white van through pedestrians on London Bridge and then proceeded on foot to Borough Market where the stabbed people with knives. Eight people were killed and another forty-eight were injured. The attackers were inspired by and pledged their allegiance to the so-called Islamic State. Two weeks later, a self-radicalized forty-seven-year-old British man used a van to attack a group of Muslims leaving a Finsbury Park Mosque in London after morning prayers, killing one and injuring eleven. The man shouted "I'm going to kill all Muslims." The two cases present mirror images of each other, not only in terrorist tactics but also in terms of radicalization following a perceived threat and adoption of an ideology that drives them to action. The notion of "mutual radicalization" is useful in this context as it conceptualizes radicalization as part of an *escalating social feedback loop*, rather than an individual process "influenced" by social factors. Both events feed into the radicalization of each group, driving polarization of the two toward a common end of violent. In a less extreme example, Drury and Reicher (Chapter 2) illustrate how social activists come to accept protestor violence after being confronted with the police's violence against them.

Extreme cases of radicalization represented by terrorism must also be contextualized within more mundane forms, which they build on top of and contribute to. Whole populations can become more extreme in their attitudes and behavior under conditions of instability. The extremist crowds that characterize Le Bon's (1885/2002) theory probably require this element of outside threat to come into being. Robespierre was famously against the death penalty at the onset of the French Revolution, but later as leading member of the "Committee for Public Safety" he became the principal engineer of the "Terror" that guillotined thousands of people. In our own day and age, as immigration increases and terrorist attacks become more frequent what was considered extremist only years earlier became naturalized as normal: It has for example become routine to refer to poor migrants in terms of "hordes," "plague," "invasion," and "criminality." Various right-wing movements (represented by Trump, Le Pen, U-KIP, etc.) have pushed the limits of what could be openly said about immigrants, in particular Muslims. Following the Finsbury Park terrorist attack, some right-wing groups in Denmark even called the perpetrator a "freedom fighter"! Although these political attitudes are calls for withdrawing into and fortifying national borders, they tap into a global, radicalizing political discourse. In this way, *banal radicalization*[8] is not only happening within national borders but is connected at an international level. Although most people that identify with it will express their attitudes in discourse and voting behavior, a select few will take it further to commit terrorist actions.

Thus, in a globalized world we need to think in terms of networked crowds rather than simply crowds physically gathered in the same place. With current technologies of intercommunication, a group of likeminded people using common phrases, images and symbols can easily form across national borders. The so-called Islamic State for example, is a diffuse global network and not simply a group localized in Syria and Iraq. It is fed both in terms of military personnel and financed from this network. Moreover, it has learned to use globally diffused images of, for example, the destruction of the ancient site of Palmyra to illustrate its strength and propagate its radical Islamist message. This is an "imagined community" (Anderson, 1983) more like Christendom in the era of the crusades or communists at the time of the Spanish Civil War than the modern nationalist form. Through its communication network, the Islamic State has also inspired lone individuals to commit terroristic attacks in their home countries, following instructions distributed on its online forums. Fighting this sort of organization requires much more than dropping bombs – even if it is defeated militarily, committed

---

[8] Ignacio Bresco should be credited with suggesting the use of the term *banal radicalization*. It is a modification of Billig's (1995) concept of *banal nationalism*, a less visible and more mundane form of nationalism that is for this reason equally if not more dangerous.

members will simply blend in with the local population and work behind the scenes. Instead, the war will be won by winning over its members through effective counterimages and ideas. As such, wars of the future will be fought on the ground of ideas as much as military force. Even at the time of the French revolution, British historian Eric Hobsbawm (1962) reminds us that "(France's) armies set out to revolutionize the world; its ideas actually did so" (p. 77).

Conclusion

Crowd psychology offers a useful framework to approach revolutions old and new. Its ideas of how groups are forged and directed through the use of suggestion, images and slogans helps to explain the communication processes effectively used by leaders to bolster their cause and guide their followers. All groups create collective imagery to forge affective bonds that hold them together. Flags, ritual ceremonies, overgeneralized words like "freedom," memories of heroic figures and great events submerge members of a group within a common stream of affect and ideas, and can be used to mobilize them to action in a suggested direction. An attack on these group symbols becomes a direct attack on the group itself. Under conditions of threat and group suggestion, people become all the more extreme. In today's world, we can understand radicalization processes through networked crowds that capture new members through effective imagery and other symbols, fostering imagined communities that transcend national borders. As such radicalization needs to be approached as a part of a wider social and communicative process rather than simply individual pathology. History has shown us that revolutions and radicalism can spread through powerful imagery and ideas, as has happened following the French Revolution, in for example 1848, 1989, 2011 and more recently with the so-called Islamic State. On a final note, it is worth stressing that Le Bon's (1885/2002) theory of crowds has been remembered in a one-sided fashion: for him, crowd mentality could lead individuals to commit terrible acts of violence but also to great heroism, even to the point of sacrificing themselves for the common cause.

REFERENCES

Anderson, B. (1983). *Imagined Communities*. London: Verso.
Bartlett, F. C. (1923). *Psychology and Primitive Culture*. Cambridge: Cambridge University Press.
Billig, M. (1995). *Banal Nationalism*. London: Sage.
Carretero, M., and van Alphen, F. (2018). History, collective memory or national memories? How the representation of the past is framed by master

narratives. In B. Wagoner (Ed.), *Handbook of Culture and Memory*. Oxford: Oxford University Press.

Connerton, P. (1989). *How Societies Remember*. Cambridge: Cambridge University Press.

Feber, D. P. (1996). Suggestion: Metaphor and meaning. *Journal of the History of the Behavioural Sciences*, 32, 16–29.

Halbwachs, M. (1925/1992). *On Collective Memory*. Chicago: University of Chicago Press.

Hobsbawm, E. (1962). *The Age of Revolution: 1789–1848*. London: Weidenfeld and Nicolson.

Le Bon, G. (1885/2002). *The Crowd: A Study of the Popular Mind*. New York: Dover.

Mitchell, W. J. T. (2005). *What Do Pictures Want? The Lives and Loves of Images*. Chicago: University of Chicago Press.

Moscovici, S. (1981). *The Age of the Crowd: A Historical Treatise of Mass Psychology*. Cambridge: Cambridge University Press.

(1986). Discovery of the masses. In C. F. Grauman and S. Moscovici (Eds.), *Changing Conceptions of Crowd Mind and Behavior* (pp. 5–25). New York: Springer.

(2000). *Social Representations: Explorations in Social Psychology*. Cambridge: Polity.

(2008). *Psychoanalysis: Its Image and Its Public*. Cambridge: Polity.

Reich, W. (1946). *The Mass Psychology of Fascism*. New York: Orgone Institute Press.

Ritchie, D. (2012). Metaphors and stories in discourse about personal and social change. In B. Wagoner, E. Jensen, and J. A. Oldmeadow (Eds.), *Culture and Social Change: Transforming Society through the Power of Ideas* (pp. 99–118). Charlotte, NC: Information Age.

van Ginneken, J. (1992). *Crowds, Psychology and Politics, 1871–1899*. Cambridge: Cambridge University Press.

Wagoner, B. (2017). *The Constructive Mind: Bartlett's Psychology in Reconstruction*. Cambridge: Cambridge University Press.

Part II

Evolution and Involution in Social Transformations

6 Social Engineering and Its Discontents
The Case of the Russian Revolution

Sierra Campbell and Fathali M. Moghaddam

> The Revolution at the present moment could be consolidated only on the basis of social transformations that correspond to the will of the majority... and to Russia's level of economic development... an attempt to transcend these limits and, by force, to impose on the country the will of the socialist minority would bring about the collapse of the Revolution.
>
> – Irakli Tsereteli

This assessment by Tsereteli (1881–1959), a leading revolutionary politician in the Petrograd Soviet in 1917, underlines the challenge clearly seen by revolutionaries, including Vladimir Lenin (Kowalski, 1997, p. 247), at the time of the 1917 Russian Revolution: there were limits to how fast and how much change could be imposed on the majority of Russians. The "will of the majority" involved not only the motivation but also the ability to change styles of thought and action. The Russian Revolution was the result of a long "lead up" period of development during which contradictory and competing economic, political, and social forces were at work (Wood, 2003). The revolutionaries recognized that it could take even longer to bring about the behavioral changes they believed necessary to create the people who could participate in and sustain the new communist society. The central challenge for the revolutionaries became *political plasticity*, the malleability of political behavior (Moghaddam, 2016).

In their search for more effective means by which they could more rapidly increase the political plasticity of ordinary people, the communists identified the new science of psychology as an important tool. At the time of the Russian Revolution, psychological science was coming under the domination of behaviorism, a school of thought that was in important ways in line with communist assumptions about human nature. In particular, the behaviorists and communists both gave highest importance to the role of the environment in "shaping behavior," and to the Lockean idea that humans are born as tabula rasa and are highly malleable. When in 1913 John Watson (1878–1958) launched the behaviorist manifesto in

103

the US, his assumptions about human plasticity were in line with those espoused by leading communist thinkers, such as Leon Trotsky (1879–1940):

What is man? He is by no means a finished or harmonious being. No, he is still a highly awkward creature. Man, as an animal, has not evolved by plan but spontaneously, and has accumulated many contradictions. The question of how to educate and regulate, of how to improve and compete the physical and spiritual construction of man, is a colossal problem which can only be understood on the basis of socialism. We can construct a railway across the Sahara, we can build the Eiffel Tower and talk directly with New York, but surely we cannot improve on man. Yes we can! To produce a new, "improved version" of man – that is the future task of communism. And for that we first have to find out everything about man, his anatomy, his physiology and that part of his physiology which is called his psychology. Man must look at himself and see himself as a raw material, or at best as a semi-manufactured product, and say: "At last, my dear homo sapiens, I will work for you." (quoted in Figes, 2002, p. 447)

Although the political end goals of behaviorists working in capitalist America and communist revolutionaries attempting to lead change in Russia were in some important ways different, they both believed in the power of the environment to reshape human behavior. Writing about Russian psychology, Luria (1928) makes the following observation, "Russian psychology has been under considerable influence from the American behaviorists" (p. 347). Since behaviorism was influenced in important ways by Russian researchers, particularly Vladimir Bekhterev (1857–1927) and Ivan Pavlov (1849–1936), the Russian communists were able to rely on their indigenous Russian "behaviorists" as a scientific basis for their programs. Parallel to this development was the spread of psychoanalysis in Russia (Miller, 1998), but our focus in this discussion is on behaviorism, particularly as developed in the US. Of course, as the adoption of "Taylorism" (the job design and mass production ideas of the American engineer Frederick Taylor, 1856–1915) shows, the Russian communists were not reluctant to import ideas from the US if it suited their political purposes. Taylorism was based on psychological assumptions in line with behaviorism.

In this chapter, we explore the historical intersection between psychological science, and behaviorism in particular, and Russian communist revolutionaries.

Russian Revolution

Prior to 1917, Czar Nicholas II ruled Russia, under conditions of government corruption and widespread economic hardship. Russia's tragic entry into World War I, and the food shortage that resulted from the ill-fated war efforts, only heightened civil unrest. Beginning on March 8, 1917, demonstrators, consisting mostly of striking industrial workers, took to the streets of St. Petersburg (then called Petrograd) for what became known as the February Revolution. Although the government deployed army troops to suppress the uprising and some opened fire on and killed a number of protestors, the uprising could not be quelled, and on March 12, Czar Nicholas II was forced to resign (Trotsky, 1930/2008, p. 105). The Czar had been abandoned even by his military generals, who "had lost faith in Nicholas's leadership or his ability to organize the rear for victory over Germany... The overthrow of the monarchy was followed rapidly by the disintegration of military discipline, of the war economy, and of the food supply system... there was abundant class hatred stored up to set the country alight once controls were removed" (Lieven, 2015, pp. 352–353).

Following the Czar's resignation, the Petrograd Soviet (the term "Soviet" at this stage of the revolution meant "revolutionary committee," typically of workers, peasants, and soldiers; Wood, 2003) and a provisional government temporarily shared power; however, the provisional government had little support among Russian citizens. Also, despite his slogan "All power to the Soviets," Lenin suspected that many Soviets were infiltrated by anti-Bolshevik elements, "in most of the Soviets of Workers' Deputies our party is ... a small minority, as against *a bloc of all* the petty-bourgeois opportunist elements" (statement from Lenin, April 4, 1917, in Kowalski, 1997, p. 52). There was a dramatic and sudden collapse of major institutions, including the church, the security system, and the legal system. Authority figures and the gentry lost their status and influence. Real power was transferred to the Soviets (Figes, 2002, pp. 436–437). By early November, the Bolshevik Party, under the leadership of Vladimir Lenin, seized power in the name of these workers, peasants, and soldiers and established the "Dictatorship of the Proletariat" in what came to be known as the October Revolution, or the Bolshevik Revolution.

The Bolsheviks came to power in Russia for the same reason that particular revolutionary groups have climbed to power in other countries: they were the most effectively organized, determined, and ruthless. The Bolsheviks were a minority in 1917, just as the Islamic fundamentalist followers of Khomeini had been a minority in Iran in 1978–1979, but they were the ones most willing to do whatever was required to grab and keep hold of power. The Bolsheviks positioned themselves as the champion of the people, even though their goal was not to establish a democracy. If their goal had been to create a democracy, "Creating a peasant-based democracy almost from scratch in a country as enormous as Russia was a daunting task" (Lieven, 2015, p. 353). Next, we consider what the Bolsheviks did want.

What the Bolsheviks Wanted to Change

The Bolsheviks launched a "war against all privilege" as a path to the communist utopia, and as a practical means of funding their efforts to change society. The focus turned to how people would think and behave in this ideal society, as well as a push for programs that could lead to behavioral transformation (Stites, 1988, p. 13). This creation of a revolutionary culture and a new society required the rejection and removal of old norms "by means of destroying odious images, idols, icons, and structures and by a sweeping negation of cultural and social values" (p. 61). Influenced heavily by Marx (and after around 1925 Engels), the revolutionaries at the time hoped to establish social justice through the rejection of private wealth and the enforcement of equality by transforming, for instance, old work habits and old forms of domesticity. Moreover, "Experiment in the Russian Revolution took on flesh in the decade or so after 1917 when various kinds of people, exhibiting varying levels of consciousness, began 'living the revolution' by renouncing the old and trying out the new," demonstrating the push common to all utopias to negate the present order and make way for future visions (p. 61). This denunciation of the old and taking up of the new permeated into idealized forms of communal housing, more mechanized labor, and the rejection of private wealth. Although the revolutionaries hoped for this new internationalist, collectivist, proletarian society, they also recognized that citizens' thought and behavior would need to change before this transformation could occur, and they, therefore, turned to psychological science as a tool for achieving their goals. But they began by "cleaning out" what they considered the antirevolutionary psychologists; in 1922 the Moscow Psychological Society was disbanded and many "old style" Wundtian psychologists were exiled (Kozulin, 1984).

The revolutionaries hoped to condition citizen behavior in order to create a utopian society characterized by collectivism, the rejection of private wealth, and the enforcement of equality. Herschel and Edith Alt (1964) elaborate on this goal: "The new social order will be cooperative rather than competitive; altruistic rather than selfish. "From each according to his abilities, to each according to his needs," will be the governing maxim. Man will be motivated by enlightened self-interest that will identify the good of one with the good of all and harmony between man and man will prevail" (p. 19). At the beginning of the revolution, the pace of the realization of these goals was "falter-ing and uncertain," forcing the revolutionaries to re-evaluate their abil-ity to rapidly alter citizen behavior, even with the aid of psychological techniques. During the civil war the Bolsheviks had used violence to influence behavior, but after 1920 there was a greater reliance on social means of creating change. Either way, they learned that controlling social change and behavior was extremely difficult and not often successful. Because of this, "the vision of society and of man and how fast they would be realized were both amended, allowing for a transition of indef-inite duration from the imperfect to the perfect" (p. 20). To advance this transition from the imperfect, privatized, and "selfish" society into a communist ideal, the Bolsheviks attempted to condition citizen behav-ior by denouncing private wealth and the bourgeois class, restructuring labor, rejecting symbols of the old society, and transforming home life, education, and other forms of propaganda.

Denunciation of the Bourgeois Class

Because the Bolsheviks achieved power monopoly after 1917, they had the opportunity to conduct large-scale experiments toward reaching their communist utopia, characterized by the rejection of private wealth and the celebration of manual labor. To reach these utopian ideals nation-ally, the Bolsheviks, for instance, employed the Red Guards and groups of armed workers to invade the homes of the "leisured classes" and seize their property. Moreover, the Bolsheviks moved those of the urban poor classes into the homes of these elite and forced the elite to do man-ual labor jobs like clearing snow or trash from the streets (Figes, 2002, p. 437). Based on the behaviorist ideals that gained popularity at the time, the Bolsheviks believed that altering citizens' environment would alter their behavior. By moving entire groups of people and making demands of the elite, the Bolshevik leaders hoped that changes would take place in how people thought and that citizens as a whole would become more collective in nature and more able to successfully transi-tion to a communist society. They attempted to speed up this process by eliminating wave after wave of opponents and replacing them with their supporters, or at least people of proletariat origin they believed would become supporters.

Restructuring of Labor

Because of their rejection of an elite class and celebration of manual labor, Taylorism – which focuses on scientific management to promote productivity – was also popular among Lenin and the Bolsheviks. Lenin "saw Taylorism's 'scientific' methods as a means of discipline that could remold the worker and society along more controllable and regularized lines" (Figes, 2002, p. 463). Inspired by American industrialists like Henry Ford, the Bolshevik engineer, poet, and head of the Central Institute of Labour Aleksei Gastev was one of the most radical proponents of Taylorism at the time and "envisaged the mechanization of virtually every aspect of life in Soviet Russia, from methods of production to the thinking patterns of the common man" (p. 463). Possibly the first to use the term "biomechanics," Gastev developed a "vision of a future communist society in which man and machine merged" (pp. 463–464). In an attempt to mechanize as much of Soviet life as possible, Gastev conducted experiments in which identically dressed workers would receive orders from machines and internalize the machinelike rhythm of basic skills like hammering, chiseling, and filing so that they would eventually "end up acting like machines" or a sort of "human robot" (p. 464). Idealizing manual labor and productivity, Lenin, Gastev, and other Bolshevik leaders hoped the use of Taylorism's scientific methods could reshape the behavior of individual workers as well as Soviet society at large.

Transformation of Domesticity

Other environmental changes the Bolsheviks implemented included the transformation of living spaces. At the beginning of the revolution, in many cases the Bolsheviks gave families single rooms in old apartment blocks and assigned them to share kitchens and bathrooms with other families in an attempt to transform not just the political regime but also the mentality of everyday citizens to become more collective. The more radical Soviet architects pushed for the complete remove of private space in these community houses in which families would not only share kitchens and bathrooms but also sleeping space as well as property and domestic chores like childcare and cooking (Figes, 2002, pp. 445–446). Despite the frequency of these communal houses in utopian imagination, the houses that were built fell just short of completely communal spaces with private living spaces for families but communalized bath houses, dining rooms, kitchens, and schools (p. 446).

In many cases, the Bolsheviks transformed the country palaces and grand urban houses of the gentry to create communal living spaces, where sometimes hundreds of families would crowd into what was once space reserved for one aristocratic family (p. 447). This transformation of domestic spaces from palaces to communal apartments, a kind of Soviet "war against palaces," was a way of rejecting the national symbols and privilege of the old society, and it was also part of the Soviet plan to engineer a more collective style of behavior among its citizens. As Figes (2002) explains, "By forcing people to share communal flats, the Bolsheviks believed that they could make them communistic in their basic thinking and behaviour. Private space and property would disappear, the patriarchal ('bourgeois') family would be replaced by communist fraternity and organization, and the life of the individual would become immersed in the community" (p. 445). This notion that the regime could train individuals, through reorganizing use of the built environment in this example, to move away from the old society's private forms of domesticity into a more collective way of life was a common thread through the Russian Revolution (as well as some other major cases, such as revolutions in France 1798 and Iran 1979).

Rejection of Symbols of the Old Society

The attempt to change behavior also occurred through the removal of symbols of the old system. In addition to confiscating and restructuring palaces, the revolutionaries also destroyed many palaces and museums, changed the names of many roads and cities, and even altered forms of art, architecture, clothing designs, and designs of household objects. Believing that the environment shapes consciousness and behavior, the Bolsheviks focused on re-shaping the environment. By getting rid of symbols of the old system and altering citizens' everyday environment, revolutionaries believed they were liberating citizens and making them better able to adopt the new, communist system (Figes and Kolonitskii, 1999). This reliance on environmental factors – like living spaces, private property, workplaces, and household objects – in the hopes it would alter citizens' human nature ties back once again to the behaviorist views of the time that the environment shapes behavior, rather than human behavior being preprogrammed.

Transformation of Education and Other Propaganda

The Bolsheviks also attempted to shape citizen behavior through the transformation of the education system, with the goal of developing a mass consciousness grounded in revolutionary values. Educational achievement not only acts as a source of individual success or opportunity for upward social mobility but also "is a basic requisite for assuring that the potential of skill, talent and energy is fully utilized, and as such is a road to national well-being" (Alt and Alt, 1964, p. 219). Emphasizing

equality of educational opportunity and education of all citizens, the Bolsheviks saw education as a means to increase productivity, promote social
mobility, and shape the minds of both current citizens and future generations. This is evident through the Bolsheviks' push for increased literacy
as well as their very carefully designed educational communication in an
attempt to "indoctrinate" or directly influence the thoughts and beliefs
of citizens (p. 44).

This careful use of communication to diffuse revolutionary values and
cultivate social cohesion was evident not only within the educational system but also in other forms of propaganda, especially art. "The Con-
structivists, the Futurists, the artists aligned to Proletkult and the Left
Front (LEF), Vsevolod Meyerhold in the theater, or the Konok group
and Eisenstein in cinema" all shared similar communist values and aim
to revolt against bourgeois art (Figes, 2002, p. 447). Tying back to the
behaviorist beliefs discussed earlier, these artists aimed to use new art
forms to condition citizens into changing in line with communist values, especially relying on mechanistic art including "cinematic montage,
biomechanics in the theatre, industrial art, etc." (p. 448). Artists such
as the poet and engineer Gastev also valued the "scientific" methods
of Taylorism and recognized the importance of art in influencing citizen
behavior and thought regarding productivity and collectivism. Moreover,
"Since they believed that consciousness was shaped by the environment,
they focused on forms of art, like architecture and documentary film,
photomontage and poster art, designs for clothes and fabrics, household objects and furniture, which had a direct impact on people's daily
lives" (p. 448). One artist that was especially prolific in this Soviet propaganda was Vladimir Mayakovsky (1893–1930). As a prominent Futur-
ist, Mayakovsky produced poetry, work in theater, journalism, radio
songs, propaganda posters, and state advertising jingles and slogans, all
of which were largely political in nature. Mayakovsky and other artists at
the time rejected the "bourgeois art traditions" of the past and attempted
to condemn the "selfish," privatized old way of life in their work.

The Bolsheviks recognized that the peasants and middle class of Russia at the time were unequipped to make the desired transition to a new,
more collective, way of life; they would need to train citizens to behave
differently if they were to attain their communist ideals. This is why they
found hope in the studies of Pavlov and relied heavily on the explicit and
direct use of psychological science to influence human behavior through
the denunciation of private wealth and the elite, mechanized labor, more
communal living spaces, rejection of symbols of the old society, education reform, and art and other forms of propaganda.

Behaviorism as a Tool for Change

Many parallels can be drawn between the beliefs of behaviorists and of communists during the Russian Revolution. Both supported the belief that nothing in human nature is preprogrammed. Communists, for instance, rejected the common argument that innate greed is good and drives society. They rejected the argument that human beings are naturally programmed for a capitalist society and naturally motivated to work hard for personal gain. These revolutionary ideals that nothing, including capitalist tendencies, is preprogrammed and is only the result of environmental factors align largely with the tenets of behaviorism. Moreover, the revolutionaries, like behaviorists, believed they could radically reshape citizens' environment and it would result in radical behavior change.

Although Russian revolutionary leaders had historically been skeptical of psychology because it was not considered a "hard science," they became convinced of the usefulness of behaviorism and other "scientific" approaches to behavior, as reflected by their support for the Bekhterev Psychoneurological Research Institute, and the journal *Overview of Psychiatry and Medical Psychology*. Pavlov was treated with some suspicion because he was not considered supportive of the regime, but in order to stop him from emigrating he was given preferential treatment and the publication and propagation of his work was supported. Realizing that citizens were unequipped to make the desired transition to a more collective way of life on their own, Russian revolutionaries turned to psychological science and particularly the research of behaviorist psychologists in an attempt to train citizens to behave differently and ultimately attain their utopian ideals. They believed that they could employ behaviorist findings in their attempts to condition citizen behavior.

The Russian revolutionaries were explicit in their use of psychology in the government and their attempts to change citizen behavior directly through psychological methods. Lenin spoke of Pavlov's research as "hugely significant for our revolution" (Figes, 2002, pp. 446–447). This was because Pavlov's research on classical conditioning and the role of environment on behavior was central to the Bolsheviks' plan to re-shape human behavior among Russian citizens.

At the time, there existed some debate about how to achieve this new revolutionary society. Some maintained the belief that the new Soviet society could be built from the "rubble" of the old Russian society. On the extreme left, however, many pushed for the destruction of the old world, agreeing with Mayakovsky that the classics were "old aesthetic junk" and "it's time for bullets to pepper museums" (Figes, 2002, pp. 449–450). As Trotsky explained in *Results and Prospects*, the communist utopia could not be created within the old society: "If socialism aimed at creating a new human nature within the limits of the old society it would be nothing more than a new edition of the moralistic utopias. Socialism does not aim at creating a socialist psychology as a pre-requisite to socialism but at creating socialist conditions of life as a pre-requisite to socialist psychology" (Trotsky, 1906/2010, p. 109). Moreover, many revolutionaries felt the new Soviet society needed to be pure and therefore purged of any historical and national aspects that were once revered. This new Soviet society would be characterized as internationalist, collectivist, and proletarian, and this began through the development of proletarian science, proletarian philosophy, and even proletarian art (p. 450). The new experimental forms of art, for instance, demonstrated this shift to a new society: "There were films without professional actors (using "types" selected from the streets), orchestras without conductors and "concerts in the factory," with sirens, whistles, hooters, spoons and washboards as the instruments" (p. 449–450). However, the realities of this transformation to a collective society were evident not only in the new forms of art but also in the redevelopment of domestic space, the transformation of education, and the destruction of symbols of the old society with the hopes that these transformations would also transform citizen behavior.

Psychological Research at the Time of the Russian Revolution

By the beginning of the twentieth century, the introspective methods used in "mainstream" psychology – as represented by Wilhelm Wundt (1832–1920) and his disciples (such as Tichener, 1867–1927, and other nineteenth-century structuralists) – had reached a major roadblock on the issue of "imageless thought" (see Moghaddam, 2005). Some laboratories reported that thought could only take place with images, but other laboratories reported that "imageless thought" can and does take place. No solution to this question seemed possible using introspection, since reports from opposing camps could not be objectively tested or verified. This situation created a backlash against introspection and an opportunity for the rise of an alternative school of thought: behaviorists claimed that in order to become a science, psychology must reject "introspection into the mind" and only focus on observable behavior. As Mills (2000) explains,

Early behaviorists shared a common set of concerns, in which negative considerations outweighed positive. All denied any intrinsic life to the mind, none believed that the mind was psychology's primary area of study, and all believed that introspection was a futile and misleading way of gathering psychological data... The early behaviorists, with some exceptions, all shared the faith that behaviorist doctrine could be directly applied to human beings and that experimentation with humans provided a direct route to knowledge. Almost all also believed that psychological research would have direct social implications. (p. 3)

Although behaviorism is in some respects a peculiarly American school of thought, having dominated psychology in the US for most of the first half of the twentieth century, the research of the Russian researchers Vladimir Bekhterev (1857–1927) and Ivan Pavlov (1849–1927), influenced by the ideas of Ivan Sechenov (1829–1905), serves as the foundation for this school (Razran, 1965). Bekhterev's contributions were in several areas, including the establishment of the first laboratory of experimental psychology in Russia, localization of psychological activities in the brain, and research on the conditioned reflex. Although it could be argued that Bekhterev's research on reflexes was closer to the American behavioral orientation, it is Pavlov and not Bekhterev who is remembered in twenty-first-century American psychology. For example, the most popular general psychology books used in the US (e.g., Kalat, 2017) discuss Pavlov but not Bekhterev. Pavlov was researching the digestive system when he stumbled onto the basic principles of what came to be known as classical conditioning. Pavlov realized that dogs instinctively associate seeing their food dish with being fed and therefore drool when they see their food dish. However, Pavlov also realized that he could train the dogs to associate any object (as a conditional stimulus) with being fed and it would trigger the same response of drooling (conditional response). By training dogs to drool when seeing the lab assistant or when hearing a bell ring, Pavlov demonstrated that behaviors are responses to stimuli and can be learned and, therefore, controlled. This study supported the behaviorist assertion that one can explain and even control behavior solely in terms of conditioning or environmental forces.

Earlier in the century, Karl Marx and Friedrich Engels derided this idea of physiological reductionism as a form of oversimplification of behavior. Marx and Engels attempted to develop a comprehensive framework for understanding society and human behavior. Influenced by the Hegelian idea that all phenomena owe part of their characteristics to context, Marx and Engels rejected the idea that science, or psychology specifically, could be understood without taking into consideration its social and historical context. Despite working within an antireductionist ideology, Russian revolutionaries found Pavlov's research appealing because of its seeming objectivity. Pavlov seemed to be demonstrating, using objectively verifiable empirical methods, that behavior can be shaped using stimulus-response associations. Because he replaced unproven introspection with a physiological correlation between stimuli and response and turned these ideas into a "hard science," Pavlov's work persuaded the Bolshevik leaders.

By the Russian Revolution, Pavlov was a renowned scientist, having won the Nobel Prize in Physiology in 1904, being named a Foreign Member of the Royal Society in 1907, and having won the Royal Society's Copley Medal in 1914. At the start of the Soviet rule, Pavlov sought to emigrate from the Soviet Union and wrote a number of letters in dissent of the government (Todes, 1995, p. 380). Despite the contentious relationship between Pavlov and the Soviet government, it was clear that the Bolshevik leaders valued and relied on Pavlov's work. This acceptance of Pavlov's work and theories was demonstrated through Lenin signing a 1921 decree for the publication of Pavlov's lectures in recognition of his outstanding contributions to science as well as Pavlov's treatment as an "exceptional case" among opponents of the regime. In the early 1920s, adequate food rations were scarce and living conditions were poor. However, because Pavlov was considered an exceptional case, the Soviet government doubled the food rations for Pavlov and his family and helped to fund Pavlov's scientific facilities. This preferential treatment of Pavlov despite his dissent demonstrated the Bolsheviks' not only acceptance of but appreciation for Pavlov's work (Joravsky, 1981, p. 15), as well as maintaining their image as supporters of science.

Behaviorists in the US

While Pavlov's studies became famous in Russia in the late nineteenth century and early twentieth century, similar shifts toward behaviorism were occurring in Europe and the US. A major event was the launching of the so-called behaviorist manifesto by Watson (1913), with the following claims:

1 Psychology is a purely experimental branch of natural science.
2 The theoretical goal of psychology is the prediction and control of behavior.
3 The science of psychology must discard all references to consciousness.
4 Both animals and humans must be studied using only objective and uniform procedures.

Watson suggested that while field studies only provided small insight, laboratory studies on controlled behavior provided useful insight into the causes of behavior. Watson's major studies were focused on conditioned emotional responses. His first attempt at experimentally producing a specific emotion consisted of using a bright light as a conditioned stimulus and a loud sound as an unconditioned stimulus. This was in attempt to explain the fear response from lightning but its results were inconclusive (Mills, 2000, p. 73). However, his next study on experimental production of emotions, known as the Little Albert experiment, proved more successful. Watson used a white rat as a conditioned stimulus and a loud sound (made by hitting a steel bar with a hammer) as an unconditioned stimulus. Little Albert, the eleven-month-old test subject, originally responded positively to the white rat; however, after the white rat and loud sound were repeatedly associated, Little Albert began responding with distress and discomfort when exposed to the rat. Although this study could not measure Little Albert's feelings or demonstrate the experimental induction of fear, it did demonstrate that Pavlov's belief of learned behavior applies not only to dogs but also humans (p. 74).

Through his work with conditioning, Watson came to the conclusion that conditioning techniques can be applied to human behavior in attempts to solve human problems and that "the goal of psychological study is the ascertaining of such data and laws that, given the stimulus, psychology can predict what the response will be; or, on the other hand, given the response, it can predict the nature of the effective stimulus" (Mills, 2000, p. 74). Watson hoped to use these theories on conditioning to either replace or improve human instincts as he believed proper training could lead to the suppression of potentially harmful tendencies and the enhancement of potentially beneficial human tendencies (p. 69).

The behaviorist belief in the enormous possibilities of people "becoming anything they want to be," based on environmental shaping, was in line with the ideas of Russian revolutionaries. They too believed they could construct a new version of man. Russian revolutionaries argued that this new construction of human nature was limited by individual struggle, the stratification of workers, and the influence of the bourgeoisie. Consequently, socialism would be unable to create a new version of man within the limits of the old society and, rather, would have to create socialist conditions of life before creating a socialist psychology (Trotsky, 1906/2010).

Other Attempts to Use Psychology to Change Behavior

The Soviet Union is not alone in its political use of psychology. Governments in modern societies, such as the UK and the US, are also using psychology to try to change human behavior in line with their ideological goals. Influenced by the work of John Watson in the 1910s and then later by B. F. Skinner in the 1930s, psychologists began to study the ideas of behaviorism and radical behaviorism and even apply these ideas to the behavior of people. Behaviorism and radical behaviorism emphasize the ways in which environmental factors influence all behavior (Leigland, 2010, pp. 210–211). As Taylor (2004) explains, "The assumption of solidity [with respect to the brain] is simply incorrect. Brains change all the time: everything you perceive, every stimulus received by your senses, changes your brain. Sometimes the change can be dramatic" (p. 115). Most changes are small, short-lived, unnoticed, and unintentional; however, this understanding of conditioning and of the plasticity of the brain has demonstrated the feasibility of controlling the brain and has been used to intentionally alter individual's thinking and behavior. Behavior conditioning "is a vast domain that includes some methods – persuasion, education, propaganda, child rearing, advertising – the practice and objectives of which are not always sinister and unliberating" (p. 52).

Behaviorism has also been adopted as a model for organizing social life by some in Western societies. Bertrand Russell attempted to socialize his children using behaviorist laws of learning, with tragic consequences (see Monk, 2000). Entire communities have been developed using behaviorist ideas, such as the Twin Oaks utopia inspired by B. F. Skinner's *Walden Two* (1948/1962) and founded on the behaviorist belief that a "positive, healthy environment" can shape human behavior (Kapur, 2016). Much like the Russian revolutionaries' goals earlier in the century, Twin Oaks hoped to use the environment to encourage humans to place the community or collective over the individual. However, human emotions, motivations, and incentives – which are hard to overcome and have historically acted as dilemmas for utopian ideals – largely hindered the goals of Twin Oaks. In Twin Oaks, as well as later utopias like Oneida and Acorn, the community was unable to overpower the self-centered nature of their utopian members – evident through actions like hoarding supplies for one's self or one's family rather than prioritizing the community – which has proven fatal to their goal of shaping a society of collective ownership (Kapur, 2016).

In the twenty-first century, governments in both the US and the UK have attempted to shape behavior through environmental stimuli, assumed to lead to "brain changes," described by Thaler and Sunstein (2008), both unintentional and intentional, as "nudges." They elaborate, "Sometimes massive social changes, in marketing and politics alike, start with a small social nudge. Humans are not exactly lemmings, but they are easily influenced by the statements and deeds of others" (pp. 53–54). Unintentional, everyday nudges are apparent through people being more likely to smile when they see people smiling in a movie scene, yawning when they see others yawn, eating more when eating with a group, and performing academically similar to their roommates in college. In addition to these unintentional nudges, individuals also use social influences intentionally or strategically, especially in politics and marketing.

In particular, advertisers are entirely aware of the power of social influences. Frequently they can emphasize that "most people prefer" their own product, or that "growing numbers of people" are switching from another brand, which was yesterday's news, to their own, which represents the future. They try to nudge you by telling you what most people are now doing. (pp. 64–65)

Political parties and candidates employ similar tactics, emphasizing how people are turning to their candidates with the hope that this will persuade others to follow the trend. These advertisers and political campaigners are what Thaler and Sunstein (2008) refer to as "choice architects," or individuals who are responsible for "organizing the context in which people make decisions" as every detail of an individual's environment – even those that seem small or insignificant – can play a role in influencing an individual's thoughts and behavior (p. 3). In addition to advertisers and political campaigners, Thaler and Sunstein illustrate the abilities of different choice architects to shift behavior through social nudges through the examples of encouraging tax compliance, increasing the preservation of petrified wood in national parks through specifically worded signs, and socializing nondrinking.

Recognizing the feasibility in controlling and altering thoughts and behavior, the US Armed Forces has also employed this tactic of social nudging, through the use of Psychological Operations (PSYOP), for instance. The US has used PSYOP strategies during World War II, the Cold War, the Vietnam War, and the Gulf War as well as more recently during conflicts in Grenada, Haiti, Bosnia, and Kosovo (Defense Science Board [DSB], 2002, p. 7). The DSB (2002) has recognized the potential power of PSYOP strategies:

Used properly, PSYOP can help, in the words of the Chinese philosopher Sun Tzu, "subdue the enemy's army without battle." Especially in an era when any loss of life is politically sensitive, the ability of PSYOP to be a "combat reducer" and save the lives of U.S. troops and citizens, as well as opposing force personnel, is exceedingly important. PSYOP forces offer U.S. policymakers and warfighters a more discreet and often more politically palatable tool than conventional military activities, which are primarily designed to bring the adversary to heel through death and destruction. (p. 11)

These strategies often consist of information dissemination through newspapers, magazines, leaflets, loud speakers, and television or radio broadcasts and involve influencing local and international media organizations. This dissemination of selective information is expected to influence the emotions, opinions, and ultimately behavior of the audience, including foreign individuals, organizations, and governments during conflicts (p. 23).

Clearly, unintentional social nudging is widespread, and intentional governmental use of psychological techniques to influence individual behavior is not limited to the Russian Revolution. What distinguishes the Russian revolutionaries' uses of psychology from other societies' uses of psychology, however, is the extent of the change and the goals of the psychological techniques. As Thaler and Sunstein (2008) suggest in *Nudge*, the changes intended in these societies are small and the interventions are small (i.e., changing the format of questions on questionnaires). The intervention in the Soviet Union, on the other hand, was extremely large and the goals radical. What is common to all the programs for behavior change is the limitation of political plasticity: thought and action in political behavior is not infinitely malleable, and even high levels of control over society (as achieved by the Russian revolutionaries) does not necessarily lead to success for behavior change programs.

The central role of political plasticity, as well as limits on the of malleability of styles of thinking and action, are also underlined by the other case studies in this book – including in the widely different contexts of Canada, Egypt, Greece, Iran, and Ireland. As indicated by Drury and Reicher, the historical and psychological research suggests that deeper engagement in change processes, so that participants have some sense of agency and control, increases the probability that they will also undergo changes at the personal level (see Moghaddam, 2002, for a broader discussion of psychology and change).

Concluding Comment

Although the Bolsheviks hoped to use the behaviorist laws of learning to move society toward a communist utopia, these large-scale experiments quickly turned into a campaign of mass terror. Bolshevik leaders encouraged peasants and workers to denounce their neighbors for counterrevolutionary behavior. Moreover, many common behaviors, including hiding property, keeping secrets, and being a non-conformist in social behavior, were interpreted as counterrevolutionary and resulted in arrest (Figes, 2008). Citizens were under constant scrutiny, even in private spaces, for behavior deemed counterrevolutionary and were constantly fearful of arrest as the regime quickly filled the prisons.

Not only did these attempts at re-shaping human nature result in mass terror throughout the revolution, they also failed to successfully create an idealistic communist society. The Bolsheviks, even with the use of behaviorist techniques, were unable to successfully implement the collective ideals they had imagined. One caveat, however, to this write-off of the Bolsheviks' attempt to mold citizen behavior as a failure is that the Bolsheviks were only able to alter certain aspects of the environment. Just as the US does not reflect capitalism in its purest form, because of governmental interference, the Soviet Union did not perfectly reflect communist teachings or communism in its purest form. During the implementation of communism in the Soviet Union, the system was corrupt and imperfect. Because the Bolsheviks never attempted communism in its purest form, it is hard to determine whether the use of psychological techniques was unsuccessful because of the techniques used or because of the corruption of the system. Nevertheless, it is clear that the revolutionaries relied on behaviorist ideals to alter citizens' environment with the hopes of altering their behavior, re-shaping human nature, and creating a new, collective society but were unable to reach this desired communist utopia.

The Russian revolutionaries' use of behaviorist theories is especially relevant today when considering the number of ways in which not only psychologists but also marketers, politicians, and governments use psychology today. This use of psychology to manipulate thought and behavior is evident in studies like those conducted in 2014 to test how manipulated emotional exposure through social media leads people to alter their behavior (see Kramer, Guillory, and Hancock, 2014). It is also evident through US intelligence agencies' discovery of Russian governmental interference in the 2016 US presidential election, as Russian actors used selective information in an attempt to alter US citizen thought and behavior (reported by the US Intelligence Chief; Harris and Sonne, 2017). Whether intentional or unintentional, and constructive or destructive in nature, it is clear Soviet revolutionaries relied on behaviorist ideals in order to develop a utopian society and that these uses of psychology to alter thought and behavior are still attempted today.

REFERENCES

Alt, H., and E. Alt. (1964). *The New Soviet Man—His Upbringing and Character Development*. New York: Bookman.

Defense Science Board (2002). Report of the Defense Science Board Task Force on the creation of all forms of information in support of Psychological Operations (PSYOP) in time of military conflict. Washington, DC: Office of the Under Secretary of Defense for Acquisition, Technology and Logistics. http://permanent.access.gpo.gov/websites/dodandmilitaryejournals/www.acq.osd.mil/dsb/reports/psyop.pdf.

Figes, O. (2002). *Natasha's Dance: A Cultural History of Russia*. New York: Henry Holt.

   (2008). *The Whisperers: Private life in Stalin's Russia*. New York: Picador.

Figes, O., and Kolonitskii, B. (1999). *Interpreting the Russian Revolution: The Language and Symbols of 1917*. New Haven, CT: Yale University Press.

Harris, S., and Sonne, P. (2017). Intelligence chief defends finding Russia meddled in election. *Wall Street Journal*, January 6. www.wsj.com/articles/intelligence-officials-to-testify-as-senate-examines-russian-hacking-1483612205.

Joravsky, D. (1981). Cultural revolution and the fortress mentality. Paper presented at the conference on the Origins of Soviet Culture, Kennan Institute for Advanced Russian Studies and the Wilson Center.

Kalat, J. W. (2017). *Introduction to Psychology*. 11th ed. Boston: Cengage Learning.

Kapur, A. (2016). The return of the utopians. *The New Yorker*, October 3. www.newyorker.com/magazine/2016/10/03/the-return-of-the-utopians.

Kowalski, R. (1997). *The Russian Revolution 1917–1921*. London: Routledge.

Kozulin, A. (1984). *Psychology in Utopia: Toward a Social History of Soviet Psychology*. Boston: MIT Press.

Kramer, A. D. I., Guillory, J. E., and Hancock, J. (2014). Experimental evidence of massive-scale emotional contagion through social networks. *Proceedings of the National Academy of Sciences*, 111(24), 8788–8790.

Leigland, S. (2010). Functions of research in radical behaviorism for the further development of behavior analysis. *Behavior Analyst*, 33(2), 207–222.

Lieven, D. (2015). *The End of Tsarist Russia: The March to World War I and Revolution*. New York: Viking.

Luria, A. R. (1928). Psychology in Russia. *Pedagogical Seminary and Journal of Genetic Psychology*, 35, 347–355.

Miller, M. A. (1998). *Freud and the Bolsheviks: Psychoanalysis in Imperial Russia and the Soviet Union*. New Haven, CT: Yale University Press.

Mills, J. A. (2000). *Qualitative Studies in Psychology: Control: A History of Behavioral Psychology*. New York: NYU Press.

Moghaddam, F. M. (2002). *The Individual and Society: A Cultural Integration*. New York: Worth.

   (2005). *Great Ideas in Psychology*. Oxford: Oneworld.

   (2016). The road to actualized democracy: A psychological exploration. Niels Bohr Lecture in Cultural Psychology, Aalborg University, Denmark.

Monk, R. (2000). *Bertrand Russell: The Ghost of Madness*. London: Random House.

Razran, G. (1965). Russian physiologists' psychology and American experimental psychology: A historical and systematic collation and a look into the future. *Psychological Bulletin*, 63, 42–64.

Shubin, A. (2001). Russian Revolution and the Bolshevik dictatorship. *Journal of Russian and East European Psychology*, 39(6), 41.

Skinner, B. F. (1948/1962). *Walden Two*. New York: Macmillan.

Stites, R. (1988). *Revolutionary Dreams: Utopian Vision and Experimental Life in the Russian Revolution*. Cary, NC: Oxford University Press.

Taylor, K. (2004). *Brainwashing: The Science of Thought Control*. New York: Oxford University Press.

Thaler, R. H., and Sunstein, C. R. (2008). *Nudge: Improving Decisions about Health, Wealth, and Happiness*. New Haven, CT: Yale University Press.

Todes, D. (1995). Pavlov and the Bolsheviks. *History and Philosophy of the Life Sciences*, 17(3), 379–341.

Trotsky, L. (1906/2010). *The Permanent Revolution and Results and Prospects*. With an introduction by L. Nichol. Seattle, WA: Red Letter Press.

(1930/2008). *History of the Russian Revolution*. Chicago: Haymarket Books.

Watson, J. B. (1913). Psychology as a behaviorist views it. *Psychological Review*, 20, 158–177.

Wood, A. (2003). *The Origins of the Russian Revolution 1861–1917*. 3rd ed. London: Routledge.

7 Political Plasticity and Revolution
The Case of Iran

Fathali M. Moghaddam

The 1979 revolution in Iran was one of the major revolutions of the twentieth century, a stunning turning point in modern Iranian history, and a life-changing event for me personally. I had been a student in England during the years leading to the revolution, and I was one of the hundreds of thousands of Western-educated Iranians who rushed back to Iran when the Shah was finally ousted in 1979. We returned with great hope, enormous enthusiasm, and with eagerness to dedicate ourselves to building a more open, democratic Iranian society. Women and men engineers, medical doctors, dentists, social scientists, architects, artists, writers... I met Western-educated returnees with so many different, much-needed high-level specializations and skills, eager to help Iranian society move forward on a democratic path. There seemed to be real possibilities for national development and democratic reform. Despite this great promise, we failed to move forward toward democracy. How did Iran move from the dictatorship of the Shah to the dictatorship of the mullahs? What went wrong? In this chapter, I will use a new conceptual lens to address these questions.

Of course, I am one among many who have examined this issue from different angles over the last few decades (e.g., Buchan, 2013; Fischer, 1980), but the puzzle of why Iran went from dictatorship to dictatorship, rather than progress closer toward democracy, is complex and worthy of serious re-examination from new perspectives. This is because the puzzle of the failed Iranian revolution is part of the puzzle of the failure of numerous other major revolutions. Again and again, we find that revolutions that overthrow dictatorships lead to a continuation of dictatorship in other forms: the French revolution (1789) leading to Napoleon declaring himself emperor, the Russian Revolution of 1917 leading to Stalin's reign of terror and eventually the twenty-first-century Putin dictatorship, the Arab Spring (starting in 2010) leading to new dictatorships in Egypt and elsewhere. The same is true of revolutions in smaller countries, such as the revolution in Cuba (1953–1959) leading to the continuous dictatorship of the Castro family since the 1960s. There are a few more hopeful cases, such as the revolution in Tunisia (2010–2011) resulting in a more democratic society (although Tunisia is under constant violent attacks from Islamic fundamentalists, who are determined to crush democratic tendencies there). However, the overall trend in the last few centuries is that revolutions that overthrow dictatorships, in both Islamic and non-Islamic societies, tend to end more like Iran than Tunisia – closed and despotic.

In this analysis, I critically reassess the "failure of revolution" to move societies from dictatorship to democracy through the conceptual lens of *political plasticity*, the malleability of collective and individual political behavior (Moghaddam, 2016). The basic question raised by the concept of political plasticity is: how fast can change take place in collective and individual political behavior? In developing a framework for political plasticity, the first task is to specify the target of change, or what is to be changed. This "target" of change is either a bit of cognition or a bit of action that is political, in the sense that it is about politics and/or has political consequences. For example, the bit of cognition or action could pertain to leader-follower relations. Political plasticity points to the challenge of changing the normative system that regulate political actions and cognitions. The concept of political plasticity enables us to analyze revolutions with a focus on change. After all, understanding change processes is at the heart of better understanding revolutions. But this confronts us with a challenge, because change processes have received very little serious research attention in psychological science (Moghaddam, 2002).

Psychological Science and Change

In applied domains, such as clinical psychology, change is of central concern. After all, psychological therapy involves trying to understand changes that have taken place, such as changes underlying a shift from adaptive behavior to dysfunctional behavior, in order to bring about healthy, functional behavior. For example, an individual who was healthy becomes clinically depressed, and the therapist attempts to help the patient move out of depression to healthy functioning again. Not surprisingly, the most in-depth pioneering discussions of psychological change have been produced by therapists, such as the Paolo Alto group (Watzlawick, Weakland, and Fisch, 1974). A small number of psychological researchers have been concerned with change in national and communal development. For example, Taylor and de la Sablonnière (2014) made a seminal contribution by exploring how researchers can intervene in Aboriginal communities to bring about constructive social change.

Although clinicians, educational psychologists, organizational psychologists, and researchers interested in minority communities have in practice been concerned with understanding and bringing about change, very few research psychologists have focused on change (the work of Taylor and de la Sablonnière, 2014, is an exception). The reasons for this are rooted in the history of psychology, and particularly the attempt to establish psychology as a science concerned with discovering the causes of behavior (Moghaddam, 2005). The German psychologist Wilhelm Wundt (1832–1920) is regarded as the father of experimental psychology, because he established the first laboratory of psychology (1889) and launched a program of experimental research to explore some aspects of psychological experiences. From the late nineteenth century, most psychological research has been conducted in the laboratory, through experiments lasting about an hour, with university students are participants. This is even true for so-called cross-cultural research (Moghaddam and Lee, 2006).

The assumption has been that in order to become a science, psychologists must discover the causes of behavior, and the best way to do this is to study the "causal link" between independent and dependent variables under controlled laboratory conditions, in experiments that typically last an hour or so. Obviously the study of change requires research methods that allow for the study of psychological processes that last much longer than an hour. Furthermore, change in human relations is seldom explained by the kinds of mechanistic cause-effect relations studied in psychology experiments (see discussions of causation in Harré and Moghaddam, 2012).

Thus, in order to better understand change, psychologists need to adopt methodologies and concepts that can be applied to questions arising from longer-term processes, such as those involving revolutions. In this discussion, I am specifically concerned to address the question of why revolutions fail to bring about changes toward democracy. I propose that the concept of political plasticity can help us in this task.

Political Plasticity

The concept of political plasticity is new, but that of plasticity is well established in psychological science. At least from the 1940s when Hebb (1949) made his seminal contribution to brain research, the idea of neural plasticity has been (implicitly or explicitly) central to psychology and neuroscience. Contemporary research continues this tradition (Huttenlocher, 2012; also see the journal *Neural Plasticity*). The concept of plasticity has recently been extended to broader behavioral areas, such as developmental plasticity (Griebel, Pepperberg, and Oller, 2016) and "teaching an adult brain new tricks" (Thomas and Baker, 2013). Some passing attention to plasticity is also reflected in discussions of culture and psychology (see papers in Gelfand, Chiu, and Hong, 2014; Levinson and Gray, 2012), and cross-cultural studies point to behavior plasticity by highlighting the limitations of mainstream Western models of behavior (e.g., Henrich et al., 2005). However, in the present chapter, my goal is to elaborate a framework for explicitly applying the concept of plasticity to political behavior. In this effort, we must keep in mind that political behavior necessarily involves collective processes.

As we move from the micro to the social level, the implication is that we should focus on changes in collectives and networks, not just on individual units in isolation. Of course, this basic idea is already well known in neuroscience research. Hebb's (1949) seminal contribution was to recognize the central role of cell assemblies, and the possibilities for the continuous shaping and re-shaping of neural networks. Rather than trying to understand single cells in isolation, he postulated the workings of collections of cells. Hebb's law leads to a picture of neural networks as continuously changing, as cells fire to different degrees and different combinations, and those cells that "fire together, wire together." Contemporary research endorses and extends this view, with a focus on the impact of context on plasticity (Baroncelli et al., 2010; Green and Bavelier, 2010; Voss et al., 2013). Thus, the idea that networks and context are important is already well established in discussions of "plasticity" at the micro level.

A Conceptual Framework for Political Plasticity

As a first step toward a better understanding of change processes in political behavior, I put forward seven basic rules that regulate political plasticity. The first five rules are about the nature of change itself; the next two rules are about connectivity between bits of cognition and/or action that are the targets of change.

Rule 1: Change processes are of two main types, within and between systems (Moghaddam, 2002).

In the political domain, most change is within-system rather than between systems. We often overlook this, because surface level changes mislead us. This is particularly because the rhetoric of revolutionaries is misleading and is intended to create the impression that between-system change has been achieved. For example, in Iran the 1979 revolution involved within-system change, not between-system change. That is, dictatorship as a system of government did not change, leader-follower relations in Iran did not change, only the individuals filling the roles of leader (dictator) and followers changed. The leader (dictator) changed from the Shah to the Supreme Leader, but the belief that the leader (dictator) must be obeyed unquestioningly did not change. Consider the case of Ahmed, who lives in Iran and prior to the revolution of 1979 believed (cognition) that the Shah of Iran was selected by God, and in action Ahmed obeyed the commands of the Shah. This theme of "divine right of kings" was also propagated by the Shah through his speeches and books (e.g., Pahlavi, 1960), strengthening the beliefs and actions of individuals who thought and acted like Ahmed.

The idea that the leader (irrespective of whether it is the Shah or the Supreme Leader) is the representative of God on earth, and that his followers must obey leadership commands, did not change after the revolution. Instead of the Shah, Khomeini and his successors filled the position of "representative of God," and they propagated the belief system of being God's representative through their sermons and books (e.g., Khomeini, 1960).

Rule 2: The characteristics of collective processes are more than the sum of smaller units. Of course, this reminds us of the Gestalt motto, "The whole is more than the sum of its parts." This is also in line with more recent proposals that "more is different" (Anderson, 1972), and that we should attend to the process of emergence (Kim, 2006), while avoiding simplistic assumptions about causation in how collective processes arise.

The idea that "more is different" suggests that the characteristics of collective human movements, such as those associated with revolutions, cannot be derived from studies of individual behavior. Behaviors which are centrally important in revolutions, such as conformity and nonconformity, obedience and disobedience, and leader-follower relations, have characteristics that can only be understood by studying collective behavior – in "real world" contexts whenever possible. "More is different" when it comes to these behaviors; the properties that emerge are not causally explained by referring back to the characteristics of individual persons.

Rule 3: Smaller units, such as individual persons, can only bring about change by acting as part of, and being connected to, a larger collective. Thus, an individual can be part of change through being part of collective processes. This change will largely depend on relations between smaller units, as well as processes within smaller units

In general, collective processes are far more difficult to change, because they can only take place when a sufficient number of other people change in the same direction and to similar degrees. This is the main reason why political revolutions seldom take place "from below": large numbers of people have to come to believe that the regime is unstable and illegitimate (following social identity theory, see Moghaddam, 2008, Chapter 5), and take similar collective action on this basis. The state and various elite groups with vested interest in the status quo use the media, the education system, and every other means available to fight against such beliefs spreading and becoming collectively accepted and acted upon (Moghaddam, 2013).

Rule 4: Change at macro levels does not necessarily bring about change at micro levels. An example of this is when a revolution topples a regime, but relations within a family and gender relations in the larger society stay the same. Another example is the resistance of bureaucracy to change after a revolution.

With respect to family and gender relations, those surrounding Ahmed and his wife behave toward them in ways that supports the belief that it is the wife's duty to obey her husband. Like a tight grid surrounding Ahmed and his wife, social relationships hold their actions and cognitions in place. With respect to connections within individuals, Ahmed's belief and his wife's belief that wife must obey her husband is connected with values and beliefs historically integral to Iranian culture, which is strongly patriarchal and hierarchical. Ahmed and his wife were socialized within this culture and there is intense pressure on both of them to conform to its core tenets. Of course, change in the family unit is particularly important because it is the training ground for the next generation.

The example of bureaucracy is perhaps even more profound and underestimated: the resistance of bureaucracy to change. The impact of this resistance is clear after changes in government through regular democratic elections: new governments discover that in order to implement their "new" policies, they have to work with the "same old" bureaucracy. The result is often that through the influence of the "same old" bureaucracy, nothing much actually changes. In the next section, I further discuss the role of bureaucracy after the Iranian revolution.

Rule 5: Lack of change at the micro level can limit or even reverse change at the macro level.

Plus ça change, plus c'est la même chose (The more things change, the more they stay the same) is a saying that often comes to mind after even major political revolutions. People I interviewed in Iran after the 1979 revolution often reported having this experience. In some respects, so much was changed by the revolution: the names of places (streets, buildings, and so on), the ways in which people addressed one another ("brother" and "sister" became common terms of reference, advertising supposed equality of status), how people dressed (the hijab for women, more scruffy "revolutionary" clothing for men) – just about everything seemed to have changed. However, people also had an uncanny sense that at a deeper level not much had changed. For example, although we addressed one another as "brother" and "sister," some "brothers" had a great deal more power than other people, and everyone was forced to unquestioningly obey those in power.

Rule 6: Political plasticity is regulated by *embeddedness*, the depth of connections holding a bit of cognition or action in place.

Embeddedness is a characteristic of, first, connections between the individual and others and, second, connections within individuals. The first type of connection is social and involves collective processes; the second type of connection takes place within persons, and involves cognition and biological processes.

In placing the relationship between the individual and others, social relationships, prior to the relationships of factors within individuals, I am following a Vygotskian perspective increasingly well known in psychological research (Harré and Moghaddam, 2012). In this approach, the assumption is that the original source of psychological experiences is the world outside, and not within persons. This includes consciousness and the self-concept, which arise through social interactions. Thus, from this perspective, consciousness and conceptions of the self, arise out of social interactions and the world "out there," and not from processes within isolated persons.

Rule 7: The depth of embeddedness is dependent on, first, resiliency and, second, quantity of connectivity.

Resiliency of connectivity concerns how robust and strong a particular connection is (between an individual and others in the case of social embeddedness, and between factors within individuals in the case of intrapersonal embeddedness). *Quantity of connectivity* concerns how many connections there are (again, between an individual and others in the case of social embeddedness, and between factors within individuals in the case of intrapersonal embeddedness).

Higher levels of resilience and higher quantities of connectivity mean that it is more difficult to change behavior against the trend set by the context. This is why those who want to enforce conformity and obedience insist that individuals take part in collective behavior. For example, in Iran the mullahs insist that prayers have greater *savaab* (religious value) when worshippers participate in collective prayers, rather than praying in private. Participation in collective prayers means that worshippers can be influenced by preachers, who preach sermons endorsed by the government, and can be monitored more closely.

Democratic Citizenship, Democratic Leadership, and the Iranian Revolution

After a revolution that results in the toppling of a dictatorship, there is a brief "opportunity bubble," a period during which leaders and followers can successfully change in the necessary ways and transition toward a more democratic society. However, historical examples have shown that it is extremely difficult for pro-democracy forces to constructively take advantage of this "opportunity bubble." In this section, I explore events following the revolution in Iran as a case study with instructive lessons for how followers and leaders can influence a potential transition from dictatorship to democracy.

In the months following the collapse of the monarchy in Iran in 1979, there was a brief period when no one political group monopolized power in the country. The situation was in some respects chaotic, because the regular Iranian military and police forces had collapsed. The Shah's feared security police (SAVAK) had also melted away. The most senior officers in all the different security forces had either fled, were in hiding, or had been killed or captured. "Security" was being maintained by disorganized neighborhood groups, so-called committees consisting of groups of men (in a few cases, I came across women associated with these "committees," but they tended to be in supporting rather than direct combat roles) often attached to local mosques. These men were usually armed with weapons captured from the regular military and police forces.

There were numerous different groups competing for power across the country in the postrevolution period in Iran. When I drove from England, across Europe and Turkey, into Iran in April 1979, in order to reach Tehran I had to pass through hundreds of makeshift checkpoints, each manned by armed groups of men, often answering to different local and regional authorities. In several places on this one thousand kilometer journey from the Turkish border to Tehran, I was given papers by one group guaranteeing safe passage to Tehran, only to have the next armed group tear up or disregard my papers. The situation was the same in Tehran, where every neighborhood was controlled by a different "security group."

The national political scene was similarly chaotic and characterized by competition for power. There were numerous political groups in open competition with one another, from the Soviet backed communist party (Tudeh), to secular nationalist parties, to moderate Islamic parties, to fundamentalist Islamic parties. In early 1979, the most well-organized and well-armed political group was the Mujahedeen Khalgh, a left-leaning Islamic group. Their spiritual leader was Ayatollah Taleghani. The Shah's regime referred to this group as "Islamic communists." However, by the summer of 1979 Ayatollah Khomeini's antidemocracy hardline followers had gained a great deal of power and influence, particularly by taking over many of the local armed "committees" that controlled security at the neighborhood level and were directly linked to local mosques.

Through gaining control of mosques and "committees" connected with them, Khomeini's hardline followers gradually acquired a national network of power and influence. Moreover, through the high level of attention he had gained from international media and his domination of the national political scene, Khomeini arrived at two major goals: first, not only did the division between politics and religion collapse, but politics became absorbed within religion. Second, the traditional "multivocal" system of Shi'a Islam was transformed gradually, until there was only one leader and one voice that everyone was now forced to obey. In traditional Shi'a Islam, all ayatollahs have the right to give their interpretations of the Koran and provide directives in their different voices to followers (see Moghaddam, 2016). However, with the rise of Khomeini to become "Supreme Leader" and "source of emulation" (*marji taghlid*), with absolute religious and political power combined, differences of opinion between ayatollahs was no longer tolerated, because everyone had to obey Khomeini. But it took some time to achieve this power monopoly, and there was a surprising level of freedom in the early days of the revolution.

Early Days of Freedom

It was an exciting time to be in Tehran in the spring of 1979, because there was now a high level of freedom and a vibrant and productive press. Numerous news outlets were competing for influence in a relatively open atmosphere. There was an amazing variety of creative activity, from a population that had been inhibited for so long. Using theater, painting, poetry, pamphlets, newspapers, graffiti, public debates – in whatever way possible for them, people with different political opinions were expressing themselves. Women were politically active in public and at that time were not forced to wear the *hejab*. I witnessed many instances when women made public speeches without wearing the hejab, often taking progressive positions on political and social issues, including gender relations. A wide variety of minority ethnic groups also became more politically active, with the Kurds being the most important. By the summer of 1979, there seemed to be some potential for Iranian society to move forward toward greater openness and democracy.

But a more critical look at the situation suggests that at a deeper level, there were severe limitations in the changes taking place. We had smashed down the Shah's framework which restricted freedom, but we had not managed to develop and make functional a widely shared normative system supportive of democracy. There were signs that a new framework for restricting freedom was growing, even in the midst of our celebrations. First, and perhaps most importantly, the style of leadership had not changed. Just as before the revolution, Iranians had to be completely and unquestioningly obedient to the Shah, now Khomeini's supporters demanded that everyone be unquestioningly obedient to the new "Supreme Leader." Through a gradual process, by the end of 1979 it had become unacceptable to publicly question any of Khomeini's decisions. Whatever the Supreme Leader said was now treated as sacred and holy. It was not just incorrect to question Khomeini's decisions, it was a sin. His extremist followers reacted with violence against anyone who dared even debate the merits of his leadership. I witnessed violent attacks on individuals who dared to publicly criticize Khomeini. Thus, although the Shah was dethroned, the relationship between "the" leader and his followers had not changed.

The Stability of Leader-Follower Relations

A major factor in the stability of leader-follower relationship before and after the revolution was Khomeini's personality: dogmatic, authoritarian, ultra-conservative, intolerant of ambiguity, ethnocentric, and highly motivated to concentrate power in this own hands. He "knew" the correct path, and he was not willing to tolerate any questioning or explorations of alternative paths. This follows a pattern of the personality of other leaders who have come to power after revolutions, such as Stalin in Russia, Castro in Cuba, and Mao in China. These leaders are all determined to achieve and maintain absolute power, and not to develop inclusive, collaborative power sharing arrangements with those who differ in their opinions. Moreover, these leaders are determined to rule absolutely and dogmatically, for as long as they are physically capable. They do not believe in term limits when it comes to their own leadership. Of course, the common personality characteristics of these leaders help them to be ruthless in their grab for power, but not to lead society toward openness and democracy after they come to power.

A second factor in the stability of leader-follower relationship before and after the revolution was the style of followership among the Iranian masses. Iranian society has been governed in a dictatorial manner for thousands of years, with a few brief periods of pro-democracy activism among a broader population, such as in the early twentieth century and in the early 1950s and later 1970s. Decision-making in Iran has not traditionally been "participatory," in the sense that the masses have been told how to behavior and what choices to make, rather than being given the means and opportunities to make up their own minds. By "means and opportunities" I refer to the creation of a context in which ordinary people have the opportunity to learn the skills needed to participate in open debates, and to make up their own minds on important issues. Nowhere was this absence or limitation more obvious than in the universities, where students had not been given the opportunities to develop skills in critical thinking, not only at the individual level, but also at the collective level and communal life.

"Open and free discussion" can only take place when the individuals in the discussion have the necessary cognitive and social skills to participate in and support such discussion. It is not enough to smash down the security system and laws that restrict free speech; it is also necessary to develop a citizenry that has the skills to constructively take part in speaking freely. But in Iran and other dictatorial societies, the family, the school system, and all other mechanisms of socialization had evolved to function within a dictatorship. These mechanisms of socialization needed to change to be able to teach young people to serve as democratic citizens. We were expecting such change in families, schools, universities, and the like to take place overnight.

I began teaching at universities in Tehran as soon as higher education institutions re-opened. All such institutions had been closed for several years in the chaos and fighting leading to the revolution. In the "spring of revolution" in 1979, the universities re-opened and students poured back, eager to take advantage of "revolutionary freedoms" and participate in a truly "revolutionary" university system. I found the students at Tehran University and the National University to be individually extremely bright; this was to be expected given the very high level of competition to enter these institutions. However, these extremely intelligent students lacked an important skill: the ability to engage in critical but constructive discussion in a group setting, with others who differ in their political, religious, and cultural views. It was not the fault of the students; they simply had not been educated to take part in such debates. Also, they were used to uncritically memorizing and regurgitating what the teacher and what their books told them, just as in the larger society people had been socialized to obey the dictates of the leader, whether it was the Shah or Khomeini.

The revolution provided an opportunity for the Iranian population to start to learn a new pattern of leader-follower relations; to be openly critical toward the leadership, to publicly debate the merits of different decisions. But the development of these skills needed time, because such changes in the collective styles of cognition and action are not possible in the short-term. People need enough time to acquire new skills, learn to constructively debate, experiment and make mistakes, and to trust that they can collectively reach better decisions. At least decades are needed to make this kind of collective progress after an antidictatorship revolution, even when the education system and social and political programs are being reformed in line with democratic goals. The probability of the necessary time and opportunity becoming available would have increased through a leadership motivated to achieve participatory decision-making, and inclusiveness. Unfortunately, Khomeini was motivated to achieve change in the opposite direction, and he attracted an extremist antidemocratic group of followers who concentrated more and more power in the hands of the Supreme Leader.

The key to understanding the antidemocratic nature of Khomeini's approach to government is the concept of *velayat-e-faghih*, endorsed by him and his followers. The basic idea of *velayat-e-faghih*, which is now enshrined in the constitution of Iran, is that society will be directed by a Supreme Leader, or a group of such leaders if one "supreme" person is not generally recognized. This Supreme Leader comes from the religious establishment and has complete power over all institutions, groups, and individuals, within and outside government. For example, the Supreme Leader has the last word on who will be president, prime minister, cabinet member, irrespective of how the people vote. This is why is was perfectly legal, according to the Iranian constitution, for the Supreme Leader to appoint Mohamed Ahmadinejad as president in 2009, even though the majority of people voted for another candidate (the other candidate and his followers were locked up and have not been heard of since).

Some supporters of *velayat-e-faghih* attempt to legitimize this idea by arguing that it is in line with Plato's notion of rule by "philosopher kings." They neglect a basic Platonic qualification for the philosopher king: not being motivated to hold power. The widespread and extreme corruption that now characterizes Iranian society reflects a greed for power that emanates from the Supreme Leader and his associates, and spreads to the rest of society.

Throughout 1979 there was a roll back of freedoms in Iran, and the most visible sign of this was women being pushed back under the hejab and out of the public sphere of activity. Women were physically pushed out of public life, and at the same time it became very difficult to raise questions about government policies endorsed by Khomeini. The universities provided some resistance to the gradual suffocation of freedoms, but the launch of the so-called Cultural Revolution in 1980 closed all universities. This so-called Cultural Revolution was a copy of what took place in China in the 1960s. In both Iran and China, an old leader (Khomeini in Iran, Mao in China) directed young fanatics to attack and close down universities and disperse the faculty to be "re-educated" in the larger society. In both Iran and China the old leader prevailed and increased his political control, but at an enormous economic cost to the nation, because entire generations of the best trained professionals and specialized experts were lost. After the death of Mao, China changed direction and has enjoyed rapid economic development. Iran has remained on the same path and stagnated, mired in corruption and extreme inequalities.

Bureaucracy, Change, and Stability

The complex relationship between bureaucracy and democracy has received some attention (Gormley and Balla, 2013), but I believe the role of bureaucracy in limiting progress toward democracy has been underestimated. This is particularly the case after revolutions, when bureaucracy tends to act as an anchor, remaining out of sight beneath the water surface, while at the same time serving to prevent movement. This "stabilizing" role has been easier to hide because bureaucracy is supposed to be politically neutral.

In theory, political leaders are supposed to use bureaucracies as tools to achieve their political goals, as instruments to implement political programs. Thus, in democracies national elections can change the political leaders in charge of government policies, but a change of government is not supposed to result in a change of the civil servants and the officers of the "government bureaucracy." The government civil service is supposed to serve whichever party comes to power, without political bias. But even if the bureaucracy is unbiased toward the major political groups, which probably is not the case, the bureaucracy has a definite and strong bias in favor of itself. This is clear to those of us who have watched the growth of bureaucracies in higher education over the last few decades.

The "self-preserving" bias of bureaucracy became apparent to me in Iran after the revolution. When universities were forcibly closed through the so-called Cultural Revolution in Iran in 1980, I resigned from university teaching. I saw the "Cultural Revolution" as a political move by hard-liners against the best interests of the country and did not want to be part of a program that seemed (and proved to be) antidemocratic. After my resignation, I went to both Tehran University and the National University to collect the pay that I was owed. It seemed that my task would be simple: all teaching and research had been halted, and all students and faculty had been kicked out of the universities. The only people on campus were university administrators. I imagined that these administrators had nothing to do, because students and faculty were absent, all classes and research had come to a halt, and I would quickly complete my business with the administrators. Of course, I could not have been more wrong. The university administrators on both campuses were very busy; it became clear that they did not need students or faculty to keep busy. They did not need classes or research at all; they were self-contained and self-preserving. They had created new work for themselves and it was difficult to find administrators who were not attending meetings, keeping one another busy. It took several weeks for me to make appointments and apply for the money owed to me.

The "self-preserving" and "stabilizing" role of bureaucracy has been recognized by those interested in change, and radical leaders such as Mao and Khomeini instinctively recognize the dangerous "anchoring" or "stabilizing" influence of bureaucracy. Of course, Mao, Khomeini, and other radicals have not been interested in moving societies toward democracy; they attack bureaucracies, professionals, and experts because they want to control them and subvert them to the radical political agenda. On the other hand, those interested in moving societies toward greater openness and democracy see the same "anchoring" role of bureaucracy as creating challenges.

In the next section, following earlier discussions on the psychology of democracy (Moghaddam, 2016) I outline the characteristics individuals need to acquire in order to be able to constructively participate in and support meso- and macro-level changes toward democracy.

The Goals of Change

The three steps to successfully implementing social change through minority influence: (1) identify and regroup the minority members needed to implement

Figure 7.1 Key characteristics of the democratic citizen

minority influence; (2) define constructive new community norms; and (3) take action to implement these new norms. (Taylor and de la Sablonnière, 2014, p. 152)

From the pioneering work of John Dewey (1916/2012) to twenty-first-century thinkers (Noddings, 2013), education is seen to be a major engine of change in the process of democratization and the socialization of democratic citizens. However, more attention needs to be given to the psychological characteristics of individuals that such "education for democracy" is intended to bring about. In the following scheme (Figure 7.1), the first three psychological characteristics concern critical self-reflection ("I could be wrong," "I must critically question everything, including the sacred beliefs of my society," "I must revise my opinions, as the evidence requires"). The next three goals concern change through openness to others ("I must seek to better understand those who are different from me," "I can learn from those who are different from me," "I must seek information and opinions from as many sources as possible"). The next two are about change through new experiences, created both for oneself and for others ("I should be actively open to new experiences" and "I should be open to creating new experiences for others"). Of course, the danger arising from the first eight goals is that the individual falls into a relativistic mindset and comes to believe that all values are equal. The final two goals are designed to avoid such a relativistic outcome, because they are goals based on the idea that there are absolute principles of right and wrong ("there are principles of right and wrong" and "not all experiences are of equal value").

These cognitive and activity goals provide direction and answer the question: political plasticity toward what end? Specific educational and training programs can be designed to help institutions and individuals move closer to these goals. Some such programs already exist and need to be extended and used more widely, beyond the confined of elite schools. For example, the first goal of habitually adopting the mindset that "I could be wrong" is already part of programs that teach young people to become open-minded researchers, capable of applying critical thinking skills and raising new questions. Consequently, some of the basic programs and tools needed to move toward the goals I have outlines are already in place in the education system.

Concluding Comment

The example of Japan after the Second World War demonstrates that under certain conditions, societies and individuals can experience democratic change in a matter of decades. These conditions, in the case of Japan, included absolute control over change processes by a foreign power determined to bring about democratic change, a high level of education among the Japanese population, and the complete military defeat and powerlessness of Japanese society, which meant it was not capable of resisting the imposed change. These conditions rarely come about in history. Far more typical is the kinds of conditions that came about after the Iranian revolution of 1979, when a dictatorship was overthrown and there was a brief "opportunity bubble" of less than a year for pro-democracy forces to shape the direction of society. Unfortunately, a variety of factors, including the leadership of Khomeini, speeded up movement back to dictatorship rather than toward democracy.

Those interested to promote democracy around the world must give far more attention to political plasticity, and particularly how to help societies and individuals achieve greater political plasticity after revolutions. Only through increased political plasticity will we be able to avoid the enormous disappointments that revolutions have led to, such as after the collapse of the USSR and the re-emergence of dictatorship in Russia, what took place after the Arab Spring, and the example of Iran I have discussed in this chapter. But a better understanding of political plasticity requires a greater focus on longer-term collective and individual processes outside the laboratory, something that psychological researchers are now better equipped to achieve (Harré and Moghaddam, 2012).

REFERENCES

Anderson, P. W. (1972). More is different: Broken symmetry and the nature of the hierarchical structure of science. *Science*, 177, 393–396.
Baroncelli, L., Braschi, C., Spolidodo, M., Benegesic, T., Sale, A., and Maffei, L. (2010). Nurturing brain plasticity: Impact of environmental enrichment. *Cell Death and Differentiation*, 17, 1092–1103.
Buchan, J. (2013). *Days of God: The Revolution in Iran and Its Consequences*. New York: Simon and Schuster.
Dewey, J. (1916/2012). *Democracy and Education*. New York: Simon and Brown.
Fischer, M. M. J. (1980). *Iran: From Religious Dispute to Revolution*. Cambridge, MA: Harvard University Press.
Gelfand, M. J., Chiu, C.-Y., and Hong, Y. Y. (Eds.) (2014). *Advances in Culture and Psychology*. Vol. 4. New York: Oxford University Press.
Gormley, W. T., and Balla, S. J. (2013). *Bureaucracy and Democracy: Accountability and Performance*. 3rd ed. Los Angeles, CA.: Sage.
Green, C. S., and Bavelier, D. (2010). Exercising your brain: A review of human brain plasticity and training-induced learning. *Psychology and Aging*, 23, 692–701.
Griebel, U., Pepperberg, I. M., and Oller, D. K. (2016). Developmental plasticity and language: A comparative perspective. *Topics in Cognitive Science*, 8, 435–445.
Harré, R., and Moghaddam, F. M. (Eds.) (2012). *Psychology for the Third Millennium*. Santa Barbara, CA.: Sage.
Hebb, D. O. (1949). *The Organization of Behavior: A Neuropsychological Theory*. New York: John Wiley.
Henrich, J., Boyd, R., Bowler, S., Camerer, C., Fehr, E., et al. (2005). "Economic man" in cross-cultural perspective: Behavioral experiments in 15 small-scale societies. *Behavioral and Brain Sciences*, 28, 795–855.
Huttenlocher, P. R. (2012). *The Effects of Environment on the Development of the Cerebral Cortex*. Cambridge, MA: Harvard University Press.
Khomeini, R. (1960). *Islamic Governance*. Privately published.
Kim, J. (2006). Emergence: Core ideas and issues. *Synthese*, 151, 547–559.

Levinson, S. C., and Gray, R. D. (2012). Tools from evolutionary biology shed new light on the diversification of languages. *Trends in Cognitive Sciences*, 16, 167–173.

Moghaddam, F. M. (2002). *The Individual and Society: A Cultural Integration*. New York: Worth.

(2005). *Great Ideas in Psychology*. Oxford: Oneworld.

(2008). *Multiculturalism and Intergroup Relations: Psychological Implications for Democracy in Global Context*. Washington, DC: American Psychological Association Press.

(2013). *The Psychology of Dictatorship*. Washington, DC: American Psychological Association Press.

(2016). *The Psychology of Democracy*. Washington, DC: American Psychological Association Press.

Moghaddam, F. M., and Lee, N. (2006). Double reification: The process of universalizing psychology in the Three Worlds. In A. Brock (Ed.), *Internationalizing the History of Psychology* (pp. 163–182). New York: New York University Press.

Noddings, N. (2013). *Education and Democracy in the 21st Century*. New York: Columbia University.

Pahlavi, M. R. (1960). *Mission for My Country*. New York: McGraw-Hill.

Taylor, D. M., and de la Sablonnière, R. (2014). *Toward Constructive Change in Aboriginal Communities*. Montreal, Canada: McGill-Queens University Press.

Thomas, C., and Baker, C. I. (2013). Teaching an adult brain new tricks: A critical review of evidence for training-dependent structural plasticity in humans. *NeuroImage*, 73, 225–236.

Voss, M. W., Vivar, C., Kramer, A. F., and Van Praag, H. (2013). Bridging animal and human models of exercise-induced brain plasticity. *Trends in Cognitive Neuroscience*, 17, 525–544.

Watzlawick, P., Weakland, J. H., and Fisch, R. (1974). *Change: Principles of Problem Formation and Problem Resolution*. New York: W. W. Norton.

8   The Velvet Revolution of Land and Minds

*Tania Zittoun**

A sociopolitical revolution is a complex phenomenon, taking place in history, implying legal, political, and human transformations. The term "revolution" itself comes from Latin, where it is built as *Re-volvere*, literally, to roll back. It has both been used to designate the closure of a cycle as in the return of the celestial bodies (eleventh century), and that of "great changes in affairs," and especially politics (fourteenth to fifteenth centuries). The term is thus etymologically built on a tension between what regularly comes back, and what is connected to a major rupture (Rey, 1998, p. 3238). Given its political and historical importance, the term has become a notion in the social sciences. Hence, the following attempt to give a definition:

> Providing one clear-cut definition of revolution proves hard due to their historical variability. One particularly important distinction, however, is between social and political revolutions. Social revolutions involve sweeping change in economic, social, cultural, as well as political institutions ... Revolutions that involve only the transfer in political power are known as political revolutions. (Harrison, 2014, p. 1673)

As it has been the task of sociologists, philosophers, political scientists as well as of economists to define the concept in the light of the variations of causes, shapes, speeds, and outcomes of revolutions in human history, I will leave further definition problems to them. I will work with a simple understanding of a Revolution as sociopolitical phenomena – deliberately combining the two categories above – as in "any major social and political transformation, sufficient to replace old institutions and social relations, and to initiate new relations of power and authority" (Blackburn, 2014). However, I will also bear in mind the fact that a revolution means something that simply revolves, that is, comes back to its initial position after a long trajectory.

---

* I would like to thank Milan Mazourek for his precious help in understanding and writing about the history of Czech Republic and Ivana Marková for inspiring some ideas presented here and for her feedback on this essay.

140

What can sociocultural psychology say about such phenomenon? Sociocultural psychology has given itself as goal to understand humans as beings of culture (Bruner, 1990; Cole, 2007; Valsiner, 2012, 2014a). Such perspective has invited us to consider people within their webs of social relationships, as they interact with material and symbolic objects, in specific social and cultural settings, as well as their relation to less visible cultural phenomena such as fiction and religion. A sociopolitical revolution is, from that perspective, simply another type of cultural phenomena (Valsiner, 2014c). As any other, it is deeply historical – it happens at a specific moment of people and groups' lives, it unfolds through time, and mostly demands an acceleration of changes normally taking places; it is determined by activities and meanings conferred to situations by people; and it is socially and culturally situated. The main challenge, for cultural psychologists, is however to be able to combine an analysis of changes in the social and cultural field – for instance, the revolution that changes a political or economic system – and an analysis of how people experience the world (Ratner, 2012). For, if our sociocultural analysis still claims to be a psychology, it has to give us access to how specific persons live these changes, and how sociocultural changes and human development mutually constitute each other (Hviid, 2015; Rosa, 2007; Zittoun et al., 2013).

In this chapter, I propose to examine the so-called Velvet Revolution in Czechoslovakia in 1989. I will briefly sketch a history of the country, and present the revolution itself. I will then propose a few theoretical elements which, from a sociocultural psychological perspective, allow us to read the conditions in which the Velvet Revolution took place. Looking at some of its consequence in people's lives, I thus hope to identify some features of a sociocultural psychology of revolution.

A Very Short History of the Czech Republic

Situated in the middle of Europe, between Germany, Austria, and Poland and what today is Slovakia, Czech Republic was part of the Austro-Hungarian Empire. With three major rivers taking their sources in the country, mountains rich of minerals, plains, and hills, the region was rich and well developed: representing 21 percent of the lands of the Austro-Hungarian Empire, it was responsible for 60–70 percent of its industrial capacity (Machonin, 2000, p. 107). Composed of the regions of Bohemia, Moravia, Czech Silesia, and Slovakia, Czechoslovakia was created as independent country in 1918 after World War I. Tomáŝs G. Masaryk, a former philosopher and educationalist, became president of a democratic First Republic. The state became one of the most successful industrial countries of the region, with its very good public transport and educational system, its factories producing metals, shoes (Bat'a), weapons (Škoda), as well flourishing arts and architecture.

With the rise of Hitler to the power in neighboring Germany in 1933, the course of history drastically changed. Misusing the principle of self-determination defined by the Atlantic charter in 1941, Hitler steered nationalistic movements in the Sudeten lands, large border zones of Czechoslovakia (about a third of the country's surface) in which a German population were installed since the thirteenth century as part of the development of the land. The conflict in a bilingual population of Czech and German origin escalated, and was used as a pretext for the policy of appeasement which was finalized as part of the Munich agreement in September 1938. Czechoslovakia was strongly advised by its European allies to renounce to these lands without military resistance, in exchange of the guarantee of Czech sovereignty over the remaining of the country. The Sudeten lands were annexed by Germany, and six months later in March 1939, Czechoslovakia was fully turned into a German protectorate. This episode let a painful memory to Czech citizens – that of, although having been ready to resists, losing their sovereignty – and an enduring feeling of having been betrayed by Western allies. The ruling of Czechoslovakia allowed Germany to access the rich resources of the country, as well as to use it as platform to the East.

In September 1939, Hitler invaded Poland thus starting World War II. Czechoslovakian territories were "liberated" in 1945, from the southwest by the American Third Army under the lead of General Patton, and from the North an East by the First Ukrainian Front under Marshall Konev. Following the Yalta agreement in February 1945, as part of the postwar settlements, Czechoslovakia fell in the zone under Soviet influence, and thus behind the Iron Curtain (e.g., Cornej and Pokorny, 2004). Postwar Czechoslovakia has then known various periods, starting with a quasi-democratic period from 1945 to 1948, year in which the Communists took over. A very harsh Soviet-style collectivization and restructuration of the society immediately followed, with arrests, confiscations, political executions, concentration camps, forced labor, torture, etc. After the end of the Stalinist cult in 56, the communist policy progressive loosened its grip on society, which led to the Prague spring in 1968, a very creative period for arts and culture. This was broken down by the invasion of the armies of the Warsaw pact in 1968, which installed the process of "normalization" – aiming to "normalize" the communist state of affairs, this time replacing physical violence against citizens by psychological and economical pressure. Finally, in the 1980s, in parallel with other movements in the eastern bloc (Perestroika in the USSR,

Solidarnosc in Poland, etc.), a combination of popular movements and political transformation allowed for the so-called Velvet Revolution – the end of communist rule and the election of Václav Havel, a dissident theater author and philosopher, as president.

Tensions between Czechs and Slovaks present since the creation of the country resulted in the peaceful division of the country in two, the Czech and the Slovak republics on January 1, 1993. Since that, Czech Republic continued its orientation toward liberal democracy and joined NATO in 1999 and the European Union in 2004. Currently, Czech Republic has a rapidly growing overall economy although inequalities also increase within the overall population (Birčiaková, Stávková, and Antošová, 2014; Kahanec et al., 2012).

The Velvet Revolution

The Velvet Revolution – *sametová revoluce* – took place in 1989 in Czechoslovakia; it is often described as an exemplary nonviolent revolution, made by people under the leadership of the intellectual figure of Václav Havel, and bringing the end of communism in Czechoslovakia. That revolution is both a political and socioeconomic change, and a return to a democracy, as the country had known during the twenty years of the First Republic under the other intellectual leadership of Masaryk.

The events have often been summarized as follows (Radio Prague, 1997; Wikipedia, 2015). On November 16, 1989, a student demonstration took place in Bratislava to commemorate the fiftieth birthday of the death of the student Jan Opletal on November 17, 1939, followed by persecutions of students and the closure of universities in Czechoslovakia by the Nazis. The demonstration attracted a great number of students; the police was present but did not intervene. A similar event grouped fifteen thousand students in Prague on November 17; this time, the police ended up the demonstration with violence, beating students. This immediately caused a massive reaction: theater and arts went on strike, later joined by factory workers; public discussions were organized; and a Civil forum (*Občanské fórum*, which had a Slovak equivalent), defending nonviolence, was created. The latter asked the government to resign. Massive demonstrations (up to five hundred thousand people) followed in the next few days, followed by more general strikes. One of the very iconic scene of that time is that of these hundreds of thousands peaceful demonstrants on Prague's main square, Wenceslas square – the equivalent of the Champs-Elysees – all shaking their keys. Eventually, the president Gustáv Husák announced his resignation on December 10.

Obviously, the revolution was not only "caused" by the peaceful demonstration, how romantic the idea might appear. External economic and political games were getting to a tipping point, and internal dynamics were active for forty years.

On the external side, the world balance was changing in the late 1980s, with the end of the Cold War, and overall a general weakening of the Soviet influence. The Perestroika had started mid-1980s under Gorbatchov; following this closely, the Czech population started to express more openly its discontent or its support to dissidents such as Václav Havel; students demonstration had started in January 1989, and a series of gathering repressed by the police had started on a regular basis on the center of Prague, while demonstrants became bolder with time (Drury, Reicher, and Stott, 2012; Zantovsky, 2015). Early November 1989, East Germans escaped to West Germany through the Czech embassy, and then the Berlin Wall collapsed on November 9. Hence, on the European map, the loss of communist influence in Czechoslovakia was part of a more general change, probably anticipated if not supported by the need of the communist countries to join the general economical market. In the light of these changes, the Communist authorities could not decide to react violently to the November demonstrations (Cornish, 2012; Zantovsky, 2015).

On the internal side, forty years of communism had let Czechoslovakia exhausted, and its previously flourishing economy was now bloodless. The general climate was depressed after the many waves of severe repression, intimidation, arrests, censorship, blatant inequalities, etc. This is what we now need to closely consider. Before doing so, I will need to introduce a few theoretical concepts to work with.

A Sociocultural Understanding

Addressing a revolution from a sociocultural perspective requires identifying theories or models appropriated to articulate collective and psychological change. Here, I will draw on a series of simple principles.

First, a revolution can be described from a developmental science perspective as change that demands a massive reorganization of a given system (Valsiner et al., 2009; Zittoun et al., 2013). A social, political, and economic transformation cannot be explained in terms of linear causality (Kohler, 2014); rather, it is made possible through complex configurations of events and facts. Such complex transformations have been described in the social sciences in terms of catalytic phenomena. "Catalysis" is a chemical reaction that occurs in specific conditions in a temporarily bounded system, where an accelerated reaction takes place thanks to the presence of a catalyst, which first brings elements to synthesize into temporary compounds, before constituting a new substance, while leaving the catalyst unchanged (Valsiner, 2014b). Catalysis can be used as a metaphor in psychology (or as a "nomad concept"; Kohler, 2014, p. 33). Dynamic changes, as well as the catalysis metaphor, can be used at different levels of description – social, interpersonal or intrapsychological (Cabell and Valsiner, 2014; Kadianaki and Zittoun, 2014; Valsiner and Cabell, 2012). Here, we will use the metaphor to describe a sociocultural change.

When talking about psychological transformation, I will use the notions of "rupture" to designate events perceived by a given person as questioning the taken-for-granted of her experience, and of "transition" to name the developmental dynamics hence generated and by which the person adjust her conduct to the new situation, until a new balance is found (Zittoun, 2006b; Zittoun et al., 2013; Zittoun et al., 2012). Here as well, of course, there is no single causality: what a person perceives as change does not "cause" psychological transformation; certain conditions facilitate change, and some elements can play the role of "semiotic regulators" and catalysts – for instance semiotic resources (Kadianaki and Zittoun, 2014).

However, in order to combine an analysis of changes at a sociocultural and at a psychological level, we need to identify both a frame to articulate these phenomena, and a common denominator – a "substance" that circulates at both level and through both levels. The general principle that articulates both phenomena can be that of "dialogicality." Inspired by Bakhtin, it mainly designates "the capacity of the human mind to conceive and communicate about social reality in relation or opposition to otherness" (Marková, 2003). Dialogism itself and it can be conceived of as ontological, epistemological, and ethical stance (Zittoun, 2014). From a dialogical perspective, we can conceive how not only verbal utterance, but more generally, any movement of mind and the flow of consciousness is responding or anticipating other events, and how these are also always related to inner-dialogues, relations to present or distant others, cultural elements, social representations, and more diffuse values and discourses, in their respective social and cultural anchorages (Grossen, Florez, and Lauvergeon, 2014; Grossen and Salazar Orvig, 2011; Zittoun and Grossen, 2012). What is the "substance" of the dialogues, what circulates from social representations to mind, is made out of signs – it is of *semiotic* nature (Valsiner, 1998, 2001, 2006; Zittoun, 2006b, 2009, 2011).

With these two theoretical principles – dialogicality and semiosis – we have the means to theorize the mutual constitution of the politics and the mind. In other words, we can grasp dynamics by which social and political systems, shaping the semiosphere (Lotman, 2000) – expressed in discourses, structuring everyday life, organizing the urban space or the nature of formal and informal relations – also progressively shape and guide individual psychological life. In a well enough functioning society, semiotic streams circulate from society and its institutions to people's lives and back. People internalize some aspects of the shared culture, and in unique ways constitute their personal culture. This is the basis of their externalization in that society and can participate to its evolution (Valsiner, 2007; Zittoun and Gillespie, 2015a).

However, for some minority groups, or in some forms of society, there is a mismatch between shared and personal cultures: the society proposes norms, values, and discourses that people cannot internalize, or that are too contrary to their personal culture, and also often denies the latter. People's personal culture and system of values thus becomes dissonant with the collective and shared one. Although we all experience such dissonances, these are very clear in the case of migration (Gillespie and Zittoun, 2013; Lawrence, Benedikt, and Valsiner, 1992; Schuetz, 1944; Zittoun, 2006a; Zittoun and Gillespie, 2015b), and also, in case of radical political change and, as here, in the case of totalitarian state. In addition, the societal organization and its institutions also exerts physical and symbolic power on people, constraining their access to semiotic resources, limiting or forcing actual conduct, or deny recognition.

This raises the question of how people can develop a meaningful action in such environments. For this, we need to introduce to more concepts. The first one is that of "engagement":

In existential philosophy the concept of engagement was introduced aiming to reinstall personality development in the concrete world. When engaged, human beings got "involved in the situation, thereby changing it, and thus creating a future for themselves as persons" (Lübcke, 1999). In a developmental perspective, engagements can be seen as situated zones of potential development. It unites potential interests of the child [or the person] with certain aspects of the environment... In engaged situations human beings move and are "moved." (Hviid, 2008, p. 184)

Engagement thus designates that what moves people, that is, dynamizes their conduct; it allows conduct to make sense to the person in a given situation, and be future oriented. In that sense engagement is one of the conditions of development.

"Imagination" is the second notion we need to understand what is at stake for people in given social and political environment. Imagination is disengaging from the here-and-now of a proximal experience, which is submitted to causality and temporal linearity, to explore, or engage with alternative, distal experiences, which are not submitted to linear or causal temporality. An imagination event thus begins with a decoupling of experience and usually concludes with a re-coupling. (Zittoun and Gillespie, 2016, p. 40)

Imagination is a core psychological dynamic, which allows enriching our daily life, in daydreaming, anticipating, creating, or remembering (Zittoun et al., 2013; Zittoun and Gillespie, 2016). The material of our imagining is given by personal past experiences, experiences of others, cultural elements, or any available semiotic materials, newly recombined and enrich in unique fashion by one's experience (Vygotsky, 1931; Winnicott, 2001). Imagination can bring us to new conduct – building a shelve or going on holidays – but also, be the means to resist imprisonment or labor camp, or bring to social change (Zittoun and Gillespie, 2016). Conversely, totalitarian states precisely aim at controlling people's access to resources so as to constrain imagination (Marková, forthcoming).

From a sociocultural perspective, then, dialogical dynamics allow understanding the mutual constitution of society and mind, through the circulation of semiotic streams. In most cases, there is some degree of homology between shared and personal culture. Yet also, there can be discrepancies which can be more or less acceptable. We also see that people's conduct needs to follows their engagements for life in society to make sense; imagination can in that sense either support these meaningful engagements, or at the contrary, deploy is alternative realities, detached from these. These few ideas are the basis of our more psychological reading of the dynamics leading to the Velvet Revolution – which will of course only address some aspects of its complexity.

The Amphibian Society

In order to understand the revolution that allowed Czechoslovakia to restore its democratic tradition, one needs to examine the social organization in the country under communism and its psychological implications. In order to do so, and guided by the ideas outlined above, I draw on a series of texts by Czech social scientists, novelists and commentators.

My main argument, based on coinciding various authors' descriptions, is that the at the dawn of the Revolution, the population was not only generally depressed because of forty years of deprivation of civil rights, as in any totalitarian state. Moreover, a long-standing irritation had developed, first because people's real engagements had been systematically unacknowledged, denied, if not destroyed, and second, because people as well as institutions had to adopt a publically suitable discourse and actions to cover basic needs and avoid further problems, while developing in private an alternative life infused with their imagination. This can be shown by following three aspects of life in society: people's possession, people's engagements, and people's discourses. In each case, the social system creates conditions in which people cannot internalize and make theirs the societal values, and a state of dissociation develops.

First, Mlčoch, an economist forbidden during the communist period, reads the evolution of the country as a transformation around the semiformal institution of ownership. As he summarizes here, the historical sketch above could also be read as a story of organized systematic dispossession:

> During the last three generations in the former Czechoslovakia – that means from its very beginning – great number of changes and reversals in ownership relations, violent interventions into property rights took place. The terrible instability of institutions – of all of them, but of ownership institutions particularly – is probably one of the most important features of the history in our countries. I can only mention here the first land reform from the First Republic when the land of feudal landlords was expropriated. The Second Republic and the Protectorate were stigmatized with the impact of the Nazi ideology, the robbery of the Jewish and also Czech possessions and their transfer into German hands. Then the postwar period with the first Nationalization Decrees, with the violent transfer of the German population – the expulsion and expropriation of Germans, the confiscation of possessions of war traitors and collaborators. Now we get to the February 1948, to the communist Nationalization Decrees, to the massive expropriation with which the process of realization of the Marxist ideology started. (Mlčoch, 1995, p. 144)

Very concretely, it means that whatever people or families had developed and accumulated over time as result of work, interest, or capacity, thinking about their future of that of their children – a house, a sewing machine, a cow, or savings – was taken away from them during communist years. People who grew under the Nazi Germany and lived their adult lives under communism thus remember having lost two or three times their own goods and savings. This situation was among others reflected on housing issues (Šmídová, 2000).

Second, along the same line, the socialism imposed in Czechoslovakia by Soviet Russia denied people the right to choose their life trajectories according to their interests and abilities. People who did not comply with the regime usually ended up working in unqualified manual occupations regardless of their expertise (e.g., doctors, artists, or scientists working as porters, responsible of heating rooms or destroying garbage) (e.g., Hrabal, 1993; Křesadlo, 2015; Viewegh, 2015). Conversely, people with lower expertise but strong allegiance to the Party would get higher positions, with collective responsibilities. Also, young people were oriented toward studies according to the need of the economy, not their own interests or engagements; in some case access to education was denied to them as retaliation against their families. At a collective level, this brought to an economic and cultural "stagnation" (Machonin, 2000, p. 112). At a more individual level, many people resign to dull life occupations, while investing "hobbies" or side activities; many invested in their flourishing "cottage life" that allowed parallel modes of sociality (Reidinger, 2008); others could get very depressed or simply alcoholics. A minority of the population engaged in "dissident" activities – that is, refused to renounce to their freedom of thinking and speech – risking repression for themselves and their relatives. For instance they published Samizdat (forbidden texts circulating on homemade press), sent their texts abroad (Zantovsky, 2015), planned informal gathering to debate and learn, together or with foreign intellectuals (Day, 1999), or organized and attended forbidden or undergrounds concerts and arts (Hagen, 2012). (Of course, there was still a portion of the population satisfied with these arrangements; also, people who grew as children these years have very often good memories of the collective activities organized for them by factories or state companies.)

Third, at a more organizational level, in companies and public institutions, "planning was an extensive cooperative game based on a deep dichotomy of actual and official rules" (Mlčoch, 2000, p. 31). Hence, on the one side, the discourse proposed was taking the shape of the socialist language of planning for the collective good; on the other side, the real socioeconomic game was a structure of informal power and networks, with its privileged and subordinated. Thus, here again, the economy progressively was dissociated between an official discursive game, and actual practices – where, in everyday life, people could survive on the basis of informal networks and shadow economy.

From such a reading, it appears that Czechoslovakia in the 1980s was tired and affected by forty years of a regime which demanded, for most people, a double mode of existence. The public life was for many a game to be played, minimally as a way of lip service (e.g., having a communist membership card in order to accede higher education) or as much more sophisticated game. People's actual engagements, that is, their existential interests and emotional commitments, took, for the most part, informal or private channels: hobbies, informal networks, and close relationships. People's imagination could also mainly develop through lines forbidden by the society and its institutions, through forbidden music, capturing TV channels from the West, or hoping to escape or for the end of the Regime. In his novel showing the moral compromising to which the regime led people, Křesadlo thus uses the expression "amphibians" to designate a dual-mode "lifestyle of those who participated in church singing as well as communist society" (Křesadlo, 2015, p. 217) – and the expression can probably be extended to other modalities of double life. It is against this double life that dissidents and especially Václav Havel, drawing on a Czech moral tradition going from Jan Hus to Jan Patočka, developed an ethical posture demanding to "live in truth" (Koha̒k, 1989; Marková, 2008; Zantovsky, 2015).

Hence, our sociocultural reading highlights a state of society where people function at two contrasting levels, and where the collective values and principles do not reflect and cannot guide people's engagements and imagination. There is thus dissociation, or a gap between societal values and personal culture, shared meaning and personal sense making. Paradoxically, it is precisely this gap that creates the space in which, in the right catalytic conditions, change can take place. In other words, revolution can be seen as a form of societal catalysis, resulting from a long cultivated inner-societal disruption. Here, the geopolitical conditions of 1989 offered the environment for the catalytic process. In that sense, the demonstrations of the Velvet Revolution were the temporary compound of such longer process, and Václav Havel played the role of catalyst.[1] The catalysis eventually resulted in a new societal order and political power – the reinstallation of a democracy.

The Revolution and Ruptures in Life Trajectories: From Amphibian Lives to the Big Pond

At a sociocultural level, the Velvet Revolution had relatively clear outcomes: the Communist power abdicated, after having installed Václav Havel at the presidency of the country. Havel called elections soon after and was indeed confirmed in its role by the population. He soon constituted a government of former artists and intellectuals, mainly dissidents, which had now the hard duty to fully transform a society. In inner politics, this implied to change the social system, the whole economical system, the cultural life, the education, etc. (Zantovsky, 2015). This period has thus rightly been called that of societal transformations (rather than transition) (Machonin, 1997).

[1] Václav Havel was described by his biograph as playing the role of "'carbon,' a chemical element capable of linking with many others to create a compound of irresistible strength, filled with contradictions yet stable enough to set in motion the momentous transformation that led ahead" (Zantovsky, 2015, p. 299).

At the level of people's lives, however things were not so clear: "the direct participants [of the social change], however, only perceive muddled and badly demarcated social events, which surprise them with ever new uncertainties"(Kabele, 2000, p. 126). Filling lives with uncertainties, the revolution was also the cause of many ruptures – the loss of a job, the end of certitudes, the possibility to travel or to become one's own boss – and thus initiated many transitions. In that sense, the corollary of our previous argument would be that the transition in people's life, triggered by the revolution, offers them the occasion to reunify their double life – to move away from an amphibian life.

Drawing on the longitudinal documentaries by Elena Třeštíkova, *Manželské etudy po dvaceti letech* (studies of marriage twenty years later, 2006), documenting the everyday life of six couples, married in the same town hall in Prague in 1980, and followed until 2005 (Třeštíkova, 2009), I have tried to analyze the nature of the transitions experienced by people following the Velvet Revolution (Zittoun, 2016a, 2016b; Zittoun and Gillespie, 2016). I here indicate some elements that support the idea that the dynamics generated by the revolution allowed, for some, to develop a more integrated life.

Although the life conditions of the six couples were very similar at the beginning of the married life – precisely because of housing and work conditions – what distinguished mostly the six involved young men were their hobbies.

In what appears as a form of compensation for the lack of freedom on the vocational front, most of the men in the couples have substantial hobbies, for which they spent a certain numbers of weekly hours. Hobbies open new spheres of experience that partly escape to the constraints of political guidance. They are also spheres in which playfulness and creativity can be let free . . .

Pavel from the very beginning is doing theater, where is play and sings, and hockey in the winter and football in the summer. He will keep doing theater all his life and keeps doing regular sports as well. His wife, Ivana, likes her husband's hobbies and assist to the theater pieces. She does a bit of gym as well.

Václav likes to work with wood – furniture, construction; outside of his work as teaching architecture, he develops a workshop. After the revolution, he becomes the owner of a large furniture store; his wife Ivana supports him. She, on the other side, develops all kind of skills – she knits, paints small frames, does small objects with various materials and fabric; for a short period after the revolution she will open a boutique for such object but will have to close it.

Jiří collects taps of bottles which he exchanges with colleagues, and plays cards with them (it has no significance upon the couple as he and Marcela early divorce). She, on the other hand, likes to take care of horses, and attends country concerts and hikes.

Antonín likes to build up cars; he competes on a rally, and also learns to take care of animals to improve the couple's food income. Mirka, his wife, just sees these hobbies as taking her husband away from the chores and the daughter. She is disappointed by his interest for farm animals and resents him for his passion for cars, and eventually forbids her husband to continue rallying. She mainly mentions her pleasure in dancing. As an older couple they both take care of a small garden.

Stanislav is extremely absorbed in building electronic artifacts – transistors, small computer, and telescopes – and also in his motorbike. He keeps on such leisure all his life, building his own hi-fi stereo, a low consuming house ... His wife, Zuzana, complains as the hobbies prevent him to participate to house chores, discussion and family life – but never seems to ask him to reduce his hobbies. She on the other hand only mentions reading some young people's magazine, and later in her life, watching TV series.

Vladimír develops and interest for photography next to his work, and the couple decides that the wife, Zuzana, will bring the main income while he can develop his skills – first trying to enter the FAMU, a prestigious art school, then working as a freelance photographer. (Zittoun, 2016a)

These hobbies took a very different importance in people's lives after the revolution. In effect, the transition in people's lives allowed for many the possibility to explore how to reunify diverse aspects of one's experience, with various trial and failures.

The skills developed as hobbies in men's youth under communism will become central in their later professional life. Václav, who likes working with wood, opens as furniture shop; Antonín, who likes playing with car pieces, will open a garage and later becomes specialized in selling wheel rims; Stanislav fabricates as satellite which enables him to capture foreign channels, and so learns German – which eventually will bring him to be translator; Vladimír who likes photography turns it into his job. Pavel discovers billiard in 1995, falls in love with the sport, and eventually turns it into his main occupation. All these men will, at one point or another, say that they are lucky enough to do their "dream work." (Zittoun, 2016a)

Of course this short summary of our analysis of six life stories (Zittoun, 2016a, 2016b) has no value of demonstration. Also, many people found themselves in difficult situation after the revolution, and felt missing the means to understand, if not participate to, a liberal society defined by very different rules than life under communism. This for instance has brought many parents to feel difficulties to support their children discovering a liberal, democratic society as young adults (Macek, Ježek, and Vazsonyi, 2013; Roberts, 2008). However, the fact is that in these six life stories, like in probably many others, the revolution liberated very powerful engagements in activities so far taking place in the shadow of society, as amphibian activity. These supported strong enough imagination of oneself in the liberal society, to bring people to engage strongly in new activities. This in itself supports our initial point: in effect, for such engagement to surface, these must have been active and repressed for long.

If the Velvet Revolution can be seen as the expression of these long-repressed engagement and imagination, it seems that the modalities of communism established in a society that had a long tradition of democracy and used to be governed by intellectual figures (Holý, 1996) contained the condition of its own destruction. The following interpretation can thus be proposed: in the right catalytic conditions, people's need to find some coincidence between inner life and societal value, personal and shared culture, finally generated a series of reactions that allows for deep social transformation and personal transitions.

Thinking through Revolutions

Each revolution is unique. Here, by retracing the history of Czech Republic, my aim was to show the underlying and accumulated streams of meaning and values that shaped people's lives: the memory of having been a flourishing democratic state, or the feeling of betrayal by former allies. These constitute the cultural and historical conditions in which forty years of communism were imposed, denying people's engagements and obliging imagination to develop in the margin of society – which eventually triggered the Velvet Revolution, a process of social transformation that could be described as catalytic, with its specific choices of nonviolence and truth as ethical and political values. Such sociocultural reconfigurations triggered transitions in people's lives, who could renounce to an "amphibian" experience toward a more integrate life.

However, some elements proposed for this analysis could be used to read other situations. The sociocultural framework sketched here proposes to consider both social and cultural conditions in a given environment, and the conditions in which people live their daily life. From a dialogical perspective, these are deeply related, and constitute the frame within which meaning and dynamics of recognition take place. Our proposal is to pay attention to the possible discrepancies between people (or subgroups) and the general cultural guidance – values, promoted actions, etc. We also considered people's engagements and imagination as core psychological needs. The question thus becomes, is a given societal environment offering people the possibility to freely develop their life trajectories according to their engagements, and space for develop imagination in such a way that it enriches life in society? If not, a disruption can progressively develop, which is likely to create a space for change. How this change takes place then becomes politics and history.

154   *Tania Zittoun*

REFERENCES

Birčiaková, N., Stávková, J., and Antošová, V. (2014). The impact of economic development in the Czech Republic on the income inequality between groups of households. *Procedia Economics and Finance*, 12, 57–65.

Blackburn, S. (2014). Revolution. In *The Oxford Dictionary of Philosophy*, 2nd ed. Oxford: Oxford University Press. www.oxfordreference.com/view/10.1093/oi/authority.20110803100417811.

Bruner, J. S. (1990). *Acts of Meaning*. Cambridge, MA: Harvard University Press.

Cabell, K. R., and Valsiner, J. (2014). Systematic systemics: Causality, catalysis, and developmental cybernetics. In K. R. Cabell and J. Valsiner (Eds.), *The Catalyzing Mind* (pp. 3–13). New York: Springer. http://link.springer.com/chapter/10.1007/978-1-4614-8821-7_1.

Cole, M. (2007). Phylogeny and cultural history in ontogeny. *Journal of Physiology–Paris*, 101(4–6), 236–246.

Cornej, P., and Pokorny, P. C. (2004). *Brief History of the Czech Lands to 2004*. 1st ed. Prague: Prah.

Cornish, F. (2012). Collectives may protest, but how do authorities respond? In B. Wagoner, E. Jensen, and J. A. Oldmeadow (Eds.), *Culture and Social Change: Transforming Society through the Power of Ideas* (pp. 39–51). Charlotte, NC: Information Age.

Day, B. (1999). *The Velvet Philosophers*. London: Continuum.

Drury, J., Reicher, S. D., and Stott, C. (2012). The psychology of collective action. In B. Wagoner, E. Jensen, and J. A. Oldmeadow (Eds.), *Culture and Social Change: Transforming Society through the Power of Ideas* (pp. 19–38). Charlotte, NC: Information Age.

Gillespie, A., and Zittoun, T. (2013). Meaning making in motion: Bodies and minds moving through institutional and semiotic structures. *Culture and Psychology*, 19(4), 518–532.

Grossen, M., Florez, D., and Lauvergeon, S. (2014). Dealing with clients' diversity in test situations: Client categorisations in psychologists' accounts of their practices. *International Journal of Educational Research*, 63, 15–25.

Grossen, M., and Salazar Orvig, A. (2011). Dialogism and dialogicality in the study of the self. *Culture and Psychology*, 17(4), 491–509.

Hagen, T. (2012). From inhibition to commitment: Politics in the Czech Underground. *EastBound Journal of Media Studies*, 3, 2–34). http://eastbound.eu/site_media/pdf/EB2012_Hagen.pdf.

Harrison, O. (2014). Revolution. In T. Teo (Ed.), *Encyclopedia of Critical Psychology* (pp. 1673–1677). New York: Springer.

Holý, L. (1996). *The Little Czech and the Great Czech Nation*. Cambridge: Cambridge University Press.

Hrabal, B. (1976/1993). *Too Loud a Solitude* (M. H. Heim, Trans.). St Ives, UK: Abacus.

Hviid, P. (2008). "Next year we are small, right?" Different times in children's development. *European Journal of Psychology of Education*, 2(23), 183–198.

(2015). Borders in education and living – a case of trench warfare. *Integrative Psychological and Behavioral Science*, 50, 1–18.

Kabele, J. (2000). The devilish cocktail of the Velvet Revolution: The social transition of society in the biographical narratives of several Czech sociologists. In Z. Konopásek (Ed.), *Our Lives as Database: Doing a Sociology of Ourselves: Czech National Transitions in Autobiographical Research Dialogues* (pp. 125–136). Prague: Univerzita Karlova V Praze, Nakladatelestvi Karolinum.

Kadianaki, I., and Zittoun, T. (2014). Catalysts and regulators of psychological change in the context of immigration ruptures. In K. R. Cabell and J. Valsiner (Eds.), *The Catalyzing Mind* (pp. 191–207). New York: Springer. http://link.springer.com/chapter/10.1007/978-1-4614-8821-7_10.

Kahanec, M., Guzi, M., Martišková, M., Paleník, M., Pertold, F., and Siebertová, Z. (2012). Gini country report: Growing inequalities and their impacts in the Czech Republic and Slovakia. Gini Country Report czech_slovak. Amsterdam: Amsterdam Institute for Advanced Labour Studies. https://ideas.repec.org/p/aia/ginicr/czech_slovak.html.

Kohák, E. V. (1989). *Jan Patočka: Philosophy and Selected Writings*. Chicago: University of Chicago Press.

Kohler, A. (2014). Cause and catalyst: A differentiation. In K. R. Cabell and J. Valsiner (Eds.), *The Catalyzing Mind* (pp. 33–70). New York: Springer. http://link.springer.com/chapter/10.1007/978-1-4614-8821-7_10.

Křesadlo, J. (2015). *GraveLarks* (V. Z. Pincava, Trans.). London: Jantar.

Lawrence, J. A., Benedikt, R., and Valsiner, J. (1992). Homeless in the mind: A case-history of personal life in and out of a close orthodox community. *Journal of Social Distress and the Homeless*, 1(2), 157–176.

Lotman, Y. M. (2000). *Universe of the Mind: A Semiotic Theory of Culture* (A. Shukman, Trans.). Bloomington: Indiana University Press.

Macek, P., Ježek, S., and Vazsonyi, A. T. (2013). Adolescents during and after times of social change The case of the Czech Republic. *Journal of Early Adolescence*, 33(8), 1029–1047.

Machonin, P. (1997). *Social Transformation and Modernization: On Building Theory of Societal Changes in the Post-Communist European Countries*. Prague: Sociologické nakladatelství.

(2000). Modernization theory and the Czech experience. In L. Mlčoch, P. Machonin, and M. Sojka (Eds.), *Economic and Social Changes in Czech Society after 1989: An Alternative View* (pp. 103–226). Prague: Karolinum Press.

Marková, I. (2003). *Dialogicality and Social Representations: The Dynamics of Mind*. Cambridge: Cambridge University Press.

Marková, I. (2008). A dialogical perspective of social representations of responsibility. In W. Wagner, T. Sugiman, and K. Gergen (Eds.), *Meaning in Action: Constructions, Narratives and Representations* (pp. 253–170). New York: Springer.

Marková, I. (forthcoming). *The Dialogical Mind: Common Sense and Ethics*. Cambridge: Cambridge University Press.

Mlčoch, L. (1995). Morality of privatization in the Czech case. *Society and Economy in Central and Eastern Europe*, 17(5), 144–151.

(2000). Restructuring of property rights: An institutional view. In L. Mlčoch, P. Machonin, and M. Sojka (Eds.), *Economic and Social Changes in Czech*

Society after 1989: An Alternative View (pp. 71–102). Prague: Karolinum Press.

Radio Prague (1997). RP's history online – Velvet Revolution. http://archiv.radio .cz/history/history15.html.

Ratner, C. (2012). *Macro Cultural Psychology: A Political Philosophy of Mind*. New York: Oxford University Press.

Reidinger, M. (2008). Islands of bourgeois self-realization in a sea of changes: A century of Czech cottaging (PhD diss.). http://search.proquest.com/ psycinfo/docview/621740283/B35E657801AF4AF9PQ/8.

Rey, A. (Ed.) (1998). *Le Robert: Dictionnaire historique de la langue française*. 3 vols. Paris: Dictionnaires le Robert.

Roberts, K. (2008). *Youth in Transition: Eastern Europe and the West*. London: Palgrave Macmillan.

Rosa, A. (2007). Acts of psyche: Actuations as synthesis of semiosis and action. In J. Valsiner and A. Rosa (Eds.), *The Cambridge Handbook of Sociocultural Psychology* (pp. 205–237). Cambridge: Cambridge University Press.

Schuetz, A. (1944). The stranger: An essay in social psychology. *American Journal of Sociology*, 49(6), 499–507.

Šmídová, O. (2000). Housing stories: Family strategies related to the property maintenance and transfer. In Z. Konopásek (Ed.), *Our Lives as Database: Doing a Sociology of Ourselves: Czech National Transitions in Autobiographical Research Dialogues* (pp. 89–123). Prague: Univerzita Karlova V Praze, Nakladatelestvi Karolinum.

Třeštíkova, H. (2009). *Manželské etudy + po dvaceti letech. 2 dokumentarní cykly* [Studies of marriage + twenty years later: 2 documentary cycles]. Prague: Česká televize/Negativ s.r.o.

Valsiner, J. (1998). *The Guided Mind: A Sociogenetic Approach to Personality*. Cambridge, MA: Harvard University Press.

(2001). Process structure of semiotic mediation in human development. *Human Development*, 44, 84–97.

(2006). The semiotic construction of solitude: Processes of internalization and externalization. *Sign Systems Studies*, 34(1), 9–35.

(2007). *Culture in Minds and Societies: Foundations of Cultural Psychology*. New Delhi: Sage.

(Ed.) (2012). *The Oxford Handbook of Culture and Psychology*. Oxford: Oxford University Press.

(2014a). *An Invitation to Cultural Psychology*. London: Sage.

(2014b). Breaking the arrows of causality: The idea of catalysis in the making. In K. R. Cabell and J. Valsiner (Eds.), *The Catalyzing Mind* (pp. 17–32). New York: Springer. http://link.springer.com/chapter/10.1007/978-1-4614-8821-7_10.

(2014c). Understanding political processes: A new arena for cultural psychology. In T. Magioglou (Ed.), *Cultural and Political Psychology. A Societal Perspective* (pp. ix–xii). Charlotte, NC: Information Age.

Valsiner, J., and Cabell, K. H. (2012). Self-making through synthesis: Extending dialogical self theory. In H. J. M. Hermans and T. Gieser

(Eds.), *Handbook of Dialogical Self Theory* (pp. 82–97). Cambridge: Cambridge University Press. www.cambridge.org/aus/catalogue/catalogue.asp? isbn=9781107006515.

Valsiner, J., Molenaar, P. C. M., Lyra, M. C. D. P., and Chaudhary, N. (2009). *Dynamic Process Methodology in the Social and Developmental Sciences.* 1st ed. New York: Springer.

Viewegh, M. (2015). *Bliss Was It in Bohemia* (D. Short, Trans.). London: Jantar.

Vygotsky, L. S. (1931). Imagination and creativity of the adolescent. www.cddc .vt.edu/marxists/archive/vygotsky/works/1931/adolescent/ch12.htm#s02.

Wikipedia. (2015). Velvet Revolution. https://en.wikipedia.org/w/index.php? title=Velvet_Revolution&oldid=694436502.

Winnicott, D. W. (2001). *Playing and Reality.* Philadelphia: Routledge.

Zantovsky, M. (2015). *Havel: A Life.* London: Atlantic Books.

Zittoun, T. (2006a). Difficult secularity: Talmud as symbolic resource. *Outlines: Critical Social Studies,* 8(2), 59–75.

(2006b). *Transitions: Development through Symbolic Resources.* Greenwich, CT: Information Age.

(2009). La circulation des connaissances: un regard socioculturel. *Revue Économique et Sociale,* 67(2), 129–138.

(2011). Freud and cultural psychology. In S. Salvatore and T. Zittoun (Eds.), *Cultural Psychology and Psychoanalysis: Pathways to Synthesis* (pp. 67–86). Charlotte, NC: Information Age.

(2014). Three dimensions of dialogical movement. *New Ideas in Psychology,* 32, 99–106.

(2016a). Imagining self in a changing world – an exploration of "studies of marriage." In M. Han and C. Cunha (Eds.), *The Subjectified and Subjectifying Mind* (pp. 85–116). Charlotte, NC: Information Age.

(2016b). Reflexivity, or learning from living. In G. Marsico, Ruggero Andrisano-Ruggeri, and S. Salvatore (Eds.), *Reflexivity and Psychology* (pp. 6:143–167). Charlotte, NC: Information Age.

Zittoun, T., Aveling, E.-L., Gillespie, A., and Cornish, F. (2012). People in transitions in worlds in transition: Ambivalence in the transition to womanhood during World War II. In A. C. Bastos, K. Uriko, and J. Valsiner (Eds.), *Cultural Dynamics of Women's Lives* (pp. 59–78). Charlotte, NC: Information Age. www.infoagepub.com/products/Cultural-Dynamics-of-Womens-Lives.

Zittoun, T., and Gillespie, A. (2015a). Internalization: How culture becomes mind. *Culture and Psychology,* 21(4), 477–491.

(2015b). Transitions in the lifecourse: Learning from Alfred Schütz. In A. C. Joerchel and G. Benetka (Eds.), *Biographical Ruptures and Their Repairs: Cultural Transitions in Development* (pp. 147–157). Charlotte, NC: Information Age.

(2016). *Imagination in Human and Cultural Development.* London: Routledge.

Zittoun, T., and Grossen, M. (2012). Cultural elements as means of constructing the continuity of the self across various spheres of experience. In M.

César and B. Ligorio (Eds.), *The Interplays between Dialogical Learning and Dialogical Self* (pp. 99–126). Charlotte, NC: Information Age.

Zittoun, T., Valsiner, J., Vedeler, D., Salgado, J., Gonçalves, M., and Ferring, D. (2013). *Human Development in the Lifecourse: Melodies of Living*. Cambridge: Cambridge University Press.

9   Wordsworth's Insurgency
Living the French Revolution

Duncan Wu

Wordsworth's life story is routinely told through the lens of *The Prelude*, a poem conceived and written in the early 1800s. Because it appears to be autobiographical, it tends to be treated as if it were factually correct, and because it falsifies, omits, and elides, the effect has been to distort our understanding of him, particularly his early life. For example, his carefully placed account of youthful exhilaration at hearing of Robespierre's death, in *Prelude* Book X, has tended to encourage biographers and critics to suppress the thought that Wordsworth might have been one of Robespierre's supporters – which, of course, reflects the design of the mature poet, who is intent not on reporting the mess and randomness of life as it played out at the time, but on using it to create the idealized world of the poem.

A more glaring example would be that crisis in Wordsworth's early life which inspired his long pamphlet in defense of the French Revolution, entitled "A Letter to the Bishop of Llandaff . . . By a Republican." Wordsworth's "Letter" is untypical in numerous respects, not least its hostility toward a prominent figure in the Anglican church, Richard Watson, Bishop of Llandaff, who in the 1770s expressed sympathy for the American Revolution and became a respected liberal spokesman on issues of the day. He was one among many who, in the 1780s, welcomed the French Revolution but who, in early 1793, was so shocked by the execution of Louis XVI as to renounce all sympathy with it.

Louis was executed on January 21; within weeks, Llandaff reprinted a sermon which had first seen the light of day in 1785, adding to it an "Appendix" in which he publicly deplored Louis's death as "sanguinary, savage, more than brutal," before declaring:

I fly with terror and abhorrence, even from the altar of Liberty, when I see it stained with the blood of the aged, of the innocent, of the defenceless sex, of the ministers of religion, and of the faithful adherents of a fallen monarch. – My heart sinks within me, when I see it streaming with the blood of the monarch himself. – Merciful God! strike speedily, we beseech thee, with deep contrition, and sincere remorse, the obdurate hearts of the relentless perpetrators and projectors of these horrid deeds, left they should suddenly sink into eternal and extreme perdition, loaded with an unutterable weight of unrepented, and, except through the blood of Him whose religion they reject, inexpiable sin. (Watson, 1793, p. 19)

Watson was a respected figure, even among conservatives: he was not only a Bishop but a member of the House of Lords, hardly someone whose views could be discounted. That can only have made the appearance of these words the harshest of blows for those who wanted to see the end of monarchical rule and inequalities of property and class by which it was accompanied. One of them was the twenty-two-year-old Wordsworth. He had a huge investment in the revolution: a French girlfriend, Annette Vallon, who, at the time he returned to Britain in late 1792, was pregnant with their daughter. His intention in returning to London was to make what money he could from the two poems he had completed in France, and then use it as the means of taking care of his young family. But events intervened. Louis's execution led swiftly to the French declaration of war with Britain on February 1, 1793, and reciprocal British declaration on February 11, making further traffic between the two countries impossible.

Wordsworth's situation was already precarious. He was orphaned at the age of thirteen, though his guardians ensured he went to Cambridge University in the hope he would find a living as a curate. Not only did he leave without taking his degree, he went native in revolutionary France, getting involved with a woman who was also a Roman Catholic. Only ignorance of that can have encouraged his Uncle William Cookson, who happened also to be George III's personal chaplain, to offer Wordsworth a title for religious orders, and then, as late as early 1793, attempt to provide him with a situation as tutor to the son of Lord Belmore (see Reed, 1967, pp. 132–133; Selincourt, 1967, p. 103, Dorothy Wordsworth to Jane Pollard, July 10 and 12, 1793). When Cookson discovered his nephew's depredations, he broke off all contact with him, later complaining he was "a great supporter of French principles" (Farington, 1978–1998, p. 6:2303, entry for April 21, 1804).

To some extent our understanding of this passage in his life has to be speculative because, without reference to *The Prelude*, the evidence is partial. One of the most authentic glimpses of him comes from his sister, who told Thomas De Quincey that Wordsworth's London friends were particularly concerned for his state of mind: "Every night they played at cards with him, as the best mode of beguiling his sense of distress" (Lindop, 2000–2003, p. 19:392). It is an uncharacteristic image, but provides a glimpse of Wordsworth's increasingly fugitive state of mind in the first half of 1793.

Llandaff's pamphlet was welcomed by reviewers: the *European Magazine* for February 1793 declared that "no one deserves greater praise than the Bishop of Llandaff" (*European Magazine*, 1793, p. 111). Wordsworth may have seen its laudatory remarks on this man of "moderate sentiments," because the *European* was the periodical to which he had contributed his first published poem in 1786, and he is likely to have kept up with it. It was a touchstone for informed Whig opinion, and its praise of Llandaff told everyone that support for the French was no longer acceptable. That was the context in which Wordsworth found himself defending the Revolution in a long essay that quoted Llandaff's horrified condemnation of regicide, only to respond

What! have you so little knowledge of the nature of man as to be ignorant, that a time of revolution is not the season of true Liberty. Alas! the obstinacy & perversion of men is such that she is too often obliged to borrow the very arms of despotism to overthrow him, and in order to reign in peace must establish herself in violence. (Owen and Smyser, 1974, p. 1:33)

This is the poet who in later years would be known for his poems about the redemptive potential of flowers and trees; the importance of love between people; and the moral principles by which humanity should be guided. Yet here he justifies the use of violence in the name of revolution. Wordsworth echoed Thomas Paine, who justified bloodshed during the storming of the Bastille by asking: "When men are sore with the sense of oppressions, and menaced with the prospect of new ones, is the calmness of philosophy, or the palsy of insensibility, to be looked for?" (Paine, 1791, p. 35). But Wordsworth goes further. He is not merely dismissing the cultivated inertia of the revolution's many bourgeois supporters, such as Llandaff, but defending "the very arms of despotism" – a word carrying implications similar to "tyranny" and "dictatorship" in the twenty-first century. Wordsworth continues:

This apparent contradiction between the principles of liberty and the march of revolutions, this spirit of jealousy, of severity, of disquietude, of vexation, indispensable from a state of war between the oppressors and the oppressed, must of necessity confuse the ideas of morality and contract the benign exertion of the best affections of the human heart. Political virtues are developed at the expence of moral ones; and the sweet emotions of compassion, evidently dangerous where traitors are to be punished, are too often altogether smothered. But is this a sufficient reason to reprobate a convulsion from which is to spring a fairer order of things? (Owen and Smyser, 1974, p. 1:34)

That question is rhetorical because, so far as Wordsworth is concerned, the answer must be "no": the smothering of compassion is a fair price for such "virtues" as those sought by revolutionaries. Moral scruples would only obstruct the punishment of traitors. And the mention of "traitors" would have made any French reader think of one man: Louis XVI. For that was the tag most frequently attached to him after his abortive attempt to flee to the Franco-German border in June 1791, where he hoped to join the counterrevolutionary army. The implication of Wordsworth's comment is that it was right Louis be stopped before he reached the frontier, and that he be executed for his attempted betrayal. Indeed, he makes clear from the outset of his "Letter" that he regards Louis as deserving of the fate meted out to him. Ferocity of character, as Wordsworth terms it – in effect, the ruthlessness demanded of the regicide – is held to be a strength, not a weakness. This argument, as Quentin Bailey has noted, echoes sentiments uttered by Saint-Just and Robespierre in the 1792 National Convention, the principal actors with whom Wordsworth aligns himself (Bailey, 2011, p. 97). All of which raises the interesting possibility – underexplored by scholars – that at the moment Wordsworth wrote his response to Llandaff he was an unashamed apologist for Robespierre.[1] Not only that but when, in the "Letter," Wordsworth wrote that "The animal just released from its stall will exhaust the overflow of its spirits in a round of wanton vagaries, but it will soon return to itself and enjoy its freedom in moderate and regular delight" (Owen and Smyser, 1974, p. 1:38), he provided a defense for the Paris mob – the sans-culottes who continued to play a crucial role in the revolution.

One problem is that we do not know exactly when Wordsworth was writing – a factor that bears on interpretation. Llandaff's "Appendix" appeared on January 30, 1793,[2] so it must have been after that – but when? The early spring of 1793 was a period of intense turmoil in France, as Girondins and Montagnards battled for supremacy both within the National Convention and the provinces. Wordsworth's editors suggest he completed the "Letter" in February or March (Owen and Smyser, 1974, p. 1:20), and perhaps he did. But there is nothing to prove he did not write it as late as April or May, when he would have read in British newspapers about the radicalization of the Committee of Public Safety and adoption of Article 1 of France's new constitution

[1] David V. Erdman once speculated that Wordsworth wanted "to be . . . a successful Robespierre," a thought he declined to develop; see Erdman (1986, p. 216)

[2] I am indebted to Owen and Smyser's (1974, p. 1:19) useful introduction to the "Letter."

(sometimes described as the Jacobin constitution) by the National Assembly; the prosecution of Marat for sedition by the Paris Commune and his acquittal; and the march on the Convention of May 1. Perhaps, as he wrote the "Letter," he was aware of the purge of leading Girondins on June 2 – figures newly identified as traitors.[3] To someone who argued compassion should not be allowed to obstruct the enactment of admittedly "despotic" measures, all those developments might have seemed defensible. Wordsworth is usually associated with the moderate Girondins, but in defending regicide – and, possibly, their purging – he stood in opposition to their more moderate stance.[4] That in turn lends support to the notion that, at the moment he wrote the "Letter," Wordsworth occupied a position more extreme than he had done in France. And perhaps it makes sense that in a place alien, even hostile, to the Revolution, Wordsworth reacted by entrenching himself deeper in pro-revolutionary ideology than ever before. Regardless of his view of Robespierre, Wordsworth's "Letter" defends the Montagnards' right to use whatever violent means were necessary to consolidate revolutionary gains.

The dating of the "Letter" to some time after Wordsworth heard of the purge – say, the third week of June 1793 – would make its writing, and the sentiments within it, more inflammatory than they would have been in early March. My aim here is to understand the extent of his radicalization. The nature of the evidence makes it impossible to achieve this in any absolute sense, much relating to his time in France having been destroyed because it related to Wordsworth's parentage of Anne-Caroline Vallon – something he and his executors preferred to keep private.

That is a shame not least because his distinction as a protagonist in the pamphlet debate of 1793 stems from the personal context out of which the "Letter" was written. He had gone to Orléans in late November 1791, taken up residence in Blois in early 1792, and not returned to Britain until November or December – almost the last point at which it was possible for him to have made the journey home. He had mixed with those involved in the revolutionary struggle and perhaps helped them work toward their goals. He had known such thinkers and writers as Antoine-Joseph Gorsas (see Roe, 1988, pp. 40–41), spent time in the

---

[3] Reed (1967, p. 142) dates composition of the "Letter" to June "or shortly after."

[4] For Wordsworth and the Girondins, see most notably Reed (1967, p. 137) and Roe (1988, p. 43). James A. W. Heffernan has flirted with the idea that Wordsworth was more amenable to Robespierre's ideology than others have wanted to admit, though he does so through the distorting lens of *The Prelude*; see Heffernan (1992).

National Convention[5] and the Jacobin Club (see Reed, 1967, p. 125), and in later years described himself as "pretty hot" in the swiftly developing events that led to Louis's execution (Wu, 1993, p. 161). Among his associates may have been the young James Watt Jr., from Glasgow, who delivered a speech to the Jacobin Club, having been introduced to it by Robespierre; was described by his own father as "a violent Jacobin" (see Levere, 2007, p. 167), and denounced in the House of Commons by Edmund Burke.[6] Back in London, it must have been at first upsetting, then infuriating, for Wordsworth to find his countrymen full of antirevolutionary jingoism and alarmed by the specter of regicide (which inspired civil war in Britain more than a century before), at the very moment when, in his eyes, they should be rejoicing at the death of the French monarch, and contemplating the joyous possibility of bringing the Hanoverian succession to its long-overdue conclusion. Hardly anyone with the skills to respond to Llandaff had anything like that perspective; indeed, it must have seemed to him he was alone in understanding those who faced insurrection within their own land while powerful enemies gathered on their frontiers, as they grappled with the insuperable task of constructing a democratic form of government, something that had not previously existed anywhere in Europe.

Fathali Moghaddam has written persuasively about the stages by which individuals become radicalized in times of revolution, each characterized by certain psychological processes, his aim being to explain the conditions that produce terrorism. In applying those insights to the case of Wordsworth, one must exercise caution. Wordsworth was never guilty of any act we would now describe as terrorist, and Moghaddam bases his thesis on a largely contemporary analysis. But to an extent, it is possible to see aspects of Wordsworth in the portrait he paints. For one thing, Moghaddam argues that the perception of injustice initiates radicalization of the individual psyche.[7] Wordsworth's denunciation not only of the ancien régime but of the institution of monarchy more generally is based on that perception: "there was not a citizen on the tenth of august who, if he could have dragged before the eyes of Louis the corpse of one of his murdered brothers, might not have exclaimed to him, Tyran, voilà ton ouvrage" (Owen and Smyser, 1974, p. 1:32), he

---

[5] See William Wordsworth to Richard Wordsworth, December 19, 1791, in Shaver (1967, p. 71).

[6] Reed (1967, p. 125) uses the word "possibly" when reporting this, and Roe (1998, pp. 44–45) helpfully assesses the evidence. For Burke's denunciation, see Muirhead (1858, pp. 492–493).

[7] I refer here to Moghaddam (2005, pp. 161–169). Moghaddam's thesis is applied in Moghaddam et al. (2016, Chapter 19).

writes in the "Letter." Wordsworth is recalling the attack on the Tuileries of August 10, 1792, in which four hundred citizens lost their lives, and quotes the words of Grégoire, Bishop of Blois (who Wordsworth knew[8]), delivered to the National Convention on November 15 – which Wordsworth probably witnessed (see Roe, 1988, pp. 66–67). Grégoire blamed the king for the slaughter of more than four hundred people, so justifying Louis's execution. Wordsworth's "Letter" does not stop there. It contains its author's "grand objection to monarchy" (that "The office of king is a trial to which human virtue is not equal") before going on to deplore "arbitrary distinctions" such as "stars, ribbands, and garters, and other badges of fictitious superiority" (Owen and Smyser, 1974, pp. 1:41, 44) – in short, the entire system by which British society functioned.

The next stage in Moghaddam's analysis concerns the individual's perception of the various options for fighting unfairness. In selecting the medium of the written word, Wordsworth placed himself at risk. He would have known of the royal proclamation against seditious writings passed by Pitt's government in May 1792, which called on magistrates to prosecute authors, publishers, and distributors, and which precipitated Thomas Paine's departure for revolutionary France in September. He would also have been aware that publisher Richard Phillips was prosecuted for publishing *The Rights of Man* in January 1793 and sentenced to eighteen months in prison. That was a terrible warning, but it tells us that Wordsworth may have felt he no longer had anything left to lose and regarded the written word as his ultimate court of appeal. If so, it underlines the desperation of his perceived position.

Moghaddam points out that radicalization is fostered when injustice is compounded by the failure of society to provide "solutions to . . . unjust treatment" (Moghaddam, 2005, p. 163). That serves to remind us of the connection between the "Letter" and Wordsworth's personal situation. He was trapped in his native land against his will, prevented from joining his young French family, and had no course open besides composition of an essay designed to reveal to enlightened Whigs the necessity of regicide. That, as much as anything, illustrates the extent to which, for Wordsworth, his personal tragedy was entwined with the rapidly evolving political situation.

In early July the oldest of his friends took him on a walking tour – again, one assumes, as a means of distracting him from the distress which threatened to overwhelm him. They traveled to the Isle of Wight where,

---

[8] Roe outlines the argument that Grégoire was an influence on Wordsworth; see Roe (1988, 66ff.).

for a month, Wordsworth watched the "anchored Vessels" of the British fleet preparing to fight the French. Inspired by that sight, he composed his first poem in months, which began as a description of the landscape before turning to more pressing concerns:

> But hark from yon proud fleet in peal profound
> Thunders the sunset cannon; at the sound
> The star of life appears to set in blood
> Old ocean shudders in offended mood
> Deepening with moral gloom his angry flood.[9]

The sun sets "in blood," a harbinger of carnage; the ocean "shudders" with horror; while the cannon thundering from the heart of the fleet sound like the "peal" of a bell that tolls for those who are about to die.

It is a vision of apocalypse, a correlative of the emotional turmoil he was now feeling, which even elements such as the sun and ocean are powerless to prevent. Nothing more conclusively reveals how far he had moved beyond the point at which he could have conceived the "Letter." That document retains a vestigial hope in his ability to persuade readers of the justice of the republican cause. But the visionary of the Isle of Wight had moved beyond that: he accepts the inevitability of war and its consequences. Perhaps he was aware of the restructuring of the Committee of Public Safety, the body that would rule France during the Terror, and collapse of the Girondin faction – events that would have made a shrewd reader of current events realize the revolution was drifting beyond the point at which it was possible to defend it.

Wordsworth was not a terrorist, but his situation during the first half of 1793 has echoes in that described by Moghaddam. Moghaddam's thesis is that the path from extremism to terrorism is one of a progressive narrowing down of possibilities: he uses "the metaphor of a narrowing staircase leading to the terrorist act at the top of a building" (Moghaddam, 2005, p. 161). That sense of possibilities having been gradually shut down, leaving little option but to become more extreme, more radical, and more reckless is the dominant impression produced by a study of the state of mind that led to the "Letter." Isolation, frustration, growing anger, and the pain of separation from his young family in France were the elements by which Wordsworth was radicalized. Depending on when exactly it was written, there are grounds for thinking it may have been designed as the vehicle for a defense of the Jacobins, even the sans-culottes.

---

[9] The transcription is mine; see Wu (2002, p. 87). See also Landon and Curtis (1997, pp. 743–744).

Though he never published it, Wordsworth did not destroy it, even if in later years he had no wish to show it to anyone. More extreme than Paine's *Rights of Man*, particularly in its denunciation of the British class system, the "Letter," had it been published, would have made him an enemy of the state, and ruined his life as well as that of anyone who helped print, publish, and distribute it. Few years had to pass before he understood how well-advised was its withholding, and that must in turn have instilled in him a caution that fostered the distrust of revolution, skepticism of the republican ideology of which he was once such a fierce exponent, and – ultimately – the decided (if eccentric) conservatism by which he was known to Byron, Keats, Shelley, and Hazlitt. It was a curious outcome for someone who, at one stage, had been so radicalized as to argue for the application of despotic measures in support of the revolution – not something he wished either his contemporaries, or posterity, to know about, which was why, when writing *The Prelude*, he omitted it.

REFERENCES

Bailey, Q. (2011). *Wordsworth's Vagrants: Police, Prisons, and Poetry in the 1790s.* Farnham, UK: Ashgate.

de Selincourt, E. (Ed.) (1967). *The Letters of William and Dorothy Wordsworth: The Early Years 1787–1800.* Rev ed. Oxford: Clarendon Press.

European Magazine (1793). Review of Richard Watson, Bishop of Llandaff, a sermon preached before the Stewards of the Westminster Dispensary. February, 111–113.

Farington, J. (1978–1998). *The Diary of Joseph Farington* (K. Garlick, A. Macintyre, and K. Cave, Eds.). 17 vols. New Haven, CT: Yale University Press.

Heffernan, J. A. W. (1992). History and autobiography: The French Revolution in Wordsworth's *Prelude*. In J. A. W. Heffernan (Ed.), *Representing the French Revolution: Literature, Historiography and Art* (pp. 41–62). Hanover, NH: University Press of New England.

Landon, C., and Curtis, J. (1997). *William Wordsworth: Early Poems and Fragments, 1785–1797.* Ithaca, NY: Cornell University Press.

Levere, T. (2007). Dr Thomas Beddoes (1760–1808): Chemistry, medicine, and books in the French and chemical revolutions. In L. M. Principe (Ed.), *New Narratives in Eighteenth-Century Chemistry*, pp. 157–176. Dordrecht, Netherlands: Springer.

Lindop, G. (Ed.) (2000–2003). *The Works of Thomas de Quincey.* London: Pickering and Chatto.

Moghaddam, F. M. (2005). The staircase to terrorism: A psychological exploration. *American Psychologist*, February–March, 161–169.

Moghaddam, F. M., et al. (2016). Globalization and terrorism: The primacy of collective processes. In A. G. Miller (Ed.), *The Social Psychology of Good and Evil*, 2nd ed. (pp. 415–440). New York: Guilford Press.

Muirhead, J. P. (1858). *The Life of James Watt.* London: John Murray.

Owen, W. J. B., and Smyser, J. W. (Eds.) (1974). *The Prose Works of William Wordsworth*. 3 vols. Oxford: Clarendon Press.

Paine, T. (1791). *The Rights of Man*. 6th ed. London: J. S. Jordan.

Reed, M. L. (1967). *Wordsworth: The Chronology of the Early Years, 1770–1799*. Cambridge, MA: Harvard University Press.

Roe, N. (1988). *Wordsworth and Coleridge: The Radical Years*. Oxford: Clarendon Press.

Watson, R. (1793). *A Sermon Preached before the Stewards of the Westminster Dispensary*. 2nd ed. London: Cadell and Evans.

Wu, D. (1993). *Wordsworth's Reading 1770–1799*. Cambridge: Cambridge University Press.

(2002). *Wordsworth: An Inner Life*. Oxford: Blackwell.

10   Between the Guillotine and the Velvet Revolution
What Is at Stake?

Jaan Valsiner*

At stake are human lives. Revolutions – like wars – are acts of devastation. Such devastation is enthusiastic – for the actors who take the side of the revolution. They hope to build something new – a Paradise, a "new society," communism, or "democracy." They feel they have all the right to topple the old regimes for the sake of the future. And then – once they find out that they have been moved from an old regime to a new one – they are justifiably disappointed (Moghaddam, Chapter 7). Dreams are crushed. The new regime may look similar to the old one – or be even worse.

For the others – opponents of revolutions, or neutral bystanders, and anybody else – that enthusiasm is inherently disruptive. It is a form of violence for no reason, a kind of rape. At the least they are brought out of their previous social roles within a society and forced to alter their conduct – with, or without, altering their belief systems. They face variable fates. They may be executed, imprisoned, or expelled as "enemies of the revolution" or they somehow survive. In this context, the values of human beings are reduced to their presumed social roles and ideological commitments. Humanity ends where ideologies rage, and the axes of revolutions begin to hit. The behavioristic credo (Campbell and Moghaddam, Chapter 6) of the revolutionary justice systems leaves only few options for survival – accept, or go – to exile, into underground, or to the gallows. Revolutions polarize the relations between human beings.

Revolution is a social turmoil – the societal equivalent of an earthquake or tsunami in the geological world. Yet the terms used tor its descriptions seem to be graded in implicit affective valuation: "revolution" (positive), "revolt" (ambivalent), "uprising" (also ambivalent), "insurgency" (negative), "takeover of power" (negative), and "act of terrorism" (very negative). All of these labels refer to one or another relation that the label-user puts onto the societal upheaval.

* I am indebted to *Danske Grundforskningsfond* for continuous support of the Niels Bohr Professorship Centre in Aalborg that has made the writing of this text possible.

169

The only one of these labels that guides the listener toward a positive affective relation to the happening is that of "revolution." The social events in France between 1789 and 1799[1] – filled with devastation, terror, and reconstruction effort that at times took ridiculous forms – is still somewhat romantically viewed in positive terms and treated as the *Revolution* that brought the values of liberty, equality, and fraternity to the European social consciousness for the time to follow. Revolutions after it are compared with this "mother of revolutions" – even from the side of their opponents. The "Bolshevik Revolution" in Russia can easily be viewed in romantic (even if dismissive) ways that overlooks the "acts of terrorism" ("the Red Terror," "the White Terror") that it included. The purpose sanctifies the means – as Ignatius Loyola famously suggested – so that the killing of people in the hope of building a communist society for all that remain (and stay loyal) is satisfied. No surprise that revolutions are large-scale behavioristic experiments (Campbell and Moghaddam, Chapter 6). To move from such experiments to societies of new – democratic – characteristics may be similar to the scenario where Burrhus Skinner would be elected to the position of the former doves in the "Skinner Box" and become involved in active pecking, while the previously busy pigeons now would assume the democratically elected "leadership role" in conducting experiments on that *Homo sapiens* learning to peck in right ways to be remunerated by chicken wings, or even maybe be given a hamburger for his success. Democratic societies involve such peaceful transformations – but behavioristic experimenters with such societies are unlikely to give up their positions in control.

Waiting for Democracy Is Like Waiting for Godot

Samuel Beckett was probably a better psychologist than most of the formally certified specialists all over the world. His play – *Waiting for Godot* – has become a classic in European theater since World War II. In it, two persons are involved in a colorful but beautifully useless dialogue about their waiting for a mysterious third (referred to as "Godot") who, of course, fails to arrive. The play is one in which nothing happens, but yet keeps audiences glued to their seats. Such image of waiting for something ephemeral fits much of Occidental social dialogues about democracy that is about to arrive if only the conditions were favorable.

---

[1] When Napoleon Bonaparte "*took power*" (i.e., we do not think that he *made another* "revolution"). Likewise, most of us would feel ill at ease if the 1933 Nazi "takeover" of the German political system were to be presented as "national-socialist *revolution*." The inherent affective quality of the label "revolution" – in contrast with "uprising" or "revolt" remains tied to the ideological position of the evaluator.

The audience – and here we can think first of all the television audience watching discussions the soon to arrive democracy in a troubled country of "the others" – is equally captured by the idea that "it must come." If a revolution happens in a country outside of the cultural historical sphere of such waiting discourses, or if the efforts of these countries are made to produce democracy by eliminating current "autocratic" leaders, it is not the democracy but a new form of autocracy that re-emerges.

Moghaddam (Chapter 7) gives us a rich personal account about the realities in Iran at the time of the 1979 revolution. What is surprising in this account is the sincere hope – by many – that democracy would come naturally if only the dictator is removed. The inherent ideal status of democratic governance is assumed – it is the "natural order" that has been violated by "dictatorial takeovers" that, if gone, would be restored or naturally develop into, a democratic form of governance. This is most certainly not the case[2] – the ways of "being democratic" require very special ways for human beings *to be in their worlds*. As Moghaddam points out,

"Open and free discussion" can only take place when the individuals in the discussion have the necessary cognitive and social skills to participate in and support such discussion. It is not enough to smash down the security system and laws that restrict free speech; it is also necessary to develop a citizenry that has the skills to constructively take part in speaking freely.

It is interesting to consider the varied contexts of "open and free" discussions. Personal characteristics and personal will to be open does not guarantee democracy – it requires a similar stand from others, and a social normative setting that supports it. Public encounters are always framed by the particular social-political atmospheres of the wider society which set up border zones for the acceptable "free exchanges" between interlocutors. In the context of a democratic society such discussion about the "benefits of autocracy" would be unappreciated. On the opposite side – in autocratic societies – any "free discussion" of democracy can be suspect or outright dangerous for the discussants. Furthermore, such "quasi-free" forms of "discussions" are also negotiated arenas for granting the popular support for autocratic societies.

Different psychological know-how may fit different societal systems. Campbell and Moghaddam (Chapter 6) have outlined the "behavior management" nature of the buildup of the Soviet empire from above.

---

[2] As many removals of dictator-like leaders – Josip Broz Tito, Muammar Gaddafi, Saddam Hussein, and others – show. The realistic result of such elimination of dictators is fragmentation of society, emergence of local self-governing and border-controlling systems, and restoration of an autocratic form of governance in some format.

The behavioral control ideas had circulated between Russia and North America. The general credo was borrowed from Russian physiology, only to be re-imported in Russia under its new disguise of "behavioral science," at the times when the postrevolutionary free (but poor) society was moving toward a new version of autocracy dominated by Joseph Stalin. Yet they overlook the co-presence of "top down" mechanisms and peer mechanisms in supporting the autocratic social systems. The two systems are set up to work together by providing incentives for the peers in getting them small competitive privileges ahead of others, thus fortifying the top-to-down social control hierarchy. Such unity of top-to-down (vertical) and peer-to-peer (horizontal) power negotiation channels were the main mechanism to eliminate the possible transition into democracy in the history of Russia. At the time of the Soviet Union, it was exemplified in the late 1920s and early 1930s in the process of establishing the "Stalinist control" over the society. This happened largely through the guidance of actions in the horizontal channel, evident in the various "public discussions" of the value of different theoretical perspectives in psychology and philosophy. All these took a similar form – administrative decisions of reorganizing an institution (e.g., Institute of Psychology in Moscow), followed by giving the power to develop a "new kind" of science to young peer groups, which then entered into competition with one another for gaining privileges from the state. The ideological leadership only needed to privilege one of the fighting cliques over others at their political convenience. Thus, in general,

> The alignment of the content material used in the "horizontal" channel with that in the "vertical" one, by scientists' own initiative, was building on the rich traditions in Russian history of *defining freedom of action by individuals as their obligation to act in the expected manner, as defined by the state.* (Valsiner, 1988, p. 90, emphasis added)

Here, historically, "rights" were "duties" – and the latter were set by the rulers and consensually accepted by the ruled. There is something to learned about the mechanisms of restoration of autocratic systems after the chance for democracy is vanishing – through the activities of the (seemingly) "free" discussions of peers who set their competitive goals, looking for the blessings of the authorities. It seems that most revolutions entail a similar structure of "popular endorsement" of the newly emerging autocracies.

Thus, the establishment of democracy is a very fragile enterprise that not only depends on the personological roots ("democratic personality") but is constructed by the politically acting persons in line with their current political interests. Hence a "democratic leader" can under some circumstances become a totalitarian dictator, or vice versa. A person who has spent his or her life making deals in the business world would easily turn one's leadership role into a dictatorship, while a king who inherits absolute power can under appropriate circumstances become a democratic leader of his own country.[3]

Personal Plasticity and Its Political Framings

Personal characteristics of democratic conduct are the cornerstones for political plasticity. The "wheel of 10 commandments" (Moghaddam, Chapter 7) is interesting in its charting out the basic parameters for political plasticity. These demands are similarly applicable on the societal and personal levels. As Moghaddam elaborates upon the system that is given in the form of a "wheel,"

the first three psychological characteristics concern critical self-reflection ("I could be wrong," "I must critically question everything, including the sacred beliefs of my society," "I must revise my opinions, as the evidence requires"). The next three goals concern change through openness to others ("I must seek to better understand those who are different from me," "I can learn from those who are different from me," "I must seek information and opinions from as many sources as possible"). The next two are about change through new experiences, created both for oneself and for others ("I should be actively open to new experiences" and "I should be open to creating new experiences for others"). Of course, the danger arising from the first eight goals is that the individual falls into a relativistic mindset and comes to believe that all values are equal. The final two goals are designed to avoid such a relativistic outcome, because they are goals based on the idea that there are absolute principles of right and wrong ("there are principles of right and wrong" and "not all experiences are of equal value").

Combining Absolute Principles

There is an interesting suborganization within the "wheel" – two out of ten statements are generically ontological (X = "There are principles of right and wrong" and Y = "not all experiences are of equal value"). The combination of these two gives us a realistic texture of flexible inequalities in the world of normativity. For instance:

1 "Principle X is RIGHT but it is not equal to the supremacy of Principle Y (that is NOT RIGHT)" → this combination leads to the ideologically based effort toward righteousness by a person or group of persons under conditions of the political dominance of Principle Y.

[3] Simeon II – born 1937 – was King of Bulgaria as child of six to nine years of age and was elected to serve as prime minister from 2001 to 2005.

The activities if the Greenpeace as an organization may serve as a concrete example here in their organization of protest actions that cross the lines of local legalities in order to catch media attention to promote the right principles.

2 "Principle X is WRONG (i.e., there are only right principles) and it is dominant over Principle Y that is RIGHT" → The communist or wahhabist principles of social organization dominate over the principles of "basic human rights" – or, with Orwellian twist – "all animals are equal but the ones who belong to the Party are more equal than others – *because they are right.*"

3 "Principle X is WRONG and Principle Y is WRONG": complete anarchy where nothing is right or wrong and all experiences are of equal value. This may be approximated by a hippie lifestyle.

4 "Principle X is RIGHT and Principle Y is RIGHT" leads to a society where individual experiences become evaluated as to their being right or wrong. The Inquisition explored the presence of demons (the wrong) in the nightmares of the persons who report illegitimate sexual encounters in their dreams.

Note that in this extension of the two ontological principles – combining then in a usual 2 × 2 fashion, none of the combinations provide us with a via regia into a democratic for of social organization. The "anarchistic solution" (number 3) seems closest – but it lacks structure. Other three have structure – but they do not fit the ideals of democratic governance of a society

Foundations for Democratic Conduct

There needs to be a personal counterpart to the normative organizational system of a society. This is reflected in Moghaddam's "wheel" on the form of the other eight components of the "wheel" are directly *personally normative*, taking the form of "I must" or "I should," "I could" or "I can":

> I could be wrong
> I can learn from those who are different from me
> I must critically question everything, including the sacred beliefs of my society
> I must revise my opinion as the evidence requires
> I must seek to understand those who are different from me
> I must seek information and opinions from as many sources as possible
> I should be actively open to new experiences
> I should be open to creating new experiences for others

Would following the last eight suggestions guarantee that a person would act in ways called "democratic"? Certainly such person will be highly flexible in one's ways of being and considerate of others' perspective. But would that flexibility lead to assuming of a democratic orientation in relation to others in interpersonal encounters? My answer to this question is no. The eight suggestions are necessary, but not sufficient, conditions for a person to begin to feel into the world through a democratic mindset.

The missing sufficient condition is goals-oriented feeling into the Other, and respect for the Other's difference from the Self. The democratic ways of personal being start from the basic Self<>Other relationships, linking *Einfühlung* – feeling into the Other and through that – into oneself, with the meaning of the unconditional acceptance of the Other as an equal fellow human being – even under the conditions of social power role difference, or even in the case of complete disagreement in the particular matter of the difference. This is a very tough criterion – accepting the Other as respectable and autonomous agent – despite principal disagreement. Yet this would be the necessary and sufficient condition for the democratic way of social action.

Any society operating on principles of democracy can build only on the majority of the persons in it adopting this democratic conduct base. This implied in the very notion of democratic transfer of social power, where one gives into election results that can bring an opposition party to power and the current governing one into opposition, without animosity and protests or violent refusal to give up power.[4] Eventually this may lead to the collective action of political plasticity that would – by electoral consensus rather than bureaucratic rules – transform an autocratic governance structure into a democratic one. In other words how would the position of the Supreme Leader be not only transformable from a single person to a group of persons, but to the *whole set of citizens* in a given country or *polis*?[5] And as a corollary what are the limiting factors against the diffusion of such collective leadership role to all citizens? In whose interest is it that such sharing of the symbolic – also translated

---

[4] In our recent political arena of discourses we encounter – with increasing frequency – the protests by the losing sides of elections of "vote rigging" by the winning side. Such accusations – phrased in the language of maintaining fairness and legality of the power transfer- are actually border zones of the range of democratic social change. The next stage of the end of democracy would be the case where the loser in election refuses to give up the previous power role. Yahyah Ammeh's case in Gambia in 2017 is an extreme example.

[5] It is worth reminding ourselves that the models of Ancient Greek democracies involved only the participation of citizens of the given *polis*, which were otherwise slaveholding societies.

into material – power with all legitimate participants would *not* happen? The answer may be in the following of the always present "rules and instructions" – an interesting set of commodities that are produced by the anonymous factory we label "bureaucracy."

Bureaucracy and Democracy

Any society is an administrative enterprise and thus includes a special category of workers who inhabit the bureaus of the administrative institutions, bureaucrats. They are little people with much power, encoded into the myriad of formal rules. They are the gatekeepers of regulations and forms that ordinary citizens have to fill in to survive in the society. Moghaddam (Chapter 7) emphasizes the need to understand their ways of functioning:

> I believe the role of bureaucracy in limiting progress toward democracy has been underestimated. This is particularly the case after revolutions, when bureaucracy tends to act as an anchor, remaining out of sight beneath the water surface, while at the same time serving to prevent movement. This "stabilizing" role has been easier to hide because bureaucracy is supposed to be politically neutral.

He is right on target – any political system, from the most autocratic to the "most" democratic, give rise to some system of middlemen (and middlewomen) in the form of government bureaucracies. These are at times nicely labeled as *civil servants*, although the notion of "civil" here may be seriously doubted by any outsider, who trying to enter the given country and is faced with visa acquisition processes. (Adichie, 2009).

Bureaucracy is a local form of autocracy that camouflages itself as a "service" to any form of governance. As such it successfully survives any kind of regime change. Even after revolutions it becomes reconstituted in some form. Its versatility of survival is linked with its organizational promises for any political governance organization. It is their role to set up order for ordinary living in local places, along the lines of governmental guidelines.

Political Plasticity as a Result of *Gegenstand*

Moghaddam's (Chapter 7) political plasticity concept might be the first theoretical framework in our contemporary social sciences that has a chance of making sense of both the successes (which are rare) and failures (which dominate histories of revolutions) of efforts to transform autocratic political systems into new forms of governance – mostly different forms of democracies. All these efforts are characterized by

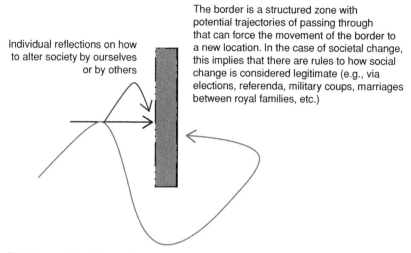

Individual reflections on how to alter society by ourselves or by others

The border is a structured zone with potential trajectories of passing through that can force the movement of the border to a new location. In the case of societal change, this implies that there are rules to how social change is considered legitimate (e.g., via elections, referenda, military coups, marriages between royal families, etc.)

The history of the given society sets up expectations that the border zone is a structure of constraints that include potential conditions for its transformations, like "is a military coup possible in this country, given its history?" The person who acts for societal change internalizes these, and relates to these, accepting, ignoring, counteracting or in another way

Figure 10.1 Triple *Gegenstand*: Societal change in action, reflection, and imagination

relating with resisting forces (Chaudhary et al., 2017) that take the general form of a *Gegenstand* (Figure 10.1).

The notion of *Gegenstand* – brought back from the historical dustbin of philosophy – allows us to simultaneously consider a phenomenon as structured and as that structure is in the process of being transformed. The *Gegenstand* is a system of potential transformation – the border in its center may – but need not – be moved to another location, passed through, or around. All this happens with the unity of three processes – a *force vector* (oriented toward the border), the *counterforce vector* (maintaining the border in its place), and the *reflection vector* (reflecting upon the encounter of the forces on the border). The particular state of the phenomena is a resultant of the interplay of these three vectors. Social action by a person is oriented toward a border maintained by some counterforces to that action. The person's reflection about the feasibility and dangers of the action may lead him or her into various outcomes of the action itself – from martyrdom for an idea to the triumph of the given utopia. Revolutionaries may perish – or succeed – yet the Gegenstand structure remains as the organizing framework for potential new action.

Some reflections upon the *Gegenstand* structure are excluded from the outset. Any decision of political participation in efforts of societal change involves the history of precedents for such change. If that history entails transfers of power via electoral democracy that trajectory of changing society may predominate. For example, when I used to ask my American students whether they have ever thought of the *possibility* that power in Washington, DC, might be transferred through a military coup the universal and resolute answer has been "no!" The first (and only) military takeover of power in North America was the American Revolution in the eighteenth century. In contrast, over the same two centuries such changes in power have been recurrent in Central and South American countries. Usually the military regimes later transfer power peacefully to some civilian administration, which is followed by some other military takeover at a later time.

Sometimes political leaders who start from military takeovers end up being elected to power by electoral vote.[6] Such cases illustrate the possibility of social power transformation within the same society in multiple forms. Still – whichever form is being put into action – there is always some person (or persons) who take (or are given) the leadership role in it. In this personification of social transformations, Napoleon Buonaparte, Vladimir Lenin, Adolf Hitler, Mahatma Gandhi, Václav Havel, and the Supreme Leader all play similar roles. They serve as personal links between social ideologies and personal value systems That link becomes projected into the given society at the given time of transformation. The specifics of such projections are not substitutable with one another. Imagine Mahatma Gandhi becoming the Supreme Leader in Iran in the 1980s, or Napoleon taking a nonviolent action path in France in 1799. Yet all versions of personal leadership roles are located on the "equifinality zone" (Sato et al., 2016) of a society undergoing a major social transformation. Political plasticity has personal grounding.

Returning to Figure 10.1, we can observe such personal grounding in two locations. First, the personal life course history of any person living in a society ("amphibian" or "autocratic" or "democratic," or any other kind) at some time becomes loosely connected with the realm of possibilities that are considered as options for social change. The cultural history of the given society is presented in history textbooks – what is on one side

---

[6] Hugo Chavez (1954–2013) in Venezuela is a good example here. He founded Movimiento Bolivariano Revolucionario 200 – a clandestine revolutionary group – in 1982. It planned and carried out a military takeover effort in 1992 – that failed, and Chavez was imprisoned. After getting out from the prison he founded a new party in 1997 and was elected president in 2000.

of the Atlantic Ocean presented as "discovery" (of the Americas) is presentable as "occupation" on the other (Carretero, 2011). Political street demonstrations with confrontations with the guardians of power may be a natural pastime in some society, and a great aberration of the social order within the personal feelings of people in another.

Secondly, the personal reflection upon "my own relation with the revolution" (or societal transformation in general) are crucial for social participation in its different forms. The transformation of a hobby into opening of a new business is a personally courageous step (the business may thrive, but equally likely could end up in bankruptcy) of personal consequences.

The Normative Background of Political Plasticity

Political plasticity is well situated in the history of ideas of the social sciences. Moghaddam's seven rules that elaborate political plasticity are based on the traditions of John Dewey (the notion of embeddedness in Rules 6 and 7), Gestalt psychology (of the Ehrenfels tradition – Rules 2 and 5), organismic systems theory (Rules 1–4). The result is a dynamic scheme that allows one to look at the various interconnected levels of social organization of the life course changes under revolution. Thus, the different transformation of hobbies into businesses in the Czech "Velvet Revolution" (Zittoun, Chapter 8) and Wordsworth's passionate defense of his French connections (Wu, Chapter 9) involve the meeting places of new opportunities that revolutions provide and personal strivings. The critical moment in the system is the heterogeneity of the plasticity between the levels of society, social groups, and individuals.

At the personal level, the moves into democracies are not easy to live with. While on the one hand a move from a totalitarian state to a democratic brings with it much awaited opportunities, for some persons it also brings a responsibility to find one's own place under conditions of societal uncertainty. A Hungarian adolescent Attila told his story of deep disinterest in the new democratic political system in Hungary, failing to find ways to trust its declared positive social agenda (Valsiner, 1997). On the opposite side, William Wordsworth attacked his English countrymen for failing to see the deep poetry of revolution (Wu, Chapter 9). Social changes are personally felt through – often with a result of passionate making of ideological oppositions. For many in a "democratic society" it is that – or any other – form of a society that is a "problem." This may be the case for different religious "out groups" (such as early Christianity in the Roman Empire in the fourth century AD), or of emerging political opposition groups that aspire the takeover of political power.

Escalations from Revolutions: From Hobbies to Businesses, Including "Terrorism"

Ordinary human beings need to survive any societal turmoil – and they do. Revolutions transform the semiospheres of the societies, leading to new cultural codes. Yet these codes are, as Zittoun (Chapter 8) points out, constructed by persons who transform their personal activities into one or another societal and economic form. Moving away from the "amphibian society," where human beings participate in political life through tactics of re-direction of interests, imitation of loyalties, and conversions to follow the ruling ideologies, to a "pond" of market-driven social actions is a complicated transition. Some make it productively – the hobbies developed in the "amphibian phase" of the Czech society set the stage for readiness for the "pond." Others – such as elder persons whose life courses had become bounded to the old times – are left with retrospective nostalgias.

Personal externalizations of values – taken into actions under conditions of revolutions – are heterogeneous. Revolutions allow for externalizations of personal credos – ranging from indiscriminate violence of revolutionary "guards" to heightened creativity of artists during revolutionary times. *Both* construction and destruction processes are unleashed from their confines of social normativity at the times of revolutionary upheavals. Such upheavals can be seen as heterotopias – "other places" – in the sense of Michel Foucault (1998). A place becomes "other" to its neighboring place once the latter's normative structure is broken in an act of standing against it (*Gegenstand*) so that it moves or breaks. A period of revolutions is a temporal heterotopia, of a society in movement from the previous shores to new imaginary ones – be those of communism, capitalism, or a religiously overwhelmed society. The revolutionaries are adventurers and pirates on a kind of social vessel. In Foucault's terms,

The sailing vessel is the heterotopia par excellence. In civilizations without ships the dreams dry up, espionage takes the place of adventure, and the police that of the corsairs. (p. 185)

And police most usually indeed takes over once the society reaches a safe haven of prosperity. Totalitarian systems of governance have been the rule rather than exception worldwide, and continue to be so in contemporary large corporations. Personal adaptations to their demand conditions are inevitably variable. The Gegenstand structure of a totalitarian society is a fruitful breeding ground for a variety of constructive adaptations that may render the person nonparticipation in the political life of society, yet let them construct personally meaningful and socially active lifestyles in biergartens, pubs, bordellos, *dachas*, and family gatherings. It is that side of personal relating with the revolutions that needs careful study:

> Our proposal is to pay attention to the possible discrepancies between people (or subgroups) and the general cultural guidance – values, promoted actions, etc. We also considered people's engagements and imagination as core psychological needs. The question thus becomes, is a given societal environment offering people the possibility to freely develop their life trajectories according to their engagements, and space for develop imagination in such a way that it enriches life in society? If not, a disruption can progressively develop, which is likely to create a space for change. How this change takes place then becomes politics, and history. (Zittoun, Chapter 8)

The space for change is a clandestine preparation for moving ahead under the conditions of society-in-change. Some personal hobbies become economic enterprises under new conditions. Other new hobbies develop – as the case of self-initiated terrorist acts show. One young man cooks a dinner in his kitchen to satisfy his girlfriend – and another prepares a bomb to be taken to public places (where – as he thinks – the "infidels" gather) to blow them up, often together with the creator of such device. Acts of terror for the public are planned first in private and often require a goals-oriented personal value construction that involves giving up one's life. This act of constructive self-destruction cannot be explained by any behavioral training schedules (Campbell and Moghaddam, Chapter 6) and requires a frame of reference that is largely absent in contemporary social sciences – the focus on how imagined futures guide actions toward the future. The history of humankind is filled with examples of self-sacrifice for the future of somebody else – ranging from organ donors to assassins and *kamikaze* pilots. Our contemporary recurrent acts of terrorism are not innovations of twenty-first-century political systems.

What Makes Terrorism Possible – and Effective – in Society?

Terrorism needs to be viewed from a business standpoint. Its destructive acts are signs – indexical signs (the fact of destruction here and now is a sign of impact) that become symbolic (in the context of value attached to it). As such, terror acts are events of creation of social capital in our era of media dominance. When in the premedia era of autocratic political systems it was the role of assassins to attempt to implement social change, in our times that function is taken over by suicide bombers blowing themselves up in places of maximum possible devastation of the lives

of ordinary persons, who have no direct links with the supposed "problems" in the society against which the bombers claim to fight. We can
consider the emergence of the social role of suicide bombers as a result
of the democratization of the role of assassins.

Terrorism is a media event. Its societal functions are made possible by
the dramatic reporting of terrorist acts by the mass media, linked with
the feelings of horror in the psychological worlds of ordinary human
beings who depend upon the media and are utilized by them for the
benefit of their own symbolic role in society.[7] There is a simple – yet
impossible – solution. The social power of terrorist acts would vanish if
the media stopped paying attention to them. The power of terrorists is
not in the act of killing but in the act of reporting it – to the terrified
TV audiences and blog-participants. We are all de facto accomplices of
the terrorist acts by failing to neutralize the obviously deeply emotionally
disturbing outcomes of their destructive acts.

Of course there is the issue of agency – terrorism needs actors – and
the actors need to glorify their killing of other, and of themselves. Becoming involved in preparing a terrorist act can be therefore compared to
becoming involved in a hobby – only one with fatal outcomes. This goes
beyond the construction of thrills and adventures (Lightfoot, 1997) as it
involves personal life philosophies of the highest existential order – that
of life and death of the agent him or herself.

Terror events as public signs have also been organized from the other
side – that of the holders of political power – in the form of public executions. The widespread social practices of beheadings, quarterings, and
burning alive the opponents of the power holders in history can be seen
as similarly goals-oriented uses of the symbolic power of terror for social
purposes. It is one task to get rid of one's opponents by killing them, but
doing this in dramatic ways in front of public has different functions in

---

[7] I am writing this precisely next day after the Westminister Bridge terror act in London
(March, 22, 2017) where a man in a car crushed a number of ordinary people walking
on the bridge, and then proceeded to kill an unarmed policeman with a knife, before
being shot dead by security guards. The important feature of this (and most other) acts
of such kind is their recurrent representation by the media in all versions of horrifying
details- eyewitness accounts, official declarations of sympathy, reporting vigils, etc. All
these reports – while obviously giving information about what happened – operate as
feed-forward signs for further promotion of the feelings of fear and apprehension – precisely what the attackers and their sponsors plan to have. An effective solution would
be to limit the news reports to two occasions – reporting precisely what happened, and
results (later) of the expert analysis of why it happened. That would undermine the goals
of the attackers – but would also undermine the goals of the journalists. This tactic – of
eliminating the symbolic power of the media has been practiced in war situations, where
the media can report only faraway bomb blasts from the battlefields from the relative
safety of their hotel balconies to where the military command confines them.

which the very act of visible killing is expected to produce psychological impacts for the internalizing minds of the people in the audience. The invention of the guillotine and its use during the French Revolution (Smith, 2003) brought these existential assumptions to the very edge of the *Einfühlung*-without-sympathy of the ones who carried out the "revolutionary justice" of chopping off the heads of the "enemies" by the new "painless" killing machine. The need to assume that the killing is "painless"[8] together with the social need to kill ("the enemy") is an existential tension for the executioners[9] – many of whom ended up being killed by the same machine and the new political powers that designated them as "enemies." Such tensions could feed into passionate support for the "revolutionary executioners" – such as Wordsworth's youthful letter to Bishop Llandolf indicates (Wu, Chapter 9). The adamancy of such passionate statement can be viewed in terms of over-compensatory result for personal feelings of tension in the periphery[10] of the revolutionary killings. Or in other words, the symbolic goals of public executions or terrorist attacks are shown to have reached their goals in *both* passionate declarations of their "righteousness" as well as equally passionate denunciations of these acts.

Conclusions: Ways Forward

What can be taken forward from the present discussion? Discourses about revolutions may carry an overly misleading flavor of the tragedies for people and dramas for societies that undergo such changes. At such times, rage dominates. Yet neither revolution nor its rage can explain either – both are processes of transformation that are made deeply affective by the rage. We need a calm explanatory system for the inevitably noncalm events.

Moghaddam (Chapter 4) sets up the groundwork for such system by outlining the basic features of "democratic personality." Charting out these features in the twenty-first century is an important social goal that

---

[8] This assumption was contested by reports of the continuing minimal functioning of the severed heads – which could still show signs of reflexes of eye blinking or muscle contraction at the time when the executioner was *displaying the head to the attending public* (Smith, 2003, p. 39). The administrative practice of "decorating" public places with heads of the executed opponents on poles (the fate of Oliver Cromwell's head is a good example here) of such display – as well as is in itself a powerful indexical sign to feed into symbolic internalization processes.

[9] Similar psychological tensions have been described for hunters (Willerslev, 2007).

[10] It is usually the persons in the periphery (audiences – immediate ir mediated, i.e., TV audiences) – rather than the center – of social events who display exaggerated affective messages for, or against, these events. The actual persons involved in the center – the executioners and the executed – are set up in their roles by their social norm systems.

is paralleled in history – after World War II – by the efforts to outline the features of the opposite case – the "authoritarian personality" (Adorno et al., 1950) with a similar social need to understand how the human psyche functions under extreme conditions. Our century gives us signs of democracies becoming new forms of autocracies – some led by "supreme leaders" and others by (equally "supreme") mass media channels.

In the latter case, an interesting reversal of the legal presumption of innocence occurs. In the democratic systems of governance, a person is innocent until proven guilty. In the media reporting of various possible misdemeanors, the person is assumed to be guilty until proven innocent. The latter may take a long time, while the public symbolic execution of the highlighted suspected person is instant. In the media-saturated society of today, twitter assumes the role of the guillotine.

It is precisely here where the contextualization of the "democratic personality" needs to happen. *Under which conditions* of societal organization (catalytic conditions; Cabell and Valsiner, 2014) would a "democratic personality" turn into its opposite ("autocratic personality") or begin to function actively but aimlessly in the society of endless discussions and committee meetings that lead to no change but occupy one's mind? Under which conditions would the "democratic personality" become harmful for other people? Democracy is no final solution but a way of operating in a society. It is an expensive form of social system, with constant threats to its extinction from all sides.

In contemporary times of hypernetworking, it is the linkages between rights and duties that come to the forefront of moving into new forms of societies. The basic right in democracies – freedom of speech – needs to be distinguished from the indiscriminate use of that freedom. Democratic society need not become a logocratic society where bloggers, tweeters, and Facebookers determine the fate of complex social issues. The right to freedom of speech needs to be complemented by the duty not to use that freedom for socially trivial purposes. The rage of revolutions might end in meaningful silences when a society is actually transformed into a new state.

REFERENCES

Adichie, N. (2009). The American Embassy. In *The Thing around Your Neck* (pp. 128–141). New York: A. Knopf.
Adorno, T. W., Frenkel-Brunswik, E., Levinson, D. J., and Sanford, R. N. (1950). *The Authoritarian Personality*. New York: John Wiley.
Cabell, K., and Valsiner, J. (Eds.) (2014). *The Catalyzing Mind*. New York: Springer.
Carretero, M. (2011). *Constructing Patriotism*. Charlotte, NC: Information Age.

Chaudhary, N., Hviid, P., Marsico, G., and Villadsen, J. (Eds.) (2017). *Rhythms of Resistance*. New Delhi: Springer.

Foucault, M. (1998/1966). Different spaces. In J. Faubion (Ed.), *Essential Works of Foucault* (pp. 2:179–185). Princeton, NJ: Princeton University Press.

Lightfoot, C. (1997). *Culture of Adolescent Risk-Taking*. New York: Guilford Press.

Sato, T., Mori, N, and Valsiner, J. (Eds.) (2016). *Making of the Future: Trajectory Equifinality Approach*. Charlotte, NC: Information Age.

Smith, P. (2003). Narrating the guillotine: Punishment technology as myth and symbol. *Theory, Culture and Society*, 20(5), 27–51.

Valsiner, J. (1988). *Developmental Psychology in the Soviet Union*. Brighton, UK: Harvester Press.

    (1997). Attila tells his story...but do we listen? *Polish Quarterly of Developmental Psychology*, 3(4), 245–249.

Willerslev, R. (2007). *Soul Hunters: Hunting, Animism, and Personhood among the Siberian Yukaghirs*. Berkeley: University of California Press.

Part III

Representations of and in Revolution

11   Image Politics of the Arab Uprisings

Sarah H. Awad and Brady Wagoner

Contemporary social upheavals involve the production of images by various social groups to propagate particular versions of social reality, which are in turn interpreted, challenged, rejected, accepted in part or in entirety, and used by individuals and groups on the ground. Images are tools used to create meaningful signs in the environment. Through them we act and position ourselves, and in turn they act back upon us. The Arab uprisings that commenced in 2011 across the Middle East and North Africa provide an illustrative example of these dynamics of images in revolutions. Images depicting the brutality of the authorities and the "martyrs" of the revolutions were commonplace and transmitted globally. Tahrir square in Cairo itself became a kind of visual theater, with news cameras looking down on it from the heights of buildings around the square. Thus, revolutions such as this are not only visually productive, but are in themselves visual to a great extent.

Political conflicts in today's visual culture become power struggles over presence and visibility. Authoritarian regimes assert their political dominance by controlling visual production, while the opposition seeks the right to be visually present in the city space and beyond. The right to place images in public space becomes significant beyond the meaning of the images; it becomes important also because an image in public space represents the power of the group that has placed the image and successfully defended the public space in which the image is seen. This chapter aims to unpack the politics of images by analyzing examples from revolutionary street art and government images in Egypt. The focus will be on four key functions of images in politics: *to create visibility, to mobilize, to position,* and *to commemorate.* These functions are exemplified by analyzing the transformation of urban images in four case studies: the authority figure, the flag, the tank, and bullets. The methodological framework draws on the social life of images and the social actors involved. Images have social lives that include their *emergence, reception, diffusion, transformation,* and *destruction.* By following images' continuous transformation in the urban space, this chapter analyzes the potential use of images for bringing about social change within shifting power dynamics.

Images as Politics

Politics involves power struggles over presence, visibility, and recognition within an established order. The politics of visual culture concerns the contestation over the representation of society and who is permitted to represent it (Ranciere, 2004). Authoritarian regimes assert their political dominance by having control over visual production and consumption, while the opposition seeks democratic representation in visible spaces; political agency constitutes possessing the ability to be seen and the right of presence and ownership of public space (Khatib, 2013). Power in that sense is in ownership over visual representation in public sphere. Images in this context are thus an integral part of the everyday politics. Consider the power images have had in representing what is happening in the Middle East today, from those driving compassion toward children in Syria's war, through those used to trigger fear of the refugees, to those produced by the so-called Islamic State *Daesh* propagating terror.

Likewise, visual images have constructed much of the local as well as global perception of the Arab uprisings since 2011. They have shaped what we remember of the events as well as how we remember them, such as the masses of protestors filling city squares and street art expressing their sentiment. These images communicated across language barriers, portraying events as they unfolded in such a way that people around the world could both witness these historic moments and stand in solidarity with, or in opposition to, millions of people. Images of masses in the streets and squares inspired more protestors to join the movement. This happened not only locally but also globally, for different causes that nonetheless shared the guiding idea of "power to the people." This slogan encompassed opposition to multiple systems of injustice, such as freedom from authoritarian regimes, social and economic inequality of the 1 percent versus the 99 percent, and humanitarian appeals against violence and torture.

The very act of taking to the streets makes a conflict visible (Doerr, Mattoni, and Teune, 2014), and marking a wall with political graffiti is a call for recognition and resistance to the monopoly the authority holds on public space (Awad, Wagoner, and Glaveanu, 2017; Awad, 2017). Protestors do not just proclaim space, but also produce spaces with new symbols that challenge existing representations (Lefebvre, 1991). Having a physically active presence in public spaces that people are only permitted by the state to use passively becomes a visual, political act (Bayat, 2013).

It was images that first ignited the anger and solidarity that led to the Arab uprisings. From early 2011, images of Mohamed Bouazizi from Tunisia, Khaled Said from Egypt, and Hamza al-Khatib from Syria were catalysts for local movements as well as global attention as they became symbols of state injustice. Bouazizi set himself on fire in protest of police harassment and humiliation, while Said was beaten to death in broad daylight by police for exposing corruption (more on this below), and al-Khatib was killed under torture by security forces after he wrote "the people demand the fall of the regime" (a common phrase during the uprisings) on a public wall. Their images transformed police violence from a state-controlled act into visual evidence in the hands of protestors (Khatib, 2013).

In modern media-saturated societies, images become a field of knowledge in their own right. The production, circulation, and interpretation of images are part of the collective elaboration of meaning and thus intrinsically political (Rogoff, 1998). Revolution street art and graffiti in the Middle East created influential images of the Arab uprisings. Activists' use of these aesthetic means of protest, transformed art from being class-based capital tied to amusement and wealth (Bourdieu, 1984), to a tool of resistance alongside gas masks in the midst of protests and clashes. The messages communicated on the wall were used to assert a counternarrative of events, mobilize and unite people around revolutionary goals, reconstruct representations of the authority figures challenging their power, and socially document and remember events as were seen and felt in the street (Awad, 2017; Awad and Wagoner, 2015; Awad, Wagoner, and Glaveneau, 2017). Images from the Arab uprisings are of protestors taking ownership of representing themselves and constructing a social reality to present to the world, as well as responding to other actors' narratives.

Revolution can thus be seen as a dramatized performance using powerful symbols to win over audiences that are both national and international. The first day of protest during the 2011 Egyptian revolution was carefully choreographed to take place on "national police day," which commemorated how the police stood up to the British occupation. In so doing, it put in stark relief the arbitrary and brutal police of contemporary Egypt that would attempt to squash the protest with the heroic role they played in the past. The strategy of the protest was to meet at peripheral spaces of the city – thereby dividing police attention – and moving toward the central point of the city, Tahrir square (which appropriately means "liberation" in Arabic). Tahrir square was of key importance precisely because of its visibility. During the protests that followed over the eighteen days until Mubarak was removed and beyond, Tahrir became a kind of political theater in which the revolutionaries could effectively spread various images of the government's attempts to break up the movement. These were taken by cellular phones and increasingly by news channels perched in the buildings surrounding the square. Standing in the middle of the square one could see innumerable cameras looking down. News channels the protestors disagreed with got an endless barrage of laser pointers directed up at them to break their image, as part of the protest.

Visual Culture: Thinking through Images

Images create affective symbols as they circulate, embodying multiple meanings. A symbol is a sign which carries multiple meanings and significance: one meaning is indicated being the obvious "face value" of the symbol (i.e., what it denotes), and another is the "hidden value" (i.e., its connotations) which produces a largely affective response without being definitely or purposively attended to (Bartlett, 1924; Wagoner, 2017). For example, the image of Khalid Said's mutilated face after he was beaten by police in Egypt took on the hidden value of fighting police corruption and injustice more generally. It became a rally point around which a group could organize itself and expand its membership. Police brutality was nothing new, but was normally directed at the poor and was now made visible. Said's case was special in that he was from the middle class and was killed in front of others in broad daylight. Thus, he could more easily serve as a symbol uniting all Egyptians against the police.

The image of Khaled Said as well as many other revolution images traveled to different contexts creating symbols of solidarity among different countries. Figure 11.1 shows the portrait of Khaled Said painted on a fragment of the historical Berlin Wall, symbolically merging two separate contexts of struggle together, as part of the Freedom Park Project. The photo was painted by Andreas von Chrzanowski (Case), and the Arabic calligraphy at the bottom was written by Mohamed Gaber (Gue3bara), reading "We are all Khaled Said," which was the name of the Facebook page made in his honor and used to call for and organize the protests of January 25, 2011. The image of Said's mutilated face fulfills the four functions of images we highlight, namely, to create visibility, mobilize, position, and commemorate. We will briefly outline each function here

Figure 11.1 Khaled Said's image on a piece of the Berlin Wall
Photo credit: First Author, Berlin, April 2017

in turn and later further elaborate them in relation to case studies of different kinds of images created during the Arab uprisings.

Create Visibility

To represent in politics means to stand in for a group of people in negoti-ations with other groups (i.e., as a representative), while in psychology its meaning concerns a symbolic depiction of some object. The two mean-ings of "represent" convergence in the politics of images. For example, images of Khaled Said represents the concrete person killed by police on the one hand, but also the revolutionaries and their demands for "life, freedom and social justice." This public representation of an image can bring visibility to a social movement's cause. Whether a photo or a piece of art, images are communicative devices that make visible to an object, a subject, or an idea, and the group that produced it. Images are different from text in the immediacy by which they make absent objects present, their capacity to make abstract entities concrete, and to create fictional characters that embody generalizations and stereotypes (Lonchuk and Rosa, 2011). Moscovici (1984) has argued that they give a "figurative nuclei" to social representations, working to naturalize our everyday knowledge and give shared reference points for a group to communicate and organize itself.

Images borrow from currents of ideas and values already existing within a society, but can also negotiate them, reconstruct them and create new ones. This power to represent and make visible gives images the capacity to produce spaces that embody the group who made them. Who is allowed, and what is allowed, to be visible creates spaces of power, inclusion, and exclusion. Images tell us something about where we are, hint at the power dynamics, and make us feel foreign or at home (Lonchuk and Rosa, 2011). Misrepresented groups often strive with the use of images to create visibility, proclaim city space, and create an atmosphere of solidarity to re-affirm their denied recognition. Regimes, especially authoritarian ones, monopolize visual culture in order to control how society is represented. This is done by producing images that communicate power and indicate who belongs and who does not.

Mobilize: Shaping Emotions and Motivating Action

Two modes of thought that govern human psychology are conceptual reason and ideational images. While the former creates a more distant and evidence-based relation to reality, the latter is vivid, emotional and directly suggests action (like an idea implanted by a hypnotist) (see also Wagoner, Chapter 5). Le Bon (1895/2002) argued that the statesmen should govern the masses by appealing to the latter mode of thought through evoking powerful images, rather than by providing them with reasoned arguments. Although we can criticize his one-sided view of the public, he was clearly on to something with regards to the power of images to move masses. Thus, beyond representation and recognition an image can easily be embodied as an affective symbol that mobilizes us to actions by appealing to our emotions. The perceiver of an image may be moved to engagement and self-transformation by appropriating a powerful image in a work of art (Dewey, 1934/2005), or to collective action through various symbols expressing outrage, and calling us to action.

The power of the image over the human mind resides in its silence, impassiveness, and insistence on repeating the same message, in its capacity for absorbing human emotions and projecting them back as a demand for reflection (Mitchell, 2005). In revolutions, images ignite emotions and rally people in the streets. As already mentioned, it was images of Mohamed Bouazizi in Tunisia and Khaled Said in Egypt that sparked revolutions in each country. In the immediate aftermath of Mubarak's being pushed out of the presidency, cities of Egypt were filled with empowerment and solidarity street art, including national flags, fists clenched in the air and the Christian cross and Islamic crescent placed together. Moreover, through circulation of images on television and the Internet, mobilization transcended geographic distance to spread revolutionary euphoria from one country to another.

Position

Images also function as condensed symbols that make arguments vis-à-vis other alternative positions within a society. Through these arguments people position themselves and others in relation to different social issues, ascribing various rights and duties to different social actors (Harré and Langenhove, 1998). The actors are also positioned as upholding or violating those rights and duties. In the online page calling for the Egyptian uprising, the photo of Khaled Said was placed beside his mutilated face after the attack, with the slogan "we are all Khaled Said." His young familiar look and the slogan explicitly positioned the perceiver as sharing the vulnerability to the police's arbitrary aggression. The visual expressed outrage at the violation of people's rights to justice and safety, and the duty to stand in solidarity against the injustice. Furthermore, it positioned the authority as having failed in its duty to protect its people.

In this context, the putting forward of arguments takes the form of a dialogue between social actors. As will be illustrated in the "tank" example further below, an effective visual image not only asserts the producer's argument, but also provokes its audience to position themselves within the argument. It creates both attention and tension, posing a challenge to the viewer. If the image is too familiar the viewer will only see it as a cliché, and if it is too unfamiliar the viewer will reject it outright. To create perceptual, emotional, and representational tension for the viewer the image needs to balance between the known and unknown, old and new. It involves representing the existing social reality, while simultaneously communicating something new that violates that reality (Marková, 2003). Thus, by following images as they respond to one another we can track how different positions evolve within an ongoing social dialogue.

Commemorate

Images also simplify events into symbolic icons that become part of our collective memory, as has happened with Khalid Said's image becoming an iconic visual to commemorate the injustice leading to 2011 uprising in Egypt. Our spatial framework is filled with images that trigger selective events of the past and certain ways of remembering them. Those images become symbolic actors on the historical stage; feeding into the stories we tell ourselves (Mitchell, 1984) and representing the affective relationship a community has with its past (Halbwachs, 1950). Images of the past are continuously reproduced and reconstructed to feed into the demands of the present and the desired future of different social actors. These images can then be used as analogies to understand a host of current events and concerns. As the psychologist Frederic Bartlett (1932, p. 219) explained, "by the aid of the image ... a man can take out of its setting something that happened a year ago, reinstate it with much if not all of its individuality unimpaired, combine it with something that happened yesterday, and use them both to help him to solve a problem with which he is confronted to-day." In this account, there is a dynamic relationship between past and present; the past is used to serve current needs and is reconstructed on that basis. Thus those having the power of image production and circulation have the power over stabilizing certain narratives of the past, thereby shaping the imagined future. Power determines which aspects of the past are circulated as visual representations (Rogoff, 1998).

Studying the Transformative Nature of Images

To research these different functions of images, we need to not only look at the production and perception of image, but also at the process the image goes through in the public sphere, *its social life*. Images are not static objects finding a place in a single context; they have social lives that include how they are produced, received, diffused, transformed, and destroyed. By following the images' continuous reconstruction, we highlight processes of dialogue between different social actors and concomitant social changes in society. Following image's transformation is also informative as to the intertwining of different public and private spheres, as well as the online and physical spaces through which an image travels. Many of the protest images were carried from squares to news and online media, while images and caricatures from social media where used in revolution graffiti and street art. This highlights the enduring power of images that travel, comment on each other, and continuously respond to the dialogues ongoing in society. Images are also understood as situated within particular sociocultural contexts through association with a complex stock of cultural knowledge and identifications, which affects how they are interpreted and re-appropriated by different social actors (Mitchell, 1994).

Images as tools for social and political action, involve different social actors, who take up the different roles of image producer, receiver, transformer, and destroyer, depending on the context (Awad, Wagoner, and Glaveneau, 2017). For example, during the uprising every protestor in a sense was an image producer, broadcasting to a local and global audience through social media. Also, a revolution mural in the street has the artist as its producer, and pedestrians and the government as its audience and potential censors. While for a political campaign poster the producer could be the authority for which pedestrians are the audience. The audience in each case could change the image, reproduce it, transfer it to another medium, or destroy it. The destruction or censorship of images is indicative of the political atmosphere and what is tolerated by the government or the general public. Revolution graffiti in Egypt was not only whitewashed by local government officials but also often sprayed over or scratched out by pedestrians who disagreed with the content displayed in what they identified as "their" neighborhood area. Government censorship is different, however, in that it not only destroys images in the streets and censors their reproduction, but also goes after image producers and circulators through arrest and issuing laws criminalizing their actions (Awad, 2017).

This framework offers one way of looking at image politics, analyzing: How do images *emerge* through actors' production efforts? How are they *received* according to each social actor's position and background? How then are images *diffused* and circulated within a context? What transformations do they go through in this process? Why do some images gain visibility and go viral while others have shorter life spans? What images catch people's attention?

Having highlighted our focus of the four functions and the methodological focus on the transformative process of images, we illustrate the above with four case examples, each representing one of the functions mentioned above: the authority figure, the flag, the tank, and the bullets. The data presented below builds on a more elaborate ethnographic data set collected from Egypt over the period from 2014 to 2017 that includes; interviews with street artists and pedestrians, city walks, photo documentation and visual analysis, as well as archived material from news and social media (see Awad, Wagoner, and Glaveanu, 2017; Awad, 2017).

The Authority Figure: Images as They Create Visibility and Produce Spaces

Images of authority, especially in authoritarian regimes who have monopoly over the visual culture, create spaces with homogenous clear messages about power. In these contexts, as Foucault (1977) points out, the citizen is continuously the object of the gaze of the state, whether physically through surveillance, or symbolically through the watchful eye of the leader's image in public and private space. Here the image of the authority figure represents not only his person and leadership but also the state and what it stands for. Through the distribution and circulation of those images in city space they create strong visibility, displaying power and control. It is not surprising that the visible presence of the ruler, whether king, emperor or statesmen, has been a common motif throughout world history.

In the Middle East, the face of the president or king is a prominent feature in public space (in many homes as well, the intrusion of the state is such that people feel obliged to show images of the leader). This personification of politics is common because it is easier to understand a man than a political program; leaders take on the role of associating politics with their personas, displaying charismatic nationalistic attributes that appeal to their supporters (Khatib, 2013). Producers of such images are normally governmental institutions, placing the image of the leader in numerous strategic spots beginning from primary school classes in public schools socializing young citizen early on to the "father" of the nation. The role of production is not only top down however; the authority image's social life extends to being reproduced and circulated by "loyal" citizens, displaying them in their businesses and homes. It is an act of support and alliance but also in many cases protection from the system. Khatib (2013) further explains that people post authority's images not because they love them, but because the system is self-enforcing and people are accustomed to it; they have internalized its control.

Of interest here is the transformation this image underwent during the political unrest and the alternative spaces that were created. During the uprisings, the image of authority could be seen as what Mitchell (1986) refers to as a site of special power that must be destroyed or exploited to reverse its idolism. The "divine" attributes of the authority images were contested and destroyed to bring about the questioning of their power and the possibility of toppling their regimes. This could be seen during protests in caricature images of leaders mocking them and revolution street art visually putting the power of those leaders in confrontation with the power of the people. The divine image was further reversed by media images after regime change and the removal of those leaders. One clear example is that of the violent killing of Qaddafi in Libya: media images of his corpse transformed him from a superior being into a nonhuman object in the hands of his killers (Khatib, 2013). Also in Egypt, one widely circulated media image representing the victory of the uprising was a picture of children in a public school taking down the oversized image of Mubarak from their classroom. By this destruction of the authority's physical and representative body, the revolution thereby denaturalizes the existing social order.

In his over thirty years as Egypt's president, Mubarak created an image of himself as a war hero, a leader of the Arab world, and promoter of Egypt's economic development. Anything that contradicted this image was censored to keep a coherent public discourse. The limited space that was left for "freedom of expression" targeted other government officials and ministers, while keeping Mubarak and his family out of any public ridicule. In the Middle East Peace Talks in 2010, a news image of Barak Obama in the lead, following him Binyamin Netanyahu, Mahmoud Abbas, Mubrark, and King Abdullah II slightly behind was taken of the event. The next morning state run newspaper *Al-Ahram* published the photo after editing it to place Mubarak at the forefront of those key figures. Interestingly this decision to alter the photo did not seem to come from the president office but rather the newspaper editorial staff. The editor-in-chief defended the image by saying it was a metaphoric edit, only meant to illustrate Egypt's leading role in the peace process (*Guardian*, 2010). This again reflects an internalized understanding of the visual discourse, what can be represented and how, when the real image did not match the conventional representation of the president, it was altered, so as to fit the image people should be seeing.

Revolution street art created a public field visibility through which this divine status was contested and debated, not only for Mubarak but also for the leaders who followed him: Tantawi, Morsi, and El Sisi. The same function of image as a tool for representation and creating visibility was used to reconstruct the visual representation of power. Several street art paintings were about flipping the powerful traditional portrayal of Mubarak, to represent him as weak and scared in front of the power of the people. Irony was also a common tool in graffiti and street art images. Artists appropriated the traditional divine portrayal of authority, and re-represented it with a twist to bring about an opposite meaning, thus potentially triggering reflexivity in viewers (see also Wagoner, Awad, and Bresco, forthcoming). These images did not only mock the leaders but also those who glorify them. Figure 11.2 uses traditional imagery of holding high the glorified framed image of the leader. But by changing the face of the leader and the follower to chimpanzees, it represents the blind and irrational devotion of followers for their simple-minded leader.

The transformation of the leader's image into graffiti images ridiculing him, represents a visual reversal in public space. Even though these practices were there before the revolution, they were in what Scott (1990)

Figure 11.2 Painting by artist Naguib at Tahrir Square, September 2014
Photo credit: First Author

terms, offstage hidden transcripts, where the hegemonic visual representation of authority is only mocked and degraded in private social gatherings and online media. The revolution provided a space for those hidden
transcripts and backstage performances to be spoken directly and publicly in the face of power. This created new spaces with reconfigured
boundaries of what could, and could not, be said in urban space.

   This revolutionized urban space was not long lived. Since El Sisi took
office in 2014, there has been a tightening security grip on such forms of
expression. This censorship not only applies to graffiti images, but also
to images produced on social media. Because images on social media
are harder to control, authorities often go after the image producers. In
2015, Amr, a twenty-two-year-old serving his compulsory military year,

was sentenced by military court to three years in prison for creating a picture of El Sisi with huge black Mickey Mouse ears and sharing it on Facebook. The prosecutors used screenshots from social media as evidence, arguing Amr posted a series of disrespectful images of the president that violate the expected moral behavior and push the boundaries beyond acceptability (Farid, 2015). This example, explicitly expresses authority's tight "moral" control over visual representation. In spite of these examples of ironic reversal, or perhaps because of them, the glorification of Sisi in images still persists. El Sisi is often portrayed with angle wings or a superman suit by his supporters in the street, in newspapers, and online. Those images reinforce the image of El Sisi as a national hero and savior of Egypt, such that those who suggest otherwise are labeled as enemies of the nation. These glorifying images however continue to trigger further ironic counterimages by the opposition.

The Flag: Images as They Shape Emotions and Mobilize

The famous images igniting the different Arab uprisings mentioned in the introduction are clear illustrations of how certain images move us beyond mere recognition, to affective reactions and in many cases mobilize action. We will discuss here an example of how even the most diffused and banal images can start a new social life following major events to mobilize people toward certain feelings, affiliations, and actions. National flags take up a novel symbolic meaning in times of turbulence. As powerful symbols of national identity they can be used to mobilize collective action toward a common goal. In moments of revolutions, triggered by the disruption of routines, people psychologically invest significant emotional energy into the symbols of nationhood (Giddens, 1985). It is thus not surprising that during and immediately after the eighteen days of the 2011 Egyptian Revolution that flags were being painted and waived all over the country. However, four years later the same flag would take on an opposite meaning.

Unlike the common use of the Lebanese flag after the civil war as a symbol of unity, the Egyptian flag was not a common daily object to be displayed and flagged. It was only apparent around football matches and on poles in government offices and schools. Protest in the years prior to the uprising in 2011 mostly used signs with their demands, without evoking a visual of the flag.

In 2011, an image of a protestor climbing up to a light pole and waving the Egyptian flag in Tahrir square with the background of thousands of protestors became a powerful symbolic image of the uprising: It connoted the slogans "power to the people" and solidarity under one national cause of "bread, freedom, and social justice." A group of protestors walking through neighborhood streets waving the flag and calling on people to join was a common practice during the eleven days of protest in 2011 before Mubarak's removal. In contrast, pro-Mubarak protest groups could easily be identified by the large portrait images of him that they carried. At this time, hanging the flag from a residential balcony was a sign of support for the revolution. Moreover, many of the revolution graffiti images used the Egyptian flag as a symbol of national unity and empowerment.

Fast forward to 2014 after military takeover and president El Sisi getting into power. At this time, a flagpole was erected in the center of Tahrir square (Figure 11.3b) after dispute over what memorial can represent the revolution (see Awad, 2017). However, this time the flag was met with much skepticism from activists, who saw it as backstabbing those who lost their lives in the square during protests and an appropriation of the protest square by the new government. The flagpole was referred to as a "khazou," roughly translated as "an impalement." In a previous study, when participants were shown images of the flag on a billboard with the statement "in the love of Egypt," they all readily identified it as a pro-military government image (see Awad, 2017). Also waving the flag in the street or hanging it from ones balcony now had the opposite meaning of supporting military rule.

How did a symbol, so common and culturally diffused, come to be appropriated to mobilize for such opposite causes in such a short time? How did the government monopolize the image of the flag right after the revolution, such that it became an automatic identifier of the regime instead of a revolutionary symbol?

The military backed government after the revolution quickly reaffirmed full control of the representation of the nation using collectively held symbols such as the flag and generic statements that define nationalism and love of one's country. After the military takeover, the image of the flag was quickly appropriated to mean counterrevolution. Hanging the flag was used to proclaim space for the authorities rather than the people. The military also heavily used it in a visual campaign to act in patriotic solidarity with the government against terrorism. The flag became the symbol of the army's dedication to the people in what the campaign refers to as two revolutions, first against Mubarak in 2011, and second against Muslim Brotherhood president Morsi. The appropriation of the flag was the visual part of the nationalistic discourse widely communicated in official media and city space after the revolution: to be a loyal Egyptian patriot is to support government, opposition is about

(a)

(b)

Figure 11.3 Tahrir Square (a) after Mubarak steps down in 2011 and
(b) in May 2015
Photo credit: (a) Mohamed Abdel-Ghany and (b) First author

being a traitor to the country in a time of instability and its fight for safety against terrorism.

In this example, the flag's use goes beyond its pragmatic communicative message to being a signal of spatial borders and affiliations. It performs a further symbolic function of being a "condensation symbol" and "a focus for sentiment about society" (Firth, 1973, p. 356). Flags symbolize the character of a nation, and this character varies by who is waving it, where, and how. Flags come to take those meanings from their poles standing in the street, from being waved by a loyal citizen or a protestor, or from being waved in a football match. In those instances, it carries more of an affective rather than an informational message. The numerous flags we see today are un-saluted, un-waved, and unnoticed. They are banal daily reminders of nationhood, being neither consciously remembered nor forgotten (Billig, 1995). The flag becomes embodied by meanings now prescribed to it by the new authority, erasing its earlier meaning. It is only the flags now being waved or saluted that ought to be noticed.

The same flag still frequently appears in the daily life, saluted by children in school every morning, waved at football matches, and standing tall on government flagpoles. However, following its social life over the last few years in Egypt illustrates shifts in power and how the meaning of patriotism has changed, from being a protestor to a citizen loyally following his/her duty to the authority.

The Tank: Images as They Position

While images represent, create spaces and mobilize, they subsequently pose arguments for a certain position, displaying the producer's stance on a contentious topic. For example, images of different protests in the uprisings positioned protestors as either freedom fighters or terrorists and foreign agents causing civil wars. The choice of which images got coverage in the media, what photo angle is taken of a protest, and the content of each image posed an argument for or against the protest action. Similarly, photos of Syrian refugees and their circulation in European media make an argument for their helplessness or present them as a potential threat to European culture and security.

An illustrative example of this argumentative function of images is in the layers of graffiti on one wall beneath 6 October Bridge, at Zamalek in Cairo from 2011 to 2013. This example also highlights the social life of images methodology mentioned above, and the analytical value of following the transformation of one image through different actors. The continuous line of argument in this image's social life concerns the contentious military role in the revolution, symbolized by the tank. Was the military a savior of the 2011 revolution or did they take advantage of the situation for their own gain? Does the tank symbolize protection or brutality? This question remains in people's minds, especially given the current military backed regime ruling Egypt.

The visual dialogue started with a street art image drawn by artist Ganzeer and his friends in May 2011 (Figure 11.4a). The image shows a tank facing a young man on a bicycle carrying a breadbasket. The boy serves as a representative of the working class, which revolution aimed to protect with the demands for "bread, freedom and social justice." It is also noteworthy that the word for "bread" (*aish*) in Arabic also means "life." Immediately we are struck by the disproportionate power of the two actors. Moreover, the positioning of the tank face-to-face with the boy and his bicycle subtly makes the argument that the army, who at that moment is supported by many Egyptians and seen as protector, could at any moment turn its weaponry against them.

Soon after in October 2011 tanks did turn against civilians in a violent crackdown on a protest in an event known as the Maspero Massacre. During the event tanks intentionally ran over protestors killing dozens. This was the first transparent sign that the military's self-proclaimed role as protectors was problematic. In January 2012, another artist, Mohammed Khaled, transformed the tank and bicycle image to document the massacre, painting civilians falling under the moving tank with a pool of blood underneath them (Figure 11.4b). Around the bread seller, protestors were added holding "vandetta" masks, an international symbol of resistance. The argument is clear: the military are killers and citizens have the duty to protest against the violations of their rights.

Actors from an opposing position quickly countered this argument. Ten days later, a pro-army group called "Badr Battalion" erased most of the new additions to the image (Figure 11.4c). The tank now stands idly besides protestors with the slogans "the army and the people are one hand" and "Egypt for the Egyptians." The latter is a slogan from 1880s that was used for pro-nationalist anticolonial campaigns and was later appropriated by the military when they seized power in 1952. The protestors are now transformed into patriotic civilians cheering for the tank with flags in hand instead of the vendetta masks. The image makes the argument that citizens should be patriotic by supporting the military which will lead to social stability. As described above, the meaning of the flag is already changing to signal this support.

In response to this, a street art group named "Mona Lisa Battalion" erased what the pro-army group had done and drew different motifs in front of the tank, including a sketch of military leader Tantawi's face as

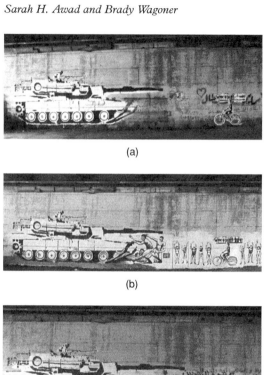

(a)

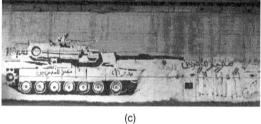

(b)

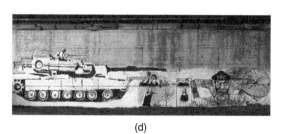

(c)

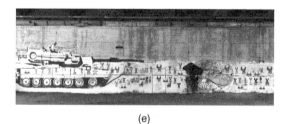

(d)

(e)

Figure 11.4 Transformations of the "tank and bicycle" mural from 2011 to 2013
Photo credit: (a,d) Suzee in the City (suzeeinthecity.wordpress.com), (b,c) Mia Grondahl and (e) Bahia Shehab

petals of a flower faced with a famous Egyptian actress holding a rifle against it (Figure 11.4d). Also to the right artist Mohamed Khaled drew a green army monster devouring a protestor with blood pouring out of its mouth.

The authorities responded by white washing the wall, leaving only the tank, and using black paint to erase the army monster. Yet again, a new coat of paint was added by artist Bahia Shehab; using her calligraphy project *A Thousand Times No*, she stencil sprays the wall with different Arabic calligraphy styles of the word "no." Underneath each "no" is a different message, such as "No to dictators," "No to military rule," and "No to violence." Shehab has created a series of graffiti images using different Arabic calligraphy styles of the word "no" and used them to spray paint a series of quotes objecting Egyptian authorities in streets of Cairo (see www.ted.com/talks/bahia_shehab_a_thousand_times_no).

Similar to other revolution street art, the wall was completely white-washed in June 2013 by local authorities. The image, its layers of repro-ductions, and its final erasing tell a story of contention political argu-mentation. Each transformation of the image positioned the actor from the symbol of the tank, as well as their position from the previous argu-ment, and with minor changes to the paintings transformed the message several times to opposite meanings.

The Bullets: Images as They Commemorate and Document

Commemorating and documenting the killing of civilian lives through the traces of bullets has been a common practice in the aftermath of col-lectively felt violence and has become part of contemporary war tourism. In Lebanon, nearly three decades after the civil war, the few remaining buildings and ruins by the Green Line in Beirut – the line that divided the city in two during the war – are still covered in bullets. In the absence of a war memorial, their walls become the primary places of memory for the war. Today there are different attempts at preserving them in the form of official memorials of the conflict (see Fordham, 2017). More recently, bulleted walls and ruins in Iraq and Syria continue to tell a story of the wars ongoing there. In many instances, those walls are used as a canvas for street art interventions adding stories of defiance and hope to the imprints of violence.

In Egypt, the remembrance of the lost lives in the 2011 uprising was one of the main themes of revolution street art. Many revolution murals commemorated the revolution "martyrs" using two visual mem-ory functions: honoring the victim and documenting the injustice. The first commemorates and pays respect to the deceased through drawing

Figure 11.5 Martyr mural depicted through Christian iconography, downtown Cairo, October 2013
Photo credit: Abdo El Amir (Hamdy & Karl, 2014)

their portrait, often adding symbols that subsume their death within a higher divine cause. For example, angel wings and phrases from Quran or Bible frame death within religious notions of martyrdom, granting them a place in heaven as having fought for the revolution. Figure 11.5 is a mural in memory of Marian, an eight-year-old girl who was shot multiple times by an unknown gunman while she was on her way to a wedding in a Coptic orthodox church (Hamdy and Karl, 2014). Even though the circumstances of her death were different from protestors who died in clashes with the police or military, her image joined those of the revolution victims in the center of revolution street art in downtown Cairo. The mural depicts the bullets in Marian's body visually referencing St. Sebastian, who is commonly depicted tied to a tree and shot with arrows in Christian iconography. The wings, hallow, the colorful bullets to the right, and the bullet marks appearing like sun flowers to the left all communicate meanings of sacrifice that give to her a holy status.

The second visual function used in commemorating civilian lives was that of social documentation of their killing incident and holding the perpetrators accountable. In some instances the painting was done in the same physical location where the person was killed so as to create an instant place reminder. Figure 11.6 shows a photograph and stenciled

(a)

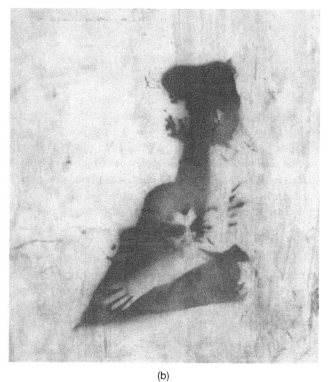

(b)

Figure 11.6 Photographs depicting (a) the shooting of activist Shaimma al-Sabbagh and (b) the stencil graffiti sprayed at the site afterward

Photo credit: Islam Osama

image of the shooting of Socialist Popular Alliance Party activist Shaimaa al-Sabbagh during a peaceful demonstration in memory of the demonstrators killed in January 25 revolution. The photograph was taken right after she was shot, while her colleague was trying to carry her. The photo created a powerful mnemonic by capturing the iconic "about to die" moment. News photos as such document the sequencing of an event while strategically freezing it at its most visually powerful moment. "Just before death" photos create iconic representations of events for remembrance as they position the event at the "about to" moment (Zelizer, 2004).

The sprayed stencil then took this iconic visual representation and "marked" it onto the walls of the physical location where she was killed. The stencil transformed a news photo that went viral on social media and newspapers into a graffiti symbol, which in turn was diffused on city walls and social media. This continuous social life of image serves documentation and remembering into the future.

Discussion: Long Live the King . . . Down with the King . . . Long Live the King . . .

Political upheavals involve struggles of different groups for representation and visibility, mobilization of masses, positioning within dominant discourses, and a presence in collective memory. With regards to all of these functions, images have a privileged place over written discourse. Visuals reach audience in a timely and affective manner, in many instances transcending language and cultural barriers. Throughout this chapter, we have proposed that following those visuals provides one way of looking at cultural and political transformations associated with political upheavals. Through the social life of images, we observe the different functions they serve, the different social actors involved, and their circulation in context.

As illustrated in the examples, visuals are attractive resources for authoritarian regimes to stabilize their homogeneous discourse and display power over knowledge, history, and public space. But those same visual resources create risks for regimes, as they play a central role in igniting revolutions by highlighting the injustices of the system, representing the established image of authority, and giving visibility (and power) to the masses. During revolutions, a social rupture occurs that opens up a gap of opportunity to reconfigure established boundaries and create spaces of contestation and positioning. In return counterrevolutions attack those spaces and visuals through destruction, censorship, and alternative production. Following this contentious and continuous process of change tell stories of political struggles as they are occurring. Thus, the analysis shows the spaces of control and censorship, as well as of agency and resistance.

The different image functions discussed in this chapter highlight the different social and political implications they have on society.

First, the function of *visibility* and its illustrative example of the authority figure shows different means and forms of visibility. Traditionally regimes' exercise of power has been linked to the authority's public display of superiority and power, visibility then was about the visibility of the few in power to the masses. Surveillance technology later changed the form of visibility to be a tool of control: the masses being continuously watched by the few. The display of authority then became about the normalizing power of the gaze: the citizens internalizing the control through believing that they are always watched (Foucault, 1977). Contemporary new media is further redefining visibility, making those in power, rather than those over whom power is exercised, the primary focus of a new kind of visibility, posing "fragility" to the divine image of authority. The same tools used to promote and celebrate political leaders, are used to attack and denounce them, and previously hidden political practices and events are exposed publicly to a much wider audience across space and time (Thompson, 2005). Those new tools and access to visibility also come with their own risks of misuse, which will be further discussed below in terms of rights and duties.

New communication channels and online media are inevitably changing the power dynamics of visual culture, creating new fields of action and interaction, in which relations of power can shift quickly, dramatically, and in unpredictable ways as we saw in the example of Egypt. Under the current government in Egypt, the personification of the leader still persists from government-produced images as well as from supporters who are looking for the savior image of a leader. However, there is an inevitable effect of the spaces of contestation that the uprising has opened, which challenge the authority's ability to convey a one-way visual representation. The image of El Sisi is met with contestation by the opposition mostly online but also in street graffiti, utilizing ironic appropriation of his image and speeches, and triggering reflection on the official discourses (Wagoner, Awad, and Bresco, forthcoming). The authority still has the most power over visuals in public space, while the opposition is steered toward online media. However, the borders between these mediums are becoming more and more permeable, with images traveling between while changing shape and meaning in the process.

Second, the *mobilizing* potential of images has been apparent throughout history. Flags and religious symbols have been frequently used to motivate people to go off to war and give their life for the higher cause represented by the symbol. These images are powerful group motivators because they speak primarily to our emotions rather than our reason. Through them we enter into a collective stream of feelings and ideas that bind us with others in common cause; this is why they are essential devices for protest crowds and political rallies (see Wagoner, Chapter 5). In the example of the Egyptian flag, we see how the sentiments and group boundaries have changed alongside shifting events and power dynamics. While before the revolution flags only functioned as powerful symbols of solidarity toward a common end in football matches, during the eighteen days of protest and its immediate aftermath the flag absorbed the revolutionary euphoria and became a key symbol bringing Egyptians together as equals protesting in the streets and squares. The flag was not only waved but wore on ones body and painted all over the city. Part of the military's taking back control of the country meant transforming the affective meaning of the flag. Considerable resources were spent on billboards, monuments, and celebrations that implicitly connected the flag with support for military rule. These efforts paid off such that today those waving the flag are more likely to be motivated against people protesting the government than with them.

Third, looking at how images *position* different actors during times of change and create contested spaces of argumentation highlights different venues of agency and social action. Looking at individuals in those contexts as reflexive agents, when confronted with various discourses they actively acquire different positions and those positions in turn influence certain actions (Harré, Lee, and Moghaddam, 2008). In the example of the Tank mural, we see that discourses and positioning do not only take place in language, but also in the images we see everyday in the streets of our cities. Images continuously present the multiple realities of a time and their social life shows the negotiation, conflict, and competition taking place between the different positions.

Of importance here are the concepts of rights and duties that are ascribed to each position and the power of different positions (Harré, Lee, and Moghaddam, 2008). While the example of the tank presents arguments between different graffiti artists in opposition and in support of the army in one physical location, the wider visual context involves positions that are widely propagated through different media platforms. On these platforms, images are continuously used to present false arguments, promote and use public ignorance, and position the producer as the source of reality and the audience as the naive and passive receiver of information. There are fabricated images of the authority figure such as in the example of Mubarak news image mentioned earlier, there are images that ignite fear such as those propagated by ISIS terrorist group, and there are images that marginalize entire groups and promote polarization in society. Those images appear to an audience as real representations of the world, and those fabrications or framing are often harder to distinguish by an audience who are less likely to spot the fake or selective representation occurring in the image process (Messaris and Abraham, 2001). In these instances, images have real moral implications in everyday life, positioning entire groups of people as "good" or "evil," "patriotic" or "traitors." They have the ability to humanize or dehumanize individuals, and to legitimize or delegitimize social struggles.

Fourth, images' function to *commemorate* and document personal as well as collective memories gives them a historical enduring role. Authority's monopoly over what visuals get circulated and what parts of recent history gets documented does not only shape the past but also the oriented future of the country. The whitewashing of the revolution street art and the lost lives in the uprisings, and replacing them with visuals of the "new stable Egypt" is a clear attempt of regulating the community's collective memory. And even though citizens appropriate those visuals and reconstruct their memories in an individual manner according to their own experiences and opinions, the monopoly over visual documentation has an enduring effect on the long term of enforcing certain memories and promoting the forgetting of others. Also those who have the power of representing the past in visual culture, have the power over dictating who is represented and included in the public sphere and who is excluded. Thus, the continuous interventions in the street and online to document the revolution from the perspective of activists has an important role in counteracting this effect and reaffirming presence and alternative narratives of the past. On the long and difficult pursuit of activist goals, these solidified images serve as important reminders for what one is fighting for.

Conclusion: Beyond the Uprising

Looking at the Arab uprisings and its different upheavals, trials, and failures through the lens of "hard" politics, may show that the people lost their opportunity for change. However, looking through the lens of visual culture as politics complicates this view to include the importance of the diffused everyday politics (Khatib, 2013). Revolutions are the heightened times where attention is brought to people's will; they are visible and dramatic. But it is in the "infra-politics of subordinate groups" that we can see the continuities of low profile forms of everyday resistance that endure in spite of the disappointments of the different revolutions (Scott, 1990). While the aspired to social changes were clearly not achieved from the revolutionary situations in Egypt, Libya, Syria, and other countries in the region, the visual culture and the actors involved in it illustrate micro processes of change in different forms of resistance to dominant powers.

The transformation of images and their implications reveals a continuous push and pull, resistance from opposition to official visual discourse and from government to alternative visual productions. It opens up the question of whether there was indeed an inevitable effect of revolutionary images in spite of the drawbacks and counterrevolutions. The different functions showed how images could be a symbolic resource for social movements as they influence the political discourse. They also showed that they could be a double edged sword; same images used to create visibility to certain groups, could be used to marginalize them, and same images used to mobilize people against injustice, could turn people numb and passive toward photos of torture and injustice.

The political potential of the different functions of images lies in the hands of the different social actors influencing the images' social lives. The examples discussed in this chapter show active producers of alternative visual culture and critical recipients of the dominant visual discourse resisting powerful ruling structures in spite of their endurance and in spite of the perceived shortcomings and failures of the uprisings. This poses moral responsibility not only on image producers but also on their receivers and gatekeepers. To the numerous images we see every day, we should question when is looking and critically appropriating an image an act of political awareness. Acts of perceiving, appropriating, refuting or destroying can all be acts of change in our visual culture. This is because the "images surrounding us do not only show how we inhabit our culture, but also how we remake it, altering the very structures by which we organize our culture" (Rogoff, 1998).

This leads us to argue that there are micro processes of social change that can be seen not only in the visual culture but also in everyday practices. From the unsuccessful revolution, groups of people have become conscious of the possibility of resistance and have learned skills for executing it. In Egypt today we do not find a completely one way, top down production of visual culture; the opposition still influences public discourse with their images, and authorities continue to respond to those images with censorship, imprisonment, and distribution of opposing images. In return, the opposition continues to use online media as well as urban spaces in spite of the risks to affirm presence in resistance to government's attempts to make the "other" invisible.

REFERENCES

Awad, S. H. (2017). Documenting a contentious memory: Symbols in the changing city space of Cairo. *Culture and Psychology*, 23(2), 234–254.

Awad, S. H., and Wagoner, B. (2015). Agency and creativity in the midst of social change. In C. W. Gruber, M. G. Clark, S. H. Klempe, and J. Valsiner (Eds.), *Constraints of Agency: Explorations of Theory in Everyday Life* (pp. 229–243). New York: Springer.

Awad, S. H., Wagoner, B., and Glaveanu, V. (2017). The (street) art of resistance. In N. Chaudhary, P. Hviid, G. Marsico, and J. Villadsen (Eds.), *Resistance in Everyday Life: Constructing Cultural Experiences* (pp. 161–180). New York: Springer.

Bartlett, F. C. (1924). Symbolism in folk-lore. In *Proceedings of the VIIth International Congress of Psychology* (pp. 278–289), Cambridge: Cambridge University Press.

 (1932). *Remembering: A Study in Experimental and Social Psychology*. Cambridge: Cambridge University Press.

Bayat, A. (2013). *Life as Politics: How Ordinary People Change the Middle East*. Stanford, CA: Stanford University Press.

Billig, M. (1995). *Banal Nationalism*. London: Sage.

Bourdieu, P. (1979/1984). *Distinction: A Social Critique of the Judgment of Taste*. London: Routledge and Kegan Paul.

Connerton, P. (1989). *How Societies Remember*. Cambridge: Cambridge University Press.

Dewey, J. (1934/2005). *Art as Experience*. New York: Berkley.

Doerr, N., Mattoni, A., and Teune, S. (2014). Visuals in social movements. In D. della Porta and M. Diani (Eds.), *Oxford Handbook of Social Movements* (pp. 557–566). Oxford: Oxford University Press.

Farid, F. (2015). Egypt Jailed a man because he made a meme of the president with "Mickey Mouse" ears. *Business Insider*. www.businessinsider.com/.

Firth, R. (1973). *Symbols: Public and Private*. London: George Allen and Unwin.

Fordham, A. (2017). In a bullet-riddled mansion, a Beirut architect envisions a museum of memory. NPR, March 30. https://n.pr/2oelJol.

Foucault, M. (1977). *Discipline and Punish: The Birth of the Prison* (A. Sheridan, Trans.). Harmondsworth, UK: Penguin.

Giddens, A. (1985). *The Nation-State and Violence*. Vol. 2. Berkeley: University of California Press.

Guardian (2010). *Al-Ahram* newspaper defends doctored photo of Hosni Mubarak. September 17. www.theguardian.com/world/2010/sep/17/al-ahram-newspaper-doctored-photo-hosni-mubarak.

Halbwachs, M. (1950/1980). *The Collective Memory* (F. J. Ditter Jr. and V. Y. Ditter, Trans.). New York: Harper and Row.

Hamdy, B., and Karl, D. (2014). *Walls of Freedom: Street Art of the Egyptian Revolution*. Berlin: From Here to Fame.

Harré, R., and Langenhove, L. (Eds.) (1998). *Positioning Theory*. Oxford: Blackwell.

Harré, R., Lee, N., and Moghaddam, M. F. (2008). Positioning and conflict: An introduction. In R. Harré, N. Lee, and M. F. Moghaddam (Eds.), *Global Conflict Resolution through Positioning Analysis* (pp. 3–20). New York: Springer.

Khatib, L. (2013). *Image Politics in the Middle East: The Role of the Visual in Political Struggle*. New York: I. B. Tauris.

Langer, S. (1953). *Feeling and Form*. New York: Charles Scribner's Sons.

  (1967). *Mind: An Essay on Human Feeling*. Vol. 1. Baltimore: Johns Hopkins University Press.

Le Bon, G. (1895/2002). *The Crowd: A Study of the Popular Mind*. New York: Dover.

Lefebvre, H. (1974/1991). *The Production of Space*. Oxford: Basil Blackwell.

Lonchuk, M., and Rosa, A. (2011). Voices of graphic art images. In M. Märtsin, B. Wagoner, E. L. Aveling, I. Kadianaki, and L. Whittaker (Eds.), *Dialogicality in Focus: Challenges to Theory, Method and Application* (pp. 129–146). New York: Nova Science.

Marková, I. (2003). *Dialogicality and Social Representations*. Cambridge: Cambridge University Press.

Messaris, P. M., and Abraham, L. (2001). The role of image in framing news stories. In S. D. Reese, O. Gandy Jr., and A. E. Grant (Eds.), *Framing Public Life: Perspectives on Media and Our Understanding of the Social World* (pp. 215–226). Mahwah, NJ: Lawrence Erlbaum.

Mitchell, W. J. T. (1984). What is an image? *New Literary History*, 15, 503–537.

  (1986). *Iconology: Image, Text, Ideology*. Chicago: University of Chicago Press.

  (1994). *Picture Theory: Essays on Verbal and Visual Representation*. Chicago: University of Chicago Press.

  (2005). *What Do Pictures Want? The Lives and Loves of Images*. Chicago: University of Chicago Press.

Moscovici, S. (1984). The phenomenon of social representations. In R. M. Farr and S. Moscovici (Eds.), *Social Representations* (pp. 3–69). Cambridge: Cambridge University Press.

Ranciere, J. (2004). *The Politics of Aesthetics: The Distribution of the Sensible* (G. Rockhill, Trans.). New York: Continuum.

Rogoff, I. (1998). Studying visual culture. In N. Mirzoeff (Ed.), *Visual Culture Reader* (pp. 24–36). New York: Routledge.

Scott, J. C. (1990). *Domination and the Arts of Resistance: Hidden Transcripts*. London: Yale University Press.

Thompson, J. B. (2005). The new visibility. *Theory, Culture and Society*, 22(6), 31–51.

Wagoner, B. (2017). *The Constructive Mind: Bartlett's Psychology in Reconstruction*. Cambridge: Cambridge University Press.

Wagoner, B., Awad, S. H., and Bresco, I. (forthcoming). The politics of representing the past: Symbolic spaces of positioning and irony. In J. Valsiner and A. Rosa (Eds.), *Cambridge Handbook of Sociocultural Psychology*, 2nd ed. Cambridge: Cambridge University Press.

Zelizer, B. (2004). The voice of the visual in memory. In K. R. Phillips (Ed.), *Framing Public Memory* (pp. 157–186). Tuscaloosa: University of Alabama.

Zittoun, T., Valsiner, J., Salgado, J., Gonçalves, M. M., Vedeler, D., and Ferring, D. (2013). *Human Development in the Life Course: Melodies of Living.* Cambridge: Cambridge University Press.

12 Constructing Cultural Pathology
The December 2008 Upheaval in the Greek Press

*Nikos Bozatzis and Christina Teliou**

> Comrade woman, comrade man.
> Revolted Greece.
> We, the smallest, from this corner of world, salute you.
> Accept our respect and our admiration
> for what you think and do.
> From far away, we learn from you. We thank you
> — Subcomandante Marcos, First World Festival
> of Dignified Rage, January 2, 2009

Over the years, the construction of crowd events and collective action in lay, media and political discourse has attracted some attention within the discursive turn in social psychology and the associated tradition of discourse-based works within the social identity theory research tradition (e.g., Drury, 2002; Drury and Reicher, 2000; Litton and Potter, 1985; Potter and Halliday, 1990; Potter and Reicher, 1987; Reicher, 1984, 1996; Reicher and Potter, 1985; Stott and Drury, 2000; Wetherell and Potter, 1988; see also Fang, 1994; van Dijk, 1989; Drury and Reicher, Chapter 2). Among other analytic angles, extant research has shed light on ways in which social actors construct versions of crowd events and collective action within evaluatively loaded descriptive practices or arguments. Analyses in this area have focused, variably, on representational resources (or *interpretative repertoires*; Potter and Wetherell, 1987; e.g., Potter and Reicher, 1987) mobilized within talk and texts, as well as on aspects of the rhetorical, argumentative organization of such discursive practices (e.g., Drury, 2002). Most importantly, such studies often highlight ways in which authorities, media or lay persons undermine, discredit or otherwise problematize collective action and crowds by *pathologizing* them. Processes of pathologization have been shown to involve the mobilization of a vocabulary and social imagery of "mobs,"

* We would like to thank the editors of this volume for their kind invitation to join in this project. Fathali Moghaddam, in particular, should also be thanked for his patience and nurturing humor at the final stages of our work. Thanks also should be extended to Vangelis Ntontis for his useful suggestions on an earlier draft of this chapter.

218

"irrationality," "contagion," and "atavism." As it has been argued (e.g., Drury, 2002; Stott and Drury, 2016; Drury and Reicher, Chapter 2), the genealogical provenance of such discursive resources can be traced back to Le Bon's (1947) popular classic *The Crowd: A Study of the Popular Mind*. Overall, social-psychological cum discourse analytic work of this mold, explicitly aims at deconstructing such representational and argumentative practices in order to salvage the option of collective action as a vehicle for radical politics and socioeconomic transformation.

This chapter draws its inspiration, political rationale, and analytic orientation from this tradition of discourse analytic and discourse-based work in social psychology.[1] Our study focuses on a series of collective action events that took place in Athens and other Greek cities in December 2008 (and, less so, in January 2009). Our analytic interest is with the ways in which these were accounted for within a segment of mainstream, national press. While our study shares the analytic concern with the workings of *pathologizing rhetoric* in accounts of collective action, our analysis takes a novel angle, shedding light on a hitherto uncharted turn that such discursive practices may take. We highlight ways in which an understanding of these mobilizations as antagonistic, radical politics is preempted through rhetorical/ideological (Billig, 1991) constructions that pathologize, in *cultural* terms, the social and political, national milieu in which these events took place: namely, modern Greece. Such rhetorical practices, we argue, attend to a certain hegemonic stake. What revolutionaries, like Subcomandante Marcos quoted above, as well as activists and (a number of) social and political theorists (e.g., Bratsis, 2010; Douzinas, 2010, 2013; Gavriilidis, 2009; Johnston and Seferiades, 2012; Kalyvas, 2010; Kornetis, 2010; Mentinis, 2010; Pechtelidis, 2011; Psimitis, 2011; Sotiris, 2010, 2013; Παπανικολόπουλος, 2016; and contributors in Dalakoglou and Vradis, 2011), welcomed, recognized, discussed or otherwise treated as insurrectionary politics, unprecedented for an EU country in recent times, came to be (re)presented as a parochial curio, allegedly stemming from the pathologies of a state, a society and a political culture in the periphery of the West.[2] The cultural pathologization of the Greek context by the

---

[1] While in social theory and political science the December 2008 upheaval drew quite some attention, social-psychological analyses are rather rare; for notable exceptions, see Baka and Garyfallou (2011) and Triga and Baka (2014); Tsalikoglou (2009) also provides for some initial reflections towards the establishment of a critical psychological research agenda in this field.

[2] It should be stressed, however, that our aim in this chapter is not to account theoretically for the reasons why the collective actions and mobilizations that unfolded in the streets, public spaces and institutional sites of Athens and other Greek cities at that period constitute an event in radical politics; neither it is our aim to enter the debate as to the type

Greek press during the very time that these mobilizations were unfolding, we argue, works against the establishment of the December 2008 upheaval as radical *politics* (cf. Kallianos, 2011) and turns it into something akin to a knee-jerk reaction against an ailing nation that needs to be "reformed," along more (neo)liberal lines perhaps, to resemble, allegedly, polities of the "advanced West" (see also, Bozatzis, forthcoming). Let us start by offering an account of the December upheaval, based, mostly, on scholarly works and participant observations.

The December 2008 Upheaval

On Saturday, December 6, 2008, early evening, a police-car was crossing a main road in the central Athens, Exarcheia district. On a crossroad, as it often happens in Exarcheia,[3] some verbal skirmish occurred between the special guard policemen in the car and a group of youth. As it transpires from later court material, despite explicit orders they received on the radio to ignore the incident and to return to their base, the two policemen parked the car some hundred meters away and walked back to the scene. There, one of them took aim and shot in the direction of a small group of youth standing in the corner.[4] The fifteen-year-old high school student Αλέξης Γρηγορόπουλος fell, fatally wounded, and died in the hands of his friends. In the hours to come, relevant information from conventional media was rather sparse. However, the news

of politics, potentialities and weaknesses that it might have presented or, indeed, missed out. Such aims would go well beyond our disciplinary scope and the limitations of in this text. Instead, our aim here is to highlight and therefore deconstruct the dominant, hegemonic, rhetorical/ideological practices that precluded and worked against a radical politics understanding of this instance of collective action.

[3] Exarcheia, located in the center of Athens, is a vibrant, densely populated district. Nearby there are quite a few University Faculties and it has been home, traditionally, to a sizable student population. The area hosts a large number of bookshops, cafes, bars and restaurants and, since the late 1970s, it is the undisputable counterculture epicenter of Athens and an urban hub that harbors and nurtures a radical, left-wing or antiauthoritarian/anarchist, political scene. For the last few decades, it is also home to considerable drug dealing. The area, in its perimeter at least, is heavily policed and its narrow streets have been the setting of numerous confrontations between the Greek riot police (M.A.T.) and youth, on various occasions. Before December 2008, perhaps the most serious and extended ones were the riots that broke out in November 1985, after the shooting and the death of another young person in the area. In the vicinity, it is located the historical building of the Athens Polytechnic, which, in November 1973, hosted a student occupation that opened the way for the fall of the military junta a few months later. Ever since, annual commemorations of this event usually end up in "επεισόδια," confrontational incidents between M.A.T. and youth, in Exarcheia and beyond.

[4] In October 2010, the police-guard, Επαμεινώνδας Κορκονέας, was convicted for murder and sentenced to life imprisonment without the possibility of a reduction in term (Xenakis and Cheliotis, 2016)

spread quickly among Athenian youth, by means of new communication technologies.[5] Some hours later, the first barricades appeared on nearby Athenian streets and what followed in the weeks to come was civil unrest, all over the country, of an unprecedented scale and duration in post–civil war[6] Greece or indeed Europe[7] (Tzatha, 2009, pp. 13–14), in her detailed account of the events, gives the following overall picture:

Until 31 January in Athens alone there were: 350 occupations of schools and thirty occupations of University Faculties, sixty-eight direct action events (attacks at police-stations, prisons or private property, sit-ins, blockades of avenues, civil disobedience, electronic civil disobedience, the firebombing of the Christmas tree in the Syntagma square), forty-six interventions/performances (interventions in theatres, shopping malls, working places, entertainment and commercial zones and media stations, redistribution of looted commerce to people on the streets, flyer distribution, concerts, dancing performances, street theatre and happenings, hanging of banners from the Acropolis), twenty-seven demonstrations (eleven resulting in riots), twenty-one rallies (four resulting in riots), twenty weblogs created on the Internet, fifteen occupations of public buildings (town halls, municipal cafeterias, headquarters of the Confederation of Greek Workers, headquarters of the Athens Journalists' Union, National Opera House, three University buildings), four general strikes, numerous graffiti and stencil on walls, shop-blinders, statues and means of transportation.

The December 2008 upheaval[8] stands out in recent Greek political history for a number of reasons that should be briefly noted here. (1) The geographical spread of protests and insurrectionary actions was unprecedented. Παπανικολόπουλος (2016) documents mobilizations in fourteen Greek urban centers, including many smaller ones, as well as an impressive diversification of the *loci* in which mobilizations occurred within greater, metropolitan Athens. (2) The intensity and the duration of the mobilizations was also unprecedented. Up to Christmas, there were demonstrations or other mobilizations taking place more or

---

[5] For the importance of media technologies in the organization and play-out of the December upheaval see Gavriilidis (2009), Milioni and Panos (2011), Mowbray (2010), Triga and Baka (2014), and Vatikiotis (2011).

[6] After the end of second world war, from 1946 to 1949, Greece went through a prolonged and destructive civil war between forces of the right and the left.

[7] Wikipedia provides a useful and relatively detailed description of the December events. https://en.wikipedia.org/wiki/2008_Greek_riots.

[8] Questions and debates over the proper naming of the collective action unfolded in December and January 2009 in Athens and other major and minor urban centers in Greece abound in the relevant, media and academic literature. The terms "riots," "revolt," "insurrection," or "events" have been used by various analysts and commentators. Without making any strong claim about our choice, our predilection, is for the term "upheaval" (see also Bratsis, 2010), largely because, we suspect, it avoids the negative connotations of the term "riots" and the rather celebratory tone of the term "revolt." In our text we also use the more neutral term "events."

less every day and there were times when some one hundred thousand people were on the streets all over the country (Kalyvas, 2010). With a short interlude during the days around Christmas and New Year's eve, the mobilizations and the overall unrest continued well into January 2009, losing though, gradually, their *momentum*. (3) When violence was part of the scene, its intensity, involving both "camps" of the confrontations, was at times staggering. According to Tzatha (2009), during the first three days of the riots, in Athens only, 435 business outlets were smashed or torched, including banks, super-markets, hotels, theaters, cinemas, multinational companies, and department stores as well as small- and medium-scale enterprises. Xenakis and Cheliotis (2016) report that the damages incurred to private property exceeded 1.5 billion euros. The same authors document hundreds of injured, on both sides of the confrontation lines; 1,800 protestors detained by the police; as well as 284 arrests in 16 cities and towns all over Greece. With the exception, perhaps, of the very first days, the mobilizations were met with excessive and more often than not indiscriminate police violence (Astrinaki, 2009) and the use of chemicals for the dispersion of protestors reached unprecedented heights. It should be noted that while in the national press, more often than not, the perpetrators of violence were deemed to be the "known-unknowns" or "hooded-ones"[9] that constitute the anarchist or antiauthoritarian *nuclei* traditionally based and frequenting Exarcheia, academic reports (e.g., Astrinaki, 2009; Dalakoglou and Vradis, 2011; Tzatha, 2009; Παπανικολόπουλος, 2016) maintain that violence, as a repertoire of collective action, whenever adopted, it involved larger segments and constituencies of the crowds protesting. (4) However, violence, as part of the protest mobilizations, was not always and certainly not exclusively on the menu. Indeed, according to the analysis presented in Παπανικολόπουλος (2016), only 18 percent of the total mobilizations recorded fell within the "violent repertoire" and this percentage falls even further, down to 5.5 percent, if the nine hundred occupations of school and one hundred occupations of university buildings are included within the total count of actions considered. The vast majority of mobilizations within the December 2008 (and January 2009) upheaval, it is argued, was of a "conventional" and "obstructive" protest type; some of these are, succinctly, captured in the quote by Tzatha (2009) above (see also Χαριτάτου-Συνοδινού, 2010). (5) When the question of who were the main actors or the prime

---

[9] "Γνωστοί-άγνωστοι" or "κουκουλοφόροι" are the terms conventionally used by the Greek media to refer to the participants of the confrontational incidents mentioned above in Note No5.

insurrectionary subject of the December events, comes to be posed, most scholarly accounts (e.g., Dafermos, 2009; Diakoumakos, 2015; Pechtelidis, 2011; Psimitis, 2011; Sotiris, 2010; and contributions in Economides and Monastiriotis, 2009) stresses its youth-centered character: school students, tertiary education students, employed, unemployed, underemployed, or precarious workers. Indeed, most of the mobilizations and certainly the more massive ones, were called upon and coordinated by an ad hoc body consisting of school student representatives. Perhaps one of the most important and, from an antagonistic politics perspective, hopeful (Kalyvas, 2010) features of the December mobilizations is that, for the first time, participated young people of an immigrant background. This cluster of the metropolitan Athens population constitutes a particularly socially disadvantaged group not only due to the high unemployment rates it suffers but also because these young persons do not enjoy citizenship rights and are frequent targets of police brutality. (6) According to some analysts (e.g., Dalakoglou and Vradis, 2011; Makrygianni and Tsavdaroglou, 2011; Petropoulou, 2010; Sotiris, 2013), the impact of December 2008 mobilizations can be discerned in organizational features of oppositional practices unfolded in subsequent years, as in the massive mobilizations against austerity. (7) The December upheaval, beyond its domestic impact, caused some commotion in European politics (Kalyvas, 2010). For example, there are media reports that the French president Nicolas Sarkozy refrained from introducing controversial educational reforms stating: "we do not want a European May 1968 in the middle of Christmas" (Bratsis, 2010). Moreover, some political scientists (e.g., Johnston and Seferiades, 2012; Kotronaki and Seferiades, 2012) draw links between the Greek December upheaval and uprisings that followed in the global arena in the next few years, as in the various "Arab Spring" outbreaks. At the very least, what is certain is that, at the time, the December mobilizations generated multiple acts of solidarity at a global level. Tzatha (2009) reports relevant, variable, actions, undertaken in 160 cities, mostly in Europe but also in as distal locations as Oaxaca, Seoul, and Wellington.

The Study and the Setting of a Critical Discursive Social Psychology Agenda

For the needs of the present study, we examined all issues of three major Greek newspapers, TO BHMA, ΕΛΕΥΘΕΡΟΤΥΠΙΑ and TA NEA, in their daily and weekend editions, for the period extending from December 7, 2008, to January 20, 2009. We focused, specifically, on editorials and opinion columns, regular ones, i.e., authored by staff-journalists, or invited ones, i.e., authored by a range of social commentators (e.g., politicians, intellectuals, experts). The three newspapers we consider were, at the time, politically affiliated to the center-left of the political *spectrum*, with TA NEA addressing and attracting mostly a lower-middle-class, popular readership; TO BHMA mostly an intellectual and upper-middle-class one; whereas ΕΛΕΥΘΕΡΟΤΥΠΙΑ used to be the more "radical" voice within the mainstream press of the center-left.[10] The reason we chose these left-of-the-center, but still mainstream and with wide circulation, newspapers, is that we wanted to check our analytic agenda against the part of the national press that is often assumed (e.g., Andronikidou and Kovras, 2012) to adopt a "permissive" attitude toward mobilizations organized or involving political forces of the left, trade unions and (new) social movements.[11] Following standard discourse analytic practices (Potter and Wetherell, 1987), all texts collected were read repeatedly in search for recurrent representational patterns (i.e., interpretative repertoires). However, our analysis, beyond the semantic content, focuses also on aspects of the rhetorical organization of these texts. Indeed, we frequently make use of the typical discursive psychology (Edwards and Potter, 1992) path of analysis that highlights parallels in "identity"/"world" making work accomplished within descriptions (e.g., Edwards, 2007). This dual analytic orientation, together with our explicit commitment to relate rhetoric to ideology (Billig, 1991), link our approach to the type of analysis advocated by Wetherell (1998) and defined as *critical discursive social psychology*. In line with critical social psychology lines of reasoning (e.g., Billig, 1987, 1991; Billig et al., 1988), we regard the authorial voices articulating and inhabiting the accounts under consideration as drawing upon long-standing "traditions of argumentation" (Shotter, 1993). Constructing socially intelligible and politically consequential accounts of the December mobilizations and the social and political context in which these took place, we argue, they invoke familiar, locally and internationally circulating, lay, media, political as well as academic, discourses of what is to be counted as "modern Greek." Most importantly, such conventional, age-long, modalities of representing the "subject matter" of the modern Greek condition correspond and avail rhetorical credentials of a particular, symbolically and ideologically valorized *positioning* (e.g., Wetherell, 1998). Let us start, then, by explicating these long-standing

[10] "Η ΕΛΕΥΘΕΡΟΤΥΠΙΑ" as well as the daily edition of "TO BHMA" did not survive the economic pressures of the then forthcoming (in its local effects) global post-2008 financial crisis and have discontinued their circulation.
[11] It should be noticed that, at the time, the ruling party in government was Νέα Δημοκρατία, a party of the Right, headed by Prime Minister Kostas Karamanlis.

traditions of argumentation about modern Greece and Greeks and the rhetorical/ideological identities at stake.

Modern Greek Cultural Dualism and the Politics of Crypto-colonialism

The ideological construction of modern Greek national discourse and identity has been the topic of a plethora of elaborate, critical works within the humanities and the social sciences (e.g., Faubion, 1993; Gourgouris, 1996; Herzfeld, 1982, 1987; Tsoucalas, 1991; Γιακωβάκη, 2006; Σκοπετέα, 1988; Τζιόβας, 1994). The modern Greek State emerged as a political entity, in the 1830s, out of the dissolving Ottoman Empire, largely due to the political will of the Great Powers of the time (Britain, France, Russia). Operating within the geopolitical logics and antagonisms of their colonial projects and aspirations, these European powers saw political advantages in supporting the Greek revolt, aiming at national independence, that broke out in the 1820s and in instituting a militarily weak nation-state, subservient to their interests. At an ideological level, these geopolitical choices were buttressed by centuries-long identity-construction processes for Europe itself. As it has been argued (e.g., Bernal, 1987), with Renaissance started a long period, culminating in the nineteenth century, through which the symbolic community of and identification with Christendom came to be gradually substituted by an emerging notion of a European identity (see also Delanty, 1995). At the core of this developing *Occidentalism* (e.g., Ahıska, 2003; Coronil, 1996), laid a powerful origin myth: the treatment of ancient Hellas as *the* primordial ancestor of modern Europe and as an absolute standard of cultural perfection. Such ideological identity-building processes went in parallel with the institutional, political and knowledge producing practices that Said (1978) describes as *Orientalism*. In the nascent era of Western geopolitical dominance, the Orient came to be *imagined-into-being*, as a surrogate, reversed cultural image of the Occident, as the cultural embodiment of *exotica*, *backwardness*, and *stagnation*.

The ideological constitution of the representational modalities of modern Greek identity are inseparably entangled in this larger hegemonic project of Western domination (Herzfeld, 1987). From the 1670s onward, scores of European travelers, intellectuals, romantic wanderers, chroniclers and admirers of *"the glory that was Greece,"*[12] stormed the lands that were to become the territory of the modern Greek nation-state

---

[12] From the 1845 Edgar Alan Poe's poem "To Helen."

(Γιακωβάκη, 2006). Moreover, large numbers of Europeans, the Philhellenes (St Clair, 1972), fought in the Greek War of Independence and even more aided the Greek struggle through publications that gradually turned the European publics in favor of this "ancient people," the "living ancestors of Europe" (Herzfeld, 1987), that were founding themselves subjugated to the "barbaric" forces of the East. Indeed, the Greek revolt was seen as a product and manifestation of the very "essence" of Occidental identity: of "love of freedom" and "individualism-as-insubordination." It was these traits that were thought as linking culturally the modern Greeks with their ancestors in a clear contrast to the "docile" Orientals (Herzfeld, 1987). However, this "favorable," Occidental, gaze came at a price. What European observers and commentators encountered in the lands they visited were ancient remnants, testimonies to a glorified past, dispersed, though, in a territory populated by Balkan communities, largely indistinguishable in lifestyles and mentalities from their "barbaric oppressors" and from other cultures of the southeastern corner of Europe and the Levant. As a result, a powerful *cultural dualism* trope came to be established for the narration of the modern Greek condition. The modern Greeks were diagnosed as culturally contaminated by centuries of subjugation to the Turks and modern Greek identity was seen as split and encompassing uneasy tensions between Occidental ("Hellenic") and Oriental ("Romeic") cultural elements (Herzfeld, 1987).

Binary oppositions, involving Oriental (or "tradition") and Occidental (or "modern") themes and perspectives, have come to inform a multitude of *realistic*, in terms of their epistemological stance, intellectual accounts of modern Greece and Greeks (for relevant critiques, see Herzfeld, 1982, 1987; Tsoucalas, 1991; Τζιόβας, 1994). For our present needs, suffice it to point out that echoes of this narrative trope can be detected in a text that, in recent years, has acquired an almost canonical *status* in Greek political science literature: Diamandouros's (1994) aptly titled "Cultural Dualism and Political Change in Postauthoritarian Greece" essay.[13] For Diamandouros, the highly contested nation-state building processes in modern Greece constituted a critical juncture that by and large defined the terms of modern Greek engagement with modernity. The tensions inherent in the transition from a premodern socioeconomic and political context to the context of a modern nation-state, argues Diamandouros, gave rise to two powerful and conflicting strands of modern Greek political culture. A "*reformist/modernizing*" one,

---

[13] Diamandouros's text was translated and published as a book in Greek in 2000 (Διαμαντούρος, 2000).

drawing its inspiration and trajectory from the novel Western experience and an antecedent, "*traditional*" or "*underdog*" one which is configured out of elements from the Byzantine and Ottoman Greek historical experiences. The former culture, Diamandouros (1994, pp. 12–13) argues, is:

[s]teeped in the Balkan-Ottoman heritage and profoundly influenced by the Weltanschauung of an Orthodox church which, for historical, intellectual, as well as theological reasons, had long maintained a strongly, and occasionally militant, anti-western stance, this is a culture marked by a pronounced introvertedness; a powerful statist orientation coupled with a profound ambivalence concerning capitalism and the market mechanism; a decided preference for paternalism and protection, and a lingering adherence to precapitalist practices; a universe of moral sentiments in which parochial and, quite often, primordial attachments and the intolerance of the alien which these imply predominate; a latent authoritarian orientation fostered by the structures of Ottoman rule and by the powerful cultural legacy of what Weber so perceptibly termed a "sultanistic regime"; and a diffident attitude towards innovation.

As for the reformist/modernizing culture's key characteristics, Diamandouros (1994, pp. 22–23) argues thus:

The younger of the twin cultures in modern Greece draws its intellectual origins from the Enlightenment and from the tradition of political liberalism issuing from it. Secular and extrovert in orientation, it has tended to look to the nations of the advanced industrial West for inspiration and for support in implementing its programs. Over time, it has been identified with a distinct preference for reform, whether in society, economy, or polity, designed to promote rationalization along liberal, democratic, and capitalist lines. Favorable to the market mechanism and supportive of the strategic use of the state to foster social and political arrangements promotive of competition and of an internationally-competitive economy, it has been more receptive to innovation and less apprehensive of the costs involved in the break with tradition. More outward-looking and less parochial than its rival, this is a culture which, on the whole, has tended to favor rather than to oppose the creation and proliferation of international linkages for Greece and to promote its integration into the international system.

According to Diamandouros, the main assumptions, characteristics, mentalities, and practices of modern Greece's twin cultures can easily be identified throughout its history; they intermingle as they are not the exclusive property of any social or political group; while at different times, one of them prevails and gives the tone to socioeconomic and political developments. According to his scheme, the reformist culture was the prevailing one from the last quarter of the nineteenth century until the 1930s; the underdog culture had the upper hand from the 1930s until the restoration of parliamentary democracy in Greece in 1974; whereas the period from the mid-1970s until the mid-1990s was marked, he argues, by a gradual phasing-in of the reformist/modernizing culture and the intense resistance of the underdog culture against the prospect of its marginalization.

Whatever may be the academic merits of *realist* intellectual accounts, like Diamandouros's one, testifying to the factual existence of twin cultures in modern Greece, such a modality of social science accounting has certainly raised important epistemological, ideological, and political questions (see, e.g., Liakos and Kouki, 2015; Ntampoudi, 2014; Stavrakakis, 2002; Xenakis, 2013; Σταυρακάκης, 2014; and, in particular, Τζιόβας, 1994). It is all too easy to see such accounts as chapters in the age-long Occidentalist saga that has prescribed for modern Greece an ideological "fate" of perennial *lacking*. Compared to "its" ancient glories and to these glories' modern day, "rightful," transplantation to Western modernity-proper, modern Greece appears trapped in a condition of an *"always-not-yet-enough-European."* From our point of view, a shift in perspective toward epistemologies that favor the analytic foregrounding of *reflexive practice* (e.g., Schatzki, Knorr Cetina, and von Savigny, 2001) as a constitutive element of *the social* and *the cultural* domain may be immensely scholarly informative. Herzfeld's (e.g., 1987, 1992, 1995, 2002) critical ethnography and critical discursive social psychology (e.g., Wetherell, 1998), as applied in studies focusing on modern Greek discursive pragmatics (e.g., Bozatzis, 1999, 2009; Μποζατζής, 2005a, 2005b) can be of use here. The social constructionist "tuning" of these perspectives allows for the "Occidental" and the "Oriental" to emerge, within the analytic sphere, as participants' orientations and not as a "binary opposition" imposed by the analyst. In that sense, they are neither cultural realities cast in historical stone, nor (cognitive) stereotypes in need to be dispelled: their reality is their reflexive deployment, by skillful social actors, in the course of unfolding practices and accounting for them, while striving for social accountability. Let us examine briefly Herzfeld's ethnographic insights in order to a get a glimpse as to how this might be shown to happen by means of a critical discursive social psychology analysis.

For Herzfeld (2002), Greek national independence, dependent as it was upon the adoption of an imported – bestowed and denied at the same time – origin myth signifies a *crypto-colonial* condition. The European gaze, which embodies a hegemonic gate-keeping of the Occidental cultural capital, gave rise, within Greece, to large-scale processes, aiming at cultural transformation. The modern Greeks (to be) learned that endless series of familiar, banal aspects of their everyday lives were of Oriental origin, therefore "alien," and in need of elimination or purification. Modern Greece and Greeks ought to be re-Hellenized. Indeed, social

history records (e.g., Πολίτης, 1993; Σκοπετέα, 1988) are ripe with doc-
umentations of large- and small-scale societal practices in which affini-
ties to an ancient Hellenic past were forged and similarities to modern
West pursued. However, in Herzfeld's ethnography, Greek social actors
do not appear as "social dupes" passively adopting the European cultural dualism narrative that counterposes the "holiness" of the Hellenic
to the "polluted" Oriental. The assumptions of this cultural dualism
narrative have been fused, Herzfeld argues, into the modern Greek discourse of *cultural imperfection.*" This is not a discourse marking passive
acceptance. It is one militating for "new beginnings," for reclaiming a
past that was simultaneously granted and denied to them. Its assumptions and hegemonic logic have become, Herzfeld argues, instruments
deployed in battles for cultural distinction in a multitude of social contexts and encounters. While Europeans saw Oriental cultural afflictions
in the modern Greek State and castigated modern Greeks for them,
Greek elites leveled the same charge to lower Greek classes for their
Oriental-looking habits; whereas, lower classes respond to their Orientalization by self-styled Occidental elites by decrying the Greek state and
its political and institutional functionaries for unmistaken *Oriental* shortcomings, rendering, say, the charge "δεν έχουμε Κράτος"[14] to a ubiquitous
argumentative verdict in everyday conversations.

For Herzfeld, perhaps the most intriguing domain in which such
symbolic confrontations and inversions come to surface is presented
by conflicting interpretations of the notion of "Greek individualism."
For the elites, as we saw, the preindependence "Greek-individualism-
as-insubordination" was celebrated as a hallmark of modern Greeks'
Occidental credentials. In post-Independence times though, from the
perspective of the state and the elites, the same cultural habits and
practices that were seen as instantiations of Occidental freedom-loving,
became hallmarks of "Oriental self-interestedness." These are exemplified in, say, everyday instances of "unruly" behaviors, "rule bending"
and "indifference to the common good" in pursuit of individual gains.
Indeed, such practices are commonly seen as a socially corrosive modern
Greek "national flaw." However, Herzfeld shows that in the rhetoric of
lay social actors, the Occidental discourse of the state about law and
order is often turned on its head. In such rhetoric, the institutional
organization of state order comes to be seen as a present-day extension
of the "alien," Ottoman rule and lay "unruly" attitudes and behaviors
are recast as a manifestations of the age-old, celebrated, and Occidental
"love for freedom" and "spirit of insubordination." In such processes,

---

[14] Literally, "we don't have a State."

Herzfeld argues, the Orientalization of the supposed harbinger of modernity and European-ness in Greece (i.e., the state, its structures and its personnel), confers Occidental credentials to the lay social actors voicing the critique. Herzfeld's ethnographic account of the symbolic battles for everyday moral accountability and the ensuing practical Orientalizations/Occidentalizations have been supplemented, in recent years, by detailed socio-psychological, discourse analytic explications, influenced by his analyses, and focusing on rhetorical/ideological pragmatics in Greek lay and media discourses (e.g., Bozatzis, 1999, 2005, 2009, 2014; Μποζατζής, 2005a, 2005b; Μποζατζής, Condor, and Levine, 2004). The analysis unfolded here follows in this emerging strand of work.

This exploration into the genealogy, representational themes and pragmatics of Greek *cultural dualism* constitutes, we argue, a quintessential background, for making analytic sense of the journalist accounts of the December 2008 events. The rhetoric deployed in the texts under consideration shall be shown to reproduce ideologically such themes and positioning processes. In that sense, it partakes into the reiteration of what Herzfeld calls the *crypto-colonial* condition of modern Greece and modern Greek identity. As Herzfeld points out, and as critical social psychologists (e.g., Billig et al., 1988) have also shown, it is the "nature" of hegemony to be predicated upon active participation within the parameters of constituted knowledge and not upon its passive acceptance. Let us now turn to our empirical analyses.

The "Cultural Pathology" Repertoire: Representations and Positioning Work

In the press material we considered, we discern a rhetorically potent and widely used interpretative repertoire. This repertoire weaves within its representational orbit imagery of widespread modern Greek cultural pathology. More specifically, it includes images, metaphors, statements, arguments, and tacit assumptions about: (1) ailing, inefficient state institutions, including the government; (2) political culture pathologies; and (3) widespread, pervasive societal decay. The pathologies attributed to state institutions, political culture, and society are discursively oriented to as commonsense *topoi* (Billig, 1987) and are mobilized, mostly, in order to make (public) sense and outline the conditions that gave rise to the December upheaval. The argument we advance is that the representations used to construct these images of modern Greek cultural pathology trace their origin and reiterate the cultural dualism discourses of Greek national identity. We argue that the evaluative journalistic descriptions we consider exemplify what Herzfeld (1995) calls processes of practical Orientalization, while, in their dialectical articulation, they lay claim to Occidental symbolic credentials for the authorial voices. Thus, they should be seen, we argue, as partaking to processes of crypto-colonial ideological reproduction even when they adopt a "sympathetic," "progressive," or, in any case, nondismissive stance toward the mobilizations. In our present analyses, we aim at documenting the relevance and the representational latitude of this repertoire and ensuing positioning processes.

Ailing, Inefficient Institutions

Given the circumstances that triggered December's mobilizations, it is not surprising that the Greek police found itself often at the argumentative sights of journalists and commentators. The metaphor of pathology was sometimes explicitly invoked:[15]

The beyond any logic execution of the 15 years old school student in Exarcheia is not just a proof of how much ill Greek Police. It is also... (Παπαχρήστος, TA NEA, 8/12, p. 11)

In this extract, it is the "illness" of the Greek police that is set to account for the "irrational execution" of Αλέξης Γρηγορόπουλος. We would like to draw some attention here to the rhetorical work accomplished with the contrast structure (e.g., Edwards and Potter, 1992) ("the execution not just a proof/it is also"). A bland formulation of the type "the execution proves how much ill Greek police is" would perhaps make that argument sound rather tentative and perhaps unwarranted; certainly would add a sense of exaggeration. The contrast structure, however, renders this first part of the overall argument of the author "just" common-knowledge: everybody can easily tell that the execution proves how much ill Greek police but it actually proves more than that. The attribution of "irrationality" to a Greek state institution as well as the complex argumentative syllogism within which this argument is framed confers credentials of rationality to the voice articulating the critique; in the manner of Herzfeld, credentials of "Occidental rationality" we should add.

In many other occasions, notions of pathology, relating to institutional malfunctioning, were conveyed by means of arguments pointing toward the police and police officers' lacking in social accountability:

[15] The texts included in the presented analysis were translated from Greek into English. In so doing, we tried to remain as faithful as possible to the Greek semantic content, at the expense, perhaps, of literary style. Whenever it was deemed necessary, as when we translated idiomatic expressions, we give the original Greek terms in square brackets.

a Police [force] that does whatever it wants and does not account [to anybody]. (Πελώνη, TA NEA, 10/12))

unsolicited avengers take the law in their hands (Πολυμίλης, ΕΛΕΥΘΕΡΟΤΥΠΙΑ, 9/12)

Critical arguments pointing toward the Greek police's lack of accountability took also a more specific turn, targeting police aggression. One way of doing that was through the invocation of a particular cultural type of personhood: the "νταής της γειτονιάς," translated here as "the bully of the neighborhood." In the following extract, the authorial voice invokes and puts the blame on such a type of personhood while, at the same time, establishes its accountability by deflecting a hearable – liberal – objection about what could be regarded as an undue critique of a (should be) respected state institution.

Every citizen can tell a story proving that Greek Police is not serious. My own adventure happened two years ago, when . . . A ridiculous incident, with a stupid and untrained policeman, which could turn into a tragedy if the woman had not managed to call me. Unfortunately, the majority of Greek policemen are untrained, rude and indifferent to the essence of their job, but eager to bully. And the special guard that murdered the kid was the "bully" of the neighbourhood; he went back to demand an explanation from these young persons that insulted him and to save face. (Πολίτης, TA NEA, 8/12)

This extract starts with the critical characterization of the police, an arguably "serious" institution, as "not serious." The author's accountability toward this dismissive critique is managed by a deft shift of footing and an extreme case formulation (Edwards and Potter, 1992): his conclusion is rendered unexceptional; it is one commonly reached by "every citizen"; everybody has an equivalent story to tell. Stories involving "stupid and untrained" policemen, "rude and indifferent to the essence of their (serious) job"; stories that may or do end in tragedies; unless a rational and bold citizen, a hero of Greek everyday life as it were, is called upon and intervenes. Otherwise, the "eagerness to bully" shown by policemen – "bullies of the neighborhood" – may find time and space to materialize. This is what happened to Αλέξης Γρηγορόπουλος, he was killed in order for a "bully" to "save face." The construct "νταής της γειτονιάς" inhabits the traditional universe of the "underdog" Greek culture; it alludes to "traditional" and parochial notions of masculinity and casual authoritarianism. The authorial voice distances itself from this spectrum of traditional subjectivity and by implication celebrates the Occidental rationality of the lay, individual Greek pitted against Orientalized state institutions and their functionaries.

At other times, though, police brutality was not seen as relating to cultural types of personhood, but to cultural types of state structures. As in the following extract.

let's assume that Αλέξης Γρηγορόπουλος, at the age of 15, was like he was accused to be! So what? Should the "pseudo-Rambo" cop pull his gun and kill him? How many thousands of kids (our kids), "offenders," like that, exist in Greek society...? Should all these kids – "scums" be "done away with" by the unsolicited, "dirty Harry" bigots of the Greek Police, who are produced – diachronically – by the system-mechanisms of State violence and repression and who are nurtured by institutional cover-up and legal impunity? "Shame, you Argives"![16] (Καραβά, TO BHMA, 11/12)

In this extract, the "diachronic" Greek "state system-mechanisms of violence and repression" are seen as responsible for the "pseudo-Rambo cop" – behaviors of police officers. Indeed, the critique does not aim at the particular officer involved in the murder but to a collective category: "the dirty Harry bigots of the Greek police." Deploying an empiricist mode of accounting (Potter and Wetherell, 1987), "state system-mechanisms of violence and repression" are seen as "producing" this type of attitudes and "nurturing" them with "institutional cover-up and legal impunity." Noticeably, the charge, leveled, assumingly, against a generic audience of authorities culminates in an admonition, articulated in Homeric language: "shame"; this is what should befall on modern Greek state structures and their political personnel. The imagery of the Greek "state system-mechanisms" makes direct references to the post–World War II times when, in Diamandouros's scheme, the "underdog" culture, in its authoritarian-Right incarnation, was having the upper hand in Greek politics. Dialectically, the authorial voice assumes an Occidental positioning favoring a reformed or reconstructed, *modernized* perhaps, modus operandi of Greek state institutions; certainly a nonauthoritarian one.

While police were a frequent target of criticism, it was not the only institution that was so. At times, it was the Greek education system or, more vaguely, Greek *paideia*[17] that was represented in terms of

---

[16] We thank George Syrimis for informing us about this standardized, in English philology, translation of the Homeric expression: "Αιδώς Αργείοι."

[17] According to the Merriam-Webster online dictionary the ancient Greek word παιδεία/paideia – still in use today – refers to "[t]raining of the physical and mental faculties in such a way as to produce a broad enlightened mature outlook harmoniously combined with maximum cultural development." In modern Greek, the semantic latitude of the term encompasses both what in English would be termed "education" and "educational system" as well as this broader ancient Hellenic meaning.

deficiencies. These deficiencies were seen as playing a serious role in the bringing about of the December events.

Paideia deficit ... In such a context, in the last years, the youth is undergoing a crisis because it is encountering a backward education ((system)), unable to guarantee for them a positive prospect for the future. (Παπαντωνίου, TA NEA, 9/12)

The author, Γιάννος Παπαντωνίου, was a former minister. He served in centrist, social-democratic (PASOK) governments of the late 1990s and early 2000s which adopted as headline in their political rhetoric the imperative of *εκσυγχρονισμός/modernization* of Greek society, state structures and political culture. In his reasoning, the December events came about as a result of failures, "in recent years" – one would suspect after the electoral defeat of PASOK in 2004 – to reform the Greek education system. This, steeped as it is in underdog, unreformed "backwardness" is not in a position to provide to the youth "positive" employment "prospects." For another commentator, a prominent journalist of the "modernizing" political logic, the Greek educational system ought to be understood in even bleaker terms,

Add to that the taste of the mincer that the educational system leaves in the mouth of every one of its victims. (Τσίμας, TA NEA, 13/12)

For him, indeed, it is these devastating failures of the Greek educational system that have, in fact, "preannounced" the December upheaval;

Because all that has been happening around us during these last few days had been pre-announced ... first, by the deep crisis in Secondary Education, by the bankruptcy of the Greek public school, by the fact that it has been discredited in the consciousness of both teachers and students and by the enraged despair that boils inside the walls of schools. (Τσίμας, TA NEA, 20.12)

The "preannouncement" argument renders the December mobilizations of the student population something to be "expected"; or, more precisely, something that ought to have been expected by any rational observer, let alone by the politicians running the government and overseeing the institutions of public education in Greece. But, evidently it was not expected and, evidently, the social actors (government) that were not in a position to anticipate it, do not share the same moral universe of Occidental rationality that the journalist implicitly claims to inhabit. With regards to the deployment of the educational deficiencies theme, the narrative pattern of Greek institutional "lacking" may be seen as taking a decisive neoliberal turn: it Orientalizes "unreformed"

state-provided education structures, at times of global neoliberal transformations which turn education from a social right to a market com-
modity. At the same time, the authorial voices articulating such a critique, enhanced by allusions to an ancient Hellenic "paideia" capital,
blur notions of Occidental rationality with notions of a neoliberal commodification ethos.

Unsurprisingly perhaps, given the center-left political affiliation of the
newspapers we consider, the then – right-wing – government was also
frequently at the receiving end of vigorous blame rhetoric. Charges of
inefficiency were mostly in order. This inefficiency, in some instances,
was explicitly framed in pathology terms, invoking images of physical
disability, impotence and ailment.

It is only that now the country is administered by a special needs government,
by an unpleasant mishmash of opportunism, incapacity and impertinence. (Θεοδωρόπουλος, TA NEA, 9.12)

The special needs government demands from them to take the responsibilities
that itself cannot take. (Θεοδωρόπουλος, TA NEA, 10/12)

if Saturday-night "belonged to Αλέξης," the government, which is shaking like a
fish and has essentially surrendered, as well as its incapacity lead us to believe
that. (Παπαχρήστος, TA NEA, 8.12)

The government, numb and puzzled as it is by the unprecedented events of the
last three days, is unable to convince that it has an organized, short term, plan
for dealing with the crisis. (Μαρνέλλος, ΕΛΕΥΘΕΡΟΤΥΠΙΑ, 10/12)

For the ex-minister we commented on above, the December events came
about as a result of task specific poor performance on behalf of the
government.

The current government ... did not undertake self-evident actions ... to train the
police [officers], so they would be in a position to cope in a peaceful and efficient way with the protests as well as with the riots by extremists and para-state
elements. (Παπαντωνίου, TA NEA, 9/12)

Whereas, in other accounts, arguments about a more general incompe-
tence of the government were voiced.

we tolerate a government that abets ((its)) authority and rushes afterwards to
apologise for something that it should have predicted, for something that it
should have anticipated ... We tolerate a prime minister who is unable to impose
State functioning in accordance with the rule of law, elementary respect for the
citizens' rights, who consistently contents himself with pompous statements and
delayed, hypocritical, apologies. (Πολυμίλης, ΕΛΕΥΘΕΡΟΤΥΠΙΑ, 9.12)

On occasion, the critique of the then government did not target simply its argued inefficiency but also involved explicit references to a public record of charges about harboring corruption-scandals as well as of unduly attempting to intervene in matters of the justice system.

> And something more: the leadership of the justice system should fulfil for once its duty! It ought to investigate this case, to press charges and set up the court immediately. Any attempt – in the standard tactic of this government – to cover it up shall have detrimental effects on social cohesion . . . And, at the end of the day, you covered-up, the wiring, the bonds, all these best men and best buddies[18]; not this one! (Παπαχρήστος, ΤΑ ΝΕΑ, 8/12)

Governmental, generalized and task specific, inefficiency and disorganization; inability to contain para-state elements infiltrating demonstrations; an incompetent, pompous, perhaps populist, certainly hypocrite prime minister; and a government, withering any sense of rule of law by intervening in the operation of the justice system in order to cover up its numerous scandals: it would not be an exaggeration to claim that what comes to be (re)presented on such occasions is, in Diamandouros's terms, an underdog culture galore. The government of the times was judged and irrevocably placed in its allocated by the Occidentalist narrative plot Oriental niche; by implication, the voices doing the judging claimed for themselves the ensuing Occidental rationality credentials.

Political Culture Pathologies

Representations of cultural pathology in our data reached far beyond the deprecation of *particular* state institutions (like the police, education, the judiciary or the then government). The repertoire of cultural pathology includes in its semantic orbit highly critical constructions of modern Greek political culture. More often than not, this was accomplished through the mobilization of charges of "corruption" and "clientalism," the cornerstones of the "underdog" Greek political culture in Diamandouros's scheme but also in other influential social science accounts of the modern Greek condition (e.g., Mouzelis, 1978). Let us look at a fuller version of an extract we saw above.

> The beyond any logic execution of the 15 years old school student in Exarcheia is not just a proof of how much ill Greek Police is. It is also a proof that in this country everything is wrong. Everything! Starting with how the rule of

---

[18] "Wiring," "bonds," "best men," and "best buddies": explicit references to political scandals that surfaced and tainted Νέα Δημοκρατία's rule at the time.

law works, how regulations are implemented, how the State institutions are assembled. Given the "who cares" [ωχαδερφισμό] and the "so what" [εντάξει μωρέ και τι έγινε] attitude that prevails everywhere, it is a miracle that, up to now, we haven't mourned more victims. (Παπαχρήστος, ΤΑ ΝΕΑ, 8/12)

As we previously saw, in this extract, the repertoire of cultural pathology kicks in with the argument that the murder in Exarcheia is a proof of the pathology of a particular state institution (the police). Nevertheless, the charge moves swiftly to encompass "everything in this country." This extreme case formulation brakes down into a three-part list (Edwards and Potter, 1992), which includes in the pathology metaphor the condition of the "rule of law" in Greece, the "implementation of regulations" and the ways in which "state institutions are assembled." In all these domains, the author testifies to the existence of a widespread attitude of indifference, on behalf of politicians and state functionaries. It is this widespread indifference to the public good that, for the author, renders the murder of Γρηγορόπουλος predictable. A similar – escalatory – argumentative logic we discern in the following extract.

The experts say that the hooded-ones are the result of the anomie in the political scene. They view the looting in which hundreds of hooded-ones engaged in in Athens and other big cities the night before last night as a result of politics – indeed of long-term politics, of the anomie in the Greek political scene, "... what leads to this [violence] is also the condition of anomie which is widespread in Greece. This has to do with the Police, which does whatever it wants to do without being held accountable. On the other hand, it has also to do with the political authority which is corrupted, lacking in efficiency and also not accountable. In Greece we break the rules, as a political class, as the State, as Universities... When you grow up in anomie and you see that the public sphere multiplies and rewards this anomic condition, you reproduce it." (Πελώνη, ΤΑ ΝΕΑ, 10/12)

Using the footing of an expert – i.e., a political scientist – the journalist relays a tale of pandemic anomie in Greece in order to account for the widespread violence and looting committed by the "hooded-ones." The tale of pandemic anomie comes in the form of a list (e.g., Edwards and Potter, 1992) that contains the domains in which anomie is to be found; it is couched in the warranting rhetoric of an empiricist account (Potter and Wetherell, 1987); and culminates with an extreme case formulation. This anomie, it is argued, is evident "in the Greek political scene"; it pertains to the police's modus operandi; it pertains to "political authority which is corrupted, lacking in efficiency and also not accountable"; and, climaxing, it pertains to the ways in which things are being done in Greece, generically: "we break the rules." It is this widespread anomie that gets to be reproduced in the actions of the "hooded-ones," supposedly, through some kind of a social learning and imitation logic. In this extract, the anomy reigning in Greek political culture is related to a more general condition of widespread anomy in Greek society. It links, in other words, the problems of Greek political culture to an imagery of wider social decay on which we comment below. Nevertheless, before moving to examine that type of imagery let us have a look at one more extract that points the finger to Greek political culture. In the article from which the following extract is taken, unfolds a similar escalatory logic about pandemic pathology in contemporary Greece. However, we focus on a particular part of that text because, within it, a genealogical explanation of Greece's political culture problems is *casually* brought up by the author.

this perspective does not explain everything. Nevertheless, it highlights one of the ingredients of the explosive mix that exploded in our unsuspecting hands one week ago. We still try – some of us – to pretend that we do not understand from where all this came about... Add to the mix the Vatopaidi affair, as a primary example of the corruption of the partisan – clientalist system that keeps alive the Ottoman tradition in the modern Greek life and confirms the pervasive sense of arbitrariness and impunity in terms of which the youth perceive public space in Greece. (Τσίμας, TA NEA, 13/12)

In the lengthy article from which this extract is taken, the author outlines his reasoning about the *familiar* sociocultural conditions that generated the December events. At some point his reasoning implicates a reference to one of the "scandals" of the then government (i.e., "the Vatopaidi affair"), which he treats as a "primary example of the corruption" of the modern Greek "partisan – clientalist system." At that point the author adds *casually*: "that keeps alive the Ottoman tradition in the modern Greek life." Nothing more needs to be added by the journalist. For modern Greeks, the "Ottoman tradition" is a well-known culprit of most faults they discern in the modern Greek condition. The gaze doing the discerning, in this case the one of the particular journalist, of course, distances itself from this Oriental tradition. His is a positioning in the best of Occidental rationality line of narrative, pinpointing to widespread and devastating Oriental inflicts tantalizing modern Greek political culture.

Societal Decay

In our data, the escalatory rhetoric that underlines much of the cultural pathology repertoire often found its point of culmination not in politics but into a charged imagery of wider social decay.

Governing . . . coma.[19] The murder of the student was probably only the trigger for the blanket of rage that has covered up Greece since Sunday morning. The cause is the generalised ambience of degeneration of the State and the institutions, the sense of societal breakdown that is experienced consciously by the older ones and unconsciously by the younger ones. (Μαρνέλλος, ΕΛΕΥΘΕΡΟΤΥΠΙΑ, 9/12)

In this extract, the murder of Αλέξης Γρηγορόπουλος is treated as "only" the trigger and not the cause of the "blanket of rage" that followed. The description of causes moves swiftly from the "generalised ambience of degeneration of the State and the institutions" to a "sense of societal breakdown." In the following extract, a similar explanatory rhetoric unfolds.

but rage is not enough. Confronted with events like these, we are obliged to try to understand what is happening. What is pushing hundreds, maybe thousands of young people to this antisocial behaviour? The problems they are confronted with, the sense of exclusion, the disappointment from school and their studies, the prospect of unemployment, all these certainly contribute to explosions of this type. But it is a mistake to believe that whoever has problems goes out on a rampage, smashing [things]. There is something deeper which is rotten in our society and in our educational system. For as long as we do not deal with it and as long as the sense of disintegration and anomie continues, the problem is going to get worst. (Anonymous, TA NEA, 10/12)

In here, a series of socioeconomic reasons are invoked and partially acknowledged as pushing "maybe thousands of young people to this antisocial behaviour." However, the real, as it were, reason is searched for into "something deeper which is rotten in our society and in our educational system." It is this "rotten" element that needs to be taken care of; it is "disintegration" and "anomie" that need to be stopped in order for the "problem" to cease getting worst. One is left with the impression that this "rotten element" alludes to something like the "essence" of the modern Greek condition. But in this extract, whatever that "rotten" "essence" could have been argued to be, it is not unambiguously pinpointed to. The next extract comes closer at fulfilling such a task.

A society of the "shot ones" [κοινωνία πυροβολημένων].[20] When: the pursuit of individual wellbeing is disassociated so cruelly and stupidly from the collective wellbeing. One, citizen blames the other in a stentorian [voice] – pointless cockfight – that it's only him to blame, without neither one of them assuming their individual responsibility. Then: everything turns into a mess. Forests get to be burned.

---

[19] The Greek word used in the original is "κώμα" which is pronounced exactly the same as "κόμμα," which means (political) party.

[20] In Greek slang, the word "shot," when used to describe a person, carries the meaning of idiocy or stupidity.

240   *Nikos Bozatzis and Christina Teliou*

The hustlers go wild. Demagogues rave. All, without exceptions, aspects of common life, are left at the mercy of luck and are impoverished. And then comes the shooting, the death. An extreme expression and a natural consequence of a society of the "shot ones." (Κουμανταρός, ΕΛΕΥΘΕΡΟΤΥΠΙΑ, 11.12)

This extract comes from an article appearing under a macabre title, blurring the act of Γρηγορόπουλος' shooting with a charge for Greek society as being a society of idiots. Familiar, by now, images and allusions to pathological political culture and societal decay come to be invoked. However, in this extract the root, as it were, of "the problem" comes to be pinpointed to: it all comes down to "the pursuit of individual well-being," at the expense of "collective well-being." Let us have a look at one more extract in which a similar reasoning unfolds.

The cop at home... It would be enough just to recount the events that one goes through, on any day, from morning until they go to sleep, to ascertain that culture and democratic spirit, respect for the others, and seriousness in thought and action are violated cruelly and are missing from the vast majority, in a society in which the neighbours in an apartment building do not even say good morning to one another and the authoritarianism of the father, the driver, the cashier, the civil servant in charge, the waiter, the policeman, the manager, the phoney politician, the bouncer as well as the kiss-my-ass attitude [γραψαρχιδισμός'] is the prevailing practice of violence within which Greeks live. This is their everyday routine, along with the search of some easy money [αρπαχτή]. some political favour, a tax-evasion, of a fiddle at the end of the day in order to confront the voracious monster of the State machinery, which, leaded by the Parliament, distributes favours [βολεύει], corrupts, engages in wrongdoings, bribes, gets rich, evades taxes, legislates shamefully in interest [νομοθετεί με παράθυρα ντροπής], takes to court as ordered, arrests selectively, creating citizens corrupted, suffering injustices, outraged. Pitted against this emetic mob, which constitutes the everyday life of the citizens, there is a guileless part [of the population]; that part which is diachronically guileless in our societies: the adolescents. And another smaller, guileless part, which is being crushed between the millstones of everyday incivility/un-culture [απολιτισιά]: the truly cultured/civilized [Πολιτισμένοι] ones. But also another part, which is getting bigger and bigger and which suffer all the more cruelly the violence of the embezzlement [οικονομισιά] and of every kind of authority: the marginalised. The immigrants, the homeless, the junkies, the unemployed, the ideologically misfits in this type of society. (παπαδόπουλος-Τετράδης, ΕΛΕΥΘΕΡΟΤΥΠΙΑ, 11/12)

In this extract, the discourse of cultural pathologization we saw unfolding in all our examples so far reaches its extremes by means of pulsating, rhetorical tension. The full choreography of the cultural pathology repertoire parades here. The "voracious monster of the State machinery"; authoritarian civil servants; corrupted politicians and political culture; images of social decay and an un-livable, violent, everyday life due to the pursuit of illegitimate, atomized, self-interests by the "vast majority" of Greeks. Against this devastating and omnipresent "everyday incivility/un-culture" of self-interested Greeks and Greek institutions stand, it is argued, only three – ideal types of – social figures: the "diachronically guileless adolescents"; the (few) "truly cultured/ civilized" citizens; and the socioeconomically and ideologically marginalized persona. Dare we suggest that the authorial voice doing the diagnosis of the root problem of modern Greek social decay (i.e., self-interestedness) stands, in the confrontation line it has skillfully drawn, opposite to the "emetic mob" of everyday Greeks? In the side of the (few) "truly civilized/cultured" ones, perhaps? Or, perhaps, in the romantic crew of the "ideological misfits in this type of society." A safe bet, we think.

The explicit invocation, in the last two extracts, of modern Greek "self-interestedness" as the root problem of modern Greece's poor cultural standing takes us back to the analytic rational developed by Herzfeld. In his manner, we treat the moral positioning claimed by such authorial voices as a claim to Occidental cultural capital. From their vantage Occidental point of view emanates a double Orientalization. The Greek State, the alleged harbinger of modernity and progress in the Greek context, transmutes into a, say, "voracious monster" and (fellow) Greeks into an "emetic mob" of "un-civilized/un-cultured" caricatures. When Greeks set to govern themselves, the Occidental essence of the modern Greek soul, i.e., "individualism-as-insubordination," turns from a national virtue to a national flaw and becomes a despicable, myopic pursuit of short-term self-interests at the expense of collective, national well-being.

The December 2008 Events in Mainstream Social Theoretical Accounts

The pathology rhetoric we highlighted in our analysis is not to be found only in journalistic accounts. It informs also mainstream *academic* treatments of the December 2008 upheaval. In April 2009, the Hellenic Observatory of the London School of Economics published a collective volume (Economides and Monastiriotis, 2009) under the vocative, in its interrogatory tone, title: *The Return of the Street Politics?* Most of the contributors in the volume answered the question in the negative. The December events did not constitute a "return to street politics." Whatever collective action these entailed, they should not be seen as an instance in radical politics aiming at the transformation of existing power relations. Despite differences in argumentative scope, a common representational thread can be discerned in these essays: the construction of a pathology ridden Greek social, cultural and political milieu.[21] The editors of the volume, in their preface (Economides and Monastiriotis, 2009, pp. viii–ix, emphasis added), set the tone thus:

> while the immediate causes of the demonstrations are clear, the deeper underlying issues remain still unfocused. What *social pathologies* and *institutional incapacities* allowed the deep causes of these events to remain subdued until recently – and to come to the surface so violently and so abruptly in December 2008?

"Social pathologies," "institutional incapacities," and, at times, imagery of a generalized, sociocultural malaise, were testified and elaborated upon by the authors of these essays as well as in other mainstream social and political works published thereafter (e.g., Andronikidou and Kovras, 2012; Gerodimos, 2015; Kalyvas, 2008). In this academic literature, however, beyond similarities in semantic content, this common representational modality informed two distinct argumentative courses.[22]

In the first one, the sociocultural and political malaise attributed to the modern Greek condition, was treated as a representational *fulcrum* in order for arguments about much-needed socioeconomic, political or cultural reforms and transformations to be voiced. The argued need for reforms and sociopolitical changes often took the shape of a straightforward neoliberal argumentative agenda. So, for Featherstone (2009, p. 2), the riots in Greece were not deemed to have much to do with the global economic crisis that erupted in 2008. They stemmed from the lingering problems of a "blocked society" and were connected to a generalized "sense of malaise." At the argumentative sights of the author was the Greek political system, which, as he argued, in the last couple of decades failed to deliver appropriate socioeconomic changes and reforms, due to clientalism, corruption, and the power of public sector trade unions. However, the argument about lingering problems in Greek political culture came also to be mobilized within a political rationale more akin to a "third-road" political agenda. In Mouzelis's (2009) elaborate account, the December events came about as a combined outcome of political,

---

[21] Notable exceptions are the essays by Gavriilidis and Tsalikoglou. The former adopts a new social movements perspective, whereas the latter argues for the need of qualitative research works that would attend to the meaning(s) of the December 2008 events for the social actors involved in them.

[22] The divergent, in terms of their political aiming, arguments advanced in mainstream social theory accounts of the December events by invocations of a cultural pathology rhetoric alert us to the possibility that in journalist discourses also different and perhaps competing political arguments can be found using more or less similar imagery. Some preliminary analyses of ours, at least, pinpoint in that direction.

socioeconomic and educational/psycho-cultural conditions. Perhaps the most important feature of his account is the element he sees as doing the linkage work between these three conditions. For the author, it is the existence of *a very weak civil society* in Greece that links these three conditions together and bestows to the December riots a "dead-end" character. In Greece, Mouzelis argues, the "party logic" penetrates all institutional spheres and undermines their autonomy and values. For the author, it is the weak civil society in Greece that gives rise to either "brainless, nihilistic" violence or to "fully justified" but "unformed" protests that do not have any transformative political potential.

In the second line of argumentation, the pathologization of Greek political culture as a means for discrediting the December upheaval takes an explicit anti-left turn. Images of sociocultural and political malaise are also central here. Nevertheless, at the argumentative sights of the relevant authors is, specifically, the alleged, post-1974 Greek political culture of tolerance toward the violence emanating from the left and anti-authoritarian circles. The argumentative upshot is twofold: ideological changes in Greece's political culture are in need as well as more "effective" policing of collective action mobilizations. In the LSE volume, fragments of this argumentative logic can be found in the contributions by Matsaganis, Kalokairinos, and Zeri. However, its intellectual champion is Stathis N. Kalyvas, professor of political science at Yale University. In an article published in the *New York Times* (Kalyvas, 2008), he dismissed the usual explanations advanced for the ongoing, at that time, events in the Athenian streets. Maladministration, corruption, diminishing confidence in the government and, even, growing economic inequalities were treated as not sufficient explanatory resources to the extent that, as he argued, Greece is hardly exceptional in terms of its problems. For Kalyvas, "these riots are a symptom of a deep cultural problem rather than a social one."

After Greece's transition to democracy in the mid-1970s, a public discourse of resistance against authority emerged and became dominant. Civil disobedience, including violent demonstrations and the destruction of public property, is almost always justified, if not glorified; the police can only be wrong: If they act too harshly they are brutal; if not, incompetent. This discourse has proven to be extremely resistant to time and momentous world events, such as the fall of the Berlin Wall, and is promoted in the media. On the one hand, several journalists came of age in the mid 1970s and are openly sympathetic to it. On the other, political entrepreneurs see it as a resource that can be used handily for political or even economic advantage... Addressing this problem requires nothing less than a deep cultural shift at the top.

Critical theory accounts of the December 2008 upheaval (e.g., Bratsis, 2010; Sotiris, 2013) have already taken to task such mainstream social theory accounts for their "inability" to theorize the December events as radical politics and for their insistence in interpreting them in terms of anomie, deviance, and political culture deficiencies. Sotiris (2013), in particular, provides a well argued for, detailed account of relevant mainstream, academic positions and a sustained critique of them drawing on the social movements literature and Marxism. While, as we stated before, it is not upon us to make an argumentative case for the reasons why the December events *are* events in radical politics, our analysis has highlighted some of the ways in which such a reading is preempted through representational modalities, themes and practices, that draw upon the cultural dualism narrative pattern. Indeed, it may well be argued that the mainstream social theory accounts of December 2008 we considered mobilize and reiterate the logic of binary oppositions for the narration of the modern Greek condition we considered above.

Epilogue

As stated in the introduction, our point of departure for the analysis presented in this text was our shared, with other social-psychological and discourse analytic strands of work, concern with the workings of pathologizing rhetoric in accounts of collective action. However, we diverged from previous analysis in that we focused and highlighted ways in which the pathologizing rhetoric in question did not concern the participants or the mobilization events per se, but the social and political context in which these took place; namely, a particular national society, (modern) Greece. By pathologizing Greek institutions, political culture and society at large, we argued, such rhetoric forestalls an understanding of the December 2008 upheaval as an "event" within a trajectory and history of radical politics (cf. Giovanopoulos and Dalakoglou, 2011; Kallianos, 2011) and turns it into a "predictable" automatic reaction against a culturally ailing societal context. In our text, we outlined the rhetorical/ideological conditions of intelligibility, as it were, of such narrative constructions. We drew heavily on critical works within the humanities and social sciences, and critical ethnography in particular, in order to account for the genealogical provenance of the representational themes we showed to be mobilized as well as for the positioning work accomplished by such representational uses. As we argued, both the critical – "pathology" – themes mobilized by the authorial voices in the accounts we considered, as well as the position from which these critiques were leveled pertain to the cultural dualism prism through which the modern

Greek condition came to be historically seen. For Herzfeld, this cultural dualism prism signifies a crypto-colonial condition; and, most importantly for our purposes, for its reproduction, it relies, among other processes, upon the thoughtful (see also Billig, 1991) deliberation and quest for social accountability of modern Greek social actors. In particular, it indeed materializes through the modern Greek the discourse of "cultural imperfection": the perennial Orientalization of certain, but shifting and variable aspects of modern Greek life, and the ensuing Occidentalization of the position from which such criticism are voiced. The fact that, at times, constructions of cultural pathology in our data seemed to advance justifications or in any case, sympathetic and nondismissive treatments of the December events should not come as a surprise. Recent ethnographic work (e.g., Theodossopoulos, 2013, 2014) has exemplified the pervasive nature of Occidentalist assumptions in Greece by highlighting their reproduction in oppositional to austerity politics discourses. Besides, it is our contention, radical politics taking the form of collective actions mobilizations and aiming at challenging deeply embedded power structures cannot rely on crypto-colonial imagery and moral posturing to do so: the empire shall always find the space to bite back.

REFERENCES

IN ENGLISH

Ahıska, M. (2003). Occidentalism: The historical fantasy of the modern. *South Atlantic Quarterly*, 102(2/3), 351–379.

Andronikidou, A., and Kovras, I. (2012). Cultures of rioting and anti-systemic politics in southern Europe. *West European Politics*, 35(4), 707–725.

Astrinaki, R. (2009). "(Un)hooding" a rebellion: The December 2008 events in Athens. *Social Text 101*, 27(4), 97–107.

Baka, A., and Garyfallou, A. (2011). Collective identity and empowerment in the December 2008 protests in Greece: A socio-psychological approach. *Journal of Critical Studies in Business and Society*, 2(1–2), 30–50.

Bernal, M. (1987). *Black Athena: The Afroasiatic Roots of Classical Civilization: Vol. 1. The Fabrication of Ancient Greece*. London: Vintage.

Billig, M. (1987). *Arguing and Thinking: A Rhetorical Approach to Social Psychology*. Cambridge: Cambridge University Press.

   (1991). *Ideology and Opinions: Studies in Rhetorical Psychology*. London: Sage.

Billig, M., Condor, S., Edwards, D., Gane, M., Middleton, D., and Radley, A. (1988). *Ideological Dilemmas: A Social Psychology of Everyday Thinking*. London: Sage.

Bozatzis, N. (1999). Greek national identity in talk: The rhetorical articulation of an ideological dilemma (PhD thesis). Lancaster University.

   (2005). Seismic affection: The cultural politics of identity construction in Greek press coverage of earthquakes in Turkey. In A. Gulerce, I. Steuble,

A. Hofmeister, G. Saunders, and J. Kaye (Eds.), *Contemporary Theorizing in Psychology: Global Perspectives* (pp. 355–364). Ontario: Captus University Press.

(2009). Occidentalism and accountability: Constructing culture and cultural difference in majority Greek talk about the minority in Western Thrace. *Discourse and Society*, 20(4), 431–453.

(2014). Banal Occidentalism. In C. Antaki and S. Condor (Eds.), *Rhetoric, Ideology and Social Psychology: Essays in Honour of Michael Billig* (pp. 122–136). London: Routledge.

(2016). Cultural othering, banal Occidentalism and the discursive construction of the "Greek crisis" in global media: A case study. *Suomen Antropologi: Journal of the Finnish Anthropological Society*, 41(2), 47–71.

Bratsis, P. (2003). Corrupted compared to what? Greece, capitalist interests and the specular purity of the State. Discussion Paper 8. London: Hellenic Observatory/European Institute, London School of Economics and Political Science.

(2010). Legitimation crisis and the Greek explosion. *International Journal of Urban and Regional Research*, 34(1), 190–196.

Coronil, F. (1996). Beyond Occidentalism: Toward nonimperial geohistorical categories. *Cultural Anthropology* 11(1): 51–87.

Dafermos, O. (2009). The society of aphasia and juvenile rage. In E. Economides and V. Monastiriotis (Eds.), *The Return of Street Politics? Essays on the December Riots in Greece* (pp. 9–13). London: The Hellenic Observatory, London School of Economics and Political Science.

Dalakoglou, D., and Vradis, A. (2011). Introduction. In A. Vradis and D. Dalakoglou (Eds.), *Revolt and Crisis in Greece: Between a Present Yet to Pass and a Future Still to Come* (pp. 13–25). London: AK Press and Occupied London.

Delanty, G. (1995). *Inventing Europe: Idea, Identity, Reality*. London: Macmillan.

Diakoumakos, G. (2015). Post-materialism in Greece and the events of December 2008. *Journal of Modern Greek Studies*, 33(2), 293–316.

Diamandouros, N. (1994). Cultural dualism and political change in postauthoritarian Greece. Estudios: Working Papers 50, Centro de Estudios Avanzados en Ciencias Sociales, Instituto Juan March de Estudios e Investigaciones.

Douzinas, C. (2010). Athens revolting: Three meditations on sovereignty and one on its (possible) dismantlement. *Law Critique*, 21, 261–275.

(2013). *Philosophy and Resistance in the Crisis: Greece and the Future of Europe*. Cambridge: Polity.

Drury, J. (2002). "When the mobs are looking for witches to burn, nobody's safe": Talking about the reactionary crowd. *Discourse and Society*, 13(1), 41–73.

Drury, J., and Reicher, S. (2000). Collective action and psychological change: The emergence of new social identities. *British Journal of Social Psychology*, 39, 579–604.

Economides, S., and Monastiriotis, V. (Eds.) (2009). *The Return of Street Politics? Essays on the December Riots in Greece*. London: Hellenic Observatory, London School of Economics and Political Science.

Edwards, D. (2007). Managing subjectivity in talk. In A. Hepburn and S. Wiggins (Eds.), *Discursive Research in Practice: New Approaches to Psychology and Interaction* (pp. 31–49). Cambridge: Cambridge University Press.

Edwards, D., and Potter, J. (1992). *Discursive Psychology*. London: Sage.

Fang, Y. J. (1994). "Riots" and demonstrations in the Chinese press: A case study of language and ideology. *Discourse and Society*, 5, 163–181.

Faubion, J. D. (1993). *Modern Greek Lessons: A Primer in Historical Constructivism*. Princeton, NJ: Princeton University Press.

Featherstone, K. (2009). Street protests in "une société bloquée." In E. Economides and V. Monastiriotis (Eds.), *The Return of Street Politics? Essays on the December Riots in Greece* (pp. 1–4). London: Hellenic Observatory, London School of Economics and Political Science.

Gavriilidis, A. (2009). [Greek Riots 2008:] A mobile Tiananmen. In E. Economides and V. Monastiriotis (Eds.), *The Return of Street Politics? Essays on the December Riots in Greece* (pp. 15–19). London: Hellenic Observatory, London School of Economics and Political Science.

Gerodimos, R. (2015). The ideology of far left populism in Greece: Blame, victimhood and revenge in the discourse of Greek anarchists. *Political Studies*, 63, 608–625.

Giovanopoulos, C., and Dalakoglou, D. (2011). From ruptures to eruption: A genealogy of the December 2008 in Greece. In A. Vradis and D. Dalakoglou (Eds.), *Revolt and Crisis in Greece: Between a Present Yet to Pass and a Future Still to Come* (pp. 91–114). London: AK Press and Occupied London.

Gourgouris, S. (1996). *Dream Nation: Enlightenment, Colonization and the Institution of Modern Greece*. Stanford, CA: Stanford University Press.

Herzfeld, M. (1982). *"Ours Once More": Folklore, Ideology and the Making of Modern Greece*. Austin: University of Texas Press.

(1987). *Anthropology through the Looking-Glass: Critical Ethnography in the Margins of Europe*. Cambridge: Cambridge University Press.

(1992). *The Social Production of Indifference: Exploring the Symbolic Roots of Western Bureaucracy*. Oxford: Berg.

(1995). Hellenism and Occidentalism: The permutations of performance in Greek bourgeois identity. In J. G. Carrier (Ed.), *Occidentalism: Images of the West* (pp. 218–233). Oxford: Berg.

(2002). The absent presence: Discourses of crypto-colonialism. *South Atlantic Quarterly*, 101(4), 899–926.

Johnston, H., and Seferiades, S. (2012). The Greek December, 2008. In S. Seferiades and H. Johnston (Eds.), *Violent Protest, Contentious Politics and the Neoliberal State* (pp. 149–156). London: Ashgate.

Kallianos, Y. (2011). December as an event in Greek radical politics. In A. Vradis and D. Dalakoglou (Eds.), *Revolt and Crisis in Greece: Between a Present Yet to Pass and a Future Still to Come* (pp. 151–165). London: AK Press and Occupied London.

Kalokerinos, A. (2009). Warped institutions, political failure and social guilt. In S. Economides and V. Monastiriotis (Eds.), *The Return of Street Politics? Essays on the December Riots in Greece* (pp. 21–25). London: Hellenic Observatory, London School of Economics and Political Science.

Kalyvas, A. (2010). An anomaly? Some reflections on the Greek December 2008. *Constellations*, 17(2), 351–364.

Kalyvas, S. N. (2008). Why Athens is burning. *New York Times*, November 11.

Kornetis, K. (2010). No more heroes? Rejection and reverberation of the past in the 2008 events in Greece. *Journal of Modern Greek Studies*, 28(2), 173–197.

Kotronaki, L., and Seferiades, S. (2012). Along the pathways of rage: The space-time of an uprising. In S. Seferiades and H. Johnston (Eds.), *Violent Protest, Contentious Politics and the Neoliberal State* (pp. 157–170). London: Ashgate.

Le Bon, G. (1947). *The Crowd: A Study of the Popular Mind*. London: Ernest Benn.

Liakos, A., and Kouki, H. (2015). Narrating the story of a failed national tradition: Discourses of the Greek crisis, 2010–2014. Χρόνος, 32.

Litton, I., and Potter, J. (1985). Social representations in the ordinary explanation of a "riot." *European Journal of Social Psychology*, 15, 371–388.

Makrygianni, V., and Tsavdaroglou, H. (2011). Urban planning and revolt: A spatial analysis of the December 2008 uprising in Athens. In A. Vradis and D. Dalakoglou (Eds.), *Revolt and Crisis in Greece: Between a Present Yet to Pass and a Future Still to Come* (pp. 29–57). London: AK Press and Occupied London.

Matsaganis, M. (2009). Facing up to the culture of violence. In S. Economides and V. Monastiriotis (Eds.), *The Return of Street Politics? Essays on the December Riots in Greece* (pp. 37–40). London: Hellenic Observatory/ London School of Economics and Political Science.

Mentinis, M. (2010). Remember remember the 6th of December . . . a rebellion or the constituting moment of a radical morphoma? *International Journal of Urban and Regional Research*, 34(1), 197–202.

Milioni, D. L., and Panos, D. (2011). New media and radical protest: Reflections from the "Greek 2008 riots." *International Journal of Media and Cultural Politics*, 7(2), 233–240.

Mouzelis, N. P. (1978). *Modern Greece: Facets of Underdevelopment*. London: Macmillan.

    (2009). On the December events. In S. Economides and V. Monastiriotis (Eds.), *The Return of Street Politics? Essays on the December Riots in Greece* (pp. 41–44). London: Hellenic Observatory/London School of Economics and Political Science.

Mowbray, M. (2010). Blogging the Greek riots: Between aftermath and ongoing engagement. *Resistance Studies Magazine*, 1, 4–15.

Ntampoudi, I. (2014). Reflections on the (Greek) underdog culture: A rebellious and radical political identity? Paper presented at the 64th Political Studies Association, Annual International Conference "Rebels and Radicals," April 14–16, Manchester, UK.

Pechtelidis, Y. (2011). December uprising 2008: Universality and particularity in young people's discourse. *Journal of Youth Studies*, 14(4), 449–462.

Petropoulou, C. (2010). From the December youth uprising to the rebirth of urban social movements: A space-time approach. *International Journal of Urban and Regional Research*, 34(1), 217–224.

Potter, J., and Halliday, Q. (1990). Community leaders: A device for warranting versions of crowd events. *Journal of Pragmatics*, 14, 905–921.

Potter, J., and Reicher, S. (1987). Discourses of community and conflict: The organization of social categories in accounts of a "riot." *British Journal of Social Psychology*, 26, 25–40.

Potter, J., and Wetherell, M. (1987). *Discourse and Social Psychology*. London: Sage.

Psimitis, M. (2011). Collective identities versus social exclusion: The December 2008 Greek youth movement. *Επιθεώρηση Κοινωνικών Ερευνών*; 136(C'), 111–133.

Reicher, S. D. (1984). The St Paul's "riot": An explanation of the limits of crowd action in terms of a social identity model. *European Journal of Social Psychology*, 14, 1–21.

(1996). "The Battle of Westminster": Developing the social identity model of crowd behaviour in order to explain the initiation and development of collective conflict. *European Journal of Social Psychology*, 26, 115–134.

Reicher, S., and Potter, J. (1985). Psychological theory as intergroup perspective: A comparative analysis of "scientific" and "lay" accounts of crowd events. *Human Relations*, 38, 167–189.

Said, E. (1978). *Orientalism: Western Conceptions of the Orient*. London: Penguin.

Schatzki, T. R., Knorr Cetina, K., and von Savigny, E. (Eds.) (2001). *The Practice Turn in Contemporary Theory*. London: Routledge.

Shotter, J. (1993). *The Cultural Politics of Everyday Life*. Milton Keynes, UK: Open University Press.

Sotiris, P. (2010). Rebels with a cause: The December 2008 Greek youth movement as the condensation of deeper social and political contradictions. *International Journal of Urban and Regional Research*, 34(1), 203–209.

(2013). Reading revolt as deviance: Greek intellectuals and the December 2008 revolt of Greek youth. *Interface: A Journal for and about Social Movements*, 5(2), 47–77.

Stavrakakis, Y. (2002). Religious populism and political culture: The Greek case. *South European Society and Politics*, 7(3), 29–52.

St Clair, W. (1972). *That Greece Might Still Be Free: The Philhellenes in the War of Independence*. London: Oxford University Press.

Stott, C., and Drury, J. (2000). Crowds, context and identity: Dynamic categorization processes in the "poll tax riot." *Human Relations*, 53, 247–273.

(2017). Contemporary understanding of riots: Classical crowd psychology, ideology and the social identity approach. *Public Understanding of Science*, 26(1), 2–14.

Theodossopoulos, D. (2013). Infuriated with the infuriated? Blaming tactics and discontent about the Greek financial crisis. *Current Anthropology*, 54(2), 200–221.

(2014). The ambivalence of anti-austerity indignation in Greece: Resistance, hegemony and complicity. *History and Anthropology*, 25(4), 488–506.

Triga, V., and Baka, A. (2014). Protesting online Facebook groups in the Greek December 2008 protests. In L. Chisholm and V. Deliyianni-Kouimtzis

(Eds.), *Changing Landscapes for Children and Youth in Europe* (pp. 152–178). Newcastle upon Tyne, UK: Cambridge Scholars.

Tsalikoglou, F. (2009). December's unquiet dreams. In E. Economides and V. Monastiriotis (Eds.), *The Return of Street Politics? Essays on the December Riots in Greece* (pp. 63–67). London: Hellenic Observatory/London School of Economics and Political Science.

Tsoucalas, C. (1991). "Enlightened concepts in the dark": Power and freedom, politics and society. *Journal of Modern Greek Studies*, 9, 1–22.

Tzatha, A. (2009). Street politics and social movements: A list of opportunities or a multitude of desires—Lessons from Greece, December 2008 (MS thesis). Utrecht University.

Van Dijk, T. A. (1989). Race, riots and the press: An analysis of editorials in the British press about the 1985 disorders. *Gazette*, 43, 229–253.

Vatikiotis, P. (2011). Networking activism: Implications for Greece. *Estudos em Comunicação*, 10, 169–218.

Vradis, A. (2009). Greece's winter of discontent. *Cities*, 13(1), 146–149.

Vradis, A., and Dalakoglou, D. (Eds.) (2011). *Revolt and Crisis in Greece: Between a Present Yet to Pass and a Future Still to Come*. London: AK Press and Occupied London.

Wetherell, M. (1998). Positioning and interpretative repertoires: Conversation analysis and post-structuralism in dialogue. *Discourse and Society*, 9(3), 387–412.

Wetherell, M., and Potter, J. (1988). Narrative characters and accounting for violence. In J. Shotter and K. Gergen (Eds.), *Texts of Identity* (pp. 206–219). London: Sage.

Xenakis, S. (2013). Normative hybridity in contemporary Greece: Beyond "modernizers" and "underdogs" in socio-political discourse and practice. *Journal of Modern Greek Studies*, 31(2), 171–192.

Xenakis, S., and Cheliotis, L. K. (2016). "Glocal" disorder: Causes, conduct and consequences of the 2008 Greek unrest. *European Journal of Criminology*, 13(5), 639–656.

Zeri, P. (2009). The riots of December: A spontaneous social phenomenon or a social movement? In S. Economides and V. Monastiriotis (Eds.), *The Return of Street Politics? Essays on the December Riots in Greece* (pp. 69–73). London: Hellenic Observatory/London School of Economics and Political Science.

IN GREEK

Γιακωβάκη, Ν. (2006). *Ευρώπη Μέσω Ελλάδας: Μια καμπή στην ευρωπαϊκή αυτοσυνείδηση (17ος – 18ος αιώνας)*. Athens: Εστία.

Διαμαντούρος, Ν. (2000). *Πολιτισμικός Δυϊσμός και Πολιτική Αλλαγή στην Ελλάδα της Μεταπολίτευσης: Πλαίσιο ερμηνείας;*. Athens: Αλεξάνδρεια.

Μποζατζής, Ν. (2005a). Αναπαριστώντας «εμάς», «αυτούς» κι «εμάς σαν αυτούς»: Ταυτότητες εν δράσει στο λόγο του ελληνικού τύπου για την κρίση των Ιμίων και τους σεισμούς στην Τουρκία. In Χ. Α. Φραγκονικολόπουλος (Ed.), *ΜΜΕ, Κοινωνία και Πολιτική: Ρόλος και λειτουργία στη σύγχρονη Ελλάδα;* (pp. 347–380). Athens: Σιδέρη.

(2005b). Πέρα από τον κοινότοπο εθνικισμό: Η συγκρότηση πολιτισμικών ταυτοτήτων στην κάλυψη των σεισμών στην Τουρκία από τον ελληνικό τύπο. In Δ. Μαρκουλής and Μ. Δικαίου (Eds.), *Πολιτική Ψυχολογία: Προβλήματα και προοπτικές*; (pp. 363–384). Athens: Τυπωθήτω.

Μποζατζής, Ν., Condor, S., and Levine, M. (2004). Η ελληνική εθνική ταυτότητα σε πλαίσια συνομιλίας: Μια ανάλυση λόγου. In Μ. Δικαίου, Π. Ρούσση, and Δ. Χρηστίδης (Eds.), *Επιστημονική Επετηρίδα Τμήματος Ψυχολογίας Α.Π.Θ.*, Στ΄ *Τόμος*; (pp. 363–384). Thessaloniki: ΑΠΘ.

Παπανικολόπουλος, Δ. (2016). *Δεκέμβρης 2008, ανάλυση και ερμηνεία: Οι αιτιώδεις μηχανισμοί πίσω από τα συγκρουσιακά γεγονότα*; Athens: Οι Εκδόσεις των Συναδέλφων.

Πολίτης, Α. (1993). *Ρομαντικά Χρόνια: Ιδεολογίες και νοοτροπίες στην Ελλάδα του 1830–1880*. Athens: ΕΜΝΕ–Μνήμων.

Σκοπετέα, Ε. (1988). *Το «Πρότυπο Βασίλειο» και η Μεγάλη Ιδέα: Όψεις του εθνικού προβλήματος στην Ελλάδα (1830–1880)*. Athens: Πολύτυπο.

Σταυρακάκης, Γ. (2014). Επανεξετάζοντας τον "πολιτισμικό δυϊσμό": Λαϊκισμός, κρίση, κανονικότητα και εθνική ιδιαιτερότητα στην Ελλάδα και τις ΗΠΑ. Paper presented at the 10th conference of the Hellenic Political Science Association, University of Athens, December 18–20.

Τζιόβας, Δ. (1994). *Η Δυτική φαντασίωση του Ελληνικού και η αναζήτηση του υπερεθνικού*. In *Επιστημονικό Συμπόσιο: Έθνος – Κράτος-Εθνικισμός*; Athens: ΕΝΠΓΠ.

Χαριτάτου-Συνοδινού, Μ. (2010). *Στάχτη και... Burberry: Ο Δεκέμβρης 2008 μέσα από συνθήματα, εικόνες και κείμενα*; Athens: Εκδόσεις ΚΨΜ.

13 Restoring Cultural Identity Clarity in Times of Revolution
The Role of Historical Narratives

*Roxane de la Sablonnière, Donald M. Taylor, and
Mathieu Caron-Diotte*

The present volume could not be more timely. We live in an era where rage and revolution are not the exception, but rather the norm. From the Middle East and Asia, to Eastern Europe, and indeed to the universal threat of terrorism in all its forms, global fear and uncertainty are pervasive. Addressing the issues raised by rage and revolution requires insights from all the social sciences, and no single discipline is positioned to provide all the answers.

Our focus in the present chapter is guided, and to some extent limited, by our own disciplinary heritage as mainstream social psychologists. As such, our attention centers on the consequences of revolution for ordinary group members, each of whom is forced to psychologically adjust if there is to be any hope of them successfully navigating the new reality that revolution brings. We begin by defining revolution and the most important psychological challenge that group members face when confronted by such collective trauma: its impact on cultural identity, and more specifically on cultural identity clarity. Our theoretical stance is that a clear cultural identity is critical for the well-being of each and every group member. A cultural identity that is clearly defined, we argue, is what provides each and every group member with a template for successfully navigating the social environment in order to "get along" and "get ahead" (Taylor and de la Sablonnière, 2014).

The goal of the present chapter is thus to explore a possible framework by which the clarity of cultural identity might begin to be restored when it is destroyed in the context of revolution. Specifically, we will argue that a group's shared historical narrative may be an important building block for rebuilding a new clearly defined cultural identity to serve as a guide for the new postrevolution environment. We argue that there are three main features of group-based collective historical narratives. First, historical narratives include key historical heroes who changed the course of history for the group, and who personify the behaviors and values that define the group. Second, historical narratives focus on pivotal historical

252

events, be they positive or negative, that define the group. Finally, each collective narrative has a trajectory of historical events and heroes that are linked together to arrive at a coherent and continuous cultural identity. These shared historical narratives can help traumatized group members who need to reconstruct their cultural identity. The group's historical narrative can provide a foundation for rebuilding identity through its concrete historical examples, and by offering the expanded time perspective necessary to help define long-term collective goals moving forward.

Revolution as Dramatic Social Change

We live in an era of widespread revolution as that term is understood by ordinary citizens, political leaders and the news media alike. Most current revolutions are of the political/military variety, and, global warming aside, even agrarian catastrophes are often militarily based. In any case, no one doubts the shattering impact that revolutions have on the elite, social structures, to say nothing of ordinary citizens. But since we are focused here on the psychological impact of revolution on ordinary group members, we need to clarify our definition of revolution. The millions of ordinary people forced to flee their homeland for survival from any number of current revolutions illustrates and speaks to the dramatic psychological impact of revolution.

At the very least, revolutions such as those of Syria, Iraq, Afghanistan, Somalia, Libya, and Yemen, to name a few, are characterized by a rapid and profound disruption of their entire political and institutional infrastructure, which all too often can be violent in nature (Heslop, 2016). In particular, revolutions induce a drastic change in the established social structures (de la Sablonnière, 2017; Heslop, 2016), which create a discontinuity in history (Parsons, 1964). According to Tilly (1996), a revolution is a drastic modification to the political, economic and social structures and institutions in a given society. Revolutions emerge from unrest and can be interpreted as a change not only in the governing body, but entire social order including beliefs, values, and attitudes (e.g., Yoder, 1926). Revolution, then, can be understood as *dramatic social change*, in the sense that it is a particular type of social change that induces a dramatic shift in the entire society.

Recently, de la Sablonnière (2017) reviewed the theoretical and empirical literature in psychology and sociology in order to formulate a typology of social change. The review focused on the types of social change that revolutions might provoke, especially from a psychological perspective. From this analysis, *dramatic social change* was defined as "a situation

254 *Roxane de la Sablonnière, Donald M. Taylor, and Mathieu Caron-Diotte*

where a rapid event leads to a profound societal transformation and produces a rupture in the equilibrium of the social and normative structures and changes/threatens the cultural identity of group members" (de la Sablonnière, 2017, p. 12; see also de la Sablonnière et al., 2009). This definition, then, points to the cultural identity of all group members as a key psychological construct that is impacted by revolution.

Revolutions clearly qualify as a dramatic social change, one that affects the entire social fabric of a social system be it a nation-state, region or community. Because individuals live within the social system, revolutions, by definition, impact each individual group member's life by impacting directly the collective identity that composes these systems; in short, their cultural identity. Because of their impact on the political, economic and social structure of a society, revolutions affect the social order, morals and values that were previously internalized by each and every group member (Heslop, 2016). Revolutions are far from being only a dramatic political change or the desperate attempt of a subgroup to better its relative position in the group's hierarchy: the ripple effect of genuine revolutions spreads to all group members thereby inducing a change in culture. Specifically, revolutions impact the cultural identity clarity of the group. That is, group members no longer have a clearly defined template to guide their own individual behavior. Even the simple prerevolution guidelines such as "If I do X, then Y will be the consequence" are no longer valid. There are no clear contingency rules, and thus more broadly, no clearly defined cultural identity.

Cultural Identity

Individuals have beliefs about which groups they belong to, usually based on those with whom they share common characteristics (Turner, 1985). Individuals may identify themselves as a representative of a particular occupation, gender, ethnic, or cultural group. Social identity is that part of an individual's "self" that is derived from the groups an individual belongs to, or more accurately, identifies with (Tajfel and Turner, 1979). Cultural identity is a form of social identity that refers to an individual's propensity to define himself or herself as a member of a particular cultural group (Sussman, 2000). Cultural identity comprises values and behaviors shared by members of a cultural group (Schwartz et al., 2013), along with their social roles and norms (Adler, 1977), and together they provide group members with a clear guide for how to navigate effectively in their world (Taylor and de la Sablonnière, 2014). Thus, cultural identity provides those group members who have internalized the culture (Ashmore, Deaux, and McLaughlin-Volpe, 2004), with a consensually defined set of valued goals that represent the worthy pursuits in life, along with the means of how to pursue them (Chandler and Lalonde, 1998). Indeed, culture guides how individuals act in the social world, how they define themselves and how they view the world (Oyserman, Kemmelmeier, and Coon, 2002). It is to be noted that the impact of culture, in comparison to other collective identities (e.g., gender, occupational), has an overarching impact on every aspect of life from the cradle to the grave (Taylor et al., 2013; Taylor and de la Sablonnière, 2014; Taylor and Usborne, 2010). Thus, in terms of social identity, cultural identity is central and salient in an individual's life. For the present chapter, we define cultural identity as *shared values by members of a cultural group, along with a consensus about the worthy pursuits in life, that provide individual group members with a clear guideline for how to navigate effectively in the world.*

Dramatic Social Change and Cultural Identity Clarity

Cultural identity, of course, is not a static monolith that is unchanging (Adams and Markus, 2001; Okazaki, David, and Abelmann, 2008). Rather, cultural identity is constantly, albeit slowly, shifting to accommodate new realities that arise from predictable and equally often unpredictable contextual factors. As contexts evolve, cultural identity, through a process of formal and informal communication, adapts. For ordinary contextual changes, cultural identity may be disrupted for a short period. However, the dramatic social change associated with revolution is of another magnitude. All of a sudden, the entire cultural identity becomes an outdated template. Cultural identity is not merely slightly clouded as might result when ordinary adaptations are needed. With revolution the entire functioning cultural identity is compromised. Thus, cultural identity becomes unclear in the context of dramatic social change (Taylor, 1997, 2002).

Cultural identity clarity is defined here as the extent to which individuals are confident about and clearly understand their cultural group's history, values, goals, attitudes, and behaviors (Usborne and Taylor, 2010; Taylor, 1997, 2002). A clear cultural identity implies that the group member believes she or he has a clear schema or template of what belonging to a particular cultural group means. For example, prior to the revolution, Syrians with a clear cultural identity would be able to pinpoint what it means to be a Syrian, what Syrian people share in common and the long-term valued goals that are promoted by their group. Indeed, many aspects of such a clear cultural identity would be so automatic and so deeply engrained that even a thoughtful Syrian might not consciously be aware of many key elements. But, while not always consciously aware, our Syrian would navigate her or his world with confidence and ease. In contrast, Syrians facing the throes of revolution would carry with them an unclear identity and therefore would be unsure about what goals to strive for, what ones are possible or even realistic, and how to conduct themselves on a daily basis.

For the displaced Syrian, the schemas and templates that were once useful would have no more value, as the social and physical environment that supported them has been drastically modified (de la Sablonnière, 2017; Moghaddam and Crystal, 1997; Taylor, 2002). Dramatic shifts in the social context, then, will first, and foremost impact group members by robbing them of a clearly defined shared template to serve as a context by which to live a meaningful life.

Research has only begun to empirically test the idea that social change impacts cultural identity clarity. In two experiments, Pelletier-Dumas, de la Sablonnière, and Duchesne-Beauchamp (2017) manipulated social change in a laboratory context. In the first experiment, participants in the experimental condition were asked to imagine a dramatic social change (the separation of Québec, which would greatly disrupt the social order in Québec). Thinking about the separation of Québec led participants to experience lower cultural identity clarity than participants who were not asked to imagine a dramatic social change (control condition). A similar pattern of results was observed in a second study that manipulated gender role changes in Québec society. In summary, there is a growing literature to suggest that dramatic social change impacts the clarity of social or group identity.

The Importance of Cultural Identity Clarity

Having established a link between revolution or dramatic social change and cultural identity clarity, a crucial follow-up question arises: What are the consequences of an unclear cultural identity? Cultural identity has serious consequences for both personal identity clarity and more broadly for psychological well-being. Taylor (1997, 2002), theorizes that a clear cultural identity is pivotal in order to allow individuals to formulate a clear personal identity for themselves. Having a clearly defined cultural identity allows every group member to have a shared template of valued goals to serve as a point of reference. Each individual group members can compare him or herself with the cultural template, to determine what makes them unique. This does not mean that every group member blindly adopts the values and scripts prescribed by the cultural template. But even those who do not will be aware of where they deviate from the template, and will know full well how other group members will respond to them. Thus, group members need a clearly defined cultural identity in order to engage the processes needed to form a clear and coherent personal identity. Finally, it is clear that a clearly defined personal identity is associated with higher levels of well-being and self-esteem (Baumgardner, 1990; Campbell, 1990; Stinson, Wood, and Doxey, 2008).

Fortunately, there is accumulating evidence that a clearly defined cultural identity allows for the generation of a clear personal identity, which in turn, is related to psychological well-being. Usborne and Taylor (2010) focused on a culturally diverse sample of undergraduate students and found that having a clear cultural identity was related to higher levels of self-concept clarity, well-being, and self-esteem. More importantly, they found that the relation between cultural identity clarity and psychological well-being was mediated by how clearly cultural group members were able to define their own personal identity. Thus, by having a clear idea of what being a member of their cultural group was, they were able to formulate a clear idea of who they were personally, which in turn, enabled them to experience higher levels of psychological well-being. This idea was further explored in a laboratory experiment (Usborne and Taylor, 2012) in which the clarity of identity for Anglophone Quebecers was manipulated. In the experiment, Anglophone Quebecers who were led to have a clear cultural identity reported higher levels of well-being, and felt more competent, compared to Anglophone Quebecers who were induced to imagine their cultural identity as unclear. Moreover, they found that the extent to which the cultural identity of their participants was clear impacted their personal identity clarity, which, in turn, affected their psychological well-being.

One of the most important components of cultural identity clarity is the long-term goals that a culture specifies as essential for group members to pursue, and the way these goals should be pursued (Taylor and de la Sablonnière, 2014). Without a clear cultural identity, individual group members are unable to determine or prioritize their own personal long-term goals. And, without clearly defined goals there, of course, can be no implementation strategy for goal success. Cultural group members can no longer derive what to strive for and how to effectively function in their social environment. For example, after a dramatic social change, any new demands that might arise from the modified social context will be unclear (Pinquart and Silbereisen, 2004). Imagine how unsettling it would be for Russian citizens after the fall of communism, as it would have been for citizens of all the former satellite nations of the former Soviet Union. The issue was not whether life for group members was better or worse, but rather, following revolutionary change, how to "get ahead." Especially uncertain would be what the new long-term goals are and how one should go about achieving them. Chandler and Lalonde (1998), echo this theme by arguing that without a clear cultural identity, individuals lose their long-term goals, which are paramount to assure that group members experience psychological well-being because of the meaning and continuity they gain from pursuing the long-term goals associated with their culture values.

Another nefarious aspect of an unclear cultural identity is that, in attempting to restore their own cultural identity clarity, individuals might make dysfunctional life choices. Individuals with an unclear cultural identity might be highly attracted to and try to join another group that can immediately provide them with a clear group identity. Research has demonstrated that when there is identity uncertainty, individuals are motivated to restore a sense of certainty by joining groups that offer a clear template of the world. One consequence of this strategy is that individuals with an unclear cultural identity are more likely to join extremist groups. These groups offer recruits a simple, clear identity (Hogg, 2004; Taylor, 2002). Joining extremist groups has the "benefit" of allowing the individual to acquire a new identity that is clearly defined, which restores a clear point of comparison to define what makes the group member unique at a personal level as well as clarifying the collective's goals. This new clear identity defines what the goals are, and how to concretely achieve them.

To date, it is clear that dramatic social change, such as revolutions, have deleterious effects on cultural identity clarity and that a clear cultural identity is crucial for the well-being of group members, and by extension society as a whole. When the clarity of cultural identity is seriously threatened, individual group members are desperate for any group identity that can offer clarity. Indeed, if no clear cultural identity is established, there is a risk of creating a cultural vacuum, leaving the entire cultural group with no clear cultural identity (Taylor, 1997). During the colonization of Indigenous peoples in Canada, White Europeans destroyed Indigenous people's cultures without offering a replacement culture (de la Sablonnière et al., 2011; Taylor and de la Sablonnière, 2014). In residential schools, Indigenous peoples were forbidden to practice their own rituals and speak their own languages. To this day, numerous problems in Indigenous communities can be traced back to the destruction of their cultural identity (e.g., Taylor, 1997, 2002; Taylor and de la Sablonnière, 2014). Thus, we now shift our attention to what we argue may be a potential tool for those faced with the dramatic social change that revolution brings: capitalizing on a cultural group's shared historical narrative.

Historical Narratives

A collective historical narrative is the story that group members tell about their group. It is a shared story that coherently links what the group agrees upon are the pivotal events in the life of the group. Most collective narratives are based on a series of agreed upon key historical events and key historical figures or heroes (Liu and Hilton, 2005). Historical events represent the turning points that profoundly shaped the history of the group (Pennebaker, Paez, and Rimé, 1997) while the historical figures or heroes represent specific individuals that heavily influenced the course of the group's history (Gengis Khan, Napoleon, Hitler, George Washington). For a historical narrative, events and key people are joined by a coherent thread that logically organizes their succession in time (Hammack, 2008), from the distant past, to the immediate past, to the present, and onward toward the future. In the present chapter, a historical narrative is defined *as a group consensus about the story shared by members of the same cultural group, reflecting their group's past, present and future.*

Our definition of a historical narrative is mainly based on the literature on temporal comparison and relative deprivation as well as on converging empirical evidence about the psychological importance of history (Liu and Hilton, 2005), context and narratives (Hammack, 2008; McAdams, 1996, 2001) for individuals. We now turn to the literature on temporal comparison that was central for developing the present theoretical perspective that proposes historical narratives as a potential tool for restoring cultural identity clarity in times of social revolution.

Temporal Comparisons and Historical Context

Humans have a fundamental need to compare themselves or their group in order to understand and evaluate their own situation (Festinger, 1954). Individuals engage in two main forms of comparison: social (Festinger, 1954) and temporal (Albert, 1977). Social comparison is the most widely used form of comparison. In social comparisons, a person compares herself or her group with another person or group. In contrast, with temporal comparison, individuals compare their present personal or group circumstance with their own personal or group situation at another point in time, either the past or anticipated future. By way of illustration, a student might engage in social comparison by comparing her or his grade on an exam with other students in the class, or evoke temporal comparison by comparing her or his grade with the grades she or he has achieved in the past. The same distinction between social and temporal comparison is applicable both to individual and group level comparisons.

Importantly, despite social comparison being the preferred form of comparison generally, temporal comparison becomes more important than social comparison for group members in times of dramatic social change, such as a revolution (Albert, 1977; Brown and Middendorf, 1996; de la Sablonnière, Tougas, and Lortie-Lussier, 2009; Mummendey et al., 1992). It would seem that dramatic social change, by definition, makes it difficult for individuals to select a stable and predictable "other," be it person or group, to compare with. Revolution dramatically alters the social structure, making people unpredictable and not good anchors for comparison. However, comparing one's chaotic present person or group situation with oneself or one's group at a different point in time allows the person to choose a comparison point where they personally or their group was anchored and stable (de la Sablonnière et al., 2009). Thus, in times of dramatic social change, the most important anchor point becomes one's personal or group situation at different points in time (de la Sablonnière, Hénault, and Huberdeau, 2009; de la Sablonnière, Tougas, and Perenlei, 2010).

It is only very recent research on temporal comparisons that allows for an appreciation of its link with collective historical narratives. Early research on comparisons neglected the central role of the social context (for an exception, see Stouffer et al., 1949). Thus, early research focused almost exclusively on investigating temporal comparisons in a decontextualized manner. That is, arbitrary and few historical points of comparison were the focus, and these were always chosen by the researcher. This practice is problematic on three fronts (de la Sablonnière, Tougas, and Perenlei, 2010; de la Sablonnière et al., 2009). First, the chosen comparison points by the researcher may not be relevant for group members because they may not represent key historical events for group members (de la Sablonnière et al., 2009; Liu and Hilton, 2005). Second, many points of comparison used in research were extremely vague. For example, questions were asked about one's "own situation in the past" (Zagefka and Brown, 2005, p. 472). The use of such vague points would likely be interpreted quite differently by individual group members; the "past" for one may be twenty years ago and for another group member two months ago. Third, many of the points of comparison used in early research represented only the "recent" past, or future points, selecting points of comparison mostly from six months to five years ago (Dambrun et al., 2006; de la Sablonnière et al., 2009; Frye and Karney, 2002; Guimond and Dambrun, 2002; McFarland and Alvaro, 2000; Ross et al., 2005; Ross and Wilson, 2002; Wilson and Ross, 2001). More distant points would never be included, even if they would be far more important for group members than recent points.

To address these shortcomings, a historical perspective has been introduced in recent research in order to genuinely respect the entire range of comparison points in the historical narrative that group members share (Bougie et al., 2011; de la Sablonnière et al., 2009). Specifically, temporal comparison was investigated by selecting multiple points of comparison, and each comparison point was not generated by the researchers, but by group members themselves. To select the key historical points that are shared by group members, researchers adapted the "Life Story Interview" (McAdams, 1996, 2001) by asking participants to list the most important historical events for their cultural group (Bougie et al., 2011) or conducted focus groups with group members to arrive at critical events (de la Sablonnière et al., 2009).

As an example of research that used this historical perspective, de la Sablonnière and colleagues (2009) began with a focus group comprising Kirghiz students in order to identify the key periods in the shared narrative of the Kirghiz people. Then, a short time after the revolution in Kirghizstan that led to the president being deposed, a different group of Kirghiz participants were asked to evaluate the situation of the Kirghiz people at each different historical period with a questionnaire. Participants then were asked to make comparisons with the present situation (the revolution) for Kirghiz people and each of the key historical points (e.g., the Pre-Soviet Period). Participants' feelings of discontent, or relative deprivation, were best predicted when taking into account all of the key events. Importantly, a stable trajectory of temporal collective relative deprivation, that is a trajectory that is characterized by less fluctuations, was associated with greater cultural identity clarity than an unstable trajectory (de la Sablonnière et al., 2009). In another study, in the South African context, a trajectory that was perceived as representative of the main historical events that defined a group was associated with higher levels of well-being, but only if the change was beneficial for the ingroup (de la Sablonnière et al., 2013). When the changes were negative for group members, a trajectory representative of the main historical events was associated with lesser levels of well-being. Historical trajectories have also been found to be associated with personal well-being (de la Sablonnière et al., 2010), collective well-being, hope, and pride (de la Sablonnière et al., 2009), as well as adjustment to change (de la Sablonnière et al., 2015). Multiple research projects, all using a historical perspective have shown that the trajectory, or the extent to which group members perceive the fortunes of their group to fluctuate in time, matters.

Research in other fields also reinforces the proposition that historical narratives are an important part of a group member's cultural identity (Assmann and Czaplicka, 1995; Hammack, 2008, 2010; Liu and Hilton, 2005; Okazaki, David, and Abelmann, 2008). For example, individuals identify more with groups with an history spanning from the past to the future (Smeekes and Verkuyten, 2015). Groups must be perceived as stable in terms of their values through time. Other scholars, such as Liu and Hilton (2005; see also Wertsch, 1997) argue that historical narratives serve the purpose of defining the group. According to their analysis, historical narratives define clearly the place of the group in the world. By having a shared knowledge about the events in which their group has been implicated, and which outgroups represent foes or allies, individuals can derive the mission of their group and how they are to act with outgroup members. Similar theorizing and empirical research (Pennebaker et al., 1997; Kammen, 2008) has underlined the role that historical events play in shaping social identities. For example, Pennebaker and Banasik (1997) argue that major historical events, such as World War II and the Vietnam war affected American identity. In sum, research clearly suggests that historical narratives may represent an important tool fort clarifying one's cultural identity.

Historical Narratives and Cultural Identity

The research we have reviewed thus far has demonstrated that there is an important value to developing a historical narrative for group members and that cultural identity clarity is a positive consequence of such an endeavor. Understanding the relation between historical narrative and cultural identity clarity is important. However, it is even more necessary to understand *how* historical narratives help build a clear cultural identity, especially in the context of revolutions or other dramatic social changes. Understanding the functions of historical narratives in terms of facilitating the formation of a clear cultural identity is crucial for developing concrete interventions designed to help communities and individual group members who are confronting the challenges that revolution brings. Here, we describe three means by which cultural narratives might promote the restoration of cultural identity clarity: a focus on historical figures or heroes, a focus on historical events, and a focus on a historical trajectory. Together, these three means can be applied to help group members clarify their "revolution-induced lack of clarity" with the help from their "past" cultural narrative, that will in turn inform their anticipated "future."

The Role of Historical Figures or Heroes

Historical narratives highlight concrete exemplars of historical figures or heroes that are "larger than life" in that they represent the best attributes that define what every member of the group strives to achieve. Social-psychological research underlines the importance of having exemplars or individuals, especially leaders, who strongly represent the group (Hains, Hogg, and Duck, 1997). Concrete historical figures provide past exemplars of individuals who personify the best that a cultural group has to offer. Reflecting on these historical figures or heroes allows ordinary group members to clearly redefine a clear cultural identity for themselves. They can do this by seeking in their reflections answers to the following questions: What were the attributes of historical heroes? What were their attitudes and how did they behave? What were their goals? And did they successfully achieve them? In referring to the historical figures and by asking these questions, a clear idea of what constitutes a good "typical" member of the cultural group in the past can be reconfigured. As the historical figures or heroes are viewed as "prototypical" of the group, comparing past heroes with present heroes or respected group representatives (Albert, 1977) helps to determine what should be strived for by all current cultural group members (Taylor, 1997, 2002). In other words, historical prototypical group members act as relevant points of comparison.

Historical figures can also be used as models. The historical figures that group members refer to may be either positive or negative. Thus, historical figures, both positive and negative, will be used as a concrete example of different values, attitudes and behaviors that are necessary to define one's cultural identity (Hammack, 2008; Liu and Hilton, 2005). Positive historical figures may be perceived as concrete role models in the context of the uncertainty that revolution brings. Seeing that cultural heroes faced extraordinary adversity may offer some hope for ordinary group members and guide them in their own behavior and in refocusing on what is most important for building an optimistic future. Positive historical heroes, with their attributes, behavior, and courage, can serve as a concrete point of comparison in order to position group members in general. In the Province of Québec, for example, René Levesque, a Québec prime minister during the Quiet Revolution, is revered as an important hero who serves as a model of courage, determination and intelligence for Quebecers. In Mongolia, because of its great military conquests and its cohesive political organization, Genghis Khan is revered by Mongolians as a symbol of the Mongolian culture and as a model for strength. One people's hero, however, can be perceived differently for other peoples. For example, in China, Genghis Khan is seen as a ruthless warlord.

In contrast, negative historical figures, can be models of what not to do, prohibiting behaviors and values to group members. For example, Hafez Al-Assad, the father of the actual leader, Bashar Al-Assad, can't be ignored by Syrians as an important historical figure that marked Syrian history, even if most Syrians do not agree with his politics (European Institute for Research on Mediterranean and Euro-Arab Cooperation, n.d.). Indeed, his reign was marked by extreme oppression. For example, he ordered the army to bomb the city of Hama in 1982 because Islamists wanted to overthrow the regime. In spite of his image that may be perceived negatively by some Syrians, he may be used as a concrete example for some group members, of how not to be.

In sum, in the context of revolution, heroes and historical figures, provide group members with access, albeit only in the abstract, to behavioral guidelines and personal qualities and traits, along with the anchor points necessary to clarify their cultural identity.

The Role of Historical Events

When revolution threatens the clarity of cultural identity, key historical events can serve as a basis for beginning the restoration of identity clarity. With both positive and negative historical events, concrete examples of what the group was and what were its underlying behaviors, values and goals can serve as a concrete guide for today's behaviors and values. As with concrete attributes of historical figures or heroes, events that occurred in the past represent concrete schemas associated with specific events that may affect how group members define themselves. Returning to these events in times of dramatic social change will certainly provide a guideline as to how to act and behave in times of hard times. It is also possible that countries that are facing a current revolution have previously faced, survived, and gone on to thrive that past revolution. The group's historical confrontation with revolution may well provide a very specific guide for group members in terms of the lack of clarity they face in their current predicament.

Focusing on past historical events, especially where a past revolution was involved would help to determine "how to" overcome individual and collective challenges. For example, how the group came to successfully overcome the chaos of past revolutions can provide inspiration as well as concrete behavioral scripts for meeting the current threat to cultural identity clarity. A group's historical narrative allows group members to determine how to attain their current and future objectives (Reicher,

2008). In a more general sense, a number of studies have demonstrated how referring to the past helps in terms of planning for the future. By reflecting on the past, individuals retrieve previous examples of situations that were similar to their future goals or situations (Schacter, Addis, and Buckner, 2007). Examples of past events are thus used to plan how to behave in possible future scenarios. For example, after being exposed to narratives about the historical resilience of their group, participants performed better on a test that was relevant to a negative stereotype about their group compared to those who were not exposed to a historical narrative, or those who were given a "negative" version of their history (Bikmen, 2015). In other words, a historical narrative can be a source of support for every cultural group member. Similarly, positive events may serve as a reminder of what constitute the long-term goals that were achieved through the determination of group members (Pennebaker et al., 1997). For example, in Syria, the Proclamation of Independence, in 1946 might be identified as a positive event. Effectively, in 1920, Syria became a territory governed by France. The people were oppressed by the regime. In 1945, after being elected, the Syrian republican government expulsed the French forces from Syria (Perspective Monde, 2016).

The fact that the group overcame such dramatic social change in the past provides a concrete example of "how to behave" in times of current change and "which values and goals" should be adopted to face the difficult situation that is currently affecting the group. In the face of a revolution that brings much uncertainty, group members can compare past historical events with the current revolution. For example, in Québec, the Conquest of New-France by England is interpreted as a dramatically negative event for Francophones (Bougie et al., 2011). Before 1760, New-France was a French controlled and populated territory, spanning from the actual Province of Québec to Louisiana. In 1760, England conquered New-France. Under English rule, French Canadians were economically and socially dominated by the English minority of Québec and faced serious assimilation threats. Referring to one's negative past underscores the progress the group has made over time when compared to the present or just before the revolution, which may provide some confidence for group members.

As well as providing a schema or a guideline for effective behavior, research has demonstrated that reflecting on past events that were extremely difficult for the group has positive consequences for current group members. In their research, Bougie and colleagues (2011) showed that Francophones who think about the conquest period by the English and the Anglophones who thought about the Quiet Revolution were reporting increased group entitativity (a sense of group cohesiveness and that the group has a real existence). In a similar fashion, the 9/11 terrorist attacks in New York led Americans to identify stronger with their national identity, increased national loyalty and led to an increase in cohesiveness among all Americans. Li and Brewer (2004) conducted a survey on American identification, loyalty, and cohesiveness among college students' one year prior to the 9/11 attacks in September 2000. At the end of September 2001, immediately after the terrorist attack on New York, Li and Brewer surveyed the same college student population, asking the same questions about identification, loyalty, and cohesiveness. They found that, compared to September 2000, their participants scored significantly higher on all of the measures. Moreover, they noted a decrease in the standard deviations on all three measures, indicating that, after 9/11, there was less variation in identification, loyalty and cohesiveness among individuals. In other words, Li and Brewer's results indicate that the dramatic event that was 9/11 led Americans to higher levels and greater uniformity of identification, loyalty and cohesiveness.

Together, research points to the important role historical events play in shaping cultural identity and in particular cultural identity clarity. Because of its positive impact, for instance on cohesiveness, it may be important for group members to reflect on these events when confronted with a current revolution that destroys every individuals' ways of life.

The Role of a Historical Trajectory

The third means by which historical narratives have the potential to restore cultural identity clarity is their ability to establish a coherent history of the group to serve as a reference point. A historical trajectory links together the historical events of a group, and their historical heroes, through a coherent thread representing its historical high points and challenges. From the most distant past to the present and onward toward the future, a historical trajectory represents a line that relates one past point to the next one and so on to the present time (revolution) and from the revolution to the expected future (both near and distant future). For example, ordinary Russians could imagine Imperial Russia (1721–1916), the Soviet Russian periods characterized by four presidents, Lenin (1917–1924), Stalin (1925–1953), Khrushchev (1954–1964), Brezhnev (1965–1982). Then, Russian people may refer to the transition period of Gorbachev and Yelstin's (1983–1999) and to the Russian Federation time with Putin and Medvedev (2000 to today). Finally, the Russian people could imagine Russia's future (e.g., in ten years). Linking the different periods represents the historical trajectory that consists of Russians' perceptions of the situation of their own group at each of these periods.

A historical trajectory provides a larger time frame than the "present," which helps individuals and groups to focus on long-term goals. Wars, revolutions, and other life-threatening situations have the effect of inducing a "present" time frame, in which individuals focus on the immediate present (Carstensen, 2006). In times of revolution, instinctively, people will be more inclined to focus on their survival and so think about the here and now. Research actually shows that in the context of dramatic events that threaten one's life and security, people are first inclined to focus on the present, and abandon their concerns about future long-term goals. However, knowing about the past is necessary for people's well-being and cultural identity clarity (de la Sablonnière et al., 2011) and thinking about the future of one's group is also important to take the necessary steps in order to improve the group's situation (Hammack, 2010; Reicher and Hopkins, 2001).

Historical trajectories serve two main functions, namely to restore coherence and comfort individuals in times where their lives might be under threat. First, by reflecting on the associations among the different historical events, it reminds people that for their group the different actions taken both in times of triumph and difficulty led to constructive consequences for the group. Specifically, historical trajectories provide group members with a coherent thread (Hammack, 2008), where the different historical events are linked together, and this can provide group members with a sense of a coherence and predictability when it is desperately needed. Coherence and predictability, even if not always in positive circumstances is what individuals need and strive for (Kahneman, 2011). Individuals no matter the circumstance will try to reduce incoherence (Festinger, 1962) and will seek any form of causal explanation to generate understanding in a context of chaos. As revolutions bring discontinuity in the social context (e.g., de la Sablonnière, 2017), ordinary group member's sense of living in a coherent and predictable world would be shattered. Historical trajectories provide the individual with a set of causes (historical events and people) that explain why things are as they are in the present, as well as linking the present events to a coherent past. Thus, group members would be able to understand the discontinuity brought about by revolution and thus re-establish some clarity by more easily interpreting their group's current situation.

Second, a historical group trajectory is helpful in that it reminds group members that existential fears have been faced and overcome in the past. Existential fears are further alleviated from the mere fact that every group member can reflect on the longevity, continuity, and resilience of their own group. The fear of death alleviated, individual group members are able to focus on developing future collective goals, and therefore influence positively cultural identity clarity. According to Terror Management Theory (Greenberg, Solomon, and Pyszczynski, 1997), our awareness of our own mortality induces existential anxiety. Therefore, when faced with changes as dramatic as revolutions, people are primed to experience existential anxiety. When reminded of their own death, individuals will involve themselves more in their own cultural group (Castano et al., 2002; Greenberg et al., 1995; Pyszczynski et al., 1996). The involvement in one's cultural group can be seen as an entity that will continue after the individual's death, giving some sense of immortality (Sani, Herrera, and Bowe, 2009). Therefore, by specifying a clear historical trajectory that begins in the distant past and connects with the future, individual group members feel that they are connected to an entity that is certain to survive and hopefully thrive into the future. This reflection on their group's historical narrative will no doubt curb the potential existential crisis that revolution brings.

In sum, the historical trajectory perspective may be useful to increase a sense of cultural identity clarity because a new purpose is given to the individual (contribute to the group's future). In fact, the historical trajectory of a cultural group would help individuals to focus on a future-oriented time perspective generally. Reflecting on the group's past (Hammack, 2010) and future (Reicher and Hopkins, 2001) can mobilize group members. And, a historical narrative that includes both the past and the future of the group will help individual group members focus on a more future-oriented time frame. Thus, reflecting on the group's trajectory, can help group members put the chaos of revolution in a broader perspective. Group members may even realize that their group can attain a positive future, and so not limit their focus indefinitely in the present uncertainty.

Conclusion

Groups of people, driven by rage, sometimes overthrow their government in order to improve their situation. Historical (e.g., American, Bolchevik and French) and contemporary (e.g., Arab Spring) revolutions are the legacy both of history and current geopolitical discourse. Some revolutions are relatively minor and thus bring a few changes to the day-to-day experience of group members. In contrast, genuine revolutions will have a dramatic impact on the entire social and political structure of a group, thus affecting everyone. Revolutions thereby threaten the clarity of cultural identity, essential for both collective and personal well-being (Taylor and de la Sablonnière, 2014). In the present chapter, we argued that, to restore a clear cultural identity in the context of revolution, it may be a useful starting point for group members to be prompted to reflect on their group's collective narrative.

We identified the main features of historical narratives that might serve as a starting point for promoting cultural identity clarity in the face of revolutionary change: historical figures, historical events, and historical trajectories. These three elements underscore "past" knowledge that can be used by group members as a comparison anchor point to rebuild a cultural identity that clarifies the group's valued long-term goals. Historical narratives help clarify cultural identity (Liu and Hilton, 2005), because they provide answers to very basic existential questions: Who are we? Where are we from? What are our goals? How should we behave? What are our attitudes? The implications of our theoretical proposition underscore the importance of having a clear historical narrative because of its impact on cultural identity clarity. Even well-intentioned revolutions, destined to overthrow dictators, are certain to have a negative impact on the cultural schemas that guide ordinary group members. Reflecting on the group's shared historical narrative in such a context of revolutionary chaos may be an important step for providing a sense of purpose and direction for coping with the new reality. The hope is that these reflections can help group members begin the process of rebuilding a clear cultural identity in the context of dramatic social change and revolution where rage if often rampant.

REFERENCES

Adams, G., and Markus, H. R. (2001). Culture as patterns: An alternative approach to the problem of reification. *Culture and Psychology*, 7(3), 283–296.

Adler, P. (1977). Beyond cultural identity: Reflections on multiculturalism. In R. W. Brislin (Ed.), *Culture Learning* (pp. 24–41). Honolulu: East-West Center Press.

Albert, S. (1977). Temporal comparison theory. *Psychological Review*, 84(6), 485–503.

Ashmore, R. D., Deaux, K., and McLaughlin-Volpe, T. (2004). An organizing framework for collective identity: Articulation and significance of multidimensionality. *Psychological Bulletin*, 130(1), 80–114.

Assmann, J., and Czaplicka, J. (1995). Collective memory and cultural identity. *New German Critique*, 65, 125–133.

Baumgardner, A. H. (1990). To know oneself is to like oneself: Self-certainty and self-affect. *Journal of Personality and Social Psychology*, 58(6), 1062–1072.

Bikmen, N. (2015). History as a resource: Effects of narrative constructions of group history on intellectual performance. *Journal of Social Issues*, 71(2), 309–323.

Bougie, E., Usborne, E., de la Sablonnière, R., and Taylor, D. M. (2011). The cultural narratives of Francophone and Anglophone Quebecers: Using a historical perspective to explore the relationships among collective relative deprivation, in-group entitativity, and collective esteem. *British Journal of Social Psychology*, 50(4), 726–746.

Brown, R., and Middendorf, J. (1996). The underestimated role of temporal comparison: A test of the life-span model. *Journal of Social Psychology*, 136(3), 325–331.

Campbell, J. D. (1990). Self-esteem and clarity of the self-concept. *Journal of Personality and Social Psychology*, 59(3), 538–549.

Carstensen, L. L. (2006). The influence of a sense of time on human development. *Science*, 312(5782), 1913–1915.

Castano, E., Yzerbyt, V., Paladino, M.-P., and Sacchi, S. (2002). I belong, therefore, I exist: Ingroup identification, ingroup entitativity, and ingroup bias. *Personality and Social Psychology Bulletin*, 28(2), 135–143.

Chandler, M. J., and Lalonde, C. (1998). Cultural continuity as a hedge against suicide in Canada's First Nations. *Transcultural Psychiatry*, 35(2), 191–220.

Dambrun, M., Taylor, D. M., McDonald, D. A., Crush, J., and Méot, A. (2006). The relative deprivation-gratification continuum and the attitudes of South Africans towards immigrants: A test of the V-curve hypothesis. *Journal of Personality and Social Psychology*, 91(6), 1032–1044.

de la Sablonnière, R. (2007). "Désélectriser" le choc culturel: le malaise identitaire chez l'intervenant. *Équilibre*, 2, 38–41.

(2017). Toward a psychology of social change: A typology of social change. *Frontiers in Psychology*, 8, 397.

de la Sablonnière, R., Auger, É., Sadykova, N., and Taylor, D. M. (2010). When the "We" impacts how "I" feel about myself: Effect of temporal collective relative deprivation on personal well-being in the context of dramatic social change in Kyrgyzstan. *European Psychologist*, 15(4), 271–282.

de la Sablonnière, R., Auger, E., Taylor, D. M., Crush, J., and McDonald, D. (2012). Social change in South Africa: A historical approach to relative deprivation. *British Journal of Social Psychology*, 52(4), 703–725.

de la Sablonnière, R., Hénault, A. M., and Huberdeau, M. É. (2009). Comparaisons sociales et comparaisons temporelles: vers une approche séquentielle et fonction de la situation unique [Social and temporal comparisons: Towards a sequential approach and function of the unique situation]. *Les Cahiers internationaux de psychologie sociale*, 83, 3–24.

de la Sablonnière, R., Pinard St-Pierre, F., Taylor, D. M., and Annahatak, J. (2011). Cultural narratives and clarity of cultural identity: Understanding the well-being of Inuit youth. *Pimatisiwin*, 9(2), 301–322.

de la Sablonnière, R., Taylor, D. M., Perozzo, C., and Sadykova, N. (2009). Reconceptualizing relative deprivation in the context of dramatic social change: The challenge confronting the people of Kyrgyzstan. *European Journal of Social Psychology*, 39(3), 325–345.

de la Sablonnière, R., Taylor, D. M., Pinard Saint-Pierre, F., and Annahatak, J. (2011). Cultural narratives and clarity of cultural identity: Understanding the well-being of inuit youth. *Primitivism: A Journal of Aboriginal and Indigenous Community Health*, 9(2), 301–322.

de la Sablonnière, R., Tougas, F., and Lortie-Lussier, M. (2009). Dramatic social change in Russia and Mongolia connecting relative deprivation to social identity. *Journal of Cross-Cultural Psychology*, 40(3), 327–348.

de la Sablonnière, R., Tougas, F., and Perenlei, O. (2009). Beyond social and temporal comparisons: The role of temporal inter-group comparisons in the context of dramatic social change in Mongolia. *Journal of Social Psychology*, 150(1), 98–115.

(2010). Beyond social and temporal comparisons: the role of temporal intergroup comparisons in the context of dramatic social change in Mongolia. *Journal of Social Psychology*, 150, 98–115.

de la Sablonnière, R., Tougas, F., Taylor, D. M., Crush, J., McDonald, D., and Perenlei, O. R. (2015). Social change in Mongolia and South Africa: The impact of relative deprivation trajectory and group status on well-being and adjustment to change. *Social Justice Research*, 28(1), 102–122.

European Institute for Research on Mediterranean and Euro-Arab Cooperation. (n.d.). Al-Assad, Hafez. www.medea.be/en/themes/biographies/abc/al-assad-hafez/.

Festinger, L. (1954). A theory of social comparison processes. *Human Relations*, 7(2), 117–140.

(1962). *A Theory of Cognitive Dissonance*. Stanford, CA: Stanford University Press.

Frye, N. E., and Karney, B. R. (2002). Being better or getting better? Social and temporal comparisons as coping mechanisms in close relationships. *Personality and Social Psychology Bulletin*, 28(9), 1287–1299.

Greenberg, J., Porteus, J., Simon, L., Pyszczynski, T., and Solomon, S. (1995). Evidence of a terror management function of cultural icons: The effects of mortality salience on the inappropriate use of cherished symbols. *Personality and Social Psychology Bulletin*, 21(11), 1221–1228.

Greenberg, J., Solomon, S., and Pyszczynski, T. (1997). Terror management theory of self-esteem and cultural worldviews: Empirical assessments and conceptual refinements. In M. P. Zanna (Ed.), *Advances in Experimental Social Psychology* (29:61–139). San Diego, CA: Academic Press.

Guimond, S., and Dambrun, M. (2002). When prosperity breeds intergroup hostility: The effects of relative deprivation and gratification on prejudice. *Personality and Social Psychology Bulletin*, 28(7), 900–912.

Hains, S. C., Hogg, M. A., and Duck, J. M. (1997). Self-categorization and leadership: Effects of group prototypicality and leader stereotypicality. *Personality and Social Psychology Bulletin*, 23(10), 1087–1099.

Hammack, P. L. (2008). Narrative and the cultural psychology of identity. *Personality and Social Psychology Review*, 12(3), 222–247.

(2010). Identity as a burden and benefit? Youth, historical narrative, and the legacy of political conflict. *Human Development*, 71(4), 173–201.

Heslop, D. A. (2016). Political system. In *Encyclopædia Britannica*. www .britannica.com/topic/political-system/Stable-political-systems.

Hogg, M. A. (2004). Uncertainty and extremism: Identification with high entitativity groups under conditions of uncertainty. In V. Yzerbyt, C. M. Judd, and O. Corneille (Eds.), *The Psychology of Group Perception: Perceived Variability, Entitativity, and Essentialism* (pp. 401–418). New York: Psychology Press.

Kahneman, D. (2011). *Thinking, Fast and Slow*. London: Macmillan.

Kammen, M. (2008). The American past politicized: Uses and misuses of history. *Annals of the American Academy of Political and Social Sciences*, 617(1), 42–57.

Li, Q., and Brewer, M. B. (2004). What does it mean to be an American? Patriotism, nationalism, and American identity after 9/11. *Political Psychology*, 25(5), 727–739.

Liu, J. H., and Hilton, D. J. (2005). How the past weighs on the present: Social representations of history and their role in identity politics. *British Journal of Social Psychology*, 44(4), 537–556.

McAdams, D. P. (1996). Personality, modernity, and the storied self: A contemporary framework for studying persons. *Psychological Inquiry*, 7(4), 295–321.

(2001). The psychology of life stories. *Review of General Psychology*, 5(2), 100–122.

McFarland, C., and Alvaro, C. (2000). The impact of motivation on temporal comparisons: Coping with traumatic events by perceiving personal growth. *Journal of Personality and Social Psychology*, 79(3), 327–343.

Moghaddam, F. M., and Crystal, D. S. (1997). Revolutions, samurai, and reductions: The paradoxes of change and continuity in Iran and Japan. *Political Psychology*, 18(2), 355–384.

Mummendey, A., Mielke, R., Wenzel, M., and Kanning, U. (1992). Die Roller sozialer Vergleiche bei der Bewertung der eigenen Lebenssituation in Ostdeutschland [The role of social comparisons in evaluating one's own living conditions in Eastern Germany]. Unpublished manuscript.

Okazaki, S., David, E. J. R., and Abelmann, N. (2008). Colonialism and the psychology of culture. *Social and Personality Compass*, 2(1), 90–106.

Oyserman, D., Kemmelmeier, M., and Coon, H. M. (2002). Cultural psychology, a new look: Reply to Bond (2002), Fiske (2002), Kitayama (2002), and Miller (2002). *Psychological Bulletin*, 128(1), 110–117.

Parsons, T. (1964). *The Social System*. New York: Routledge and Kegan Paul.

Pelletier-Dumas, M., and de la Sablonnière, R. (2017). Dramatic personal change impairs personal identity clarity: The moderating role of identity integration. Manuscript in preparation.

Pelletier-Dumas, M., de la Sablonnière, R., and Duchesne-Beauchamp, M. (2016). Dramatic social change and its impact on cultural identity clarity. Unpublished manuscript.

Pennebaker, J. W., and Banasik, B. L. (1997). On the creation and maintenance of collective memories: History as social psychology. In D. Paez, J. W. Pennebaker, and B. Rimé (Eds.), *Collective Memory of Political Events: Social Psychological Perspectives* (pp. 3–20). Mahwah, NJ: Lawrence Erlbaum.

Pennebaker, J. W., Paez, D., and Rimé, B. (Eds.) (1997). *Collective Memory of Political Events: Social Psychological Perspectives*. Mahwah, NJ: Lawrence Erlbaum.

Perspective monde. (2016). *Syrie*. http://perspective.usherbrooke.ca/bilan/pays/SYR/fr.html.

Pinquart, M., and Silbereisen, R. K. (2004). Human development in times of social change: Theoretical considerations and research needs. *International Journal of Behavioral Development*, 28(4), 289–298.

Pyszczynski, T., Wicklund, R. A., Floresku, S., Koch, H., Gauch, G., Solomon, S., and Greenberg, J. (1996). Whistling in the dark: Exaggerated consensus estimates in response to incidental reminders of mortality. *Psychological Science*, 7(6), 332–336.

Reicher, S. D. (2008). Making a past fit for the future: The political and ontological dimensions of historical continuity. In F. Sani (Ed.), *Self-Continuity: Individual and Collective Perspectives* (pp. 145–158). London: Psychology Press.

Reicher, S. D., and Hopkins, N. (2001). *Self and Nation*. London: Sage.

Ross, M., Hein, S. J., Wilson, A. E., and Sugimori, S. (2005). Cross-cultural discrepancies in self-appraisals. *Personality and Social Psychology Bulletin*, 31(9), 1175–1188.

Ross, M., and Wilson, A. E. (2002). It feels like yesterday: Self-esteem, valence of personal past experiences, and judgments of subjective distance. *Journal of Personality and Social Psychology*, 82(2), 792–803.

Sani, F., Herrera, M., and Bowe, M. (2009). Perceived collective continuity and ingroup identification as defence against death awareness. *Journal of Experimental Social Psychology*, 45(1), 242–245.

Schacter, D. L., Addis, D. R., and Buckner, R. L. (2007). Remembering the past to imagine the future: The prospective brain. *Nature Reviews Neuroscience*, 8(9), 657–661.

Schwartz, S. J., Kim, S. Y., Whitbourne, S. K., Zamboanga, B. L., Weisskirch, R. S., Forthun, L. F., et al. (2013). Converging identities: Dimensions of acculturation and personal identity status among immigrant college students. *Cultural Diversity and Ethnic Minority Psychology*, 19(2), 155–165.

Smeekes, A., and Verkuyten, M. (2015). The presence of the past: Identity continuity and group dynamics. *European Review of Social Psychology*, 26(1), 162–202.

Stinson, D. A., Wood, J. V., and Doxey, J. R. (2008). In search of clarity: Self-esteem and domains of confidence and confusion. *Personality and Social Psychology Bulletin*, 34(11), 1541–1555.

Stouffer, S. A., Suchman, E. A., DeVinney, L. C., Star, S. A., and Williams, R. M., Jr. (1949). *The American Soldier: Adjustment during Army Life*. Princeton, NJ: Princeton University Press.

Sussman, N. M. (2000). The dynamic nature of cultural identity throughout cultural transitions: Why home is not so sweet. *Personality and Social Psychology Review*, 4(4), 355–373.

Tajfel, H., and Turner, J. C. (1979). An integrative theory of intergroup conflict. In W. G. Austin and S. Worchel (Eds.), *The Social Psychology of Intergroup Relations* (pp. 33–47). Monterey, CA: Brooks/Cole.

Taylor, D. M. (1997). The quest for collective identity: The plight of disadvantaged ethnic minorities. *Canadian Psychology*, 38(3), 174–189.

(2002). *The Quest for Identity: From Minority Groups to Generation Xers*. Westport, CT: Praeger.

Taylor, D. M., Debrosse, R. G., Cooper, M., and Kachanoff, F. (2013). Cultural identity clarity. In G. Sammut, P. Daanen, and F. M. Moghaddam (Eds.), *Understanding the Self and Others: Explorations in Intersubjectivity and Interobjectivity* (pp. 143–160). New York: Routledge.

Taylor, D. M., and de la Sablonnière, R. (2014). *Towards Constructive Change in Aboriginal Communities: A Social Psychology Perspective*. Montreal: McGill-Queen's Press.

Taylor, D. M., and Usborne, E. (2010). When I know who "We" are, I can be "Me": The primary role of cultural identity clarity for psychological well-being. *Transcultural Psychiatry*, 47(1), 93–111.

Tilly, C. (1996). *European Revolutions: 1492–1992*. Oxford: Blackwell.

Turner, J. C. (1985). Social categorization and the self-concept: A social-cognitive theory of group behaviour. In E. J. Lawler (Ed.), *Advances in Group Processes: Theory and Research* (pp. 2:77–122). Greenwich, CT: JAI Press.

Usborne, E., and Taylor, D. M. (2010). The role of cultural identity clarity for self-concept clarity, self-esteem, and subjective well-being. *Personality and Social Psychology Bulletin*, 36(7), 883–897.

(2012). Using computer-mediated communication as a tool for exploring the impact of cultural identity clarity on psychological well-being. *Basic and Applied Social Psychology*, 34(2), 183–191.

Wertsch, J. V. (1997). Narrative tools of history and identity. *Culture and Psychology*, 3(1), 5–20.

Wilson, A., and Ross, M. (2001). From chump to champ: People's appraisals of their earlier and present selves. *Journal of Personality and Social Psychology*, 80(4), 572–584.

Yoder, D. (1926). Current definitions of revolution. *American Journal of Sociology*, 32(3), 433–441.

Zagefka, H., and Brown, R. (2005). Comparisons and perceived deprivation in ethnic minority settings. *Personality and Social Psychology Bulletin*, 31(4), 467–482.

14   The Shark and the Octopus
Two Revolutionary Styles

Fathali M. Moghaddam

The chapters in Part III deal with issues that at a surface level seem different, but at a deeper level they are all concerned with how collective movements develop particular behavioral styles. My focus here is on two different behavioral styles that characterize collective movements leading to revolutions, styles I call the "shark" and the "octopus." These two behavioral styles tend to remain stable over years, probably because of limits to political plasticity (Moghaddam, 2016a). However, in the longer-term shark and octopus revolutionary styles do undergo changes, at least in some cases.

The shark is a creature of continuous movement, naturally tending to roam from place to place in search of food. The shark does not make a den, it does not select a small, well demarcated space as its home. Rather, it survives by cruising through large territories of water without borders, ready to move where food can be found. Inquisitive, eager to explore, always ready to push into new frontiers, the shark is opportunistic and ready to seize on resources in new territories.

The octopus, on the other hand, is shy and reclusive. It makes a den with clear boundaries, constructed of rocks and other objects, remains isolated, and only comes out in search of food. The octopus does not roam far from its den; it prefers to remain alone in the dark, hidden away in holes and crevices.

There are essentially two types of revolutionary movements, each with their own distinct identity and culture: those that behave like a shark, and those that behave like an octopus. The shark revolutionary movements have energy and inclination that naturally drives them outward; they are expansionist and inevitably go to war with neighbors and even geographically distant competitors. By their incessant probing, forward moving, expansionist approach, shark revolutionary movements radicalize competitors, setting off a process of mutual radicalizations and successive conflicts (Moghaddam, forthcoming).

In contrast, octopus revolutionary movements generate momentum by achieving increasing control of their immediate surroundings.

Lacking the motivation to be expansionist, octopus revolutionary movements have to look inward and focus their energies and resources on radicalizing within their own group, remaining within a limited and narrow boundary. Octopus revolutionary movements are extremely secretive and reclusive; they treasure complete domination within. Their main message to the world is, "Leave us alone!"

The key difference between these two types of revolutionary movements is that the shark style feeds on expansionism and becomes energized by forward movement, whereas the octopus style at least initially concentrates on sheer survival by being inward looking. The French Revolution (1789) is the classic example of the Shark revolutionary style at the level of the nation-state, whereas (at least in its initial years) the Russian Revolution (1917) is far closer to the Octopus revolutionary style. The expansionism of the French revolution almost immediately resulted in decades of war, whereas the self-protective, inward looking style of the Russian Revolution resulted in Russia being willing to withdraw from World War I under humiliating terms. The same trend is evident in the cases of Iran and North Korea, which on a smaller scale represent classic examples of shark and octopus revolutionary movements respectively. The revolution in Iran was expansionist and was almost immediately followed by a massive war with a neighboring state, whereas since the end of the Korean War (1951–1953), North Korea has concentrated its attention and resources to keeping the revolution alive within its own borders, and keeping the rest of the world at arm's length.

After discussing examples of shark and octopus revolutionary styles, I examine a type of leadership that goes across these styles, and is also shared by other major societies, as has become more even evident since the 2016 presidential elections in the US.

The French Revolution: The First Shark Example

From the outset . . . the great continuing strand of militancy was patriotic. Militarized nationalism was not, in some accidental way, the unintended consequence of the French Revolution: it was its heart and soul. It was wholly logical that the multimillionaire inheritors of revolutionary power – the true "new class" of this period of French history – were . . . real conquerors: the Napoleonic marshals, whose fortunes made even those of the surviving dynasts of the nobility look paltry by comparison. (Schama, 1989, p. 858)

The French revolution was fueled by its own aggression, feeding off of its own forward momentum. This was a revolution that would die if it came to a standstill. Expansionist from the start, the French Revolution was always moving away from the center, from Paris, from France, and then from continental Europe to the rest of the world. Not just the ethos, but also the actions of the French revolutionaries were international – to push beyond local, regional, and national boundaries, to bring the practices and ideas of the new revolution to all humanity. The revolution would conquer, and as Schama points out, it was natural that the exporters of the revolution be military conquerors.

As an expansionist force, the French revolution was immediately seen as dangerous by neighboring rulers. They saw the shark for what it was; it would eat them, unless they killed it first. The inevitable result was war. In the years 1792–1797, the first French Republic that emerged from the revolution went to war against a coalition of powers that changed in membership, but most importantly included Britain, Prussia, and Austria as the most important members. By the end of this first French Revolutionary War, a young general named Napoleon Bonaparte (1769–1821) had firmly established himself as the supreme French military leader. There was a brief lull in fighting, broken by Napoleon's invasion of Egypt in 1798. The next year Napoleon staged a coup and made himself the First Consul of the Republic. Another coalition of nations fought against the expansionist revolutionary forces in the second French Revolutionary War, which ended in 1802. By this time, Austria and Russia had been pushed to seek peace with Napoleon, and Britain was isolated.

The expansionist, restless nature of the shark means that it is constantly on the move, creating danger for neighbors. The coming to power of Napoleon, who declared himself the first Emperor of the French in 1804, reinforced the shark character of French revolutionary. Inevitably, more wars soon followed, aptly referred to as the Napoleonic wars (1803–1815). French forces invaded country after country, sometimes invading the same territory several times after victories and defeats, spreading the legal codes and ethos of the revolution. It was the Russian winter, faced by French forces after the disastrous invasion of Russia in 1812, which finally broke the back of Napoleon's army.

But so strong was the fervor of the revolution that even after the military defeat in Russia and his exile in Elba, Napoleon was able to escape and persuade forces sent to capture him to follow him once more into battle to continue their revolution. The final defeat of French forces at the battle of Waterloo in 1815 brought to an end almost continuous fighting since 1792 – almost a quarter of a century of war. It was through this enormous war effort, involving armies of millions and dozens of nations in different coalitions, that the sheer expansionist energy of the French Revolution was finally harnessed and tamed. The French shark was caged.

The Iranian Revolution: The Second Shark Example

November 4, 1979 . . . several hundred students and activists seized the United
States Embassy, taking hostage sixty-three Americans . . . On November 6
Khomeyni accepted the resignations of Prime Minister Bazargan and Foreign
Minister Yazdi, ending dual sovereignty. The Revolutionary Council was ordered
to take over . . . The first goal of the student activists was successful: removing
the moderates . . . from the center of power, forcing the political struggle to move
faster (to keep the revolution "on course"). (Fischer, 1980, pp. 233–234)

Iranian radicalization and the consequent revolution that toppled the
dictatorship of the Shah in 1979 was and has continued to be outward
looking, expansionist, aggressively moving into new territories, and in
other ways a typical example of shark revolutionary movement. The Iranian revolution cannot be anything else: it will die if it does not keep
moving outward, because the energy of the revolution is re-generated by
its outward movement.

From the beginning, Ayatollah Ruhollah Khomeini (1902–1989) and
other extremist leaders of the revolution were instinctively motivated to
export their revolutionary ideology. The first major step in this expor-
tation process was the invasion of the US Embassy in Tehran, Iran,
embassies by convention being considered islands of their home country. This action also served to sweep aside the moderates, such as Prime
Minister Merdi Bazargan (1907–1995), who in the first year of the revolution still occupied some leadership positions. The moderates believed
it was wrong to invade the US Embassy, but could not make public their
opposition for fear of being labeled as "American stooges."

Khomeini saw himself as leading a global Islamic movement, and from
the start invested highly in exporting the revolution. Given that almost
all Iranians are Shi'a Muslims (which make up less that 10 percent of
Muslims in the world, more than 90 percent being instead Sunni Muslims) and Khomeini was a Shi'a religious leader, the most obvious places
to target first in the effort to export the revolution were societies with
significant Shi'a populations. The largest Shi'a population outside Iran
lives in southern Iraq (about 60 percent of the Iraqi population is Shi'a
Muslim), so Iraq became a prime target for efforts to export the Iranian
revolution. The ruler of Iraq, Saddam Hussein (1937–2006), a Sunni
Muslim, relied heavily on the Sunni minority to govern Iraq and was not
about to allow Iran to stir up trouble and radicalize Shi'a Iraqis. When
it was clear that the revolution might spill over from Iran to Iraq, rather
than risk a revolt by the Shi'a majority in Iraq, Saddam Hussein launched
an attack on Iran. There followed a devastating eight-year (1980–1988)
war.

The Iran-Iraq War served to sap Iran's revolutionary energy, and for a while seemed to cage this shark. In 1980–1981, I accompanied several United Nations missions to the Iran-Iraq war front and witnessed the enormous human and material costs of the war. Entire cities were flattened and millions of people were killed or seriously injured. The shark was seriously wounded and finally forced to the peace table in 1988. Khomeini declared that making peace with Saddam Hussein was like taking a poison chalice. After eight years of grinding aggression, neither side had gained an inch of ground. It took many years before Iran could mobilize its energy and seriously renew any effort to try again to export the revolution. Ironically, it was the US that created a new and far smoother path for the shark to achieve its expansionist goals.

The 2003 ill-conceived US-led invasion of Iraq, following the almost equally misguided 2001 invasion of Afghanistan, destabilized the entire Near and Middle East and provided Iran with extraordinary new opportunities to follow a shark strategy and export its brand of Islamic revolution. Because the invasion of Iraq took place with no serious planning for postinvasion Iraq, after the fall of Saddam Hussein's regime chaos ensued and a power vacuum was created, into which Iran rapidly sent people and resources. Iran took full advantage of the golden opportunity it was unexpectedly handed by the George W. Bush administration, ineptly led by Vice President Dick Cheney and Secretary of Defense Donald Rumsfeld – an opportunity that the eight-year Iran-Iraq War had failed to win for the mullahs ruling Iran.

Iran's increased influence in Iraq was helped by historical factors. In addition to the majority of Iraqis being Shi'a Muslim, the Shi'a holy cities of Najaf and Karbala are also in Iraq. Najaf is the burial place of Imam Ali (the cousin and son-in-law of the prophet Mohammad), and the holiest city in Shi'a Islam. Karbala is also an important Shi'a holy city, being the location of the Imam Hussein Shrine. Many generations of Iranians have studied and worked in Najaf and Karbala, and the ties between people in this region of Iraq and Iran are very close. In addition to these historic ties between Iran and Iraqi Shiites, ties became even stronger during the Iran-Iraq War when many leading Iraqi Shiites fled or were expelled from Iraq by Saddam Hussein and took shelter in Iran. I was living in Tehran in 1980 when the Iran-Iraq War began, and we used to refer to the Iraqi political leaders living in exile in Tehran as the "shadow Iraqi cabinet." As long as the Saddam Hussein regime survived, they remained in exile. But after the 2003 US-led invasion and the demise of Saddam Hussein's Sunni-led regime, they eagerly returned to Iraq and became highly influential in Iraqi politics – extending Iran's influence in Iraq. The shark was moving forward again.

Iran has used its success in Iraq as a platform for extending its influence in other parts of the Near and Middle East. By building up Hezbollah (a military organization, recognized as terrorist by the US, with wide ideological, cultural, and other operations, based in Lebanon) and the Qods force (the unit of Iran's Revolutionary Guards responsible for international operations), Iran has greatly increased its capability to try to export its revolution. Hezbollah and the Qods force are being used in many places abroad, in addition to Lebanon and Iraq. For example, in Syria these forces are used to prop up the dictator Bashar Assad, who is also backed by Russia; in Yemen, they are used to destabilize the Sunni government, and generate instability on the southern border of Saudi Arabia, a Sunni ally to the US and regional rival to Shi'a Iran; in Afghanistan also, Iran has extended its influence in recent decades, relying on similarities in language (Persian, the official language in Iran, is close to Dari, spoken by about 55 percent of Afghans) culture, and religion.

In addition to military operations designed to export the revolution, Iran is launching ideological assaults abroad. This is achieved by training large numbers of foreign clerics, many at the newly established Mustafa International University (MIU), to return to their countries and preach Iran's brand of revolutionary Islam. So far, forty-five thousand foreign clerics have been trained at MIU, and twenty-five thousand are being trained at present (including six thousand women). According to one authoritative source, "Other startling statistics relating to MIU include its 70 branches worldwide; regular relationships with more than a hundred other centers internationally; 150 websites; publication of 50,000 works in 45 languages as well as 70 journals; and management of 400 clubs with 8,000 members" (Khalaji, 2016, p. 5).

The French and Iranian revolutions, then, are examples of the Shark pattern of behavior, where new energy and resources are derived from expansion and continuous forward movement. In contrast, I next consider two cases of octopus revolutionary behavior, where the movement is energized by ever-increasing control of home territory.

The Russian Revolution: The First Octopus Example

The main preoccupation of those engaged in octopus style revolution is to achieve complete control in their own territory, to become the undisputed master of their own house. Their survival depends on successfully focusing their entire energy on "cleaning house." Whereas shark revolutionary movements derive their energy from expansionism and continually moving forward, octopus revolutionary movements derive their energy by achieving tighter and tighter control of their own territories. It is only after internal control is achieved that the octopus will venture further out from home.

Gaining internal control and cleaning house were exactly the challenges the Bosheviks took up in 1917. The Bolsheviks evolved to become the "majority" faction in the Marxist Russian Social Democratic Labour Party, formed in 1898 to unite the various fragmented left-wing revolutionary movements within the Russian empire. The Bolsheviks prophesied global revolution, and eventual international victory for communist revolutionaries on behalf, and through the eventual participation, of the proletariat. However, at the beginning of the twentieth century, even victory within the chaotic Russian empire seemed far off for the Bolsheviks, with their most talented leaders, including Lenin and Trotsky, exiled abroad and far removed from action in Russia.

Chaos had been created in the Russian empire by the disastrous policies of Czar Nicholas II (1868–1918), which included blundering into two major wars, first the Russo-Japanese war (1904–1905) and then the First World War (1914–1918). The Russo-Japanese war resulted in a number of surprising victories for Japan, leaving Russia utterly humiliated. The Russian experience during World War I was even worse; Russia was very poorly prepared for war when it allied with Britain and France to fight Germany, Austro-Hungary, and Italy. After some initial successes, the Russian military experienced defeat after defeat and suffered about three million casualties. Furthermore, the unpopular war created severe shortages of food and supplies and caused deep suffering in the general Russian population, leading to a number of spontaneous bread riots. During this same period, Nicholas reinstated severe political repression, after having granted the people some political freedoms in response to revolutionary anti-Czar movements in 1905. Thus, by the start of 1917 Russia was experiencing military defeat, severe economic depression and food shortages, heightened political repression, and lack of effective leadership. The Czar and the royal family were deeply unpopular, as they were blamed for the disastrous war.

The first of two important revolutions in 1917 took place in February. The main revolt centered in what is now St. Petersburg, the capital city of Russia at that time. This spontaneous revolt showed that even troops specifically tasked to defend the Czar had moved to the opposition, and there was nothing the Czar could do but to abdicate, which he did on March 15, 2017. But the collapse of the Czar's regime was not the result of revolutionary actions by workers or peasants; it was the result of

282 Fathali M. Moghaddam

soldiers refusing to fire on civilians, and the Czar losing his authority in the midst of terrible economic and social conditions worsened by the tragic war.

The abdication of the Czar created a power vacuum. Two groups took the lead in collaborating in a plan to fill this vacuum, by forming a provisional government. The first of these groups (the Petrograd Soviet) consisted of representatives from workers and soldiers. The second group was a committee of the Duma (an assembly of representatives). The Bolsheviks and other revolutionary parties refused to participate in the provisional government; in part because they were surprised by these rapid events and did not have a clear plan for moving forward, in part because in this state of uncertainty they did not want to lend credibility to the provisional government. The real power in the provisional government rested with the Petrograd Soviet, which represented the soldiers and workers who could actually carry out orders to get things done.

The situation changed for the Bolsheviks when Lenin managed to get back into Russia from his exile abroad. Stalin and other Bolshevik leaders had failed to grasp the opportunity that now lay ahead; it was Lenin who took decisive action. He attacked the idea of compromising and coming to agreement with other groups, Marxist or otherwise. He was also against waiting – he saw the chance to grab power and wanted the Bolsheviks to take decisive command.

One such action was ending Russia's involvement in the devastating war that had brought bankruptcy to the state, and famine and misery to most people in the Russian empire. Through Lenin's influence, the Bolsheviks positioned themselves favorably in the struggle for power, "In contrast to the hesitations and divisions of the other parties, the Bolsheviks, adopting Lenin's line, now urged that the Russian people should put revolution before war. A demonstration organized by Stalin on June 18 brought several hundred thousand onto the streets, with an overwhelming number of banners proclaiming Bolshevik slogans. This represented a triumph of the party against its rivals, who at once accused Lenin of planning a coup" (Bullock, 1993, p. 52).

Was it a coup that brought the Bolsheviks nearer to monopoly power in October 1917? Or was it a revolution led by the workers and peasants, as the Bosheviks claimed? The Bolshevik Party now had almost a quarter of a million members, so it had soared in popularity. Again, the key factor in developments proved to be the refusal of troops to follow orders given by the central authority. Just as in February 1917 troops had failed to follow the orders of the Czar's government to fire on demonstrators, in October troops refused to follow orders from the provisional government to suppress what was in effect a "power grab" by the Bolsheviks,

"Astonishingly, the revolution was over in less than forty-eight hours and with little bloodshed" (Bullock, 1993, p. 54).

Although they had seized the initiative, the Bolsheviks were in a very weak position. First, they were only one of a number of competing political groups. There were strong opponents, including the Mensheviks and other competing Marxist groups as well as liberal factions of the provisional government, who would try to stop the Bolsheviks achieving political monopoly. As it turned out, the existence of a strong opposition eventually led to a civil war. Second, Russia was in utter disarray. The vast majority of people were suffering from the severe food shortages and consequences of the unpopular war. Lenin and the Bolsheviks concentrated their energies on coming to power, keeping power, and increasing their control across the vast Russian empire.

The particular talents and personality characteristics of Lenin were supremely suited for the task ahead. He was extraordinarily well equipped to keep the Bosheviks focused on fighting to achieve a monopoly of state power; it was in important respects "Lenin's revolution" (Marples, 2000). An essential ingredient of Lenin's strategy to achieve and maintain power was the use of violence and terror (Ryan, 2012). Immediately following the October 1917 power grab by the Bolsheviks, the target of Lenin's violence were other groups of revolutionaries. It was precisely because the Bolsheviks did not have sufficient control over the country, and political events in particular, that they resorted to violence.

The Bolsheviks used a number of different strategies to try to gain monopoly control. The first strategy was to sign a peace treaty (the Treaty of Brest-Litovsk signed March 3, 1918) with Germany and end Russian involvement in World War I, even at the expense of making significant concessions and giving up the Baltic States to the Germans. Second, they implemented a large program of land and property redistribution, giving peasants and workers "ownership" (although this turned out to be mostly in the form of collective ownership). Third, they launched into a full-scale civil war (1917–1922) that would eventually put an end to serious political opposition in the country.

Throughout the bitter civil war, the Bolsheviks, represented by the Red Army, used the same tactics they had displayed to take power in October 1917. They used summary executions against their opposition, including Czar Nicholas and his entire family, who were killed because the Bolsheviks feared they would be "rescued" by the Whites. The British, French, and Italian governments directly and indirectly intervened in the war, hoping that the weakening or defeat of the Bolsheviks would lead Russia to reconsider and continue with the war against

Germany. However, Lenin's influence continued to lead the Bolsheviks to give highest priority to the establishment and survival of the revolutionary nation.

With the end of the Russian Civil War (1922) came not only the crushing of all groups opposed to the Bolsheviks, but also the independence hopes of Tatars, Bashkirs, and other minorities. After the death of Lenin (1924), Stalin took control under the title of General Secretary of the Communist Party's Central Committee. Perhaps the most significant lesson Stalin had learned from Lenin was that getting and keeping power inside Russia had to take precedence over everything else. Adherence to this "octopus" rule had brought success, "The Bolsheviks were the smallest of the Russian socialist parties, with no more than twenty-five thousand members at the beginning of 1917, in opposition and politically isolated for most of that year. Yet before its end their leaders had emerged, unexpectedly and almost overnight, the first socialist government in the world" (Bullock, 1993, p. 91).

The North Korean Revolution: The Second Octopus Example

On August 15, 1945, two young US colonels were directed to "...withdraw to an adjoining room and find a place to divide Korea... Given thirty minutes to do so... (the young colonels)... chose the thirty-eighth parallel" (Cumings, 2005, pp. 186–187). In this way, an arbitrary line, hastily drawn on a map by two American army officers without any consultation with Koreans, began the history of North and South Korea after the end of the Second World War (1939–1945). In order to better understand why Korea came to be divided, and how North Korea came to develop an octopus revolutionary style, we need to examine the experiences of Koreans since at least the nineteenth century.

Frederick McKenzie's books *The Tragedy of Korea* (1908) discusses the plight of modern Korea, which was exploited for many decades even before being annexed by Japan in 1910. In addition to the extreme exploitation of material resources by the Japanese in Korea, the exploitation of human resources was even more tragic. During the Second World War, an estimated 200,000–220,000 women were forcibly taken from Korea and China to serve as prostitutes to "comfort" members of the Japanese military. The stories of these abducted women are only now being told (Friedman, 2015), and this is symbolic of the still hidden tragedy of modern Korea. Although Japan was the aggressor and Korea was the victim, after the Second World War Japan was kept intact, provided considerable help, and positioned as an ally by the US (Schaller, 1997), whereas Korea, the victim of Japanese aggression, ended up being divided.

After the defeat and expulsion of the Japanese from Korea, the north of Korea was occupied first by Soviet forces and later by Chinese forces, while the south of Korea was occupied by American forces. The hastily drawn line along the thirty-eighth parallel was an attempt by the US to prevent communist (Soviet) forces from overwhelming all of Korea, which they were threatening to do. In 1946 the "Korean Workers' Party" was established, a communist party with Soviet backing. But geographically China is much closer to Korea, and the victory of Mao Zedong's (1893–1976) communist forces and the establishment of the People's Republic of China on October 1, 1949, greatly increased the ability of China to help communists in Korea. Soon Chinese communist backing replaced Soviet support, while South Korea continued to rely on American support.

War broke out between North and South Korea in 1950 and continued until 1953. The two sides were in a precarious position, because both relied heavily on foreign powers (mainly China and the US) for their survival. The heavy reliance of the regimes in North Korea and South Korea on foreign powers, and not their local populations, for their survival meant that the ordinary people of the two Koreas had little say in decision-making in their own societies. Until the 1990s, both North and South Korea remained corrupt dictatorships. However, after the demise of the Soviet Union and the end of the Cold War, South Korea gradually changed to become more open and democratic. Also, from the 1980s the South Korean economy began to outperform the North Korean economy, so that the income of South Koreans is now about twenty-eight times higher than that of North Koreans (*Economist*, 2016).

The octopus style of the North Korean revolution is in large part explained by its leadership, which has been a hereditary dictatorship since 1948. The founder of the dictatorship Kim Il-Sung (1912–1994), *President for Eternity*, handed power to his son Kim Jong Il (1941/2–2011), the *Dear Leader*, who was succeeded by his son Kim Jong Eun (probably born 1984), the *Great Successor*. Under the guise of communism and using horrific repression tactics similar to those used by Stalin in the Soviet Union, the hereditary dictatorship of North Korea has survived in part by isolating the people of North Korea and severely limiting even the most basic freedoms.

The primary motivation of the North Korean regime, like the mullahs in Iran and other dictatorial regimes, is to continue to survive. Both North Korea and Iran see the US as a hostile enemy, determined to end their "revolutionary" regimes. Whereas Iran has adopted a shark revolutionary style, pushing out and maintaining a high level of expansionist activities, most obviously in Iraq, Afghanistan, Syria, Lebanon, Yemen, but also less overtly in Qatar and various other Islamic societies, North Korea has adopted an octopus revolutionary style, looking inward and threatening the world to "stay away, or else!"

The octopus style of North Korea is two pronged: severe repression and isolationism to control the North Korean population, and nuclear weapons to keep away outsiders. At home, the North Korean population is controlled by the use of gulags, severe censorship, and an enormous security and military apparatus (Hawk, 2003). A very high number of North Koreans are enmeshed in the military: out of a population of 25 million, 1.2 million are in the military, and 7.7 million are in the reserves – so about a third of the total population are either in the military of in the reserves (Moon, 2012). By comparison, "only" about one in twelve South Koreans are in the military or in the reserves. While keeping a lid on freedoms at home, the North Korean dictatorship tries to keep the rest of the world away by continuous threats, recently using missiles that could be armed with nuclear weapons.

But we should keep in mind that the cases we have considered, including Iran and North Korea, are in some respects similar to the situation in Western democracies. An important area of similarity across societies is the role of a particular style of leadership in collective mobilization, which I discuss below.

Bombastic Leadership, the Shark, and the Octopus

The eight-year assault on your Second Amendment freedoms has come to a crashing end. You have a true friend and champion in the White House. No longer will federal agencies be coming after law-abiding gun owners. No longer will the government be trying to undermine your rights and your freedoms as Americans. Instead, we will work with you, by your side . . .
    We'll build the wall. Don't even think about it. Don't even think about it. Don't even think about it. That's an easy one. We're going to build the wall. We need the wall. – Donald Trump, in his keynote speech to the National Rifle Association, April 28, 2017

Both shark and octopus revolutionary movements face the challenge of mobilizing people. How does collective mobilization come about? This question underlies the chapters in Part III, as well as all the major social science theories attempting to explain revolutions and various other forms of collective action. For example, relative deprivation theory has led to a vast array of research trying to pin down the conditions in which subjective experiences of deprivation will lead people to take action as part of a collective movement (Moghaddam, 2008; Power, Chapter 3). One of the factors that has received too little attention in this research is leadership, and particularly the kind of leadership that relies on emotions and identity as the main strategy for communicating and mobilizing followers (Moghaddam, 2016b, Chapter 6). To demonstrate this point, I focus on the leadership of Donald Trump and Ruhollah Khomeini as examples of what I term *bombastic leadership*, which has four main characteristics: first, giving primacy to emotions and "how people feel" (see the related discussion on "emotional leadership" by Humphrey, 2002); second, appeals to identity and identification with major groups, particularly based on religion, nationality, and "blood"; third, aggressive attacks against "the establishment" and elites representing the establishment; fourth, giving priority to "big ideas" and "visions" of an idealistic future, irrespective of facts and the present reality as established by "objective" or "scientific" criteria (see also Wagoner, Chapter 5).

The victory of Donald Trump in the 2016 US presidential elections was an enormous shock and disappointment to many better-educated Americans, of all political persuasions. For example, the conservative commentator George Will (2017) wrote in the *Washington Post*, "It is urgent for Americans to think and speak clearly about President Trump's inability to do either. This seems to be not a mere disinclination but a disability. It is not merely the result of intellectual sloth but of an untrained mind bereft of information and married to stratospheric self-confidence." Numerous American intellectuals, many from the political right, have been horrified by the leadership style of Trump, his inability to speak eloquently or logically, and the general disregard of the Trump movement for "facts" and science. For his part, Trump has repeatedly attacked the media, taking particular aim at the *New York Times* and other "elite" media outlets, as the "enemy of the people." Trump has also proposed slashing finding for science and academia generally, just as research centers and universities have become bastions of the anti-Trump movement.

Listening to American intellectuals talk about Donald Trump reminds me of my experiences listening to Iranian intellectuals talk about Supreme Leader Ruhollah Khomeini in 1978–1980. Just as Trump galvanized the antiestablishment movement in the US in 2016, Khomeini became the spearhead for the anti-Shah movement in 1978–1979, the period leading up to the overthrow of the monarchy in Iran. During the first year after the revolution, Khomeini mobilized his fanatical supporters to literally wipe out all his political competitors, and by 1980 he had achieved a stranglehold over Iranian society. The hostage-taking crisis and the invasion of Iran by Iraq in 1980 provided Khomeini with the political cover he needed to brand all opposition as "spies" and/or "enemies of Islam," and to annihilate them. He achieved this feat while being mocked by better-educated Iranians for his inability to communicate with them, and for his lack of understanding of modern science.

My argument here is that in many cases, collective mobilization, including of the type that lead to political revolutions, is achieved through bombastic leadership that influences people through emotions and group identification.

Bombastic Leadership

One of the greatest examples of bombastic leadership in the twentieth-century was Mao Zedong (1893–1976), who established the Chinese Communist Party in 1921 and founded the People's Republic of China in 1949. Mao came to wield absolute power in China, but the "Great Helmsman" steered his country into one disastrous storm after another. These disasters came about because, like all bombastic leaders, Mao was extremely effective at emotionally arousing and mobilizing the masses, but because he had little regards for scientific research and planning, the national mobilizations that he achieved at best came to nothing, but mostly had terrible and enormously damaging consequences. For example, the so-called Great Leap Forward (roughly 1958–1961) was supposed to transform Chinese society, through industrialization and collectivization. But instead of resulting in increases in productivity, the outcome was disarray and lower production. This proved to be particularly harmful in rural areas, because the failures of collective farming resulted in food scarcity and widespread famine in China (Chang and Halliday, 2005).

Another example of Mao's bombastic leadership style was the so-called Cultural Revolution, which took place during the late 1960s. Mao mobilized the Red Guards and young revolutionaries to attack "the establishment" and different types of authority figures, including those in the education system. Universities were attacked and shut down, and university professors were sent out into society to be "re-educated" through ordinary work "among the people." Mao's anti-intellectual and antielite attacks set China back decades, because an entire generation of highly educated experts was in one way or another prevented from contributing to society through their specialized professional skills.

Remarkably, in 1980–1981 Khomeini copied Mao's "Cultural Revolution" in Iran, and achieved the same results. In both cases, old bombastic leaders emotionally charged and mobilized young fanatical supports to attack "experts," "scientists," "intellectuals," and professionals in general. In both cases, the bombastic leaders attacked universities in particular as "antirevolution," and closed them down so as to "re-educate" the faculty and nullify them politically. The outcome in Iran was just as disastrous for national development: an entire generation of highly trained professionals was lost, and Iranian universities have not recovered in terms of academic standards. In the case of China, it was only after the death of Mao that Chinese society was able to reinvest in higher education, train experts and professionals, and make up for lost ground in science and technology.

There are, unfortunately, almost endless examples of the "antiscience" and "antifacts" nature of bombastic leadership leading to disasters. Looking to the past, Josef Stalin's rejection of Mendelian genetics and his adoption of the bogus "scientific" doctrine of Michurinism, resulted in disasters in Soviet agriculture (see Moghaddam, 2013). Looking to the future, Donald Trump's rejection of scientific evidence demonstrating the role of humankind in global warming points to enormous disasters in the making.

Concluding Comment

The shark and octopus revolutionary styles are not fixed. There are cases in which in the first few years after a revolution, one style is followed but later there is a shift to the other style. For example, the 1917 revolution in Russia was followed by some years of octopus behavior, but particularly with the Second World War there opened up new opportunities for a shark revolutionary style to develop. The Soviet Union expanded and took over all of Eastern Europe, as well as East Germany. On the other hand, after a failed attempt at expansion early on, North Korea adopted and maintained an octopus revolutionary style until the present. Similarly, the revolutionary style of Iran has been consistently shark.

REFERENCES

Bullock, A. (1993). *Hitler and Stalin: Parallel Lives*. New York: Vintage Books.
Chang, J., and Halliday, J. (2005). *Mao: The Unknown Story*. New York: Knopf.
Cumings, B. (2005). *Korea's Place in the Sun: A Modern History*. Updated ed. New York: W. W. Norton.
Economist (2016). Bright lights, big pity. December 24, 38–40.
Fischer, M. M. J. (1980). *Iran: From Religious Dispute to Revolution*. Cambridge, MA: Harvard University Press.
Friedman, S. J. (2015). *Silenced No More: Voices of Comfort Women*. New York: Freeman.

Hawk, D. (2003). *The Hidden Gulag: Exposing North Korea's Prison Camps.* Washington, DC: US High Commission on Human Rights.

Humphrey, R. H. (2002). The many faces of emotional leadership. *Leadership Quarterly*, 5, 493–504.

Khalaji, M. (2016). *The Shiite clergy post-Khomeini: Balancing authority and autonomy. Research Notes 37.* Washington, DC: Washington Institute for Near East Policy.

Marples, D. R. (2000). *Lenin's Revolution: Russia, 1917–1921.* London: Routledge.

McKenzie, F. A. (1908/1968). *The Tragedy of Korea.* Seoul: Yonsei University Press.

Moghaddam, F. M. (2008). *Multiculturalism and Intergroup Relations: Psychological Implications for Democracy in Global Context.* Washington, DC: American Psychological Association Press.

(2013). *The Psychology of Dictatorship.* Washington, DC: American Psychological Association Press.

(2016a). Omniculturalism and our human path. *Journal of Oriental Studies*, 26, 77.

(2016b). *The Psychology of Democracy.* Washington, DC: American Psychological Association Press.

(forthcoming). *Mutual Radicalization: The Psychology of How Groups and Nations Radicalize Each Other.* Washington, DC: American Psychological Association Press.

Moon, G. I. (2012). *The Sunshine Policy: In Defense of Engagement as a Path to Peace in Korea.* Seoul: Yonsei University Press.

Petty, R. E., and Cacioppo, J. T. (1986). *Communication and Persuasion: Central and Peripheral Routes to Attitude Change.* New York: Springer.

Ryan, J. (2012). *Lenin's Terror: The Ideological Origins of Early Soviet State Terror.* London: Routledge.

Schaller, M. (1997). *The United States and Japan since the Occupation.* New York: Oxford University Press.

Schama, S. (1989). *Citizens: A Chronicle of the French Revolution.* New York: Vintage.

Will, G. F. (2017). Trump has a dangerous disability. *Washington Post*, May 3. www.washingtonpost.com/opinions/trump-has-a-dangerous-disability/2017/05/03/56ca6118-2f6b-11e7-9534-00e4656c22aa_story.html.

Index